Introducing
InnoDB Cluster

Learning the MySQL
High Availability Stack

Charles Bell

Apress®

Introducing InnoDB Cluster

Charles Bell
Warsaw, Virginia, USA

ISBN-13 (pbk): 978-1-4842-3884-4   ISBN-13 (electronic): 978-1-4842-3885-1
https://doi.org/10.1007/978-1-4842-3885-1

Library of Congress Control Number: 2018955580

Managing Director, Apress Media LLC: Welmoed Spahr
Acquisitions Editor: Jonathan Gennick
Development Editor: Laura Berendson
Coordinating Editor: Jill Balzano

Cover designed by eStudioCalamar

Cover image designed by Freepik (www.freepik.com)

Distributed to the book trade worldwide by Springer Science+Business Media New York, 233 Spring Street, 6th Floor, New York, NY 10013. Phone 1-800-SPRINGER, fax (201) 348-4505, e-mail orders-ny@springer-sbm.com, or visit www.springeronline.com. Apress Media, LLC is a California LLC and the sole member (owner) is Springer Science + Business Media Finance Inc (SSBM Finance Inc). SSBM Finance Inc is a Delaware corporation.

For information on translations, please e-mail rights@apress.com, or visit www.apress.com/rights-permissions.

Apress titles may be purchased in bulk for academic, corporate, or promotional use. eBook versions and licenses are also available for most titles. For more information, reference our Print and eBook Bulk Sales web page at www.apress.com/bulk-sales.

Any source code or other supplementary material referenced by the author in this book is available to readers on GitHub via the book's product page, located at www.apress.com/9781484238844. For more detailed information, please visit www.apress.com/source-code.

Printed on acid-free paper

I dedicate this book to my big brother, William E. Bell, who left this world too soon. I miss you, Bill.

Table of Contents

About the Author

 **Charles Bell** conducts research in emerging technologies. He is a member of the Oracle MySQL Development team and is a senior software developer for the MySQL Enterprise Backup team. He lives in a small town in rural Virginia with his loving wife. He received his Doctor of Philosophy in Engineering from Virginia Commonwealth University in 2005.

Charles is an expert in the database field and has extensive knowledge and experience in software development and systems engineering. His research interests include 3D printers, microcontrollers, three-dimensional printing, database systems, software engineering, high-availability systems, the cloud, and sensor networks. He spends his limited free time as a practicing maker, focusing on microcontroller projects and refinement of three-dimensional printers.

About the Technical Reviewer

Valerie Parham-Thompson has experience with a variety of open source data storage technologies, including MySQL, MongoDB, and Cassandra, as well as a foundation in web development in software-as-a-service environments. Her work in both development and operations in startups and traditional enterprises has led to solid expertise in web-scale data storage and data delivery.

Valerie has spoken at technical conferences on topics such as database security, performance tuning, and container management, and speaks often at local meetups and volunteer events. She holds a bachelor's degree from the Kenan Flagler Business School at UNC-Chapel Hill, has certifications in MySQL and MongoDB, and is a Google Certified Professional Cloud Architect. She currently works in the Open Source Database Cluster at Pythian, headquartered in Ottawa, Ontario.

Follow Valerie's contributions to technical blogs on Twitter at @dataindataout.

Acknowledgments

I would like to thank all the many talented and energetic professionals at Apress. I appreciate the understanding and patience of my editor, Jonathan Gennick, and managing editor, Jill Balzano. They were instrumental in the success of this project. I would also like to thank the army of publishing professionals at Apress for making me look so good in print, with a special thank you to the reviewers for their wise counsel and gentle nudges in the right direction. Thank you all very much!

I also am indebted to the technical reviewer, Valerie Parham-Thompson, for her insight and guidance in making this book the best book on MySQL InnoDB Cluster for both beginning and experienced high-availability systems developers.

Most important, I want to thank my wife, Annette, for her unending patience and understanding while I spent so much time with my laptop.

Introduction

High availability is often thought of as something you must spend a lot of time and money to get right. In the not-so-distant past, if you wanted to use MySQL in a high-availability setting, you had to learn how to configure the server by using configuration files and several unique (yet SQL) commands to make it all work. Although there were tools designed to make it easier, it was still messy and, at times, labor intensive. This all changes with MySQL InnoDB Cluster, which turns the lengthy setup and configuration into a short set of steps using an application programming interface. Yes, Virginia, there's an API for that.

As you will see, InnoDB Cluster takes MySQL high availability to an entirely different level. Never has MySQL offered such sophistication and stability for such complex subject matter. As you shall see, Oracle has spent a considerable amount of engineering, development, and quality-control time to get high availability right for MySQL.

If you have used older high-availability features in MySQL such as replication, you will be especially surprised to see how much easier it is to work with InnoDB Cluster. Even if you haven't used replication, you will discover that high availability no longer requires investing in bespoke solutions or thousands of hours of your own development time. MySQL high availability has come of age.

This book introduces you to high availability and teaches you how to set up and configure InnoDB Cluster in your environment, including how to migrate existing applications and follow best practices for using InnoDB Cluster in production.

Intended Audience

I wrote this book to share my passion for MySQL high availability. I especially wanted to show just how easy and sophisticated MySQL has become. Now, anyone can set up an InnoDB Cluster and make their applications more robust, with greater uptime and reliability than ever before. The intended audience therefore includes anyone interested in learning about MySQL high availability and InnoDB Cluster, such as database administrators, developers, and information technology managers, systems architects, and strategic planners.

How This Book Is Structured

The book was written to guide you from a general knowledge of high availability and the new features in MySQL InnoDB Cluster to detailed explanations of the components that make up InnoDB Cluster, as well as how to set up and configure it by using the new MySQL Shell. The first several chapters cover general topics, including a short introduction to high availability and InnoDB Cluster, installing MySQL, and the components for InnoDB Cluster. Later chapters present more detailed coverage of the InnoDB components, including MySQL Shell, X Admin API, MySQL Router, and more. Following those chapters is a pair of chapters that present an example installation as well as an example for building a high-availability application using InnoDB Cluster. The book concludes with notes about upgrading to MySQL 8 and best practices for using InnoDB Cluster. The following is a brief overview of each chapter in this book:

> *Chapter 1, "Introduction to High Availability"*: This chapter discusses what high availability is and how MySQL can be used to achieve high availability using the first building block of the MySQL high-availability portfolio of features. The chapter also presents a brief tutorial on how to use MySQL Replication. Understanding how to achieve high availability in MySQL by using features available before InnoDB Cluster will help clarify how InnoDB Cluster improves upon these features.

> *Chapter 2, "What is MySQL InnoDB Cluster?"*: This chapter presents an overview of InnoDB Cluster, including the evolution of InnoDB Cluster from storage engine to high-availability solution. The chapter also presents an overview of the components that make up InnoDB Cluster.

> *Chapter 3, "MySQL Group Replication"*: This chapter explores Group Replication in greater detail, to demonstrate and reinforce its concepts. The chapter also presents a guided tour of Group Replication and a hands-on walk-through of setting it up.

> *Chapter 4, "MySQL Shell"*: This chapter demonstrates how to use MySQL Shell, including installing it on Windows, as well a look at its startup options, shell commands, connections, and sessions. We'll even do a bit of interactive scripting in JavaScript

and Python. Although this chapter does not provide exhaustive coverage of all the features of MySQL Shell, it presents a broad tutorial for using it for the most common tasks in setting up and configuring InnoDB Cluster.

Chapter 5, "High Availability in a Sandbox": This chapter presents a detailed walk-through of setting up InnoDB Cluster in a sandbox (on a single MySQL server). The walk-through provides an overview of the commands needed to set up and configure InnoDB Cluster.

Chapter 6, "MySQL Router": This chapter discusses MySQL Router in greater detail, including how to set up and configure the router.

Chapter 7, "Example MySQL HA Deployment": This chapter explores a development environment using separate servers to demonstrate a generalized high-availability deployment of MySQL. The chapter demonstrates how to install MySQL on several machines, establish an InnoDB Cluster among them, and deploy a single application server to host a simple application via MySQL Router. The chapter also presents how to set up and configure InnoDB Cluster on the Raspberry Pi computer.

Chapter 8, "Example Application": This chapter presents a tutorial on how to develop a high-availability web-based application using Python and Flask. The chapter presents a brief primer on using Flask before moving on to writing a simple application for use on InnoDB Cluster and hosted on an application server with the router.

Chapter 9, "InnoDB Cluster Administration": This chapter examines the common tasks used to administer an InnoDB Cluster. The chapter also discusses how to make your InnoDB Cluster more secure by examining the administrative tasks for securing the cluster.

Chapter 10, "Planning Your Deployment": This chapter presents considerations and techniques for planning your cluster deployment. The chapter also includes information about how to plan for adopting MySQL 8 in your enterprise.

How to Use This Book

This book is designed to guide you through learning more about high availability and MySQL InnoDB Cluster, discovering the power of X AdminAPI, and seeing how to migrate existing and build new high-availability applications.

If you are new to MySQL and InnoDB Cluster, you should spend time going through the first four chapters, including installing MySQL on your own system and learning how to use MySQL Shell.

The next several chapters are designed to give you more information about the components that make up InnoDB Cluster. I consider these required reading for anyone who has not used MySQL Replication or Group Replication.

Once you are familiar with InnoDB Cluster and its components from reading the first five chapters, you can work through Chapter 6 to learn the basics of setting up InnoDB Cluster in a sandbox (on a single local machine). Chapter 7 covers MySQL Router, which is especially important for those who want to build high-availability applications.

Chapters 8 and 9 present a complete solution that demonstrates how to build a product InnoDB Cluster and a short, bare-bones, high-availability application in Python and Flask that you can run on your systems to experiment with writing applications for InnoDB Cluster. Perhaps what makes Chapter 8 especially interesting is that it demonstrates how to run MySQL on the Raspberry Pi to form an InnoDB Cluster running on five Raspberry Pi computers.

Planners may find Chapter 10 especially helpful in planning an upgrade to MySQL 8 and adapting InnoDB Clusters to your infrastructure.

Downloading the Code

The code for the examples shown in this book is available on the Apress web site, `www.apress.com/9781484238844`. You can find a link on the book's information page on the Source Code/Downloads tab. This tab is in the Related Titles section of the page.

Contacting the Author

If have any questions or comments—or even spot a mistake you think I should know about—you can contact me at `drcharlesbell@gmail.com`.

CHAPTER 1

Introduction to High Availability

Database administrators and systems architects who manage infrastructures understand the need for building in redundancy while keeping maintenance chores to a minimum. One of the tools used to achieve this is a class of features that make the server or service available as much as possible. We call this *high availability*.

High availability is not only a key factor in establishing robust, always ready infrastructures, but also a quality of robust, enterprise-grade database systems. Oracle has continued to develop and improve the high-availability features in MySQL. Indeed, these features have matured to include detailed management and configuration, status reporting, and even automatic failover of the primary server to ensure that your data is available even if the primary goes down. Best of all, Oracle has included these features in the community edition of MySQL so the whole world can use them.

MySQL high availability through the new InnoDB Cluster feature is a collection of components built on the long-term stability of MySQL Replication. The components include modifications to the server and new components such as Group Replication, a router for routing your connections, and MySQL Shell for simplified setup and configuration. Together, these components form a new paradigm in MySQL high availability.

In this chapter, you will discover what high availability is and how to achieve high availability by using the first building block of the MySQL high-availability portfolio of features. You will also see a brief tutorial on how to use MySQL Replication. Understanding how to achieve high availability in MySQL by using features available before InnoDB Cluster will help clarify how InnoDB Cluster improves upon these features.

Let's begin with a brief tutorial on high availability.

1

© Charles Bell 2018
C. Bell, *Introducing InnoDB Cluster*, https://doi.org/10.1007/978-1-4842-3885-1_1

MYSQL—WHAT DOES IT MEAN?

The name *MySQL* is a combination of a proper name and an acronym. *SQL* stands for *Structured Query Language*. The *My* part isn't the possessive form—it is a name. In this case, *My* is the name of the founder's daughter. As for pronunciation, MySQL experts pronounce it "My-S-Q-L" and not "my sequel."

What Is High Availability?

High availability is easiest to understand if you consider it loosely synonymous with *reliability*—making the solution as accessible as possible and tolerant to failures either planned or unplanned for an agreed-upon period. That is, it's how much users can expect the system to be operational. The more reliable the system, and thus the longer it is operational, equates to a higher level of availability.

High availability can be accomplished in many ways, resulting in different levels of availability. The levels can be expressed as goals to achieving some higher state of reliability. Essentially, you use techniques and tools to boost reliability and make it possible for the solution to keep running and the data to be available as long as possible (also called *uptime*). Uptime is represented as a ratio or percentage of the amount of time the solution is operational.

You can achieve high availability by practicing the following engineering principles:

- *Eliminate single points of failure*: Design your solution so that there are as few components as possible that, if they fail, render the solution unusable.

- *Add recovery through redundancy*: Design your solution to permit multiple, active redundant mechanisms to allow rapid recovery from failures.

- *Implement fault tolerance*: Design your solution to actively detect failures and automatically recover by switching to a redundant or alternative mechanism.

These principles are building blocks, or steps to take, to reach higher levels of reliability and thus high availability. Even if you do not need to achieve maximum high availability (whereby the solution is up nearly all the time), by implementing these principles, you will make your solution more reliable at the least, which is a good goal to achieve.

Now that you understand the goals or requirements that high availability can solve, let's discuss some of the options for implementing high availability in your MySQL solutions. The following sections discuss four options for implementing goals of high availability. By implementing all of these, you will achieve a level of high availability. How much you achieve depends on not only how you implement these options but also how well you meet your goals for reliability.

RELIABILITY VS. HIGH AVAILABILITY: WHAT IS THE DIFFERENCE?

Reliability is a measure of how operational a solution is over time, which covers one of the major goals for high availability. Indeed, you could say that the ultimate level of reliability—the solution is always operational—is the definition of *high availability*. To make your solution a high-availability solution, you should focus on improving reliability.

Recovery

The easiest implementation of reliability you can achieve is the ability to recover from failures. This could be a failure in a component, application server, database server, or any other part of the solution. *Recovery*, therefore, is how to get the solution back to operation in as little time and with as little cost as possible.

However, it may not be possible to recover from all types of failure. For example, if one or more of your servers suffers a catastrophic disk failure, recovery may require replacing the hardware and loss of data during the outage. For other types of failure, recovery options may permit a faster method of returning to operation. Furthermore, some components are more important and must be recoverable, so your efforts should be to protect those more important components, the database being chief among them.

For instance, if your data becomes corrupt or is lost because of hardware failure, you need to have a way to recover that data with as little loss as possible. One way to achieve that is by keeping frequent backup copies of the data that can later be restored to recover the data from loss.

Many tomes have been written about various strategies for backing up and restoring your data. Rather than attempt to explain every nuance, technique, and best practice, I refer you to the many texts available. For this book and the solutions available for MySQL, it is sufficient to understand that there are two types of backup methods—logical and physical—each with its own merits.

Logical Backup

A *logical backup* makes a copy of the data by traversing the data, making copies of the data row by row, and typically translating the data from its binary form to SQL statements. The advantage of a logical backup is that the data is human readable and can even be used to make alterations or corrections to the data prior to restoring it. The downside is that logical backups tend to be slow for larger amounts of data and can take more space to store than the actual data (depending on data types, number of indexes, and so on).

Physical Backup

A *physical backup* makes a binary copy of the data from the disk storage layer. The backup is typically application specific; you must use the same application that made the backup to restore it. The advantage is that the backup is much faster and smaller in size. Plus, applications that perform physical backups have advanced features such as incremental backups (only the data that has changed since the last backup) and other advanced features. For small solutions, a logical backup may be more than sufficient, but as your solution (your data) grows, you will need to use a physical backup solution.

Redundancy

One of the more challenging implementations of reliability is *redundancy*—having two or more components serving the same role in the system. A goal for redundancy may be simply having a component in place in case you need to replace the primary one. This could be a hot standby: the component actively participates in parallel with the primary, and your system automatically switches to the redundant component when a failure is detected. The most common target for redundancy is the database server. MySQL excels in this area with several features. One of the oldest redundancy features available in MySQL is called *replication*.

MySQL Replication is not difficult to set up for the most basic use cases, which are hot standby and backup. For these, you set up a second database server that gets a copy of all changes made on the original server. The original server is called the *master*, or the *primary*, and the second server is called the *slave*, or *secondary*. MySQL Replication is such a large topic that I've devoted a section to it later in this chapter.

WAIT, WHY ARE WE TALKING ABOUT MYSQL REPLICATION?

You may be wondering why we are discussing MySQL Replication when this book is about InnoDB Cluster. It is important to understand MySQL Replication because it is one of the fundamental components upon which InnoDB Cluster is built. Although MySQL Replication is older, has fewer features, and requires manual administration, understanding MySQL Replication will give you a much better idea of the way InnoDB Cluster works. It will also help you appreciate how much more sophisticated InnoDB Cluster is as compared to the components upon which it is based.

Redundancy can also be implemented by using additional, dedicated hardware. You could implement a redundant power option (for example, a second power supply or alternative power such as solar or battery backup), use multiple application servers, use multiple data acquisition nodes, and more. There isn't really any reason you cannot build redundancy into your solution. However, only you, the designer or administrator, will know which nodes are the most critical and therefore which ones you want to have duplicates of in case of failure.

The sophistication of the redundant mechanism is something you control and depends on how much you want to put into it. In fact, the level of sophistication of the redundancy is associated with the amount of work or expense of the implementation.

For example, you could use a spare, offline component that can be manually activated when the original fails, which is slow and requires manual intervention. Or you can use a spare, online component that can be used in place of the primary, which still requires manual intervention but is faster to recover. Or you can write your application code to automatically detect the failure and switch to the secondary, which is the best (fastest) but requires more programming and thus more work (potentially a lot more).

You can tailor your redundancy to meet your needs or abilities. You could start with simple offline spares and add greater sophistication as your solution evolves.

SO, WHAT IS FIVE NINES?

You may have heard or read about a concept called *five nines*, or 99.999% of a year uptime. A five nine solution therefore permits, at most, only 5.26 minutes of downtime per year. But five nines is just one class or rating regarding reliability that includes other categories, each related to the percentage of uptime or reliability. For more information about the available classes, see `https://en.wikipedia.org/wiki/High_availability#Percentage_ calculation`.

Scaling

Another reliability implementation has to do with performance. In this case, you want to minimize the time it takes to store and retrieve data. MySQL Replication is an excellent way to implement scalability. You do this by designing your solution to write (save) data to the master (primary) and read the data from the slave (secondary). As the application grows, you can add slaves to help minimize the time to read data. Having additional slaves allows your application to run more than one instance or even multiple connections simultaneously (one per slave at a minimum). Thus, scalability builds upon the redundancy features in MySQL.

By splitting the writes and reads, you relieve the master of the burden of having to execute many statements. Given that most applications have many more reads than writes, it makes sense to devote a different server (or several) to providing data from reading and leaving the writes to the one master server.

It is important to understand that there are two forms of scale-out: read and write. You can achieve read scale-out by using redundant readers like those you see in MySQL Replication, but achieving write scale-out requires a solution that can negotiate and handle updates on two or more servers. Fortunately, MySQL InnoDB Cluster achieves this by using an advanced form of replication called *MySQL Group Replication*. You will see more about this feature in a later section.

Of course, there are other ways to improve performance that do not require implementing MySQL Replication, but you may not achieve much benefit in the longer run.

Fault Tolerance

The last implementation of reliability and indeed what separates most high-availability solutions regarding uptime is *fault tolerance*, which is the ability to detect failures and recover from the event. Fault tolerance is achieved by leveraging recovery and redundancy and adding the detection mechanism and active switchover.

For example, you can implement fault tolerance at the database. Once again, we build on the use of MySQL Replication to achieve the switch. When the master goes down, we use the replication commands in MySQL to switch the role of master to one of the slaves. There are two types of master role change when working with MySQL: *switchover*, which is switching the role of master to a slave when the master is still operational, and *failover*, which is selecting a slave to take on the role of master when the master is no longer operational. Switchover is intentional, and failover is a reactive event.

Oracle provides a couple of tools to help you set up automatic failover. You can use MySQL Utilities (`mysqlfailover`) to monitor your master and switch to a slave when the master goes offline. For larger solutions with many servers that may also require write scale-out, you can use MySQL Group Replication, performing failover automatically as well as other more sophisticated high-availability operations. There is also MySQL Router, which is a connection router for MySQL that allows you to set up a specific set of servers to be used by the router such that the router automatically switches to another server should the current server go offline (become unreachable). Fortunately, both Group Replication and Router are part of InnoDB Cluster.

You can also implement a form of fault tolerance in your applications, but like redundancy, this requires specialized code that may be costlier to build and maintain. Even the use of a router may require modification to your application to use certain ports and other connection information. However, these are minor changes compared to writing your own fault-tolerance capabilities in your application.

CAN MYSQL REALLY REACH HIGH AVAILABILITY?

Not only can you reach high availability with MySQL, but you have many options for achieving high availability with MySQL, some from third-party vendors, as well as several tools by Oracle. Even MySQL itself is designed with the basic building blocks for high availability. However, the features of MySQL as well as the tools and solutions for high availability allow you to tailor MySQL to provide as much reliability as you need.

Now that you have a broader understanding of what high availability is and how you can achieve the principles of high availability, let's look at the high-availability features of MySQL.

Overview of MySQL High-Availability Features

MySQL has had high-availability features for some time. In fact, MySQL Replication was first introduced many years ago in version 3.23.15 and has since undergone many layers of improvements and refinements. Since then, the portfolio of MySQL high-availability features has expanded to cover many use cases, from simple redundancy (hot standby), to scale-out, to highly reliable systems.

The following is a list of the major high-availability features in MySQL. Included is a brief overview of each feature as it relates to high availability. There are many small improvements, tools, and enhancements, both in the server and in external tools, to complement these features. For example, you can monitor any of these features with MySQL Enterprise Monitor (`https://dev.mysql.com/doc/mysql-monitor/4.0/en/`).

- *MySQL Replication*: The first high-availability feature that permits duplication of data from one instance (server) to one or more additional instances (servers). The major high-availability features realized in MySQL Replication include redundancy, hot standby (recovery), backup, and read scalability.

- *MySQL Group Replication*: Built on MySQL Replication, Group Replication provides advanced server interactions permitting better redundancy with greater synchronization, automatic failover, and write scalability. Thus, Group Replication provides greater recovery and reliability than MySQL Replication.

- *MySQL InnoDB Cluster*: Built on MySQL Group Replication, InnoDB Cluster adds additional management for ease of use in leveraging a new client for administration though an application programming interface (API), application failover and routing, and simplified configuration. Thus, InnoDB Cluster provides greater high availability than Group Replication.

- *MySQL NDB Cluster*: Often confused with InnoDB Cluster, NDB Cluster is a separate product from Oracle that provides a high-availability, high-redundancy version of MySQL adapted for the distributed computing environment using the in-memory NDB storage engine (also known as NDBCLUSTER) to enable running several computers with MySQL servers and other software in a cluster.

As you can see, the list of high-availability features in MySQL is impressive. While the list is not long, the significance of these features cannot be understated. Many organizations have used MySQL Replication and NDB Cluster for many years. The additions of Group Replication and later InnoDB Cluster have proven Oracle's commitment to enterprise-grade high availability in the MySQL server.

Note   NDB Cluster is available only as part of the MySQL NDB Cluster distribution. For more information about MySQL NDB Cluster, see `https://dev.mysql.com/doc/refman/5.7/en/mysql-cluster.html`.

To fully understand the importance of and improvement gains from using InnoDB Cluster, we begin with a primer on MySQL Replication. You will learn more about InnoDB Cluster in Chapter 2 and Group Replication in Chapter 3.

MySQL Replication Primer

MySQL Replication is an easy-to-use feature and yet a complex and major component of the MySQL server. This section presents a bird's-eye view of replication to explain how it works and how to set up a simple replication topology.[1] Although this section discusses MySQL Replication under version 8.0, MySQL Replication is configured the same way in earlier versions of MySQL. The steps shown in this section to set up and configure replication can be used with older versions of MySQL. As mentioned previously, knowing how MySQL Replication works will give you a better idea of how InnoDB Cluster works.

Replication requires two or more servers. One server must be designated as the source, or primary (called the *master*). The master role means all data changes (writes) to the data are sent to the master and only the master. All other servers in the topology maintain a copy of the master data and are by design and requirement read-only servers (called *slaves*).[2] Thus, when your applications store or update data, they send it to the master. Applications you write to use the data can read it from the slaves.

Note   The terms *master* and *slave* are used exclusively in MySQL Replication and are representative of the fact that only one server can be written to and thus has the *master* copy. The remaining servers are read-only, containing a copy (replicant) of the data. These terms were changed to *primary* and *secondary* in later high-availability features to better describe the roles in the new features.

MySQL Replication supports two methods of replication. The original (sometimes called *MySQL 5.7 Replication, classic replication, binary log file replication,* or *log file and position replication*) method involves using a binary log file name and position to execute events or apply changes to synchronize data between the master and slaves. A newer method that uses global transaction identifiers (GTIDs) is transactional and therefore does not require working with log files or positions within these files, which greatly simplifies many common replication tasks. Replication using GTIDs guarantees consistency between master and slave.

---

[1]A *topology* in this sense is the set of servers participating in replication. A replication topology may also be used to describe how the servers are connected, such as a single master and one or more slaves, tiered (masters can be slaves to other slaves), and even circular (the master-slave connection forms a loop).

[2]These terms are merely representative of the roles servers play in replicating data. They are in no way associated with vile and deplorable practices that use similar terms.

WHAT'S A GTID?

GTIDs enable servers to assign a unique identifier to each set or group of events, thereby making it possible to know which events have been applied on each slave. To perform failover with GTIDs, you take the best slave (the one with the fewest missing events and the hardware that matches the master best) and make it a slave of every other slave. We call this slave the *candidate slave*. The GTID mechanism will ensure that only those events that have not been executed on the candidate slave are applied. In this way, the candidate slave becomes the most up-to-date and therefore a replacement for the master.

The copy mechanism works by using a technology called the *binary log* that stores the changes in a special format, thereby keeping a record of all the changes. These changes are then copied to the slaves and re-executed there. After the slave re-executes the changes (called *events*), the slave has an exact copy of the data. We will see more about the binary log in a later section.

The master maintains a binary log of the changes, and the slave maintains a copy of that binary log called the *relay log*, which has the same format as the binary log. When a slave requests data changes from the master, it reads the events from the master and writes them to its relay log; then another thread in the slave executes those events from the relay log.

At the lowest level, the binary log exchanges between the master and slaves support three formats:

- *Statement-based replication (SBR)*: Replicates entire SQL statements

- *Row-based replication (RBR)*: Replicates only the changed rows

- *Mixed-based replication (MBR)*: A hybrid of RBR, with some events recorded using SQL statements

As you can imagine, a slight delay occurs from the time a change is made on the master to the time it is made on the slave. Fortunately, this delay is almost unnoticeable except in topologies with high traffic (lots of changes). For your purposes, when you read the data from the slave, it likely is up-to-date. You can check the slave's progress by using the command SHOW SLAVE STATUS; among many other things, it shows you how far behind the master the slave has become. You'll see this command in action in a later section.

MySQL Replication also supports two types of synchronization. The original type, *asynchronous*, is one-way: events executed on the master are transmitted to the slaves and executed (or applied) as they arrive, with no checks to ensure that the slaves are all at the same synchronization point as the master (slave updates may be delayed when there are many transactions). The other type is *semi-synchronous*: a commit performed on the master is blocked before returning to the session that performed the transaction until at least one slave acknowledges that it has received and logged the events for the transaction.

Synchronous replication, in which all nodes are guaranteed to have the same data in an all-or-none commit scenario, is supported by MySQL NDB Cluster. See the MySQL NDB Cluster section in the online reference manual for information about synchronous replication.

Tip   For more information about MySQL Replication, see the "Replication" section in the online reference manual (`https://dev.mysql.com/doc/refman/8.0/en/replication.html`).

Now that you have a little knowledge of replication and how it works, let's see how to set it up. The next section discusses how to set up replication with one server as the master and another as the slave. You will see both types of replication used. As you will see, only a few differences exist in the way you configure the servers and start replication.

MySQL Replication Tutorial

This section demonstrates how to set up replication from one server (the master) to another (a slave). The steps include preparing the master by enabling binary logging and creating a user account for reading the binary log, preparing the slave by connecting it to the master, and starting the slave processes. The section concludes with a test of the replication system.

If you would like to experience this tutorial on your own, you should prepare two servers—either as two physical machines or two virtual machines. However, the easiest way to experiment with MySQL Replication is to set up two MySQL instances on a test system. More specifically, you will see how to run multiple MySQL servers on the same machine. To do this, you should already have MySQL installed on your system. You can follow the instructions in the online reference manual (`https://dev.mysql.com/doc/refman/8.0/en/installing.html`) if you have not installed MySQL on your system. You will see a more in-depth demonstration of installing MySQL 8.0 in the next chapter.

Note   The steps used to set up replication with binary log file and position are the same as those for using GTIDs, but the commands differ slightly in some of the steps. This tutorial shows both methods.

The steps to set up and configure MySQL Replication include the following:

1. Initialize the data directories.

2. Configure the master.

3. Configure the slaves.

4. Start the MySQL instances.

5. Create the replication user account.

6. Connect the slaves to the master.

7. Start replication.

8. Verify the replication status.

There may be other, equally viable procedures to set up replication, but the preceding steps can be done on any machine and will not affect any existing installations of MySQL. That said, it is recommended to perform these steps on a development machine to remove the risk of disrupting production systems.

The following sections demonstrate each of these steps in greater detail. While the tutorial uses multiple, local instances to demonstrate how to use replication, the procedure would be the same for setting up replication in a production environment. The details of the individual commands to use specific hosts, drives, folders, ports, and so forth are the only things that would change to use the procedure in production.

Note   The steps shown in this tutorial are run on an Ubuntu 16.04 platform. Although there are platform-specific commands and a few platform-specific options, the tutorial can be run on macOS and Windows platforms with minor changes.

Initialize the Data Directories

The first step is to initialize a data directory for each of the machines used. In this case, we will create a folder on our local machine to contain all the data directories. We will use two instances of MySQL to represent a single master and a single slave. The following demonstrates creating the folders needed. Notice that I create these in a local folder accessible to the user account I am using, not a system or administrative account. This is because we will be running the instances locally and do not need the additional privileges or access such accounts permit.

```
$ mkdir rpl
$ cd rpl
$ mkdir data
```

Now that we have a folder, <user_home>/rpl/data, we can use the initialization option of the MySQL server to set up our data directories.[3] We do this by using the special --initialize-insecure and --datadir options of the server executable. The --initialize-insecure option tells the server to create the data directory and populate it with the system data but to skip the use of any authentication. This is safe because no users have been created yet (there's no data directory!).

The --datadir option specifies the location of the data directory main folder. Because we are running this as a local user, we need the --user option. We also need to know the base directory (called basedir) from the MySQL server installed on the local machine. You can get that information from the server configuration file or by using the MySQL client (named mysql) and pass it a show command. The following demonstrates how to do this. Here, we see the base directory is /usr/. We will use this value so that the mysqld executable can find its dependent libraries and files.

```
$ mysql -uroot -proot -e "SHOW VARIABLES LIKE 'basedir'"
mysql: [Warning] Using a password on the command line interface can be
insecure.
```

---

[3]The <user_home> is a placeholder for the home folder for the current user. For example, /home/cbell.

14

```
+---------------+-------+
| Variable_name | Value |
+---------------+-------+
| basedir       | /usr/ |
+---------------+-------+
```

Finally, we use the `--no-defaults` option (which must appear first in the parameter list) to skip reading of the MySQL configuration file(s). This is necessary if we already have an instance of MySQL running on the machine or MySQL has been installed previously on the machine.

The following shows the commands needed to initialize the data directories for the master and a slave. Notice I use `slave1` for the slave. This is so you can expand the tutorial to multiple slaves should you want to experiment with adding additional slaves.

```
mysqld --no-default --user=cbell --initialize-insecure --basedir=/usr/
--datadir=<user_home>/rpl/data/master
mysqld --no-default --user=cbell --initialize-insecure --basedir=/usr/
--datadir=<user_home>/rpl/data/slave1
```

Note   You can easily expand this tutorial to use two or more slaves. Simply repeat the commands for the slave, substituting the correct port.

When you run these commands, you will see several messages printed as follows. You can safely ignore the warnings, but notice that the last one tells us that the root user does not have a password assigned. This is OK for our tutorial, but something you never want to do for a production installation. Fortunately, we can fix that easily after we start the instance.

```
$ mysqld --no-defaults --user=cbell --initialize-insecure --basedir=/usr/
--datadir=/home/cbell/rpl/data/master
2018-03-05T16:44:44.746906Z O [Warning] TIMESTAMP with implicit DEFAULT
value is deprecated. Please use --explicit_defaults_for_timestamp server
option (see documentation for more details).
2018-03-05T16:44:44.948910Z O [Warning] InnoDB: New log files created, LSN=45790
2018-03-05T16:44:45.027466Z O [Warning] InnoDB: Creating foreign key
constraint system tables.
2018-03-05T16:44:45.096708Z O [Warning] No existing UUID has been found, so
we assume that this is the first time that this server has been started.
Generating a new UUID: 82783ccc-2094-11e8-b3e3-10bf4850c554.
```

```
2018-03-05T16:44:45.100255Z 0 [Warning] Gtid table is not ready to be used.
Table 'mysql.gtid_executed' cannot be opened.
2018-03-05T16:44:45.101415Z 1 [Warning] root@localhost is created with an empty
password ! Please consider switching off the --initialize-insecure option.
```

Now that we have the data directories created and populated, we can configure the master and slave(s).

Configure the Master

Replication requires the master to have binary logging enabled. It is turned on by default in MySQL 8.0.11, but if you have an older version, you must add this option in the configuration file. In fact, we will need a configuration file for each of the instances we want to start. In this section, we concentrate on the master, and in the next we will see the configuration file for a slave.

We also need to select the port for the instance. For this tutorial, we will use port numbers starting from 13001 for the master and 13002+ for the slaves. In addition, we will need to choose unique server identification numbers. We will use 1 for the master and 2+ for the slaves.

There are other settings we will need to make. Rather than list them, let's view a typical base configuration file for a master using replication with binary log and file position. Listing 1-1 shows the configuration file we will use for the master in this tutorial.

Listing 1-1. Master Configuration File (Log File and Position)

```
[mysqld]
datadir="/home/cbell/rpl/data/master"
basedir="/usr/"
port=13001
socket="/home/cbell/rpl/master.sock"

server_id=1
master_info_repository=TABLE
relay_log_info_repository=TABLE
log_bin=master_binlog
binlog_format=row
```

Notice that the configuration file has one section named mysqld, which applies only to the MySQL server executable. Only the mysqld and related executables will read this section for values. Among those values are the common required settings for datadir, basedir, port, and socket (for *nix style platforms). Notice that these values match the settings we've discussed previously.

The next section sets the server ID, turns on the TABLE option for storing replication information, which makes replication recoverable from crashes, and turns on the binary log and sets its location. Finally, we use the ROW format for the binary log, which is a binary format and is the default for the latest versions of MySQL Replication.

If we wanted to use GTID-based replication, additional options must be set. For the master, there are only three: turn GTIDs on, set consistency enforcement, and log slave updates. The configuration file for a GTID-enabled master server is shown in Listing 1-2. Notice that the first portion of the file is the same as the previous example. Only the last few lines are added to enable GTIDs.

Listing 1-2. Master Configuration File (GTIDs)

```
[mysqld]
datadir="/home/cbell/rpl/data/master"
basedir="/usr/"
port=13001
socket="/home/cbell/rpl/master.sock"

server_id=1
master_info_repository=TABLE
relay_log_info_repository=TABLE
log_bin=master_binlog
binlog_format=row

# GTID VARIABLES
gtid_mode=on
enforce_gtid_consistency=on
log_slave_updates=on
```

For this tutorial, we will be using GTID-enabled replication, so you should create a file in the folder we created earlier named `master.cnf`; for example, `/home/cbell/rpl/master.cnf`. We will use this file to start the instance for the master in a later step.

Tip   Some platforms may fail to start MySQL if the configuration file is world readable. Check the log if your server does not start for messages regarding the permissions of files.

Now, let's look at the configuration files for the slaves.

Configure the Slaves

Whereas log file and position replication require the master to have binary logging enabled, it is not required for the slaves. However, it is a good idea to turn on the binary log for the slaves if you want to use the slave to generate backups or for crash recovery. Binary logging is also required if you want to use GTID-enabled replication. In this section, we will use binary logging on the slaves.

As we did for the master, we need to set several variables including `datadir`, `basedir`, `port`, and `socket` (for *nix style platforms). Listing 1-3 shows the configuration file for the first slave (named `slave1`).

Listing 1-3. Slave Configuration File (Log File and Position)

```
[mysqld]
datadir="/home/cbell/rpl/data/slave1"
basedir="/usr/"
port=13002
socket="/home/cbell/rpl/slave1.sock"

server_id=2
master_info_repository=TABLE
relay_log_info_repository=TABLE
log_bin=slave1_binlog
binlog_format=row
report-port=13002
report-host=localhost
```

Notice that two additional variables are set: `report-port` and `report-host`. These are necessary to ensure that commands like `SHOW SLAVE HOSTS` report the correct information; the information for that view is derived from these variables. Thus, it is always a good idea to set these correctly.

Notice also that we set the data directory to one set aside for this slave, and the server ID is changed. Finally, we also change the name of the binary log to ensure that we know from which server the log originated (if needed in the future).

If we wanted to use GTID-based replication, we would add the same set of variables we did for the master, as shown in Listing 1-4.

Listing 1-4. Slave Configuration File (GTIDs)

```
[mysqld]
datadir="/home/cbell/rpl/data/slave1"
basedir="/usr/"
port=13002
socket="/home/cbell/rpl/slave1.sock"

server_id=2
master_info_repository=TABLE
relay_log_info_repository=TABLE
log_bin=slave1_binlog
binlog_format=row
report-port=13002
report-host=localhost

# GTID VARIABLES
gtid_mode=on
enforce_gtid_consistency=on
log_slave_updates=on
```

For this tutorial, we will be using GTID-enabled replication, so you should create a file in the folder we created earlier named `slave1.cnf`; for example, `/home/cbell/rpl/slave1.cnf`. If you want to add more slaves, create additional configuration files with the same data, changing only the data directory, socket, port, server ID, and binary log file.

Start the MySQL Instances

Now we are ready to start the MySQL instances. This is easy to do because we have already created the configuration file with all the parameters we need. We need to provide the configuration file with only the --defaults-file option. The following shows the commands to start both server instances:

```
mysqld --defaults-file=master.cnf
mysqld --defaults-file=slave1.cnf
```

When you run these commands, you should run them from the folder that contains the configuration files. Otherwise, you will have to provide the full path to the configuration file. It is also a good idea to either use a separate terminal window to launch each instance or redirect the output (logging of messages) to a file, as shown in Listing 1-5. However, you may want to use a separate terminal the first time you start the server to ensure no errors. Listing 1-5 shows an excerpt of the messages printed when launching the master.

Listing 1-5. Starting the Master Instance

```
$ mysqld --defaults-file=master.cnf
2018-03-05T18:45:18.544588Z 0 [Warning] TIMESTAMP with implicit DEFAULT
value is deprecated. Please use --explicit_defaults_for_timestamp server
option (see documentation for more details).
2018-03-05T18:45:18.545466Z 0 [Note] mysqld (mysqld
5.7.21-0ubuntu0.16.04.1-log) starting as process 8477 ...
...
2018-03-05T18:45:18.697423Z 0 [Note] Server hostname (bind-address): '*';
port: 13001
2018-03-05T18:45:18.697500Z 0 [Note] IPv6 is available.
2018-03-05T18:45:18.697523Z 0 [Note]   - '::' resolves to '::';
2018-03-05T18:45:18.697569Z 0 [Note] Server socket created on IP: '::'.
2018-03-05T18:45:18.735880Z 0 [Note] Event Scheduler: Loaded 0 events
2018-03-05T18:45:18.736092Z 0 [Note] mysqld: ready for connections.
Version: '5.7.21-0ubuntu0.16.04.1-log'  socket: '/home/cbell/rpl/master.sock'
port: 13001  (Ubuntu)
```

If you plan to use a single terminal, it is recommended to redirect the output to a file named master_log.txt and use the option to start the application in another process (for example, the & symbol). The log files are updated as the server generates messages, so you can refer to them if you encounter problems. It also helps to keep your terminal session clear of extra messages. The following shows how to structure the preceding command to start as a separate process and log messages to a file:

```
$ mysqld --defaults-file=master.cnf > master_output.txt 2>&1 &
```

If you haven't done so already, go ahead and start the slave. The following is the command I used to start the slave (slave1):

```
$ mysqld --defaults-file=slave1.cnf > slave1_output.txt 2>&1 &
```

Create the Replication User Account

After the MySQL instance is started, you must create a user to be used by the slave to connect to the master and read the binary log before you can set up replication. There is a special privilege for this named REPLICATION SLAVE. The following shows the correct GRANT statement to create the user and add the privilege. Remember the username and password you use here because you will need it for connecting the slave.

The following shows the commands needed to create the replication user. Execute these commands on all your servers. Although the user is not needed for the slaves, creating it now will allow you to use the slaves for recovery, switchover, or failover without having to create the user. In fact, this step is required for permitting automatic failover.

```
SET SQL_LOG_BIN=0;
CREATE USER rpl_user@'localhost' IDENTIFIED BY 'rpl_pass';
GRANT REPLICATION SLAVE ON *.* TO rpl_user@'localhost';
FLUSH PRIVILEGES;
SET SQL_LOG_BIN=1;
```

Notice the first and last commands. These commands tell the server to temporarily disable logging of changes to the binary log. We do this whenever we do not want to replicate the commands on other machines in the topology. Specifically, maintenance and administrative commands such as creating users should not be replicated. Turning off the binary log is a great way to ensure that you do not accidently issue transactions that cannot be executed on other machines.

The best way to execute these commands is to save them to a file named `create_rpl_user.sql` and use the source command of the `mysql` client to read the commands from the file and execute them. You can quickly create the replication user on all instances with the following commands:

```
mysql -uroot -h 127.0.0.1 -e "source /home/cbell/rpl/create_rpl_user.sql"
--port=13001
mysql -uroot -h 127.0.0.1 -e "source /home/cbell/rpl/create_rpl_user.sql"
--port=13002
```

Now we are ready to connect the slaves to the master and start replicating data.

Connect the Slaves to the Master

The next step is to connect the slaves to the master. There are various ways to do this depending on which form of replication you are using. Specifically, the command to connect the slave to the master differs when using log file and position as compared to GTID replication. There are also two steps: configuring the slave to connect and starting replication. Let's look at configuring the slave with log file and position first.

Connect with Log File and Position

To connect a slave to the master by using log file and position, we need a bit of information. This information is needed to complete the CHANGE MASTER command that instructs the slave to make a connection to the master. Table 1-1 shows the complete list of information needed. The table includes one of the sources where the information can be found along with an example of the values used in this tutorial.

Table 1-1. *Information Needed for Connecting a Slave (Log File and Position)*

Item from Master	Source	Example
IP address or hostname	master.cnf	localhost
Port	master.cnf	13001
Binary log file	SHOW MASTER STATUS	master_binlog.000002
Binary log file position	SHOW MASTER STATUS	154
Replication user ID	create_rpl_user.sql	rpl_user
Replication user password	create_rpl_user.sql	rpl_pass

The information for the master binary log file can be found with the SHOW MASTER STATUS command. The following shows how to use the mysql client to execute the command and return:

```
$ mysql -uroot -h 127.0.0.1 --port=13001 -e "SHOW MASTER STATUS\G"
*************************** 1. row ***************************
             File: master_binlog.000002
         Position: 154
     Binlog_Do_DB:
 Binlog_Ignore_DB:
Executed_Gtid_Set:
```

Notice that the command also displays any active filters as well as a GTID-specific value for the latest GTID executed set. We won't need that for this tutorial, but it is a good idea to file that away in case you need to recover a GTID-enabled topology.

Tip   For wide results, use the \G option to see the columns as rows (called *vertical format*).

Now that you have the master's binary log file name and position as well as the replication user and password, you can visit your slave and connect it to the master with the CHANGE MASTER command. The command can be constructed from the information in Table 1-1 as follows (formatted to make it easier to read—remove the \ if you are following along with this tutorial):

```
CHANGE MASTER TO MASTER_USER='rpl_user', MASTER_PASSWORD='rpl_pass', \
    MASTER_HOST='localhost', MASTER_PORT=13001, \
    MASTER_LOG_FILE='master_binlog.000002', MASTER_LOG_POS=154;
```

You must run this command on all the slaves. It may be easier to save this to a file and execute it by using the mysql client as we did for the replication user. For example, save this to a file named change_master.sql and execute it as shown here:

```
mysql -uroot -h 127.0.0.1 -e "source /home/cbell/rpl/change_master.sql"
--port=13002
```

There is one more step to starting the slave, but let's first look at how to configure the CHANGE MASTER commands for GTID-enabled replication.

Connect with GTIDs

To connect a slave to the master by using GTIDs, we need a bit of information. This information is needed to complete the CHANGE MASTER command that instructs the slave to make a connection to the master. Table 1-2 shows the complete list of information needed. The table includes one of the sources where the information can be found along with an example of the values used in this tutorial.

Table 1-2. *Information Needed for Connecting a Slave (GTIDs)*

Item from Master	Source	Example
IP address or hostname	master.cnf	localhost
Port	master.cnf	13001
Replication user ID	create_rpl_user.sql	rpl_user
Replication user password	create_rpl_user.sql	rpl_pass

Notice that we need less information than for log file and position replication. We don't need to know the master binary log file or position because the GTID handshake procedure will resolve that information for us. All we need is the host connection information for the master and the replication user and password. For GTID-enabled replication, we use a special parameter, MASTER_AUTO_POSITION, to instruct replication to negotiate the connection information automatically. The CHANGE MASTER command can be constructed from the information in Table 1-2 as follows (formatted to make it easier to read—remove the \ if you are following along with this tutorial):

```
CHANGE MASTER TO MASTER_USER='rpl_user', MASTER_PASSWORD='rpl_pass', \
    MASTER_HOST='localhost', MASTER_PORT=13001, MASTER_AUTO_POSITION = 1;
```

You must run this command on all the slaves. It may be easier to save this to a file and execute it by using the mysql client as we did for the replication user. For example, save this to a file named change_master.sql and execute it as shown here:

```
mysql -uroot -h 127.0.0.1 -e "source /home/cbell/rpl/change_master.sql"
--port=13002
```

If you want to be able to use the file for either form of replication, you can simply place both commands in the file and comment out one that you don't need. For example, the following shows an example file with both CHANGE MASTER commands. Notice that the GTID variant is commented out with the # symbol:

```
CHANGE MASTER TO MASTER_USER='rpl_user', MASTER_PASSWORD='rpl_pass',
MASTER_HOST='localhost', MASTER_PORT=13001, MASTER_LOG_FILE='master_
binlog.000001', MASTER_LOG_POS=150;
# GTID option:
# CHANGE MASTER TO MASTER_USER='rpl_user', MASTER_PASSWORD='rpl_pass',
MASTER_HOST='localhost', MASTER_PORT=13001, MASTER_AUTO_POSITION = 1;
```

Now that we have our slaves configured to connect, we must finish the process by telling the slaves to initiate the connection and start replication.

Start Replication

The next step is to start the slave processes. This command is simply START SLAVE. We would run this command on all the slaves as we did for the CHANGE MASTER command. The following shows the commands for starting the slaves:

```
mysql -uroot -h 127.0.0.1 -e "START SLAVE" --port=13002
```

The START SLAVE command normally does not report any errors; you must use SHOW SLAVE STATUS to see them. Listing 1-6 shows the command in action. For safety as well as peace of mind, you may want to run this command on any slave you start.

Listing 1-6. Checking SLAVE STATUS

```
$ mysql -uroot -h 127.0.0.1 -e "SHOW SLAVE STATUS \G" --port=13002
*************************** 1. row ***************************
               Slave_IO_State: Waiting for master to send event
                  Master_Host: localhost
                  Master_User: rpl_user
                  Master_Port: 13001
                Connect_Retry: 60
              Master_Log_File: master_binlog.000002
          Read_Master_Log_Pos: 154
               Relay_Log_File: oracle-pc-relay-bin.000002
```

```
               Relay_Log_Pos: 375
      Relay_Master_Log_File: master_binlog.000002
           Slave_IO_Running: Yes
          Slave_SQL_Running: Yes
            Replicate_Do_DB:
        Replicate_Ignore_DB:
         Replicate_Do_Table:
     Replicate_Ignore_Table:
    Replicate_Wild_Do_Table:
Replicate_Wild_Ignore_Table:
                 Last_Errno: 0
                 Last_Error:
               Skip_Counter: 0
        Exec_Master_Log_Pos: 154
            Relay_Log_Space: 586
            Until_Condition: None
            Until_Log_File:
             Until_Log_Pos: 0
          Master_SSL_Allowed: No
          Master_SSL_CA_File:
          Master_SSL_CA_Path:
             Master_SSL_Cert:
           Master_SSL_Cipher:
              Master_SSL_Key:
       Seconds_Behind_Master: 0
Master_SSL_Verify_Server_Cert: No
               Last_IO_Errno: 0
               Last_IO_Error:
              Last_SQL_Errno: 0
              Last_SQL_Error:
   Replicate_Ignore_Server_Ids:
            Master_Server_Id: 1
                 Master_UUID: 82783ccc-2094-11e8-b3e3-10bf4850c554
            Master_Info_File: mysql.slave_master_info
                   SQL_Delay: 0
         SQL_Remaining_Delay: NULL
```

```
Slave_SQL_Running_State: Slave has read all relay log; waiting for
more updates
      Master_Retry_Count: 86400
            Master_Bind:
 Last_IO_Error_Timestamp:
Last_SQL_Error_Timestamp:
          Master_SSL_Crl:
      Master_SSL_Crlpath:
      Retrieved_Gtid_Set:
       Executed_Gtid_Set:
           Auto_Position: 1
     Replicate_Rewrite_DB:
            Channel_Name:
      Master_TLS_Version:
```

Take a moment to slog through all these rows. You need to pay attention to several key fields. These include anything with error in the name, and the state columns. For example, the first row (Slave_IO_State) shows the textual message indicating the state of the slave's I/O thread. The I/O thread is responsible for reading events from the master's binary log. There is also a SQL thread that is responsible for reading events from the relay log and executing them.

For this example, you just need to ensure that both threads are running (YES) and there are no errors. For detailed explanations of all the fields in the SHOW SLAVE STATUS command, see the online MySQL reference manual in the section "SQL Statements for Controlling Slave Servers" (https://dev.mysql.com/doc/refman/5.7/en/replication-slave-sql.html).

Now that the slave is connected and running, let's check replication by checking the master and creating some data.

Verify Replication Status

Checking the slave status with the SHOW SLAVE STATUS command is the first step to verifying replication health. The next step is to check the master by using the SHOW SLAVE HOSTS command. Listing 1-7 shows the output of the SHOW SLAVE HOSTS for the topology setup in this tutorial. This command shows the slaves that are attached to the master and their UUIDs. It should be noted that this information is a view and is not real-time. It is possible for slave connections to fail and still be shown on the report until the processes time out and the server kills them. Thus, this command is best used as a sanity check.

Listing 1-7. SHOW SLAVE HOSTS Command (Master)

```
$ mysql -uroot -h 127.0.0.1 -e "SHOW SLAVE HOSTS \G" --port=13001
*************************** 1. row ***************************
 Server_id: 2
      Host: localhost
      Port: 13002
 Master_id: 1
Slave_UUID: 7e71cad7-20a6-11e8-a12b-10bf4850c554
```

Here we see the slave is connected and we know from the last section that the slave status is good.

Next, let's create some simple data on the master and then see whether that data is replicated to the slave. In this case, we will create a database, a table, and a single row and then run that on the master. Listing 1-8 shows the sample data as executed on the master.

Listing 1-8. Creating Sample Data for Testing Replication (Master)

```
$ mysql -uroot -h 127.0.0.1 --port=13001
Welcome to the MySQL monitor.  Commands end with ; or \g.
Your MySQL connection id is 7
Server version: 8.0.11 MySQL Community Server - GPL

Copyright (c) 2000, 2018, Oracle and/or its affiliates. All rights reserved.

Oracle is a registered trademark of Oracle Corporation and/or its
affiliates. Other names may be trademarks of their respective
owners.

Type 'help;' or '\h' for help. Type '\c' to clear the current input statement.

mysql> CREATE DATABASE test;
Query OK, 1 row affected (0.01 sec)

mysql> USE test;
Database changed
mysql> CREATE TABLE test.t1 (c1 INT PRIMARY KEY, c2 TEXT NOT NULL);
Query OK, 0 rows affected (0.03 sec)

mysql> INSERT INTO test.t1 VALUES (1, 'Chuck');
Query OK, 1 row affected (0.03 sec)
```

To verify that the data was replicated, all we need do is issue a SELECT SQL command on the table on one of the slaves (or all of them if you are so inclined). The following shows an example of what we expect to see on each of the slaves:

```
$ mysql -uroot -h 127.0.0.1 --port=13002 -e "SELECT * FROM test.t1"
+----+-------+
| c1 | c2    |
+----+-------+
|  1 | Chuck |
+----+-------+
```

This concludes the short tutorial on setting up MySQL Replication. This section presented a brief look at MySQL Replication in its barest, simplest terms. Now, let's look at how we can script an example setup of MySQL Replication.

Example MySQL Replication Script

If you have been working with systems for any length of time, it is almost certain that you see any repetitive operation as an opportunity to write a script to make the process easier and faster to repeat. Setting up MySQL Replication in a test environment as we did during the tutorial is an excellent example where automation is possible. We will explore an example script in this section.

While there are many ways you could write a script to automate a replication environment, let's keep it simple and place all our configuration files and data directories in a single folder in our user account. For example, if we used Linux, we could create a folder named rpl and within that folder create a folder named data, which contains the data directories for the instances. The following shows how this may look:

```
/home/cbell/rpl
              |
           +---/data
              |
           +---/master
              |
           +---/slave1
              |
           +---/slave2
              |
           +---/slave3
```

We also place the configuration files, automation scripts, and any additional files that contain data we use for commands, and so forth. For example, the contents of our folder may look like the following (prior to starting replication):

```
/home/<user>/rpl $ ls
change_master.sql  create_rpl_user.sql  sample_data.sql  shutdown.sh
slave2.cnf
check_rpl.sql         master.cnf            setup.sh          slave1.cnf
slave3.cnf
```

Listing 1-9 shows a script you can use to start replication on a typical Linux platform. As you will see, the script uses several additional files such as the `.sql` files mentioned in the tutorial. To use this script, simply create those files per the instructions in the preceding tutorial. You also need to make changes to the paths to match your system. The script file is named `setup.sh`, but you can name it however you like.

Listing 1-9. Example Replication Startup Script

```
#
#!/bin/bash
#
# Introducing MySQL InnoDB Cluster - Chapter 1 : Setup Replication (Linux)
#
...
#
# Dr. Charles Bell, 2018
#
BIN='/usr/sbin'
BASEDIR='/usr/'
DATADIR='/home/<user>/rpl'
echo
echo Introduction to MySQL InnoDB Cluster - Ch01 : Setup MySQL Replication
echo
```

```
echo ====== Step 1 of 6: INITIALIZE DATA DIRECTORIES ======
echo "> Creating data directory root ..."
cd "$DATADIR"
rm -rf "$DATADIR/data"
mkdir "$DATADIR/data"
echo "> Initializing the master ..."
echo
$BIN/mysqld --no-defaults --user=<user> --initialize-insecure
--basedir=$BASEDIR --datadir="$DATADIR/data/master"
echo
echo "> Initializing slave1 ..."
echo
$BIN/mysqld --no-defaults --user=<user> --initialize-insecure
--basedir=$BASEDIR --datadir="$DATADIR/data/slave1"
echo
echo "> Initializing slave2 ..."
echo
$BIN/mysqld --no-defaults --user=<user> --initialize-insecure
--basedir=$BASEDIR --datadir="$DATADIR/data/slave2"
echo
echo "> Initializing slave3 ..."
echo
$BIN/mysqld --no-defaults --user=<user> --initialize-insecure
--basedir=$BASEDIR --datadir="$DATADIR/data/slave3"
echo
echo ====== Step 2 of 6: START ALL INSTANCES ======
echo "> Removing old socket file ..."
cd $DATADIR
rm *.sock*
echo "> Starting master ..."
$BIN/mysqld --defaults-file="$DATADIR/master.cnf" > master_output.txt 2>&1 &
echo "> Starting slave1 ..."
$BIN/mysqld --defaults-file="$DATADIR/slave1.cnf" > slave1_output.txt 2>&1 &
```

```
echo "> Starting slave2 ..."
$BIN/mysqld --defaults-file="$DATADIR/slave2.cnf" > slave2_output.txt 2>&1 &
echo "> Starting slave3 ..."
$BIN/mysqld --defaults-file="$DATADIR/slave3.cnf" > slave3_output.txt 2>&1 &
sleep 5
echo
echo ====== Step 3 of 6: CREATE THE REPLICATION USER ======
echo "> Creating replication user on the master ..."
mysql -uroot -h 127.0.0.1 -e "source /home/<user>/rpl/create_rpl_user.sql"
--port=13001
echo "> Creating replication user on slave1 ..."
mysql -uroot -h 127.0.0.1 -e "source /home/<user>/rpl/create_rpl_user.sql"
--port=13002
echo "> Creating replication user on slave2 ..."
mysql -uroot -h 127.0.0.1 -e "source /home/<user>/rpl/create_rpl_user.sql"
--port=13003
echo "> Creating replication user on slave3 ..."
mysql -uroot -h 127.0.0.1 -e "source /home/<user>/rpl/create_rpl_user.sql"
--port=13004
echo
echo ====== Step 4 of 6: START RPL ======
echo "> Executing CHANGE MASTER on slave1 ..."
mysql -uroot -h 127.0.0.1 -e "source /home/<user>/rpl/change_master.sql"
--port=13002
echo "> Executing START SLAVE on slave1 ..."
mysql -uroot -h 127.0.0.1 -e "START SLAVE" --port=13002
mysql -uroot -h 127.0.0.1 -e "source /home/<user>/rpl/change_master.sql"
--port=13003
echo "> Executing START SLAVE on slave2 ..."
mysql -uroot -h 127.0.0.1 -e "START SLAVE" --port=13003
mysql -uroot -h 127.0.0.1 -e "source /home/<user>/rpl/change_master.sql"
--port=13004
echo "> Executing START SLAVE on slave3 ..."
mysql -uroot -h 127.0.0.1 -e "START SLAVE" --port=13004
```

```
echo
echo ====== Step 5 of 6: CHECK RPL ======
echo "> Checking replication setup ..."
mysql -uroot -h 127.0.0.1 -e "source /home/<user>/rpl/check_rpl.sql"
--port=13001
echo
echo ====== Step 6 of 6: CREATE SOME DATA ======
echo "> Creating data ..."
mysql -uroot -h 127.0.0.1 -e "source /home/<user>/rpl/sample_data.sql"
--port=13001
sleep 3
mysql -uroot -h 127.0.0.1 -e "SELECT * FROM test.t1" --port=13003
echo Done.
echo
```

Listing 1-10 is an example of the output you will see when this script runs. Some of the messages from the server initiation step have been removed. Execution on your system may vary, but the listing shows the correct sequence of statements you should see.

Listing 1-10. Example Replication Script Output

```
$ ./setup.sh
Introduction to MySQL InnoDB Cluster - Ch01 : Setup MySQL Replication
====== Step 1 of 6: INITIALIZE DATA DIRECTORIES ======
> Creating data directory root ...
> Initializing the master ...
> Initializing slave1 ...
> Initializing slave2 ...
> Initializing slave3 ...
====== Step 2 of 6: START ALL INSTANCES ======
> Removing old socket file ...
> Starting master ...
> Starting slave1 ...
> Starting slave2 ...
> Starting slave3 ...
```

```
====== Step 3 of 6: CREATE THE REPLICATION USER ======
> Creating replication user on the master ...
> Creating replication user on slave1 ...
> Creating replication user on slave2 ...
> Creating replication user on slave3 ...
====== Step 4 of 6: START RPL ======
> Executing CHANGE MASTER on slave1 ...
> Executing START SLAVE on slave1 ...
> Executing CHANGE MASTER on slave2 ...
> Executing START SLAVE on slave2 ...
> Executing CHANGE MASTER on slave3 ...
> Executing START SLAVE on slave3 ...
====== Step 5 of 6: CHECK RPL ======
> Checking replication setup ...
+-----------+-----------+-------+-----------+----------------------------+
| Server_id | Host      | Port  | Master_id | Slave_UUID                 |
+-----------+-----------+-------+-----------+----------------------------+
|         2 | localhost | 13002 |         1 | d2a4b096-254f-11e8-8694-   |
|           |           |       |           | 8086f28ecc6d               |
|         4 | localhost | 13004 |         1 | d774c619-254f-11e8-894f-   |
|           |           |       |           | 8086f28ecc6d               |
|         3 | localhost | 13003 |         1 | d507b376-254f-11e8-8882-   |
|           |           |       |           | 8086f28ecc6d               |
+-----------+-----------+-------+-----------+----------------------------+
====== Step 6 of 6: CREATE SOME DATA ======
> Creating data ...
+----+-------+
| c1 | c2    |
+----+-------+
|  1 | Chuck |
+----+-------+
Done.
```

Notice at the end of the script we see the output of SHOW SLAVE HOSTS that shows all the slaves connected (you should see all three).We also see the results of a SELECT query for the test data executed on one of the slaves.

If you try this script and encounter errors, be sure to check the paths in the script to ensure that you've changed them correctly. Also, be sure to check the *_output.txt log files because the server may issue error messages that can help you fix whatever caused the error.

You may also be interested in a quick and easy way to shut down replication. Listing 1-11 shows an example script you can use with the setup script to shut down your example replication topology. Notice that we shut down in a precise order by first stopping the slave threads, then shutting down the MySQL instances, and finally removing the data directory.

Listing 1-11. Example Replication Shutdown Script

```
#!/bin/bash
#
# Introducing MySQL InnoDB Cluster - Chapter 1 : Shutdown Replication
#
...
#
# Dr. Charles Bell, 2018
#
DATADIR='/home/<user>/rpl'
echo
echo Introduction to MySQL InnoDB Cluster - Ch01 : Shutdown MySQL Replication
echo
echo ====== Step 1 of 3: STOP REPLICATION ON SLAVES ======
echo "> Stopping the slave threads on slave1 ..."
mysql -uroot -h 127.0.0.1 --port=13002 -e "STOP SLAVE"
echo "> Stopping the slave threads on slave2 ..."
mysql -uroot -h 127.0.0.1 --port=13003 -e "STOP SLAVE"
echo "> Stopping the slave threads on slave3 ..."
mysql -uroot -h 127.0.0.1 --port=13004 -e "STOP SLAVE"
echo
echo ====== Step 2 of 3: SHUTDOWN mysqld INSTANCES ======
echo "> Stopping the MySQL instance for slave1 ..."
mysql -uroot -h 127.0.0.1 --port=13002 -e "SHUTDOWN"
```

```
echo "> Stopping the MySQL instance for slave2 ..."
mysql -uroot -h 127.0.0.1 --port=13003 -e "SHUTDOWN"
echo "> Stopping the MySQL instance for slave3 ..."
mysql -uroot -h 127.0.0.1 --port=13004 -e "SHUTDOWN"
echo "> Stopping the MySQL instance for the master ..."
mysql -uroot -h 127.0.0.1 --port=13001 -e "SHUTDOWN"
echo
echo ====== Step 3 of 3: DESTROY THE DATA DIRECTORIES ======
echo "> Removing data directories and the root ..."
cd "$DATADIR"
rm -rf "$DATADIR/data"
echo Done.
```

If you are attempting to diagnose a problem with your example replication topology, you may want to comment out the last step in case there are issues in the slave threads or a query. Deleting the data directories will also delete any log files that could help with diagnosing problems. Listing 1-12 shows an example of the output of running this script.

Listing 1-12. Example Replication Shutdown Script Output

```
$ ./shutdown.sh

Introduction to MySQL InnoDB Cluster - Ch01 : Shutdown MySQL Replication
====== Step 1 of 3: STOP REPLICATION ON SLAVES ======
> Stopping the slave threads on slave1 ...
> Stopping the slave threads on slave2 ...
> Stopping the slave threads on slave3 ...
====== Step 2 of 3: SHUTDOWN mysqld INSTANCES ======
> Stopping the MySQL instance for slave1 ...
> Stopping the MySQL instance for slave2 ...
> Stopping the MySQL instance for slave3 ...
> Stopping the MySQL instance for the master ...
====== Step 3 of 3: DESTROY THE DATA DIRECTORIES ======
> Removing data directories and the root ...
Done.
```

Tip You may need to make changes to these scripts to match your platform and setup of your account. Some changes may require some work. However, the sample code for this book includes this script adapted for Linux, macOS, and Windows 10.

Now that you know more about MySQL Replication and Group Replication, let's review some of the challenges that database administrators face when administering these features.

Challenges for MySQL DBAs

You may have perceived a few things from these brief discussions about MySQL Replication and Group Replication. Among those may be the typical overwhelming feeling when you realize the setup procedure is strict and requires arcane commands. Of course, the same could be said of any system or major feature, like high availability. Fortunately, references such as this book and others can help mitigate some of the learning curve.

However, it is well-known that these high-availability features in MySQL have challenges for administrators—both systems and database alike. The following gives an overview of several categories of challenges for the purposes of preparing you for learning how InnoDB Cluster makes many of them easier.

Setup

This category covers the planning and installation of the replication-based high-availability solution. Consider needs for existing data, servers, applications, users, and administrators.

- *Setting up variables for replication*: Know how to tune replication and the servers for optimal operation.

- *Rollout of installations*: Install and set up replication on potentially hundreds of servers throughout an infrastructure, and do so with automation.

- *Integrating applications and third-party solutions*: Figure out how to integrate other high-availability components with replication and MySQL.

- *Read scaling*: Build the topology for faster application reads; read data from multiple slaves/secondaries.

- *Write scaling*: Build the topology for faster application writes; write data to more than one primary.

Troubleshooting

This category includes those tasks associated with detecting and correcting anomalies from errors, outages, planned maintenance, and more.

- *Data not replicating*: Discover and correct when data does not reach one or more servers.

- *Secondary stops with error (or unexpectedly)*: Troubleshoot and repair servers that stop replicating.

- *Errors during replication*: Recover from errors, including tasks such as recovering a server, synchronizing data, and reestablishing replication.

- *Secondary lagging behind on updates*: Determine why some servers are not updating the data as fast as others.

Maintenance

This category covers the preventative and sometimes corrective tasks associated with keeping a high-availability solution running at its peak efficiency. This category is often overlooked by inexperienced administrators and often requires advanced, paid tools in larger installations.

- *Checking performance of a server*: Ensure that all servers are operating at peak efficiency.

- *Monitoring servers in the topology*: Detect problems early, such as performance, errors, and load.

- *Upgrades to the database, MySQL, or platform*: Know how to upgrade the servers in a topology (often a major effort in large organizations).

- *Checking data consistency*: Check for data inconsistencies for a given server.

- *Synchronizing data*: Ensure that all servers have the same data as the primary.

Administration

This category covers the typical or expected tasks that occur as part of having a high-availability solution. These may include managing the server, replication, and the data in reaction to planned or expected conditions or events.

- *Conducting switchover*: The manual transfer of the primary role to a secondary.

- *Automatic failover*: The primary (write) role switches to a candidate secondary, automatically ensuring no interruption in data access.

- *Recovery of a server in the topology*: Recover a server that has failed or has corrupt data.

- *Backup and Restore*: Leverage the secondaries for offloading backup and use secondaries for restoring data.

- *Provisioning*: Add more secondaries to a topology with the goal of minimizing time to reproduce changes. Often accomplished using a backup from another secondary.

References on MySQL High Availability

If you peruse some of the lengthier works on MySQL high availability prior to InnoDB Cluster, you may find some additional, more complex challenges for specific use cases. If you would like to know more about MySQL Replication and MySQL high-availability features prior to InnoDB Cluster, the following are some excellent resources:

- *MySQL High Availability: Tools for Building Robust Data Centers, Second Edition* by Charles Bell et al. (O'Reilly, 2014)

- *MySQL Replication Simplified: Easy Step-by-Step Examples to Establish, Troubleshoot, and Monitor Replication* by Sribatsa Das (Business Compass, 2014)

- *High Performance MySQL: Optimization, Backups, Replication, and More* by Baron Schwartz et al. (O'Reilly, 2012)

- *High Availability MySQL Cookbook* by Alex Davies (Packt, 2010)

There are some rather obscure resources that are of interest to anyone wanting to know more about the details of the binary log and its format. Of course, the online reference manual has considerable documentation and should be your primary source. However, the following contain key information not found in other sources:

- `http://dev.mysql.com/doc/internals/en/index.html`

- `http://dev.mysql.com/doc/internals/en/replication-protocol.html`

- `http://dev.mysql.com/doc/internals/en/row-based-replication.html`

Tip   The source code for this book contains scripts that you can use to set up MySQL Replication and MySQL Group Replication and modify them to your needs. You can find these on the Apress web site for the book (`www.apress.com/9781484238844`).

Summary

Achieving high availability in MySQL is possible with MySQL Replication. Indeed, you can create robust data centers with replication. Better still, replication has been around for a long time and is considered stable. Many organizations have and continue to have success using replication in production—from small installations to massive installations.

Even so, there are limitations to using MySQL Replication, such as how to handle switching the master role to another machine (slave) if the master fails, how to perform this automatically, how to handle multiple write scenarios, and general troubleshooting and maintenance. Many of these have been improved in Group Replication. However, as you have seen, setup of replication requires effort and maintenance, which may be a concern to planners (for example, architects) and administrators alike.

Given the rather steep learning curve to get replication up and running and to manage it over time has become a great challenge to those unfamiliar with similar high-availability solutions. Indeed, the demand for those knowledgeable of MySQL Replication is quite high and because it is a unique skillset, hard to find.

Thus, Oracle has improved upon MySQL Replication, building on its feature set and success and folding in several other features to make an easier-to-learn and easier-to-maintain high-availability solution. Group Replication and later InnoDB Cluster is that answer and has already proven itself to be the go-to solution for MySQL high availability.

In the next chapter, you will discover more about InnoDB Cluster and how it can be used to achieve high availability.

CHAPTER 2

What Is MySQL InnoDB Cluster?

Now that you understand what high availability is and how to achieve a level of high availability with MySQL Replication, let's look at the newest evolution of high-availability features in MySQL: InnoDB Cluster.

It is a testament to the dedication of the Oracle MySQL engineers (and Oracle itself) that MySQL continues to improve with new features. The drive within the MySQL engineering division is to continue to develop disruptive database technologies for the Internet. Oracle has not only fostered this aggressiveness but also continued to live up to its promise to invest in and grow its MySQL business. This newest version, MySQL 8, proves conclusively that Oracle has fulfilled its promise to ensure that MySQL remains the world's most popular open source database system.

This new release of MySQL breaks many of the molds of previous versions, adding new, revolutionary features that change the firmament of how some will use MySQL. Indeed, the version number alone has jumped from 5.X to 8.0, signifying the jump in technological sophistication and finally breaking away from continuous development of the 5.X codebase that has lasted for over 13 years.

WHAT HAPPENED TO THE 8.0.5–8.0.10 RELEASES?

You may have noticed that the 8.0 release series is not sequential and that some interim numbered releases have been skipped. This is largely an effort to stabilize and coordinate the one product release mantra so that users can know, at a glance, what versions of which components work together. Clearly, knowing you have version 8.0.11, say, for all your MySQL components ensures that they will all work together. Gone are the days when we needed a roadmap and a Sherpa guide to discover what version of which component worked together!

One of the most exciting new features is InnoDB Cluster. This represents a huge leap forward in high availability for MySQL. Best of all, it comes standard in all releases of MySQL 8.0. Let's look at what makes InnoDB Cluster such an important feature for enterprises large and small.

Overview

The core component of InnoDB Cluster is the InnoDB storage engine. Since MySQL 5.6, InnoDB has been the flagship storage engine (and the default engine) for MySQL. Oracle has slowly evolved away from the multiple storage engine model, focusing on what a modern database server should do: support transactional storage mechanisms. InnoDB is the answer to that requirement and much more.

To better understand how we arrived at InnoDB Cluster, let's take a short tour of the other storage engines available in MySQL 8.0 and earlier releases.

What Is a Storage Engine?

A *storage engine* is a mechanism to store data in various ways. For example, there is a storage engine that allows you to interact with comma-separated values (text) files (CSV), another that is optimized for writing log files (archive), one that stores data in memory only (memory), and even one that doesn't store anything at all (blackhole). Along with InnoDB, the MySQL server ships with several storage engines. The following sections describe some of the more commonly used alternative storage engines. Note that some storage engines have been dropped from support over the evolution of MySQL, including the Berkeley Database (BDB) storage engine.

Tip   If you want to see which storage engines are available for use on your MySQL server, you can use the `SHOW ENGINES` command. See (`https://dev.mysql.com/doc/refman/8.0/en/create-table.html`) to learn more about specifying a storage engine with the `CREATE TABLE` command.

MyISAM

The *MyISAM storage engine* was originally the default in MySQL and was used by most LAMP stacks, data warehousing, e-commerce, and enterprise applications. MyISAM files are an extension of Indexed Sequential Access Method (ISAM) built with additional optimizations, such as advanced caching and indexing mechanisms. These tables are built using compression features and index optimizations for speed.

Additionally, the MyISAM storage engine provides for concurrent operations by providing table-level locking. The MyISAM storage mechanism offers reliable storage for a wide variety of applications while providing fast retrieval of data. MyISAM is the storage engine of choice when read performance is a concern.

Memory

The *memory storage engine* (sometimes called *HEAP tables*) is an in-memory table that uses a hashing mechanism for fast retrieval of frequently used data. These tables are much faster than those that are stored and referenced from disk. They are accessed in the same manner as the other storage engines, but the data is stored in-memory and is valid only until MySQL is restarted. The data is flushed and deleted on shutdown (or a crash).

Memory storage engines are typically used in situations in which static data is accessed frequently and rarely ever altered. Examples of such situations include zip code, state, county, category, and other lookup tables. HEAP tables can also be used in databases that utilize snapshot techniques for distributed or historical data access.

Merge

The *merge storage engine* (sometimes named `MRG_MYISAM`) is built using a set of MyISAM tables with the same structure (tuple layout or schema) that can be referenced as a single table. The tables are partitioned by the location of the individual tables, but no additional partitioning mechanisms are used. All tables must reside on the same machine (accessed by the same server). Data is accessed using singular operations or statements, such as `SELECT`, `UPDATE`, `INSERT`, and `DELETE`. Fortunately, when a `DROP` is issued on a merge table, only the merge specification is removed. The original tables are not altered.

The biggest benefit of this table type is speed. It is possible to split a large table into several smaller tables on different disks, combine them using a merge-table specification, and access them simultaneously. Searches and sorts will execute more quickly because there is less data in each table to manipulate. For example, if you divide

45

the data by a predicate, you can search only those specific portions that contain the category you are searching for. Similarly, repairs on tables are more efficient because it is faster and easier to repair several smaller individual files than a single large table. Presumably, most errors will be localized to an area within one or two of the files and thus will not require rebuilding and repair of all the data. Unfortunately, this configuration has several disadvantages:

- You can use only identical MyISAM tables, or schemas, to form a single merge table. This limits the application of the merge storage engine to MyISAM tables. If the merge storage engine were to accept any storage engine, the merge storage engine would be more versatile.

- The replace operation is not permitted.

- Indexed access has been shown to be less efficient than for a single table.

Merge storage mechanisms are best used in very large database (VLDB) applications, such as data warehousing with data residing in more than one table in one or more databases.

Archive

The *archive storage engine* is designed for storing large amounts of data in a compressed format. The archive storage mechanism is best used for storing and retrieving large amounts of seldom-accessed archival or historical data. Such data includes security-access-data logs. While not something that you would want to search or even use daily, it is something a database professional who is concerned about security would want to have should a security incident occur. No indexes are provided for the archive storage mechanism, and the only access method is via a table scan. The archive storage engine should not be used for normal database storage and retrieval.

Federated

The *federated storage engine* is designed to create a single table reference from multiple MySQL database systems. The federated storage engine therefore works like the merge storage engine, but it allows you to link data (tables) together across database servers.

This mechanism is similar in purpose to the linked data tables available in other database systems. The federated storage mechanism is best used in distributed or data mart environments.

The most interesting aspect of the federated storage engine is that it does not move data, nor does it require the remote tables to be the same storage engine. This illustrates the true power of the pluggable-storage-engine layer. Data is translated during storage and retrieval.

CSV

The *CSV storage engine* is designed to create, read, and write comma-separated values (CSV) files as tables. Although the CSV storage engine does not copy the data into another format, the sheet layout, or metadata, is stored along with the file name specified on the server in the database folder. This permits database professionals to rapidly export structured business data that is stored in spreadsheets. The CSV storage engine does not provide any indexing mechanisms, making it impractical for large amounts of data. It is intended to be used as a link between storing data and visualizing it in spreadsheet applications.

Blackhole

The *blackhole storage engine*, an interesting feature with surprising utility, is designed to permit the system to write data, but the data is never saved. If binary logging is enabled, however, the SQL statements are written to the logs. This permits database administrators and developers to temporarily disable data ingestion in the database by switching the table type. This can be handy when you want to test an application to ensure that it is writing data that you don't want to store, such as when creating a relay slave for filtering replication.

InnoDB

InnoDB is a general-purpose storage engine that balances high reliability and high performance. InnoDB became the default storage engine in MySQL 5.7, which means that all tables created without the ENGINE clause, are created as InnoDB tables in the InnoDB tablespace. The decision to use the InnoDB storage engine was made after several attempts to build a robust, high-performance storage engine for MySQL. Given the maturity and sophistication of InnoDB, it made much more sense to use what already existed. Plus, Oracle owned both MySQL and InnoDB.

WHY IS IT CALLED INNODB?

In the early days, the InnoDB storage engine was built and owned by a separate company called Finland-based InfoBase Oy, which named its database engine InnoDB. This was a separate product that was not part of MySQL, nor was it owned by MySQL AB (the original owner of MySQL now fully owned by Oracle). Eventually, Oracle came to own both InnoDB in 2005 and MySQL in 2010, and it made sense to combine the two efforts because they have mutually inclusive goals. Although a separate InnoDB engineering team still exists, they are fully integrated with the core server development team.

The InnoDB storage engine is used when you need to use transactions. InnoDB supports traditional ACID transactions (see the accompanying sidebar) and foreign-key constraints. All indexes in InnoDB are B-trees, and the index records are stored in the leaf pages of the tree. InnoDB is the storage engine of choice for high-reliability and transaction-processing environments.

WHAT IS ACID?

ACID stands for *atomicity*, *consistency*, *isolation*, and *durability*. Perhaps one of the most important concepts in database theory, it defines the behavior that database systems must exhibit to be considered reliable for transaction processing.

Atomicity means that the database must allow modifications of data on an "all or nothing" basis for transactions that contain multiple commands. Each transaction is atomic. If a command fails, the entire transaction fails, and all changes up to that point in the transaction are discarded. This is especially important for systems that operate in highly transactional environments, such as the financial market. Consider for a moment the ramifications of a money transfer. Typically, multiple steps are involved in debiting one account and crediting another. If the transaction fails after the debit step and doesn't credit the money back to the first account, the owner of that account will be angry. In this case, the entire transaction from debit to credit must succeed, or none of it does.

Consistency means that only valid data will be stored in the database. If a command in a transaction violates one of the consistency rules, the entire transaction is discarded, and the data is returned to the state it was in before the transaction began. Conversely, if a transaction completes successfully, it will alter the data in a manner that obeys the database consistency rules.

Isolation means that multiple transactions executing at the same time will not interfere with one another. This is where the true challenge of concurrency is most evident. Database systems must handle situations in which transactions cannot violate the data (alter, delete, and so forth) being used in another transaction. There are many ways to handle this. Most systems use a mechanism called *locking* that keeps the data from being used by another transaction until the first one is done. Although the isolation property does not dictate which transaction is executed first, it does ensure that they will not interfere with one another.

Durability means that no transaction will result in lost data nor will any data created or altered during the transaction be lost. Durability is usually provided by robust backup-and-restore maintenance functions. Some database systems use logging to ensure that any uncommitted data can be recovered on restart.

InnoDB offers several critical advantages over the older storage engines in MySQL, including the following:

- Data Manipulation Language (DML) operations follow the ACID model, with transactions featuring commit, rollback, and crash-recovery capabilities to protect user data.

- Row-level locking and Oracle-style consistent reads increase multiuser concurrency and performance.

- InnoDB tables arrange your data on disk to optimize queries based on primary keys. Each InnoDB table has a primary-key index called the *clustered index* that organizes the data to minimize I/O for primary key lookups.

- To maintain data integrity, InnoDB supports foreign key constraints. With foreign keys, inserts, updates, and deletes are checked to ensure that they do not result in inconsistencies across different tables.

Many improvements have been made to InnoDB, including a host of performance enhancements and even support for fine-tuning and more. This is clear in the way InnoDB continues to evolve with refinements in each release of MySQL. Indeed, the list of refinements has grown long since the 5.6 releases. Although most of the improvements are subtle, in the sense that you won't notice them (except through better performance and reliability, which are not to be taken lightly), most show a dedication to making InnoDB the best transactional storage mechanism—and through extension, MySQL a strong transactional database system.

The following lists some of the more interesting improvements to InnoDB that you will find in MySQL 8. Some of these may seem to be very deep into the depths of the code, but those who have optimized or otherwise tuned their InnoDB installation may need to take note of these when planning to move to MySQL 8. What is not listed here are dozens of minor defect repairs and improvements in reliability and performance.

- *Improved tablespace support*: Includes enhancements to work with the new data dictionary, relocating tablespaces, and more.

- *A new* `innodb_dedicated_server` *configuration option*: (Disabled by default) used to have InnoDB automatically configure the following options according to the amount of memory detected on the server.

  - `innodb_buffer_pool_size`

  - `innodb_log_file_size`

  - `innodb_flush_method`

- *Crash recovery*: Should the index tree become corrupt, InnoDB writes a corruption flag to the redo log. This makes the corruption flag crash-safe (it is not lost on a forced restart). Similarly, InnoDB also writes an in-memory corruption flag on each checkpoint. When crash recovery is initiated, InnoDB can read the flags and use them to adjust recovery operations.

- *InnoDB memcached plugin*: Has been improved by permitting fetching of multiple key/value pairs in a single memcached query.

- *Deadlock detection*: There are several new options, but the most promising includes an option to dynamically configure deadlock detection (`innodb_deadlock_detect`). This could permit additional tuning control for high-usage systems for which deadlock detection is a detriment to performance.

- `INFORMATION_SCHEMA` *views*: There are new views for InnoDB.

- `AUTO_INCREMENT`: There are several minor improvements with auto-increment fields, including the following:

  - The current maximum auto-increment value is now persistent across server restarts.

- A restart no longer cancels the effect of the AUTO_INCREMENT = N table option.

- A server restart immediately following a ROLLBACK operation no longer results in the reuse of auto-increment values that were allocated to the rolled-back transaction.

- Setting an AUTO_INCREMENT column value to a value larger than the current maximum is persisted, and later new values (say, after a restart) start with the new, larger value.

- *Temporary tables*: All temporary tables are now created by default in the shared temporary tablespace named ibtmp1.

Although this list seems focused on minor improvements, some of these are important to system administrators looking for help tuning and planning their database server installations. If you would like to know more about any of these improvements or see a list of all the latest changes, see the online MySQL 8.0 Reference Manual (http://downloads.mysql.com/docs/refman-8.0-en.pdf).

Perhaps the most important feature that sets InnoDB apart from the earlier storage engines in MySQL is its configurability. Although some of the early storage engines were configurable, none were at the scale that exists for configuring InnoDB. There are dozens of parameters you can use to tune InnoDB to meet your unique storage needs.

Caution   Use care when tinkering with InnoDB parameters. It is possible to degrade your system to the point of hurting performance. As with any tuning exercise, always consult the documentation (and experts) first, and then plan to target specific parameters. Be sure to tune one parameter at a time, and to test, confirm, or revert before moving on.

Although InnoDB works well out of the box with well-chosen defaults and is likely to not require much tuning for most, those who need to tune MySQL will find all they need and more to get their database systems running at peak efficiency. See https://dev. mysql.com/doc/refman/8.0/en/innodb-introduction.html for more information about the InnoDB Storage engine, including its numerous configuration and tuning options.

Tip   Another excellent source for tips and advice for configuring MySQL and InnoDB is *High Performance MySQL: Optimization, Backups, Replication, and More* by Baron Schwartz et al. (O'Reilly, 2012).

Now that you have a better understanding of the pedigree and evolution of InnoDB, let's discover what InnoDB Cluster provides.

Introducing InnoDB Cluster

One of the most exciting new features in MySQL 8.0[1] is InnoDB Cluster. It is designed to make high availability easier to set up, use, and maintain. InnoDB Cluster works with the X DevAPI via MySQL Shell and the AdminAPI, Group Replication, and MySQL Router to take high availability and read scalability to a new level. InnoDB Cluster combines new features in InnoDB for cloning data with Group Replication and MySQL Router to provide a new way to set up and manage high availability. The following list describes the components that make up InnoDB Cluster. You will learn more about these in the next section, and see details of how to configure and use each of these in later chapters as you explore InnoDB via a tutorial.

- *Group Replication*: A new form of replication that builds upon MySQL Replication, adding an active communication protocol (group membership) that permits higher levels of availability including fault tolerance with automatic failover.

- *MySQL Shell*: A new MySQL client that permits several modes of interfaces including the traditional SQL as well as JavaScript and Python scripting languages.

- *X DevAPI*: A special application programming interface for applications to interact with data programmatically.

- *AdminAPI*: A special API available via MySQL Shell for configuring and interacting with InnoDB Cluster. The AdminAPI has features designed to make working with InnoDB Cluster easier.

- *MySQL Router*: Lightweight middleware that provides transparent routing between your application and back-end MySQL servers.

---

[1]And some releases of MySQL 5.7.

You may be wondering what all the fuss is about. It appears on the surface that InnoDB Cluster is a bundle of existing features in MySQL. Although that may be a valid conclusion, the truth is there is more to the product than simply bundling things together with a new name. In this case, Oracle has added specialized administrative layers and features internal to InnoDB Cluster that improves on these products. As you will see, working with InnoDB Cluster often hides many of the details (and tedium) of working with the components individually.

Let's look at a conceptual configuration to get a sense of how the components interact. Figure 2-1 shows how these components are arranged conceptually to form InnoDB Cluster.

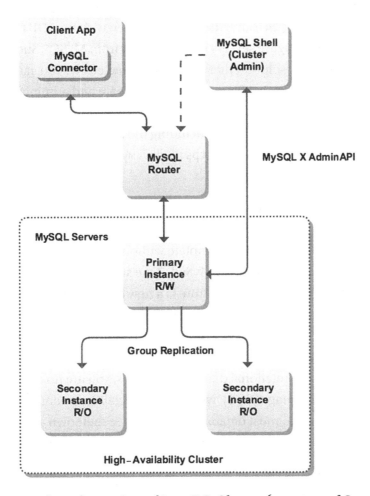

Figure 2-1. *Typical configuration of InnoDB Cluster (courtesy of Oracle)*

In this use case, a cluster of three servers is set up with a single primary (think *master* in standard replication parlance), which is the target for all writes (updates). Multiple secondary servers (slaves) maintain replicas of the data, which can be read from; these servers enable reading data without burdening the primary, thus enabling read scalability (but all servers participate in consensus and coordination). The incorporation of Group Replication means the cluster is fault tolerant and group membership is managed automatically. MySQL Router caches the metadata of the InnoDB Cluster and performs high-availability routing to the MySQL Server instances, making it easier to write applications to interact with the cluster.

You may be wondering what makes this different from a read scalability (sometimes called *read-out scalability*) setup with standard replication. At a high level, it may seem that the solutions are solving the same use case. However, with InnoDB Cluster, you can create, deploy, and configure servers in your cluster from MySQL Shell, providing a complete high-availability solution that can be managed easily. You can use the X AdminAPI (also called the AdminAPI) via the shell to create and administer InnoDB Cluster programmatically using either JavaScript or Python.

To learn more about InnoDB Cluster, including the latest features, use cases, and more, see the online documentation at `https://dev.mysql.com/doc/refman/8.0/en/mysql-innodb-cluster-userguide.html`.

InnoDB Cluster and the MySQL Document Store

A book on InnoDB Cluster would be incomplete without discussing how well InnoDB Cluster works with other new features of MySQL. One such feature is the MySQL Document Store. The MySQL Document Store is a new dynamic for MySQL that allows storage and retrieval of JSON data (called *documents*) via an application programming interface (in fact, the X DevAPI). The Document Store permits you to create NoSQL applications that work with unstructured data.

If you have worked with relational databases systems, you are no doubt familiar with Structured Query Language (SQL), which uses special statements (commands) to interact with the data. In fact, most database systems have their own version of SQL that includes commands for manipulating the data (DML) as well as defining the objects to store data (DDL), and even administrative commands to manage the server.

To retrieve data in an SQL interface, you must use special commands to search for the data and then convert the results into internal programming structures, making the data seem like an auxiliary component rather than an integral part of the solution.

NoSQL interfaces break this mold by allowing you to use APIs to work with the data. More specifically, you use programming interfaces rather than command-based interfaces.

WHY IS IT CALLED "NOSQL"?

Sadly, NoSQL can mean several things depending on your perspective, including *non-SQL*, *not only SQL*, or *nonrelational*. But they all indicate that the mechanism you're using is not using a command-based interface, and most uses of the term indicate you're using a programming interface.

In MySQL 8, access to JSON documents can be either through SQL or NoSQL using the X Protocol and X DevAPI through the X Plugin. So, although InnoDB Cluster will enhance your high-availability applications that are written for traditional SQL databases, InnoDB Cluster also works seamlessly with NoSQL applications.

Tip   To learn more about the MySQL Document Store, see my book, *Introducing the MySQL 8 Document Store* (Apress, 2018).

InnoDB Cluster and NDB Cluster

If you peruse the MySQL web site, you will find another product with *cluster* in the name. It is enticingly named *NDB Cluster*. NDB Cluster is a separate product from the MySQL server, employing a technology that enables clustering of in-memory databases in a shared-nothing system. The shared-nothing architecture enables the system to work with inexpensive hardware, and with a minimum of specific requirements for hardware or software.

NDB Cluster is designed not to have any single point of failure. In a shared-nothing system, each component is expected to have its own memory and disk, and the use of shared storage mechanisms such as network shares, network file systems, and Storage Area Network (SANs) is not recommended or supported. See https: https://dev. mysql.com/doc/refman/5.7/en/mysql-cluster-compared.html to learn more about NDB Cluster and how it relates to InnoDB.

> **Tip** To learn more about NDB Cluster, see the excellent *Pro MySQL NDB Cluster* by Jesper Krogh and Mikiya Okuno (Apress, 2017). This book covers every aspect of NDB Cluster and is a must for anyone interested in deploying and managing NDB Cluster.

Components

Now that you have a better idea of what InnoDB Cluster is, including how it evolved and its benefits for high availability, let's learn more about the components that make up InnoDB Cluster. The following sections describe each of the components at a high level. Once again, you will discover more about each in later chapters. I will present only the basics of each component, to give you an idea of its complexity and benefits.

Group Replication

If you have used MySQL Replication, you are no doubt familiar with how to leverage it when building high-availability solutions. Indeed, it is likely you have discovered a host of ways to improve availability in your applications with MySQL Replication.

WHAT IS REPLICATION, AND HOW DOES IT WORK?

MySQL Replication is an easy-to-use feature and yet a complex and major component of MySQL Server. This section presents a bird's-eye view of replication for the purpose of explaining how it works and how to set up a simple replication topology. For more information about replication and its many features and commands, see the online MySQL reference manual (http://dev.mysql.com/doc/refman/8.0/en/replication.html).

Replication requires two or more servers. One server must be designated as the origin or master. The master role means all data changes (writes) to the data are sent to the master and only the master. All other servers in the topology maintain a copy of the master data and are by design and requirement read-only servers. Thus, when your applications send data for storage, they send it to the master. Applications you write to use the sensor data can read it from the slaves.

The copy mechanism works by using a technology called the *binary log* that stores the changes in a special format, thereby keeping a record of all the changes. These changes are then copied to the slaves and executed there. After the slave executes the changes (called *events*), the slave has an exact copy of the data.

The master maintains a binary log of the changes, and the slave maintains a copy of that binary log, called the *relay log*. When a slave requests data changes from the master, it reads the events from the master and writes them to its relay log; then another thread in the slave executes those events from the relay log. As you can imagine, a slight delay occurs from the time a change is made on the master to the time it is made on the slave. Fortunately, this delay is almost unnoticeable except in topologies with high traffic (lots of changes).

It is likely that the greater your high availability needs, and the more your solution expands (grows in sophistication), the more you need to employ better ways to manage the loss of nodes, data integrity, and general maintenance of the clusters (groups of servers replicating data—sometimes called *replica sets*). In fact, most high-availability solutions have outgrown the base master-and-slaves topology, evolving into tiers consisting of clusters of servers; some replicate a portion of the data for faster throughput and even for compartmental storage.

All of these have led many to discover they need more from MySQL Replication. Oracle has answered these needs and more with Group Replication. Group Replication allows your MySQL high-availability solution to grow well beyond the confines of the original MySQL Replication feature and thus empower MySQL 8 to become an important component in high-availability database solutions.

Group Replication was released as GA in December 2016 (starting with the 5.7.17 release) and is bundled with MySQL Server in the form of a plugin. Because Group Replication is implemented as a server plugin, you can install the plugin and start using Group Replication without having to reinstall your server, which makes experimenting with new functionality easy.

Group Replication also makes synchronous replication (among the nodes belonging to the same group) a reality, while the existing MySQL Replication feature is asynchronous (or at most semi-synchronous). Therefore, stronger data consistency is provided at all times (data is available on all members without delays caused by waiting for replicas to catch up).

This is possible via a distributed state machine with strong coordination among the servers assigned to a group. This communication allows the servers to coordinate replication automatically within the group. More specifically, groups maintain membership so that the data replication among the servers is always consistent at any point in time. Even if servers are removed from the group, when they are added back, the consistency is initiated automatically. Further, there is also a failure detection mechanism for servers that go offline or become unreachable. Figure 2-2 shows how you would use Group Replication with your applications to achieve high availability.

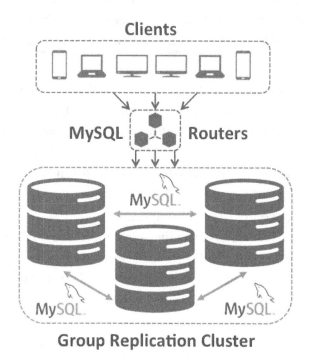

Figure 2-2. *Using Group Replication with applications for high availability (courtesy of Oracle)*

Notice that Group Replication can be used with MySQL Router to allow your applications to have a layer of isolation from the cluster. You will see a bit about the router in a later section.

Another important distinction between Group Replication and standard replication is that all the servers in the group can participate in updating the data with conflicts resolved automatically. Yes, you no longer must carefully craft your application to send writes (updates) to a specific server! However, you can configure Group Replication to allow updates by only one server (called the *primary*) with the other servers acting as secondary servers or as a backup (for failover).

The following capabilities and more are made possible using three specific technologies built into Group Replication—group membership, failure detection, and fault tolerance:

- *Group membership*: Manages whether servers are active (online) and participating in the group. Also, ensures that every server in the group has a consistent view of the membership set. Every server knows the complete list of servers in the group. When servers are added to the group, the group membership service reconfigures the membership automatically.

- *Failure detection*: A mechanism that is able to find and report which servers are offline (unreachable) and assumed to be dead. The failure detector is a distributed service that allows all servers in the group to test the condition of the presumed dead server, and in that way, the group decides whether a server is unreachable (dead). This allows the group to reconfigure automatically by coordinating the process of excluding the failed server.

- *Fault tolerance*: This service uses an implementation of the Paxos distributed algorithm to provide distributed coordination among the servers. In short, the algorithm allows for automatic promotion of roles within the group to ensure that the group remains consistent (data is consistent and available) even if a server (or several) fails or leaves the group. Like similar fault-tolerance mechanisms, the number of failures (servers that fail) is limited. Currently, Group Replication fault tolerance is defined as $n = 2f + 1$, where n is the number of servers needed to tolerate f failures. For example, if you want to tolerate up to 5 servers failing, you need at least 11 servers in the group.

For more information about Group Replication, see the "Group Replication" section in the online reference manual at `https://dev.mysql.com/doc/refman/8.0/en/replication.html`.

MySQL Shell

One of the biggest missing features in the old MySQL client (named `mysql`) was the absence of any form of scripting capability. However, it is possible to use the old client to process a batch of SQL commands, and there is limited support in the client for writing stored routines (procedures and functions). For those who wanted to create and use scripts for managing their databases (and server), in the past there have been external tools such as MySQL Workbench, but nothing dedicated to incorporating multiple scripting languages.

MySQL Workbench is a fantastically popular product from Oracle. MySQL Workbench is a GUI tool designed as a workstation-based administration tool. It provides a host of features, including tools for database design and modeling, SQL development, database administration, database migration, and scripting support with Python. For more information about MySQL Workbench, see `https://dev.mysql.com/doc/workbench/en/`.

MySQL Shell is a new and exciting addition to the MySQL portfolio. MySQL Shell represents the first modern and advanced client for connecting to and interacting with MySQL. The shell can be used as a scripting environment for developing new tools and applications for working with data. Although it does support an SQL mode, its main purpose is to permit access to data with the JavaScript and Python languages. That's right, you can write Python scripts and execute them within the shell interactively or as a batch. Cool! Figure 2-3 shows an example of launching MySQL Shell. Notice the nifty prompt that displays the MySQL logo, connection information, and mode. Nice!

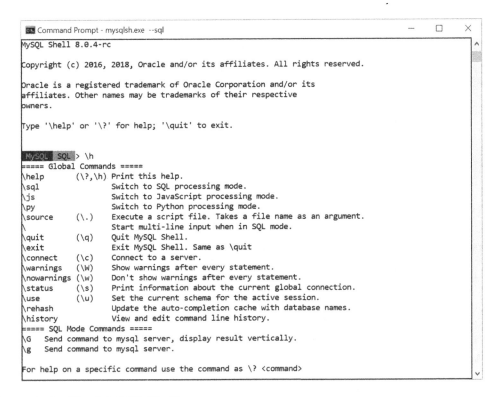

Figure 2-3. *The MySQL Shell*

MySQL Shell is designed to use the new X Protocol for communicating with the server via the X Plugin. However, the shell can also connect to the server by using the older protocol, albeit with limited features in the scripting modes. What this means is, the shell allows you to work with relational data (SQL), JSON documents (NoSQL), or both.

The addition of the SQL mode provides an excellent stepping-stone to learning how to manage your data with scripts. You can continue to use your SQL commands (or batches) until you convert them to JavaScript or Python. Furthermore, you can use both to ensure that your migration is complete.

MySQL Shell has many features, including support for traditional SQL command processing, script prototyping, and even support for customizing the shell. Most of the features can be controlled via command-line options or with special shell commands. You'll take a deeper look at some of the more critical features in later sections. For now, the following lists some of the major features of the shell:

- *Logging*: You can create a log of your session for later analysis or to keep a record of messages. You can set the level of detail with the - option ranging from 1 (nothing logged) to 8 (max debug).

61

- *Output formats*: The shell supports three format options. These are command-line options you specify when launching the shell.

    - *Table* (`--table`): The traditional grid format you're used to from the old client

    - *Tabbed*: Presents information using tabs for spacing and is used for batch execution

    - *JSON* (`--json`): Formats the JSON documents in an easier-to-read manner

- *Interactive code execution*: The default mode for using the shell is interactive mode, which works like a traditional client: you enter a command and get a response.

- *Batch code execution*: If you want to run your script without the interactive session, you can use the shell to run the script in batch mode. However, the output is limited to nonformatted output (but can be overridden with the `--interactive` option).

- *Scripting languages*: The shell supports both JavaScript and Python, although you can use only one at a time.

- *Sessions*: Sessions are essentially connections to servers. The shell allows you to store and remove sessions.

- *Startup scripts*: You can define a script to execute when the shell starts. You can write the script in either JavaScript or Python.

- *Command history*: The shell saves the commands you enter, allowing you to recall them by using the up and down arrow keys.

- *Global variables*: The shell provides a few global variables you can access when in interactive mode. These include the following.

    - `session`: Global session object, if established

    - `db`: Schema, if established via a connection

    - `dba`: The AdminAPI object for working with the InnoDB Cluster

    - `shell`: General-purpose functions for using the shell

    - `util`: Utility functions for working with servers

- *Customize the prompt*: You can also change the default prompt by updating a configuration file named `~/.mysqlsh/prompt.json` by using a special format or by defining an environment variable named `MYSQLSH_PROMPT_THEME`.

- *Autocompletion of keywords, classes, and methods*: Starting in 8.0.4, the shell permits users to press the Tab key to autocomplete keywords in SQL mode, and the major classes and methods in JavaScript and Python modes. The shell also provides code completion for known keywords, API functions, and SQL keywords.

Tip   For more information about the MySQL Shell, see the section entitled, "MySQL Shell User Guide" in the online MySQL reference manual (`https://dev.mysql.com/doc/refman/8.0/en/mysql-shell.html`).

X DevAPI

The X Developer application programming interface, or X DevAPI, is a library of classes and methods that implement a new NoSQL interface for MySQL. Specifically, the X DevAPI is designed to allow easy interaction with JSON documents and relational data. The X DevAPI has classes devoted to supporting both concepts, allowing developers to use either (or both) in their applications. The X DevAPI, together with the X Protocol, X Plugin, and clients written to expose the X DevAPI form the MySQL 8 Document Store. The X DevAPI has several powerful features, including the following:

- *MySQLX*: A module used to get a session object resulting from an X Protocol connection to a MySQL server.

- *Sessions*: A connection to a MySQL server.

- *Collections*: An organizational abstraction for storing JSON documents.

- *Documents*: JSON documents are the primary storage mechanism for data in collections.

- *CRUD operations*: Simple methods for create, read, update, and delete operations. Read operations are simple and easy to understand.

- *Relational data*: Implements CRUD operations for traditional relational data including SQL statement execution and results processing.

- *Expressions*: Modern practices and syntax styles are used to get away from traditional SQL-string-building for finding things in your collections and documents.

- *Parallel execution*: Nonblocking, asynchronous calls follow common host language patterns.

- *Method chaining*: The API is built so that methods that create or retrieve (get) an object return an instance of that object. This allows us to combine several methods together (called *method chaining*). Although method chaining is neither a new concept nor unique to the X DevAPI, it is a powerful mechanism for making our code more expressive and easier to read.

Note   The X DevAPI is available only when using the X Plugin. You cannot use the X DevAPI without the X Plugin installed, and then only through an X Protocol–enabled client or database connector.

The X DevAPI is available only through one of the clients that implement the X Protocol—specifically, any of the following. Furthermore, to use any of these clients, you must also have the X Plugin installed and configured for use on your server.

- *MySQL Shell*: https://dev.mysql.com/downloads/shell/

- *MySQL for Visual Studio*: https://dev.mysql.com/downloads/windows/visualstudio/

- *Connector/J*: https://dev.mysql.com/downloads/connector/j/

- *Connector/NET*: https://dev.mysql.com/downloads/connector/net/

- *Connector/Node.js*: https://dev.mysql.com/downloads/connector/nodejs/

- *Connector/Python*: https://dev.mysql.com/downloads/connector/python/

- *Connector/C++*: https://dev.mysql.com/downloads/connector/cpp/

> **Tip** For more information about the X DevAPI, see `https://dev.mysql.com/doc/x-devapi-userguide/en/`.

AdminAPI

The Admin application programming interface, or AdminAPI, is a library of classes and methods that implement a new management interface for InnoDB Cluster. Specifically, the AdminAPI is designed to allow easy interaction with InnoDB Cluster by using a scripting language from MySQL Shell. MySQL Shell includes the AdminAPI, which enables you to deploy, configure, and administer InnoDB Cluster. The AdminAPI contains two classes for accessing the InnoDB Cluster functionality:

- dba: Enables you to administer InnoDB clusters using the AdminAPI. The dba class enables you to administer the cluster; for example, creating a new cluster, working with a sandbox configuration (a way to experiment with InnoDB Cluster using several MySQL instances on the same machine), and checking the status of instances and the cluster.

- cluster: Management handle to an InnoDB cluster. The cluster class enables you to work with the cluster to add instances, remove instances, get the status (health) of the cluster, and more.

Because we will be working directly with the AdminAPI throughout this book, you will see more details about the methods available for each class in Chapter 5.

> **Tip** See `https://dev.mysql.com/doc/dev/mysqlsh-api-python/8.0/group___admin_a_p_i.html` to learn more about the AdminAPI.

Router

MySQL Router is a relatively new component in MySQL. It was original built for the now obsolete MySQL Fabric product and has been significantly improved and reworked for use with InnoDB Cluster. In fact, it is a vital part of InnoDB Cluster.

MySQL Router is a lightweight middleware component providing transparent routing between your application and MySQL servers. Although it can be used for a wide variety of use cases, its primary purpose is to improve high availability and scalability by effectively routing database traffic to appropriate MySQL servers.

For client applications to handle failover, they need to be aware of the InnoDB cluster topology and know which MySQL instance is the primary (write) server. Although it is possible for applications to implement that logic, MySQL Router can provide and handle this functionality for you.

Moreover, when used with InnoDB Cluster, MySQL Router acts as a proxy to hide the multiple MySQL instances on your network and map the data requests to one of the instances in the cluster. If there are enough online replicas, and communication between the components is intact, applications will be able to (re)connect to one of them. MySQL Router also makes it possible for this to happen by simply repointing applications to connect to Router instead of directly to MySQL.

Tip   For more information about MySQL Router, see `https://dev.mysql.com/doc/mysql-router/8.0/en/`.

Installing InnoDB Cluster

Recall, Oracle has chosen to build InnoDB Cluster into MySQL Server and has committed to providing InnoDB Cluster to community and enterprise customers alike. When you install MySQL, you have also installed InnoDB Cluster and all of the components needed to make it work.

In this section, you'll walk through installing MySQL on a Windows PC by using the MySQL Windows Installer. If you are using another platform, you can see the online MySQL reference manual for more details (`https://dev.mysql.com/doc/refman/8.0/en/installing.html`).

The MySQL Windows Installer (also called the *MySQL Installer*) provides an easy-to-use, wizard-based installation experience for all your MySQL software needs. While some developer-specific components may require additional installations, the installer is your one-stop site for installing the latest versions of MySQL products including the following:

- MySQL Server

- MySQL Connectors

- MySQL Workbench and sample models

- Sample databases

- MySQL for Excel

- MySQL Notifier

- MySQL for Visual Studio

- Documentation

Tip   When installing on Windows, you may be asked by Windows to approve the escalation of the installation.

The installer allows you to choose which products you want to install, and you can run the installer as many times as you want to update, add, or remove products. Furthermore, you can choose either a web-based installer or a stand-alone installer. If you have an online connection while running the MySQL Installer and you do not want to install all MySQL products (thereby downloading only what you need), choose the web installer. If you do not have an online connection while running the MySQL Installer or want to install all products now or in the future, choose the stand-alone installer.

You can download the MySQL Installer at `https://dev.mysql.com/downloads/installer/`. At the site, you will see the latest version of the installer, including an option to install 32- or 64-bit binaries. Note, however, that the installer itself is a 32-bit application.

Now, let's look at a quick, typical walk-through of installing MySQL on a Windows machine. Because the installer follows a script that changes based on your selections, installing MySQL on your PC may differ. However, the following shows the progress for installing MySQL from scratch, installing all of the products needed for InnoDB Cluster and the MySQL Document Store. We begin by downloading the installer and launching it. Figure 2-4 shows the initial license agreement screen. Notice that this is the community edition of the installer (which means it installs only the community edition products under the GNUv2 license).

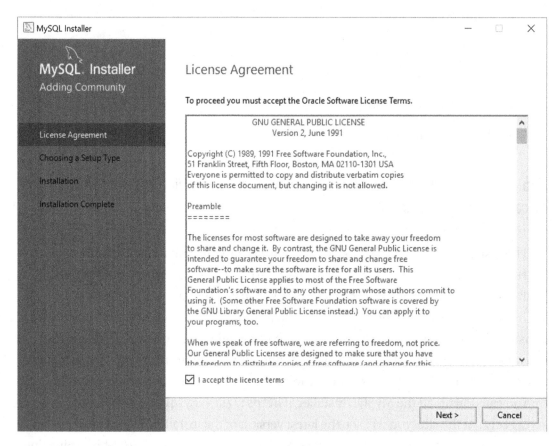

Figure 2-4. *License Agreement (MySQL Installer)*

After you have read and agree to the license, you can tick the "I accept the license terms" check box and click Next to display the Choosing a Setup Type panel, shown in Figure 2-5. This panel gives you several choices, including a developer-centric installation, installing only the server, installing only the clients, a full installation of all products, and a custom option that permits you to choose which components to install. Choose the Custom option and click Next.

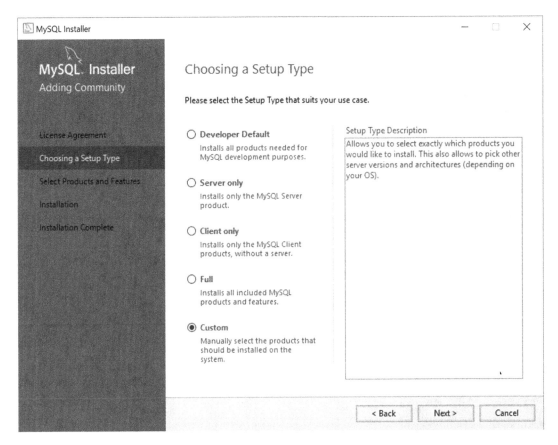

Figure 2-5. *Choose a Setup Type (MySQL Installer)*

The next panel allows you to choose the products you want to install. Figure 2-6 shows the panel with MySQL Server and the documentation selected for installation. To choose a product for installation, expand the categories in the left list, and then select the product you want to install and click the right arrow to move it to the list on the right. Those products shown in the list on the right will be installed as you proceed. For this chapter, you need only MySQL Server and the documentation. You will add other products in later chapters. When the products you want to install are listed on the right, click the Next button.

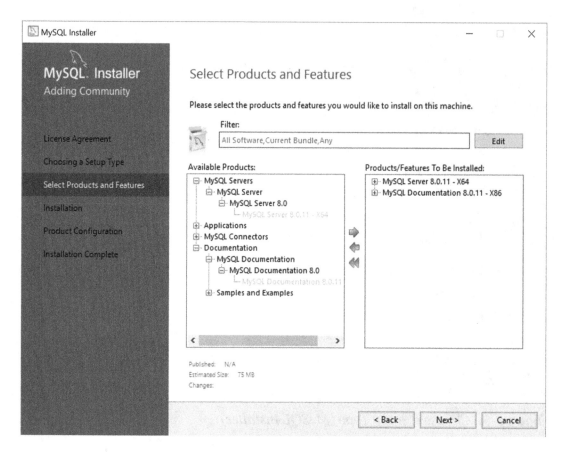

Figure 2-6. *Select Products and Features (MySQL Installer)*

The next panel is an installation summary that permits you to confirm that you have the correct products listed for installation. The panel, shown in Figure 2-7, also indicates the status so you can observe the progress of the installation. When you are ready to begin installation of the products selected, click Execute.

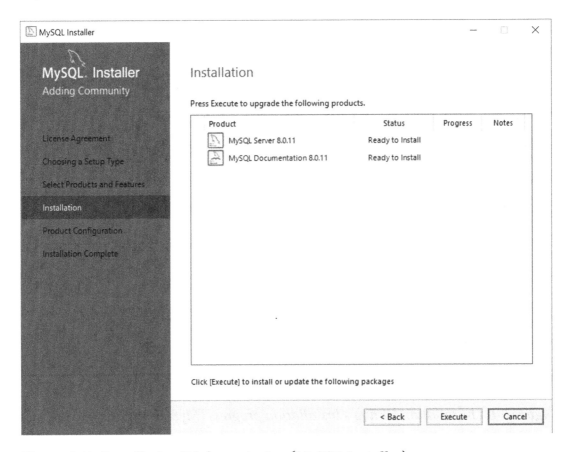

Figure 2-7. *Installation Dialog – staging (MySQL Installer)*

When installation begins, you will see the progress of each product, as shown in Figure 2-8.

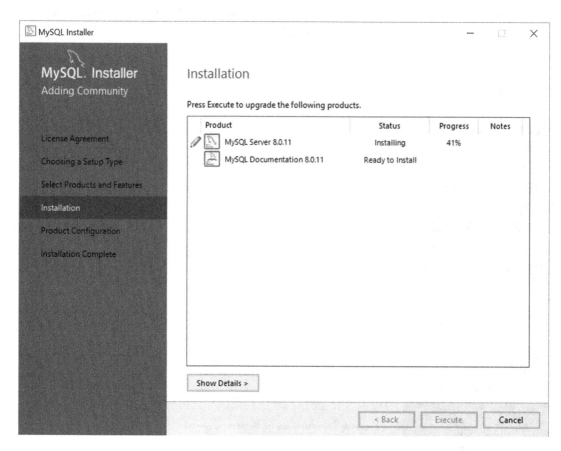

Figure 2-8. *Installation Dialog – installation progress (MySQL Installer)*

After all products are installed, the Installation panel will show the status of all installations as complete and change the buttons at the bottom to show Next, as shown in Figure 2-9. When you're ready, click Next.

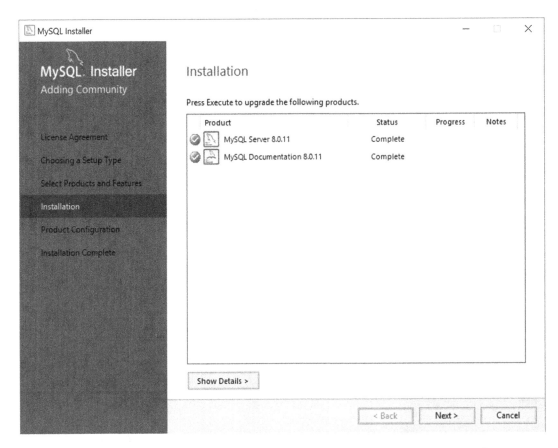

Figure 2-9. *Installation Dialog – installation complete (MySQL Installer)*

The next step in the installation is to configure any products that have post-installation options. MySQL Server is one such product that permits you to set several configuration items to complete installation. Figure 2-10 shows the Product Configuration panel. When you're ready, click Next to begin the configuration.

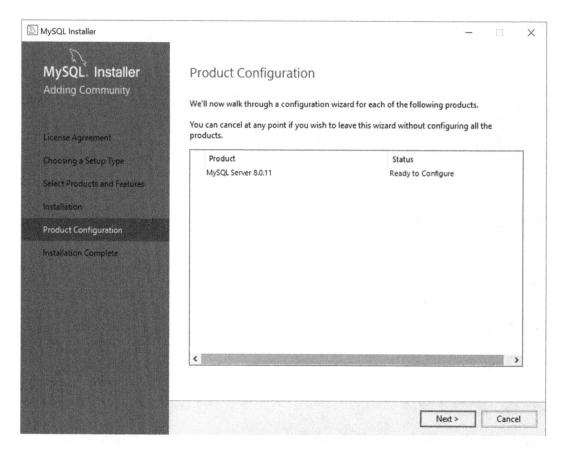

Figure 2-10. *Product Configuration (MySQL Installer)*

New in the MySQL Installer for MySQL 8.0.11 is the ability to set up a test InnoDB Cluster configuration from the installer. This can be a real time-saver if you want to install MySQL on a test server for development or experimentation. You will take a more deliberate path to set up InnoDB Cluster in Chapter 6. For now, you can leave the default selection to install a stand-alone MySQL Server instance, as shown in Figure 2-11. Then click the Next button.

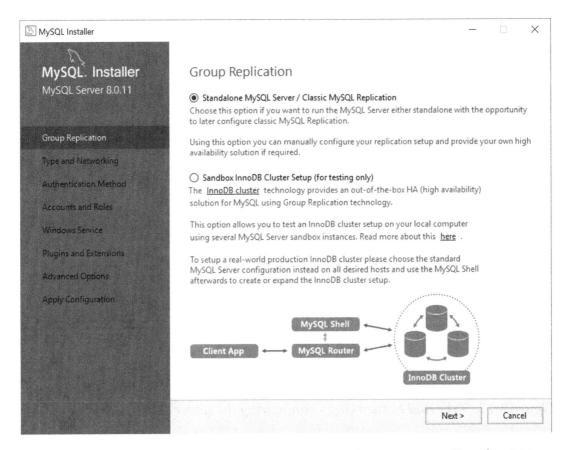

Figure 2-11. *Setup Group Replication or InnoDB Cluster in a Sandbox (MySQL Installer)*

When configuring the server, the first step is setting up the networking and configuration type. Figure 2-12 shows the Type and Networking panel that permits you to choose the type of configuration (a baseline that contains settings typical for the use case selected) and any connectivity options you wish to choose.

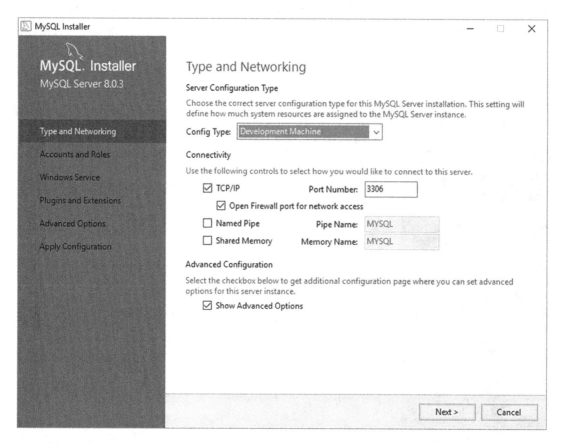

Figure 2-12. *Type and Networking – configuring the server (MySQL Installer)*

In this case, we will choose the Development Machine configuration type (the default). We'll also choose to use TCP/IP on port 3306 and open the Windows firewall to allow communication to/from the network; we do this by ticking the check boxes next to each option as shown. It is also recommended to tick the Show Advanced Options check box for further configuration. After you choose the options, click Next to proceed.

Recall that MySQL changed the default authentication plugin in release 8.0.4. Because so many installations still use the legacy authentication method, Oracle provides an option to choose the older method during installation so that your applications will continue to work with the newest version. If you want to use the newer authentication along with strong password encryption, leave the default selection, as shown in Figure 2-13. Click the Next button to proceed.

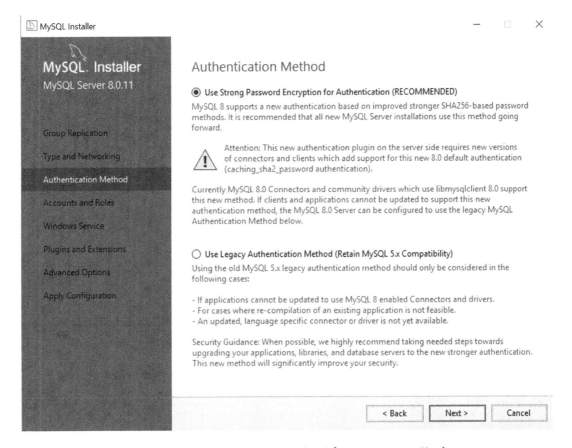

Figure 2-13. *Choosing Authentication Method (MySQL Installer)*

The next thing we need to do is choose the password for the root user account. This is the account that MySQL uses for all administrative actions. You should choose the password wisely so that you protect your server from accidental access. Figure 2-14 shows the Accounts and Roles panel. Notice that you can also set up additional user accounts at this time, which can save you time after installation. When you're ready, click the Next button to proceed.

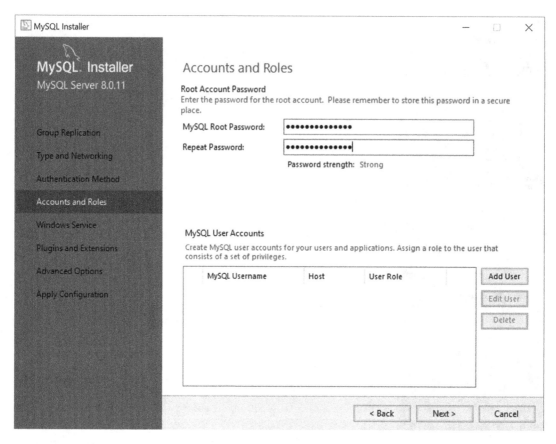

Figure 2-14. *Accounts and Roles – configuring the server (MySQL Installer)*

Next, we have the option to set up a Windows service to manage starting and stopping the server. This is recommended for anyone installing the server with expectations that it will be running from bootup. In fact, you can choose to create the service but not set it to automatically start. Figure 2-15 shows a typical selection for setting up the Windows service for the server. After choosing the options you want, click the Next button to proceed.

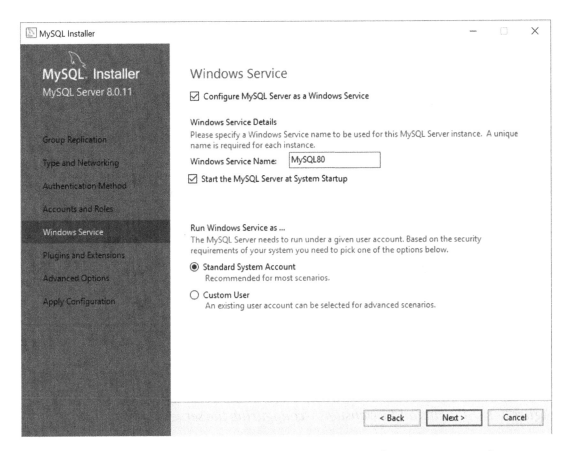

Figure 2-15. *Windows Service – configuring the server (MySQL Installer)*

Next, we can choose to enable and configure the MySQL Document Store via the X Protocol plugin. Figure 2-16 shows the Plugins and Extensions panel used to enable the plugin. We want to enable the plugin, set the port to 33060 (default), and allow the port to pass through the firewall. After choosing the options, click Next.

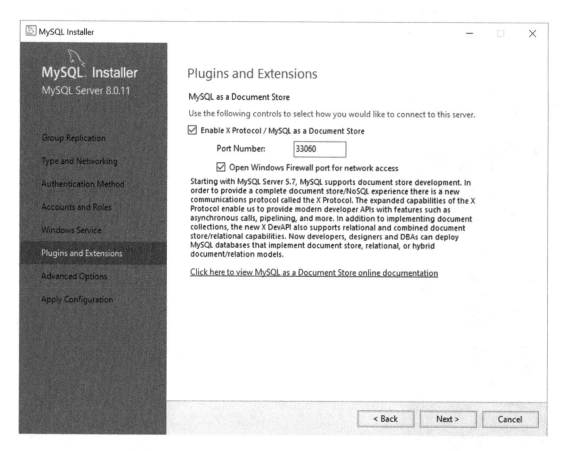

Figure 2-16. *Plugins and Extensions – configuring the server (MySQL Installer)*

Next, because we choose the advanced configuration options, we can set up various logging options including the error, query, and binary log. You should consider turning on (selecting) the general and query logs. We also must enable the binary log for use with InnoDB Cluster. Figure 2-17 shows the Advanced Options panel. Notice that you can also choose to name each of the logs and relocate them. However, for this book, you can leave the default names, which are based on the machine name. For example, this walk-through was run on a machine named OPTIPLEX-7010, so the file names have that prefix. After choosing the options, click Next.

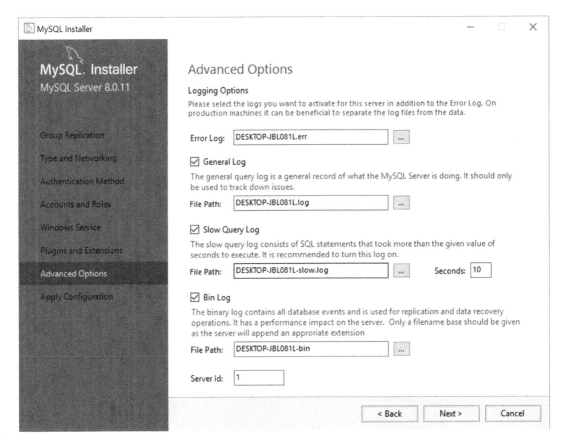

Figure 2-17. *Advanced Options (MySQL Installer)*

At this point, the installer will show you a summary of the steps to execute and permit you to start the process or go back and make changes, as shown in Figure 2-18. When you're ready, click the Execute button to proceed.

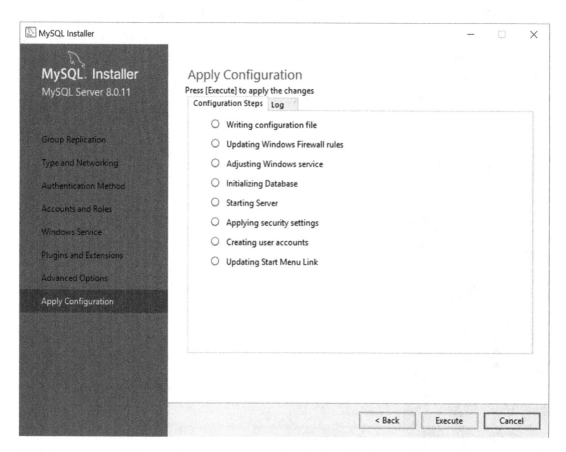

Figure 2-18. *Apply Configuration – staging (MySQL Installer)*

While the configuration process is running, the panel will change to gray out the Execute and Back buttons and show green check marks on the dots next to each step, as shown in Figure 2-19. If errors occur, the panel will show a red X and may display an error message if the error prohibits continuing.

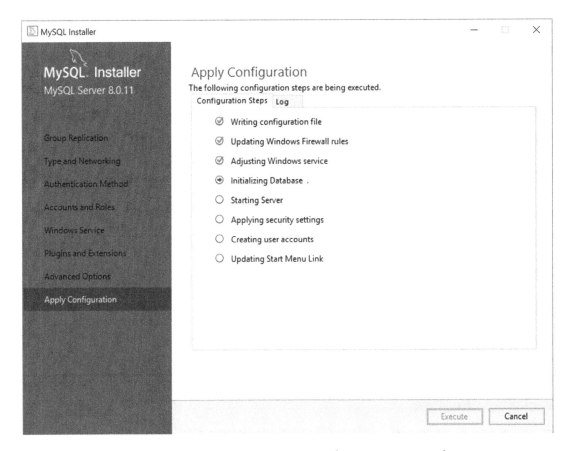

Figure 2-19. *Apply Configuration – in progress (MySQL Installer)*

When the product configurations are complete, the panel will change to show green dots next to all steps. The buttons at the bottom will change to a single button labeled Finish, as shown in Figure 2-20. When you're ready, click the Finish button to proceed.

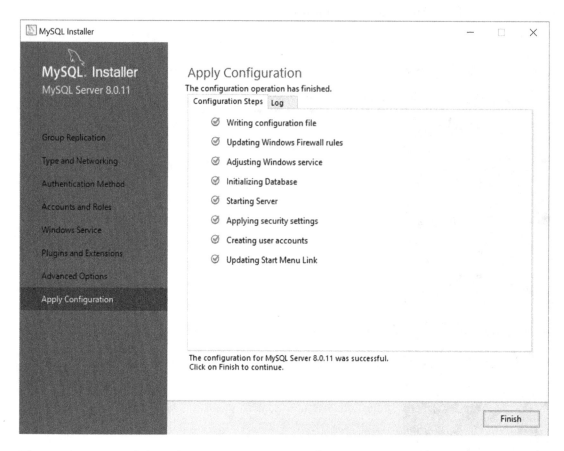

Figure 2-20. *Apply Configuration – complete (MySQL Installer)*

The next panel shows a summary of the product configuration operations, as shown in Figure 2-21.

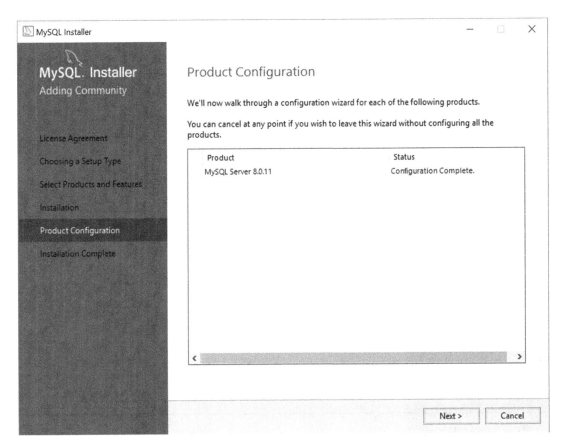

Figure 2-21. *Product Configuration – summary (MySQL Installer)*

After you have verified that there are no errors, click the Next button to proceed to the final panel, shown in Figure 2-22. You can click the Finish button to complete the installation and close the installer.

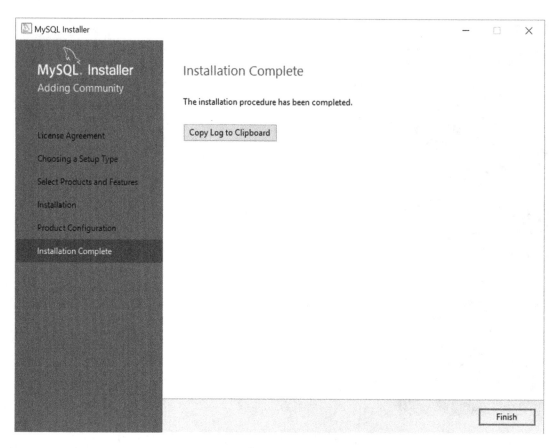

Figure 2-22. *Installation Complete (MySQL Installer)*

This concludes the walk-through of installing MySQL on a Windows PC for the first time. As mentioned, you can run the installer again to install additional products. Recall also that depending on the product chosen, the sequence of panels shown will vary.

Summary

Aside from the addition of Group Replication, InnoDB Cluster is perhaps the most important new feature for those seeking to build a high-availability solution with MySQL. Never have so many features in the server been designed to provide a robust, powerful, reliable, and easy-to-manage high-availability MySQL.

In this chapter, you learned more about the InnoDB storage engine, including the latest new features and the many components that make up InnoDB Cluster, including Group Replication, MySQL Shell and AdminAPI, and MySQL Router for application connection routing.

In the next chapter, you will kick the tires on Group Replication and learn more about this fantastic and highly complex feature. Although you will see that the AdminAPI makes configuring Group Replication easy, good systems and database administrators must know how Group Replication works so that they can continue to refine and expand their high-availability solution as well as be equipped to troubleshoot Group Replication.

CHAPTER 3

MySQL Group Replication

The very core of InnoDB Cluster is Group Replication. As you learned in the preceding chapter, Group Replication is the latest evolution of MySQL Replication, designed to make data replication more robust and reliable. Together with the modifications to the InnoDB storage engine (all under the hood and hidden away), Group Replication enables high-availability capabilities that, in the past, required specialized and sometimes customized products, middleware, and bespoke applications to achieve.

In this chapter, you will explore Group Replication from setup to an active group. This will demonstrate and reinforce the concepts of Group Replication. You may be wondering why you would want to study such a feature at the lowest, manual configuration level, especially if you have already experimented with InnoDB Cluster and MySQL Shell (via the AdminAPI).

The answer is one of robustness of knowledge. Every successful systems or database administrator must know how products work—and not just how to set them up and get them going. That is the easy part, and thanks to the AdminAPI, anyone can set up InnoDB Cluster. However, what if something goes wrong, or you need to use InnoDB Cluster (Group Replication) in a different way? Having experienced setting up Group Replication at the lowest level will give you greater insights into what to do in the future.

In this chapter, you'll take an in-depth look at what makes up Group Replication. After that, you will take a guided tour of Group Replication. Follow along as we explore one of the greatest advances in MySQL history! However, let's begin with a list of concepts and terms that make up the language of describing Group Replication.

Concepts, Terms, and Lingo

It is likely that all but the most proficient or those with the latest knowledge of MySQL will fully understand all the terms and concepts thrown around to describe Group Replication. In this section, you'll take a step back for a moment to focus on some of the

© Charles Bell 2018
C. Bell, *Introducing InnoDB Cluster*, https://doi.org/10.1007/978-1-4842-3885-1_3

terms and concepts you will encounter in this chapter and the rest of the book (or any book on MySQL high availability). This section provides a glossary of terms associated with Group Replication that you can feel free to reference from time to time.

- *Binary log*: A file produced by the server that contains a binary form of all transactions executed. The binary log file is also used in replication to exchange transactions between two servers. When used on a primary (master), it forms a record of all changes, which can be sent to the secondary (slave) for execution to create a replica (sometimes somewhat inaccurately called a *replicant*).

- *Multi-primary*: A group where writes may be sent to more than one primary and replicated among the group.

- *Failover*: An event that permits the group to recover from a fault on the primary, automatically electing a new primary.

- *Fault tolerant*: The ability to recover from a fault or error detected among the group without loss of data or functionality. Note that fault tolerance in Group Replication is limited by the number of servers in the group. See the sidebar, "How Do I Calculate the Number of Faults a Group Can Handle?" to learn how to calculate the number of faults a group can tolerate.

- *Group*: A set of MySQL servers participating in the same Group Replication communication setup.

- *Group communication*: A special mechanism that uses a state machine and a communication protocol to keep the servers in the group coordinated, including synchronization of transaction execution and selection/election of roles.

- *Instance*: A running MySQL server. Typically used to refer to one or more MySQL servers running on the same machine. This is not the same as *MySQL Server*, which often refers to the set of hardware and MySQL execution.

- *Primary*: A server in a group that is assigned the role of collecting all writes (updates) to data.

- *Relay log*: A binary log file used on a secondary (slave) to record transactions read from the primary (master) binary log cached for execution. It has the same format as the binary log.

- *Secondary*: A server in a group that is assigned the role of reader, which means applications can read data from a secondary but may not write to a secondary.

- *Single-primary*: A group configured with a single primary and one or more secondary servers. This is similar to the master/slave configuration in the older MySQL Replication feature.

- *Switchover*: A controlled maintenance event in which an administrator actively changes the primary role, removing it from one server and assigning it to another (making the new server the primary). This does not happen automatically and typically is not associated with a failure.

- *Transaction*: A set of data changes that must all succeed before the set is applied to the data. Failed transactions are not written to the database.

- *Topology*: The logical layout of servers in a replication group. Examples include the following:

  - *Single-primary*: A single server with radial connections to each slave.

  - *Tiered*: Connections of single-primary groups in which each secondary is the primary to another set of secondary servers.

  - *Multi-primary*: Each primary connects to every other primary in the group as well as the secondary servers in the group.

Note   Recall that in MySQL Replication, the primary was named *master* and the secondaries named *slaves*. Although not precisely synonymous, you can consider them so, but be sure to retrain your thought processes to use *primary* and *secondary* when working with InnoDB Cluster and Group Replication.

Overview

MySQL Group Replication is an advanced form of MySQL Replication used to implement fault-tolerant systems. The replication group (topology) is a set of servers that interact with each other through message passing. The communication layer provides a set of guarantees such as atomic messages and total order message delivery. These are powerful properties that translate into useful abstractions that you can use to build more advanced database replication solutions. Group Replication provides the following benefits:

- Removes the need for manually handling server failover

- Provides distributed fault tolerance

- Automates reconfiguration (adding/removing instances, failures, and so forth)

- Automatically detects and handles conflicts

- Provides guarantees against data loss

Group Replication builds on top of such properties and abstractions and implements a multi-master, update-everywhere replication protocol. One of the technologies that makes Group Replication possible is global transaction identifiers (GTIDs). Thus, servers that participate in Group Replication will have GTIDs enabled.

Essentially, a group is formed by multiple servers, and each server in the group may execute transactions independently. But all read/write (RW) transactions commit only after they have been approved by the group. Read-only (RO) transactions need no coordination within the group and thus commit immediately. In other words, for any RW transaction, the group needs to decide whether it commits or not, thus the commit operation is not a unilateral decision from the originating server.

To be precise, when a transaction is ready to commit at the originating server, the server atomically broadcasts the write values (rows changed) and the correspondent write set (unique identifiers of the rows that were updated). Then a global total order is established for that transaction. Ultimately, all servers receive the same set of transactions in the same order. Therefore, all servers apply the same set of changes in the same order, and they remain consistent within the group.

Group Replication provides redundancy by replicating the system state among the replication group. Should one (or more) of the servers fail, the system is still available. If enough servers fail, performance or scalability could be impacted, but the system will remain available.

This is made possible by a group membership service, which relies on a distributed failure detector that can signal when any servers leave the group, either through deliberate interaction or due to a failure. A distributed recovery procedure ensures that when servers join the group, they are brought up-to-date automatically. There is no need for manual server failover, and the multi-master update-everywhere nature ensures that not even updates are blocked in the event of a single-server failure. Therefore, MySQL Group Replication guarantees that the database service is continuously available.

It may not surprise you that setting up MySQL Group Replication resembles the process of setting up MySQL Replication. After all, Group Replication is built upon the foundations of MySQL Replication. In the next section, you will see a demonstration of Group Replication. Instead of concentrating on the same steps from the MySQL Replication tutorial, we will cover the same topics briefly and dive into the nuances specific to Group Replication.

MySQL Group Replication Tutorial

This section demonstrates how to set up Group Replication among a set of servers. As mentioned previously, Group Replication uses different terms for the roles in the group. Specifically, there is a primary role and a secondary role. Unlike MySQL Replication, in which one server is designated as the master (primary), Group Replication can automatically change the roles of servers in the group as needed. Thus, although we will set up Group Replication by identifying one of the servers as the primary, the end state of the group over time may result in one of the other servers becoming the primary.

If you would like to experience this tutorial on your own, you should prepare four servers. As in the last tutorial, we will use several instances running on the current machine. We need several instances to ensure that the group has a viable set to enable redundancy and failover. In this case, the group can tolerate at most one failure.

HOW DO I CALCULATE THE NUMBER OF FAULTS A GROUP CAN HANDLE?

The formula for determining how many failures (simultaneous or consecutive, unrecovered failures) that a set of servers can tolerate is as follows, where S is the set of servers and f is the number of failures:

```
S = 2f + 1
```

For example, a set of seven servers can tolerate, at most, three failures:

$$7 = 2f + 1$$
$$6 = 2f$$
$$2f = 6$$
$$f = 6 / 2$$
$$f = 3$$

If you want to know how many servers, s, it takes to tolerate a known number of failures, F, a little math application reveals the following. Note that you must round down any fractions. You can't have 1.5 servers fail.[1]

$$s = 2F + 1$$
$$(s - 1) = 2F$$
$$2F = (s - 1)$$
$$F = (s - 1)/2$$

For example, a set of three servers can tolerate one failure:

$$F = (3 - 1)/2$$
$$F = 2 / 2$$
$$F = 1$$

Similarly, a set of five servers can tolerate two failures:

$$F = (5 - 1)/2$$
$$F = 4 / 2$$
$$F = 2$$

The example of four servers in this tutorial can tolerate only one failure:

$$(4 - 1) / 2 = 1.5$$

or 1, rounded down

The steps to set up and configure Group Replication include the following. There may be other, equally viable procedures to set up Group Replication, but these can be done on any machine and will not affect any existing installations of MySQL. That said, it is recommended to perform these steps on a development machine to remove the risk of disrupting production systems.

---

[1]Randomly rebooting machines are not considered a fractional component here.

Note   The steps used to set up Group Replication are similar to those for MySQL Replication. In fact, except for terminology (for example, *slave* vs. *secondary*), the configuration files, and two extra steps to install the Group Replication plugin and start Group Replication on the master for the first time, the process is the same.

---

1. Initialize the data directories.

2. Configure the primary.

3. Configure the secondaries.

4. Start the MySQL instances.

5. Install the Group Replication plugin.

6. Create the Replication user account.

7. Start Group Replication on the primary.

8. Connect the secondaries to the primary.

9. Start Group Replication on the secondaries.

10. Verify the Group Replication status.

The following sections demonstrate each of these steps in greater detail running on Linux with MySQL installed. The steps are the same for other platforms, but the paths may differ slightly. Although the tutorial uses multiple, local instances to demonstrate how to use replication, the procedure would be the same for setting up replication in a production environment. The details of the individual commands to use specific hosts, drives, folders, and ports are the only things that would change to use the procedure in production.

Note   We will be using the older MySQL client (`mysql`) and SQL commands in the examples. You will see the new MySQL Shell in action in the Chapter 4 and the AdminAPI utilized in Chapter 5.

Initialize the Data Directories

The first step is to initialize a data directory for each of the machines used. In this case, we will create a folder on our local machine to contain all the data directories. We will use four instances of MySQL to represent a primary and three secondaries. The following demonstrates creating the folders needed. Notice that I create these in a local folder accessible to the user account I am using, not a system or administrative account. This is because we will be running the instances locally and do not need the additional privileges or access that such accounts permit.

```
$ mkdir gr
$ cd gr
$ mkdir data
```

Now that we have a folder, <user_home>/gr/data, we can use the initialization option of the MySQL server to set up our data directories the same way we did in MySQL Replication. Recall, we use the special --initialize-insecure and --datadir options of the server. The following shows the commands needed to initialize the data directories for the primary and secondaries:

```
mysqld --no-defaults --user=cbell --initialize-insecure --basedir=/usr/
--datadir=<user_home>/gr/data/primary
mysqld --no-defaults --user=cbell --initialize-insecure --basedir=/usr/
--datadir=<user_home>/gr/data/secondary1
mysqld --no-defaults --user=cbell --initialize-insecure --basedir=/usr/
--datadir=<user_home>/gr/data/secondary2
mysqld --no-defaults --user=cbell --initialize-insecure --basedir=/usr/
--datadir=<user_home>/gr/data/secondary3
```

Now that we have the data directories created and populated, we can configure the master and slave(s).

Configure the Primary

This step differs the most from MySQL Replication. In fact, the configuration file is quite a bit different. Specifically, we use the same variables from GTID-enabled replication in addition to several of the more common Group Replication variables that must be set. Table 3-1 lists the variables related to Group Replication and their uses. There are additional variables for controlling Group Replication. See `https://dev.mysql.com/doc/refman/8.0/en/group-replication-options.html` in the online reference manual for a complete list.

Table 3-1. *Group Replication Variables (Configuration File)*

Variable	Description
`transaction_write_set_extraction`	Defines the algorithm used to hash the writes extracted during a transaction. Group Replication must be set to XXHASH64.
`loose-group_replication_recovery_use_ssl`	Determines whether the Group Replication recovery connection should use SSL. Typically set to ON, but the default is OFF.
`loose-group_replication_group_name`	The name of the group that this server instance belongs to. Must be a valid UUID.
`loose-group_replication_start_on_boot`	Determines whether the server should start Group Replication during server start.
`loose-group_replication_local_address`	The network address that the member provides for connections from other members, specified as a host:port formatted string.
`loose-group_replication_group_seeds`	A list of group members that is used to establish the connection from the new member to the group. The list consists of the seed member's group_replication_local_address network addresses specified as a comma-separated list, such as host1:port1,host2:port2.
`loose-group_replication_bootstrap_group`	Configure this server to bootstrap the group. This option must be set on only one server, and only when starting the group for the first time or restarting the entire group. After the group has been bootstrapped, set this option to OFF.

Notice the last variable, `group_replication_bootstrap_group`. This variable is something we will set to OFF in the configuration files, but only after we have bootstrapped the group for the first time. This is one of the uses of the initial primary node—to start the group. You will see a special step that you must take the first time you boot the primary to start the group. After that, this variable must be set to OFF.

Note   Notice also the `loose-` prefix. This special prefix applies to variables and is used to instruct the server to continue to start if the plugin has not been loaded at the time the server is started. This is a precautionary measure to avoid errors during startup if something goes wrong. On a production server, you should not include the prefix, especially if Group Replication is relied upon for high availability.

To construct a configuration file for the primary, we need several things: the usual variables for data directory, base directory, and port, as well as the GTID variables and the Group Replication variables. It is also a good idea to add the plugin directory to ensure that the server can find the Group Replication plugin (you will see this in a later step), and to turn on the binary log checksum.

Because the `group_replication_group_seeds` variable needs the list of servers initially participating in the group, we must decide on the ports each server will use. The Group Replication setup requires two ports for each server: one for the normal connections and another for use with Group Replication. For this tutorial, we will use ports 24801+ for the server connections and ports 24901+ for the Group Replication ports. In addition, because we are using local instances, the hostname for all the members in the group will use the loopback address (127.0.0.1), but this would normally be the hostname of the server on which it is running. Finally, we also need to choose server IDs, so we will use sequential values starting at 1. Listing 3-1 shows the configuration file we will use for the master in this tutorial.

Listing 3-1. Primary Configuration File (Group Replication)

```
[mysqld]
datadir=/home/cbell/gr/data/primary
basedir=/usr/
plugin_dir=/usr/lib/mysql/plugin/
port=24801
socket=/home/cbell/gr/primary.sock
```

```
server_id=1
gtid_mode=ON
enforce_gtid_consistency=ON
binlog_checksum=NONE

transaction_write_set_extraction=XXHASH64
loose-group_replication_recovery_use_ssl=ON
loose-group_replication_group_name="bbbbbbbb-bbbb-cccc-dddd-eeeeeeeeeeee"
loose-group_replication_start_on_boot=OFF
loose-group_replication_local_address="127.0.0.1:24901"
loose-group_replication_group_see
ds="127.0.0.1:24901,127.0.0.1:24902,127.0.0.1:24903,127.0.0.1:24904"
loose-group_replication_bootstrap_group=OFF
```

You may notice there is no `log-bin` variable set. The server will automatically enable the binary log when it encounters the variables for Group Replication, because it is required. However, you can include the variable if you want to name the binary log files or locate them in another folder, but that is an advanced configuration option that isn't necessary for a tutorial or even a development installation.

Note   If you are running this tutorial on Windows and do not have Secure Socket Layer (SSL) installed and MySQL configured for use with SSL connections, you must remove the `group_replication_recovery_use_ssl` option.

For this tutorial, you should create a file in the folder we created earlier named `primary.cnf`; for example, `/home/cbell/gr/primary.cnf`. We will use this file to start the instance for the primary in a later step.

Now, let's look at the configuration files for the secondaries.

Configure the Secondaries

The configuration file for the secondaries is similar to the one for the primary. The only changes are to use the correct values for the instance-specific variables such as port, data directory, socket, and server ID. However, some differences exist beyond those settings. The `transaction_write_set_extraction` variable is set on the initial primary. For the secondaries, we add `group_replication_recovery_get_public_key` and set it to `ON`. This variable determines whether the secondary requests from the primary the public key required for RSA key-pair-based password exchange. This variable applies to secondaries that authenticate with the caching_sha2_password authentication plugin. Listing 3-2 shows the configuration file for the first secondary (named secondary1).

Listing 3-2. Secondary Configuration File (Group Replication)

```
[mysqld]
datadir=/home/cbell/gr/data/secondary1
basedir=/usr/
plugin_dir=/usr/lib/mysql/plugin/
port=24802
socket=/home/cbell/gr/secondary1.sock

server_id=2
gtid_mode=ON
enforce_gtid_consistency=ON
binlog_checksum=NONE

loose-group_replication_recovery_get_public_key=ON
loose-group_replication_recovery_use_ssl=ON
loose-group_replication_group_name="bbbbbbbb-bbbb-cccc-dddd-eeeeeeeeeeee"
loose-group_replication_start_on_boot=OFF
loose-group_replication_local_address="127.0.0.1:24902"
loose-group_replication_group_see
ds="127.0.0.1:24901,127.0.0.1:24902,127.0.0.1:24903,127.0.0.1:24904"
loose-group_replication_bootstrap_group=OFF
```

For this tutorial, we will be using three secondaries, so you should create a file for each in the folder we created earlier and name them secondary1.cnf, secondary2.cnf, and secondary3.cnf. Be sure to change the instance-specific variables such as the data directory, socket, port, server ID, and so forth. You must change both ports: the port for the server and the port for Group Replication.

Note   If you are running this tutorial on Windows and do not have SSL installed and MySQL configured for use with SSL connections, you must remove the group_replication_recovery_use_ssl option.

For this tutorial, we will be using three secondaries, so you should create a file for each in the folder we created earlier and name them secondary1.cnf, secondary2.cnf, and secondary3.cnf. Be sure to change the instance-specific variables such as the data directory, socket, port, server ID, and so forth. You must change both ports: the port for the server and the port for Group Replication.

Start the MySQL Instances

Now we are ready to start the MySQL instances. This is easy because we have already created the configuration files with all the parameters we need. We need only to provide the configuration file with the --defaults-file option. The following shows the commands to start the server instances used in this tutorial. Notice that a redirect is added to place the messages from the server in a log file.

```
mysqld --defaults-file=primary.cnf > primary_output.txt 2>&1 &
mysqld --defaults-file=secondary1.cnf > secondary1_output.txt 2>&1 &
mysqld --defaults-file=secondary2.cnf > secondary2_output.txt 2>&1 &
mysqld --defaults-file=secondary3.cnf > secondary3_output.txt 2>&1 &
```

When you run these commands, you should run them from the folder that contains the configuration files. Otherwise, you will have to provide the full path to the configuration file. Although the commands include the redirects, you may want to use a separate terminal the first time you start the server to ensure that there are no errors. Listing 3-3 shows an excerpt of the messages printed when launching the primary.

Listing 3-3. Starting the Primary Instance

```
$ mysqld --defaults-file=primary.cnf
2018-03-06T16:54:27.768154Z 0 [System] [MY-010116] /home/cbell/source/git/
mysql-bug-staging/build/bin/mysqld (mysqld 8.0.11) starting as process 6533
2018-03-06T16:54:29.212063Z 0 [Warning] [MY-010068] CA certificate ca.pem
is self signed.
2018-03-06T16:54:29.226500Z 0 [Warning] [MY-011071] unknown variable
'loose-group_replication_recovery_use_ssl=ON'
2018-03-06T16:54:29.226523Z 0 [Warning] [MY-011071] unknown variable
'loose-group_replication_group_name=bbbbbbbb-bbbb-cccc-dddd-eeeeeeeeeeee'
2018-03-06T16:54:29.226530Z 0 [Warning] [MY-011071] unknown variable
'loose-group_replication_start_on_boot=OFF'
```

```
2018-03-06T16:54:29.226535Z 0 [Warning] [MY-011071] unknown variable
'loose-group_replication_local_address=127.0.0.1:24901'
2018-03-06T16:54:29.226540Z 0 [Warning] [MY-011071]
unknown variable 'loose-group_replication_group_see
ds=127.0.0.1:24901,127.0.0.1:24902,127.0.0.1:24903,127.0.0.1:24904'
2018-03-06T16:54:29.226549Z 0 [Warning] [MY-011071] unknown variable
'loose-group_replication_bootstrap_group=OFF'
...
2018-03-06T16:54:29.313298Z 0 [System] [MY-010931] /home/cbell/source/
git/mysql-bug-staging/build/bin/mysqld: ready for connections. Version:
'8.0.11'  socket: '/home/cbell/gr/primary.sock'  port: 24801  MySQL
Community Server (GPL).
```

Once again, if you plan to use a single terminal, it is recommended to redirect the output to a file and use the option to start the application in another process (for example, the & symbol).

If you are following along with this tutorial and haven't done so already, go ahead and start the secondaries. After all the server instances are started, we can move on to the next step—installing the Group Replication plugin.

Install the Group Replication Plugin

After the MySQL instances are started, you must install the Group Replication plugin.[2] This requires only one command, and does not require restarting the plugin should you need to restart the server. The following shows the command you use to install the plugin. The command requires the name of the plugin along with the name of the dynamically loadable executable. In this case, the name of the plugin is group_replication, and the name of the loadable executable is group_replication.so:

```
INSTALL PLUGIN group_replication SONAME 'group_replication.so'
```

Tip   Notice the .so in the file name. This is the extension you would use for *nix platforms. On Windows, the file name extension is .dll.

---

[2]Future versions of MySQL may have the plugin loaded by default.

The following shows the command executing on the primary. Notice that there are no additional messages. To check the plugin status, use the SHOW PLUGINS command or search for the plugin in the INFORMATION_SCHEMA.PLUGINS table, as shown in Listing 3-4.

Listing 3-4. Installing and Checking the Group Replication Plugin Status

```
$ mysql -uroot -h 127.0.0.1 --port=24801
Welcome to the MySQL monitor.  Commands end with ; or \g.
Your MySQL connection id is 8
Server version: 8.0.11 MySQL Community Server (GPL)

Copyright (c) 2000, 2018, Oracle and/or its affiliates. All rights reserved.

Oracle is a registered trademark of Oracle Corporation and/or its
affiliates. Other names may be trademarks of their respective owners.

Type 'help;' or '\h' for help. Type '\c' to clear the current input statement.

mysql> INSTALL PLUGIN group_replication SONAME 'group_replication.so';
Query OK, 0 rows affected (0.09 sec)

mysql> SELECT * FROM INFORMATION_SCHEMA.PLUGINS WHERE PLUGIN_NAME = 'group_
replication' \G
*************************** 1. row ***************************
           PLUGIN_NAME: group_replication
        PLUGIN_VERSION: 1.1
         PLUGIN_STATUS: ACTIVE
           PLUGIN_TYPE: GROUP REPLICATION
   PLUGIN_TYPE_VERSION: 1.2
        PLUGIN_LIBRARY: group_replication.so
PLUGIN_LIBRARY_VERSION: 1.9
         PLUGIN_AUTHOR: ORACLE
    PLUGIN_DESCRIPTION: Group Replication (1.1.0)
        PLUGIN_LICENSE: GPL
           LOAD_OPTION: ON
1 row in set (0.01 sec)

mysql> \q
Bye
```

Notice that we get only a cursory OK message when installing the plugin. If the plugin directory in the configuration file is wrong or the plugin executable is missing, you will get errors when running this command. If this happens, use SHOW VARIABLES LIKE 'plugin_dir'; to check the plugin directory. Then shut down the server and ensure that the executable file is in the plugin directory and that the plugin directory is the correct value in the configuration file.

For the plugin status, we expect to get a row from the SELECT query and to see the status set to ACTIVE. If you see another status, be sure to check that the plugin installed correctly and that it is the correct plugin from the version of MySQL you have installed. If you have multiple versions of MySQL installed, it is easy to mistakenly point the plugin directory to the wrong plugin.

Note   You must run these commands on each server instance before starting Group Replication.

This was the extra step mentioned previously when comparing starting Group Replication to MySQL Replication. If you are following along with this tutorial, execute these statements now to install the plugin on all four instances. When the plugin is loaded on all instances, you can proceed to create the replication user on all the instances.

Create the Replication User Account

After the MySQL instances are started, you must create a user to be used by the servers to connect to each other. Recall, in Group Replication, the servers all "talk" to each other. Fortunately, the commands are the same as those we used in MySQL Replication. We need to create this user on all the server instances. The following shows the commands needed to create the replication user. Execute these commands on all your servers:

```
SET SQL_LOG_BIN=0;
CREATE USER rpl_user@'%' IDENTIFIED BY 'rpl_pass';
GRANT REPLICATION SLAVE ON *.* TO rpl_user@'%';
FLUSH PRIVILEGES;
SET SQL_LOG_BIN=1;
```

Notice the use of % in the hostname. This was done to ensure that the replication user can connect from any server. You would not normally do this for a production environment, but for a tutorial or development testing, it makes things a bit easier.

Recall, the `set sql_log_bin=0` commands tell the server to temporarily disable logging of changes to the binary log. We do this whenever we do not want to replicate the commands on other machines in the topology. Specifically, maintenance and administrative commands such as creating users should not be replicated. Turning off the binary log is a great way to ensure that you do not accidently issue transactions that cannot be executed on other machines.

The best way to execute these commands is to save them to a file named `create_rpl_user.sql` and use the source command of the `mysql` client to read the commands from the file and execute them. You can quickly create the replication user on all instances with the following commands.

Note   The paths in this section use the home directory `/home/cbell/`. Be sure to substitute the path to your user directory.

```
mysql -uroot -h 127.0.0.1 -e "source /home/cbell/gr/create_rpl_user.sql"
--port=24801
mysql -uroot -h 127.0.0.1 -e "source /home/cbell/gr/create_rpl_user.sql"
--port=24802
mysql -uroot -h 127.0.0.1 -e "source /home/cbell/gr/create_rpl_user.sql"
--port=24803
mysql -uroot -h 127.0.0.1 -e "source /home/cbell/gr/create_rpl_user.sql"
--port=24804
```

Start Group Replication on the Primary

The next step is to start Group Replication on the primary for the first time. Recall from our discussion on the Group Replication variables, the variable `group_replication_bootstrap_group` is normally set to `OFF` except on the first start of the group. Because the group has never been started, we must do so on the primary.

Fortunately, the variable `group_replication_bootstrap_group` is dynamic, and we can turn it on and off on-the-fly. We can run the following commands on the primary to start Group Replication for the first time:

```
SET GLOBAL group_replication_bootstrap_group=ON;
START GROUP_REPLICATION;
SET GLOBAL group_replication_bootstrap_group=OFF;
```

As you may recall, we set group_replication_bootstrap_group to OFF in the primary configuration file. This was so that if we restart the primary, the setting will be correct. You can set it to ON if you like, but you would have to change it in the configuration file before you restart the primary. Setting it to OFF is much safer and less work.

If you are following along in this tutorial, go ahead and run those commands on the primary now. After you finish, you'll be ready to connect the secondaries to the primary.

Connect the Secondaries to the Primary

The next step is to connect the secondaries to the primary. We use the same CHANGE MASTER command that you saw in the previous tutorial. However, we need only the replication user and password. We tell the server to connect to the special replication channel named group_replication_recovery. The following shows the command used for each of the secondaries to connect them to the primary:

```
CHANGE MASTER TO MASTER_USER='rpl_user', MASTER_PASSWORD='rpl_pass' FOR
CHANNEL 'group_replication_recovery';
```

Note   You may see a warning about using passwords in commands. This is designed to encourage you not to put the replication user and password in the file. It is more secure to use the pluggable authentication options.

Notice that we need less information than even the GTID-enabled replication. Cool! You must run this command on all the secondaries. It may be easier to save this to a file and execute it by using the mysql client as we did for the replication user. For example, save this to a file named change_master.sql and execute it as shown here:

```
mysql -uroot -h 127.0.0.1 -e "source /home/cbell/gr/change_master"
--port=24802
mysql -uroot -h 127.0.0.1 -e "source /home/cbell/gr/change_master"
--port=24803
mysql -uroot -h 127.0.0.1 -e "source /home/cbell/gr/change_master"
--port=24804
```

Now that we have our secondaries configured to connect to the primary, we must finish the process by starting Group Replication.

Start Group Replication on the Secondaries

The next step is to start Group Replication on the secondaries. Rather than use the START SLAVE command as in MySQL Replication, Group Replication uses the command START GROUP_REPLICATION. Run this on each of the secondaries as shown here:

```
mysql -uroot -h 127.0.0.1 -e "START GROUP_REPLICATION" --port=24802
mysql -uroot -h 127.0.0.1 -e "START GROUP_REPLICATION" --port=24803
mysql -uroot -h 127.0.0.1 -e "START GROUP_REPLICATION" --port=24804
```

The START GROUP_REPLICATION command normally does not report any errors, and it may take a bit longer to return. This is because a lot of things are going on in the background when the secondary connects to and begins negotiating with the primary. However, unlike MySQL Replication, you cannot use SHOW SLAVE STATUS to check the status. In fact, issuing that command will get no results. So, what do you do?

Verify Group Replication Status

Group Replication has redesigned the way we monitor replication services. Group Replication adds several views to the performance_schema database that you can use to monitor Group Replication. There is a lot of information there, and if you are interested, you can see https://dev.mysql.com/doc/refman/8.0/en/group-replication-monitoring.html to learn more about the views and what they contain.

Checking Group Replication status requires issuing queries against the performance_schema views. The replication_group_members view (table) is used for monitoring the status of the server instances that are tracked in the current view, or in other words, that are part of the group and as such are tracked by the membership service. The information is shared between all the server instances that are members of the replication group, so information on all the group members can be queried from any member. Listing 3-5 shows the command in action.

Listing 3-5. Checking Group Replication Status

```
$ mysql -uroot -h 127.0.0.1  --port=24802
Welcome to the MySQL monitor.  Commands end with ; or \g.
Your MySQL connection id is 34
Server version: 8.0.11 MySQL Community Server (GPL)

Copyright (c) 2000, 2018, Oracle and/or its affiliates. All rights reserved.
```

Oracle is a registered trademark of Oracle Corporation and/or its affiliates. Other names may be trademarks of their respective owners.

Type 'help;' or '\h' for help. Type '\c' to clear the current input statement.

mysql> SHOW SLAVE STATUS\G
Empty set (0.00 sec)

```
mysql> SELECT * FROM performance_schema.replication_group_members \G
*************************** 1. row ***************************
  CHANNEL_NAME: group_replication_applier
     MEMBER_ID: 21e6463c-4330-11e8-bc61-d4258b76e981
   MEMBER_HOST: oracle-pc
   MEMBER_PORT: 24801
  MEMBER_STATE: ONLINE
   MEMBER_ROLE: PRIMARY
MEMBER_VERSION: 8.0.11
*************************** 2. row ***************************
  CHANNEL_NAME: group_replication_applier
     MEMBER_ID: 2854aecd-4330-11e8-abb6-d4258b76e981
   MEMBER_HOST: oracle-pc
   MEMBER_PORT: 24802
  MEMBER_STATE: ONLINE
   MEMBER_ROLE: SECONDARY
MEMBER_VERSION: 8.0.11
*************************** 3. row ***************************
  CHANNEL_NAME: group_replication_applier
     MEMBER_ID: 2ecd9f66-4330-11e8-90fe-d4258b76e981
   MEMBER_HOST: oracle-pc
   MEMBER_PORT: 24803
  MEMBER_STATE: ONLINE
   MEMBER_ROLE: SECONDARY
MEMBER_VERSION: 8.0.11
```

```
*************************** 4. row ***************************
  CHANNEL_NAME: group_replication_applier
     MEMBER_ID: 3525b7be-4330-11e8-80b1-d4258b76e981
   MEMBER_HOST: oracle-pc
   MEMBER_PORT: 24804
  MEMBER_STATE: ONLINE
   MEMBER_ROLE: SECONDARY
MEMBER_VERSION: 8.0.11
4 rows in set (0.01 sec)
```

Notice that we run the SHOW SLAVE STATUS command but get nothing in return. Drat. However, when we query the view, we get a host of information including the current state of each member of the group. Interestingly, you can run this query on any member in the group. This shows how Group Replication propagates metadata to all the members in the group.

You can also narrow the output to get a more pleasing view including only the member host, port, state and role, shown here:

```
mysql> SELECT MEMBER_HOST, MEMBER_PORT, MEMBER_STATE, MEMBER_ROLE FROM
performance_schema.replication_group_members;
+-------------+-------------+--------------+-------------+
| MEMBER_HOST | MEMBER_PORT | MEMBER_STATE | MEMBER_ROLE |
+-------------+-------------+--------------+-------------+
| oracle-pc   |       24801 | ONLINE       | PRIMARY     |
| oracle-pc   |       24802 | ONLINE       | SECONDARY   |
| oracle-pc   |       24803 | ONLINE       | SECONDARY   |
| oracle-pc   |       24804 | ONLINE       | SECONDARY   |
+-------------+-------------+--------------+-------------+
```

If you want to locate just the primary, you can use the following query on any of the group members:

```
SELECT member_id, member_host, member_port FROM performance_schema.global_
status JOIN performance_schema.replication_group_members ON VARIABLE_
VALUE=member_id WHERE VARIABLE_NAME='group_replication_primary_member';
```

When you execute this query on any one of the members in the group, you will see the UUID of the primary:

```
+---------------------------------------+-------------+-------------+
| member_id                             | member_host | member_port |
+---------------------------------------+-------------+-------------+
| 21e6463c-4330-11e8-bc61-d4258b76e981  | oracle-pc   |       24801 |
+---------------------------------------+-------------+-------------+
```

You should place these SQL statements in a file named check_gr.sql so that we can use it later in a script to automate setting up Group Replication.

Now that we have Group Replication running, let's create some data. We will use the same sample data as we did in the last tutorial. However, this time, we will execute the queries on one of the secondaries. What do you expect to happen? If you're thinking in terms of MySQL Replication, you may expect the data to appear on only one of the secondaries. Let's see what happens. The following executes the data queries on one of the secondaries:

```
$ mysql -uroot -h 127.0.0.1  --port=24802
Welcome to the MySQL monitor.  Commands end with ; or \g.
...
mysql> CREATE DATABASE test;
ERROR 1290 (HY000): The MySQL server is running with the --super-read-only
option so it cannot execute this statement
```

Why did we get this error? It turns out, each secondary is started with super-read-only, which solves the old problem of users with the "super" power being able to write to replicas; super-read-only=OFF disallows anyone from writing to a replica. So, the common issue of writes sent to a slave (from MySQL Replication) is resolved. Huzzah! Use of super-read-only also indicates we are running Group Replication in single-primary mode (which is the default). You will see other modes when we explore the nuances of InnoDB Cluster in later chapters.

Returning to our test of creating some data, let's run the same commands on the primary. The following shows the expected results:

```
$ mysql -uroot -h 127.0.0.1  --port=24801
...
mysql> CREATE DATABASE test;
Query OK, 1 row affected (0.03 sec)
```

```
mysql> USE test;
Database changed
mysql> CREATE TABLE test.t1 (id INT PRIMARY KEY, message TEXT NOT NULL);
Query OK, 0 rows affected (0.04 sec)

mysql> INSERT INTO test.t1 VALUES (1, 'Chuck is here');
Query OK, 1 row affected (0.01 sec)
```

Here, we see the data was created. Now, to check the secondary. The following shows the results of running a query on the secondary. As you can see, the data has been replicated.

```
$ mysql -uroot -h 127.0.0.1  --port=24802
...
mysql> SELECT * FROM test.t1;
+----+----------------+
| id | message        |
+----+----------------+
|  1 | Chuck is here. |
+----+----------------+
1 row in set (0.00 sec)
```

You should place the four SQL commands—CREATE DATABASE, CREATE TABLE, INSERT, and SELECT—into a file named sample_data.sql, which we will use later in a script to automate setting up Group Replication.

Demonstration of Failover

Now that we have a working Group Replication setup, let's see how automatic failover works. If you haven't run the preceding tutorial and want to follow along, be sure to run the previous steps first.

Automatic failover is a built-in feature of Group Replication. The communication mechanism ensures that the primary (in a single-primary configuration) is monitored for activity and, when it is no longer available or something serious has gone wrong, the group can decide to terminate the primary connection and elect a new primary.

Let's see how this works. Recall from the preceding tutorial, we have the initial primary running on port 24801. We can simulate a failure by killing the MySQL process for that server. Because we're running on Linux, we can determine the process ID by inspecting the process ID file, which MySQL creates with the name of the machine and a file extension of .pid in the data directory. For example, the file for the primary shown in the tutorial is in data/primary/oracle-pc.pid. The file is named using the machine and stored in the data directory. The file for your system will be named differently. The following demonstrates how to find the process ID and stop it. Note that you may need super-user privileges to kill the process.

```
$ more ./data/primary/oracle-pc.pid
18019
$ sudo kill -9 18019
```

Tip On Windows, you can use the Task Manager to kill the process.

Now that the primary is down, we can view the health of the group with the previous queries. Recall, we use the check_gr.sql file that contains the queries. Listing 3-6 shows the output from the queries.

Listing 3-6. Checking Group Health After the Primary Goes Down

```
$ mysql -uroot -h 127.0.0.1 --port=24802 -e "source check_gr.sql"
*************************** 1. row ***************************
  CHANNEL_NAME: group_replication_applier
     MEMBER_ID: 2854aecd-4330-11e8-abb6-d4258b76e981
   MEMBER_HOST: oracle-pc
   MEMBER_PORT: 24802
  MEMBER_STATE: ONLINE
   MEMBER_ROLE: PRIMARY
MEMBER_VERSION: 8.0.11
*************************** 2. row ***************************
  CHANNEL_NAME: group_replication_applier
     MEMBER_ID: 2ecd9f66-4330-11e8-90fe-d4258b76e981
   MEMBER_HOST: oracle-pc
   MEMBER_PORT: 24803
```

```
    MEMBER_STATE: ONLINE
     MEMBER_ROLE: SECONDARY
  MEMBER_VERSION: 8.0.11
*************************** 3. row ***************************
    CHANNEL_NAME: group_replication_applier
       MEMBER_ID: 3525b7be-4330-11e8-80b1-d4258b76e981
     MEMBER_HOST: oracle-pc
     MEMBER_PORT: 24804
    MEMBER_STATE: ONLINE
     MEMBER_ROLE: SECONDARY
  MEMBER_VERSION: 8.0.11
```

member_id	member_host	member_port
2854aecd-4330-11e8-abb6-d4258b76e981	oracle-pc	24802

Notice that the group has automatically chosen a new primary (on port 24802) and there are now only three servers in the group. So, there is no loss of write capability. However, recall from an earlier discussion that the group can tolerate only so many failures, and after that limit is reached, the group can no longer successfully fail over, and in those cases the group may not be fault tolerant. Listing 3-7 shows the state of this same group after the second and third primary machines have been stopped. Notice that the state of the last primary is unknown.

Listing 3-7. State of the Group When No More Primary Servers Remain

```
$ mysql -uroot -h 127.0.0.1 --port=24804 -e "source check_gr.sql"
*************************** 1. row ***************************
    CHANNEL_NAME: group_replication_applier
       MEMBER_ID: 2ecd9f66-4330-11e8-90fe-d4258b76e981
     MEMBER_HOST: oracle-pc
     MEMBER_PORT: 24803
    MEMBER_STATE: UNREACHABLE
     MEMBER_ROLE: PRIMARY
  MEMBER_VERSION: 8.0.11
```

```
*************************** 2. row ***************************
  CHANNEL_NAME: group_replication_applier
    MEMBER_ID: 3525b7be-4330-11e8-80b1-d4258b76e981
  MEMBER_HOST: oracle-pc
  MEMBER_PORT: 24804
 MEMBER_STATE: ONLINE
  MEMBER_ROLE: SECONDARY
MEMBER_VERSION: 8.0.11
+------------------------------------+-------------+-------------+
| member_id                          | member_host | member_port |
+------------------------------------+-------------+-------------+
| 2ecd9f66-4330-11e8-90fe-d4258b76e981 | oracle-pc   |       24803 |
+------------------------------------+-------------+-------------+
```

Now that we've seen failover in action, let's look at how to automate this tutorial so we can experiment with it further (and easier).

DevOps Scripts

If you're like me and you want to make your development life easier, you will likely want to use a script to coordinate starting and stopping an experimental Group Replication setup. Fortunately, we can do that in this case because we are using local instances and thus know exactly what server IDs, IP addresses, and ports to use. Listing 3-8 is a script written for the Linux operating system.

Listing 3-8. DevOps Script to Start Group Replication (Linux)

```sh
#!/bin/sh
# This file contains the setup commands used to start the tests for using MEB'
# with GR. Specifically, this file contains commands to start (4) mysqld
# instances and establish group replication among them.
#
# Note: All of the files reside in a local directory such as /home/cbell/
# gr_linux. If you wish to run these commands, substitute the correct
#       directory in the commands.
#
```

```
# Note: Change the user to your user account or appropriate surrogate.
#
# The instances are primary (primary), secondary1, secondary2, secondary3
# (secondaries). Each is started with a corresponding config file, which is
# expected to be in the base directory. Each instance uses a different
# port but runs on the local machine.
#
# The steps include:
# 1) initialize the data directories
# 2) launch all mysqld instances
# 3) install the GR plugin
# 4) create the replication user
# 5) start GR
# 6) check GR
# 7) create initial data

echo ====== Step 1 of 7: INITIALIZE DATA DIRECTORIES ======

cd /home/cbell/gr_linux
rm -rf /home/cbell/gr_linux/data
mkdir /home/cbell/gr_linux/data
mysqld --no-defaults --user=cbell --initialize-insecure --basedir=/home/
cbell/source/git/mysql-bug-staging/build/ --datadir=/home/cbell/gr_linux/
data/primary
mysqld --no-defaults --user=cbell --initialize-insecure --basedir=/home/
cbell/source/git/mysql-bug-staging/build/ --datadir=/home/cbell/gr_linux/
data/secondary1
mysqld --no-defaults --user=cbell --initialize-insecure --basedir=/home/
cbell/source/git/mysql-bug-staging/build/ --datadir=/home/cbell/gr_linux/
data/secondary2
mysqld --no-defaults --user=cbell --initialize-insecure --basedir=/home/
cbell/source/git/mysql-bug-staging/build/ --datadir=/home/cbell/gr_linux/
data/secondary3

echo ====== Step 2 of 7: START ALL INSTANCES ======

cd /home/cbell/gr_linux
rm *.sock*
```

```
mysqld --defaults-file=/home/cbell/gr_linux/primary.cnf > primary_output.
txt 2>&1 &
mysqld --defaults-file=/home/cbell/gr_linux/secondary1.cnf > secondary1_
output.txt 2>&1 &
mysqld --defaults-file=/home/cbell/gr_linux/secondary2.cnf > secondary2_
output.txt 2>&1 &
mysqld --defaults-file=/home/cbell/gr_linux/secondary3.cnf > secondary3_
output.txt 2>&1 &

sleep 5

echo ====== Step 3 of 7: INSTALL THE GR PLUGIN ======

mysql -uroot -h 127.0.0.1 -e "INSTALL PLUGIN group_replication SONAME
'group_replication.so'" --port=24801
mysql -uroot -h 127.0.0.1 -e "INSTALL PLUGIN group_replication SONAME
'group_replication.so'" --port=24802
mysql -uroot -h 127.0.0.1 -e "INSTALL PLUGIN group_replication SONAME
'group_replication.so'" --port=24803
mysql -uroot -h 127.0.0.1 -e "INSTALL PLUGIN group_replication SONAME
'group_replication.so'" --port=24804

echo ====== Step 4 of 7: CREATE THE REPLICATION USER ======

mysql -uroot -h 127.0.0.1 -e "source create_rpl_user.sql" --port=24801
mysql -uroot -h 127.0.0.1 -e "source create_rpl_user.sql" --port=24802
mysql -uroot -h 127.0.0.1 -e "source create_rpl_user.sql" --port=24803
mysql -uroot -h 127.0.0.1 -e "source create_rpl_user.sql" --port=24804

echo ====== Step 5 of 7: START GR ======

mysql -uroot -h 127.0.0.1 -e "source start_gr_primary.sql" --port=24801
mysql -uroot -h 127.0.0.1 -e "source change_master.sql" --port=24802
mysql -uroot -h 127.0.0.1 -e "START GROUP_REPLICATION" --port=24802
mysql -uroot -h 127.0.0.1 -e "source change_master.sql" --port=24803
mysql -uroot -h 127.0.0.1 -e "START GROUP_REPLICATION" --port=24803
mysql -uroot -h 127.0.0.1 -e "source change_master.sql" --port=24804
mysql -uroot -h 127.0.0.1 -e "START GROUP_REPLICATION" --port=24804
```

```
echo ====== Step 6 of 7: CHECK GR ======

echo "Waiting for GR to start and reconcile..."
sleep 5
mysql -uroot -h 127.0.0.1 -e "source check_gr.sql" --port=24801

echo ====== Step 7 of 7: CREATE SOME DATA ======

sleep 30

mysql -uroot -h 127.0.0.1 -e "source sample_data.sql" --port=24801
mysql -uroot -h 127.0.0.1 -e "SELECT * FROM test.t1" --port=24801

echo ====== SETUP COMPLETE ======
```

Take some time to explore this script. You should be able to adapt it to your own platform with a few minor changes. For example, if you are using a MySQL installation other than the default, you may need to provide paths to the executables or, similarly, you may need to alter the configuration files setting the various directories.

When you execute this script, you will see output similar to Listing 3-9. Notice that this is the same output we encountered during the tutorial.

Listing 3-9. Executing the setup_gr.sh Script (Linux)

```
$ ./setup_gr.sh
====== Step 1 of 7: INITIALIZE DATA DIRECTORIES ======
2018-04-18T17:44:19.902106Z 0 [System] [MY-013169] [Server] /home/cbell/
source/git/mysql-bug-staging/build/bin/mysqld (mysqld 8.0.11) initializing
of server in progress as process 17828
2018-04-18T17:44:24.306322Z 4 [Warning] [MY-010453] [Server] root@localhost
is created with an empty password ! Please consider switching off the
--initialize-insecure option.
2018-04-18T17:44:2   9.133321Z 0 [System] [MY-013170] [Server] /home/
cbell/source/git/mysql-bug-staging/build/bin/mysqld (mysqld 8.0.11)
initializing of server has completed
2018-04-18T17:44:30.615437Z 0 [System] [MY-013169] [Server] /home/cbell/
source/git/mysql-bug-staging/build/bin/mysqld (mysqld 8.0.11) initializing
of server in progress as process 17876
```

```
2018-04-18T17:44:35.248184Z 4 [Warning] [MY-010453] [Server] root@localhost
is created with an empty password ! Please consider switching off the
--initialize-insecure option.
2018-04-18T17:44:40.080563Z 0 [System] [MY-013170] [Server] /home/cbell/
source/git/mysql-bug-staging/build/bin/mysqld (mysqld 8.0.11) initializing
of server has completed
2018-04-18T17:44:41.589196Z 0 [System] [MY-013169] [Server] /home/cbell/
source/git/mysql-bug-staging/build/bin/mysqld (mysqld 8.0.11) initializing
of server in progress as process 17925
2018-04-18T17:44:45.912417Z 4 [Warning] [MY-010453] [Server] root@localhost
is created with an empty password ! Please consider switching off the
--initialize-insecure option.
2018-04-18T17:44:50.810105Z 0 [System] [MY-013170] [Server] /home/cbell/
source/git/mysql-bug-staging/build/bin/mysqld (mysqld 8.0.11) initializing
of server has completed
2018-04-18T17:44:52.246658Z 0 [System] [MY-013169] [Server] /home/cbell/
source/git/mysql-bug-staging/build/bin/mysqld (mysqld 8.0.11) initializing
of server in progress as process 17971
2018-04-18T17:44:56.781545Z 4 [Warning] [MY-010453] [Server] root@localhost
is created with an empty password ! Please consider switching off the
--initialize-insecure option.
2018-04-18T17:45:01.652505Z 0 [System] [MY-013170] [Server] /home/cbell/
source/git/mysql-bug-staging/build/bin/mysqld (mysqld 8.0.11) initializing
of server has completed
====== Step 2 of 7: START ALL INSTANCES ======
rm: cannot remove '*.sock*': No such file or directory
====== Step 3 of 7: INSTALL THE GR PLUGIN ======
====== Step 4 of 7: CREATE THE REPLICATION USER ======
====== Step 5 of 7: START GR ======
====== Step 6 of 7: CHECK GR ======
Waiting for GR to start and reconcile...
*************************** 1. row ***************************
  CHANNEL_NAME: group_replication_applier
     MEMBER_ID: 21e6463c-4330-11e8-bc61-d4258b76e981
   MEMBER_HOST: oracle-pc
   MEMBER_PORT: 24801
```

```
  MEMBER_STATE: ONLINE
   MEMBER_ROLE: PRIMARY
MEMBER_VERSION: 8.0.11
*************************** 2. row ***************************
  CHANNEL_NAME: group_replication_applier
     MEMBER_ID: 2854aecd-4330-11e8-abb6-d4258b76e981
   MEMBER_HOST: oracle-pc
   MEMBER_PORT: 24802
  MEMBER_STATE: ONLINE
   MEMBER_ROLE: SECONDARY
MEMBER_VERSION: 8.0.11
*************************** 3. row ***************************
  CHANNEL_NAME: group_replication_applier
     MEMBER_ID: 2ecd9f66-4330-11e8-90fe-d4258b76e981
   MEMBER_HOST: oracle-pc
   MEMBER_PORT: 24803
  MEMBER_STATE: ONLINE
   MEMBER_ROLE: SECONDARY
MEMBER_VERSION: 8.0.11
*************************** 4. row ***************************
  CHANNEL_NAME: group_replication_applier
     MEMBER_ID: 3525b7be-4330-11e8-80b1-d4258b76e981
   MEMBER_HOST: oracle-pc
   MEMBER_PORT: 24804
  MEMBER_STATE: ONLINE
   MEMBER_ROLE: SECONDARY
MEMBER_VERSION: 8.0.11
+--------------------------------------+-------------+-------------+
| member_id                            | member_host | member_port |
+--------------------------------------+-------------+-------------+
| 21e6463c-4330-11e8-bc61-d4258b76e981 | oracle-pc   |       24801 |
+--------------------------------------+-------------+-------------+
```

```
====== Step 7 of 7: CREATE SOME DATA ======
+----+----------------+
| id | message        |
+----+----------------+
|  1 | Chuck is here. |
+----+----------------+
====== SETUP COMPLETE ======
```

There is also a corresponding shutdown script, shown in Listing 3-10. You can use this to quickly shut down the group.

Listing 3-10. DevOps Shutdown Script (Linux)

```
# This file contains commands to shut down and destroy the test GR cluster as
# set up by the commands in gr_meb_setup.txt.
#
# Note: the primary is expected to be p1, but it doesn't matter as the data
#       directories are destroyed at the end
#
# The steps include:
# 1) issue STOP GROUP_REPLICATION on all secondary servers
# 2) issue STOP GROUP_REPLICATION on the primary
# 3) shut down all mysqld instances
# 4) destroy the data directories

echo ====== Step 1 of 4: STOP GROUP REPLICATION ON SECONDARIES ======
mysql -uroot -h 127.0.0.1 --port=24802 -e "STOP GROUP_REPLICATION"
mysql -uroot -h 127.0.0.1 --port=24803 -e "STOP GROUP_REPLICATION"
mysql -uroot -h 127.0.0.1 --port=24804 -e "STOP GROUP_REPLICATION"

echo ====== Step 2 of 4: STOP GROUP REPLICATION ON PRIMARY ======

mysql -uroot -h 127.0.0.1 --port=24801 -e "STOP GROUP_REPLICATION"

echo ====== Step 3 of 4: SHUTDOWN mysqld INSTANCES ======

mysql -uroot -h 127.0.0.1 --port=24802 -e "SHUTDOWN"
mysql -uroot -h 127.0.0.1 --port=24803 -e "SHUTDOWN"
mysql -uroot -h 127.0.0.1 --port=24804 -e "SHUTDOWN"
mysql -uroot -h 127.0.0.1 --port=24801 -e "SHUTDOWN"
```

```
echo ====== Step 4 of 4: DESTROY THE DATA DIRECTORIES ======

cd /home/cbell/gr_linux
rm -rf data/

echo ====== SHUTDOWN COMPLETE ======
```

When you run this script, you will see only cursory statements on the progress. If you see connection errors, that's normally OK. It just means the client could not connect. In the case of running shutdown for a server that is already shut down, this is expected.

```
$ ./shutdown.sh
====== Step 1 of 4: STOP GROUP REPLICATION ON SECONDARIES ======
====== Step 2 of 4: STOP GROUP REPLICATION ON PRIMARY ======
====== Step 3 of 4: SHUTDOWN mysqld INSTANCES ======
====== Step 4 of 4: DESTROY THE DATA DIRECTORIES ======
====== SHUTDOWN COMPLETE ======
```

Tip   The source code for the book contains examples for using these scripts on Ubuntu, macOS, and Windows.

This concludes the short tutorial on setting up MySQL Group Replication. This section presented a brief look at Group Replication in its barest, simplest terms.

Summary

There is no denying that Group Replication is a leap forward in MySQL high availability. However, as you've seen in the tutorial in this chapter, it isn't simple to set up. While those familiar with working with MySQL Replication will see the process as the same with a few extra steps, those new to MySQL and high availability may feel the learning curve is quite steep.

This chapter provided a ground-floor view of Group Replication and what it takes to set it up and maintain a group initially and during a failure or two. If you're among those thinking there must be a better way, there is—and we're almost there!

In the next chapter, we will take a short break from exploring the more technical details of InnoDB Cluster and look at the exciting new MySQL client: MySQL Shell.

CHAPTER 4

MySQL Shell

One of the biggest features that may be somewhat overlooked is the new MySQL Shell. Recall, MySQL Shell is a new way to interact with your MySQL servers. It has many advantages over the previous client that was bundled with the server, the most powerful being the ability to use Python or JavaScript directly from the shell.

In this chapter, you'll explore MySQL Shell in more detail. You will learn more about its major features and options as well as see how to use the new shell to execute scripts interactively. As you will see, MySQL Shell is another critical element of the future of MySQL.

I recommend reading through the sections in this chapter leading up to the examples at least once before trying out MySQL Shell yourself. The information presented will help you adjust to using the new commands and connections, which can sometimes be a bit confusing until you understand the concepts.

Note I use the term *shell* to refer to features or objects supported by MySQL Shell. I use *MySQL Shell* to refer to the product itself.

Using MySQL Shell

MySQL Shell is a new and exciting addition to the MySQL portfolio. MySQL Shell represents the first modern and advanced client for connecting to and interacting with MySQL. The shell can be used as a scripting environment for developing new tools and applications for working with data. Cool! Figure 4-1 shows an example of launching MySQL Shell. Notice the nifty prompt that displays the MySQL logo, connection information, and mode. Nice!

© Charles Bell 2018
C. Bell, *Introducing InnoDB Cluster*, https://doi.org/10.1007/978-1-4842-3885-1_4

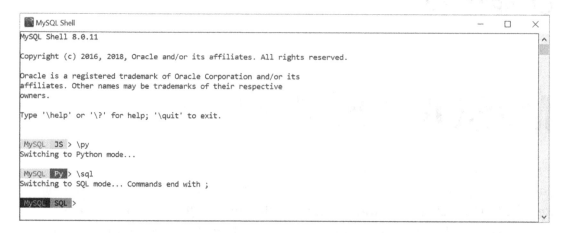

Figure 4-1. *The MySQL Shell*

> **Note**   Unlike the old client, which requires a server connection to launch, when you launch the shell without specifying a server connection, the shell will run but is not connected to a server. You must use the \connect shell command to connect to a server.

Recall from Chapter 2 that MySQL Shell is designed to use the new X Protocol for communicating with the server via the X Plugin. However, the shell can also connect to the server by using the older protocol, albeit with limited features in the scripting modes. As a result, the shell allows you to work with relational (SQL) or JSON documents (NoSQL), or both.

The addition of the SQL mode provides an excellent stepping-stone to learning how to manage your data with scripts. You can continue to use your SQL commands (or batches) until you convert them to JavaScript or Python. Furthermore, you can use both to ensure that your migration is complete.

The following sections present the major features of the shell at a high level. For more information about MySQL Shell, see the "MySQL Shell User Guide" section in the online MySQL reference manual (https://dev.mysql.com/doc/mysql-shell-excerpt/8.0/en/).

Shell Commands

As with the original MySQL client, some special commands control the application itself rather than interact with data (via SQL or the X DevAPI). To execute a shell command, issue the command with a slash (\). For example, \help prints the help for all the shell commands. Table 4-1 lists some of the more frequently used shell commands.

Table 4-1. *Shell Commands*

Command	Shortcut	Description
\		Start multiline input (SQL mode only)
\connect	(\c)	Connect to a server
\help	(\?,\h)	Print the help text
\js		Switch to JavaScript mode
\nowarnings	(\w)	Don't show warnings
\py		Switch to Python mode
\quit	(\q,\exit)	Quit
\source	(\.)	Execute the script file specified
\sql		Switch to SQL mode
\status	(\s)	Print information about the connection
\use	(\u)	Set the schema for the session
\warnings	(\W)	Show warnings after each statement

Notice that you can use the \sql, \js, and \py shell commands to switch the mode on the fly. This makes working with SQL and NoSQL data much easier because you don't have to exit the application to switch modes. Furthermore, you can use these shell commands even if you used the startup option to set the mode.

Tip   To get help with any shell command, use the \help command. For example, to learn more about the \connect command, enter \help connect.

Finally, notice the way you exit the shell (\q or \quit). If you type quit as you're used to in the old client, the shell will respond differently depending on the mode you're in. The following presents an example of what happens in each mode:

```
MySQL  SQL > quit;
ERROR: You have an error in your SQL syntax; check the manual that
corresponds to your MySQL server version for the right syntax to use near
'quit' at line 1
 MySQL  SQL > \js
Switching to JavaScript mode...
 MySQL  JS > quit
ReferenceError: quit is not defined
 MySQL  JS > \py
Switching to Python mode...
 MySQL  Py > quit
Use quit() or Ctrl-D (i.e. EOF) to exit
 MySQL  Py > \q
Bye!
```

You may see similar oddities if you are used to the old MySQL client and accidentally use an old client command, but it only takes a bit of regular use to remind you of the correct commands to use. Now, let's look at the startup options for the shell.

Options

The shell can be launched using several startup options that control the mode, connection, behavior, and more. Table 4-2 introduces some of the more common options that you may want to use. You will see more about the connection options in a later section.

Table 4-2. *Common MySQL Shell Options*

Option	Description
-f, --file=file	Process file for execution.
-e, --execute=<cmd>	Execute command and quit.
--uri	Connect via a Uniform Resource Identifier (URI).
-h, --host=<value>	Hostname to use for connection.
-P, --port=#	Port number to use for connection.
-S, --socket=sock	Socket name to use for connection in UNIX or a named pipe name in Windows (only classic sessions).
-u, --dbuser=<value>	User to use for the connection.
--user=<value>	An alias for dbuser.
--dbpassword=<value>	Password to use when connecting to server.
--password=<value>	An alias for dbpassword.
-p	Request password prompt to set the password.
-D --schema=<value>	Schema to use.
--database=<value>	An alias for --schema.
--sql	Start in SQL mode.
--sqlc	Start in SQL mode using a classic session.
--sqlx	Start in SQL mode using an X Protocol session.
--js	Start in JavaScript mode.
--py	Start in Python mode.
--json	Produce output in JSON format.
--table	Produce output in table format (default for interactive mode).
-i, --interactive[=full]	To use in batch mode, it forces emulation of interactive mode processing. Each line on the batch is processed as if it were in interactive mode.
--log-level=value	The log level. Value must be an integer between 1 and 8 or any of [none, internal, error, warning, info, debug, debug2, debug3].

(continued)

Table 4-2. (*continued*)

Option	Description
--mx --mysqlx	Create an X Protocol session (simply called "Session").
--mc --mysql	Create a classic (old protocol) session.
--ma	Create a session with automatic protocol selection.
--nw, --no-wizard	Disables wizard mode (noninteractive) for executing scripts.
--ssl-mode	Enable SSL for connection (automatically enabled with other flags).
--ssl-key=name	X509 key in PEM format.
--ssl-cert=name	X509 cert in PEM format.
--ssl-ca=name	CA file in PEM format (check OpenSSL docs).
--ssl-capath=dir	CA directory.
--ssl-cipher=name	SSL cipher to use.
--ssl-crl=name	Certificate revocation list.
--ssl-crlpath=dir	Certificate revocation list path.
--tls-version=version	TLS version to use. Permitted values are TLSv1, TLSv1.1.
--auth-method=method	Authentication method to use.
--dba=enableXProtocol	Enable the X Protocol in the server connected to. Must be used with --mysql.

Notice that there are aliases for some of the options that have the same purpose as the original client. This makes switching to the shell a bit easier if you have scripts for launching the client to perform operations. Notice also the set of options for using a Secure Sockets Layer (SSL) connection. Most of these are self-explanatory, and you've seen several of these previously. Let's now look at the sessions and connections available and how to use them. For a complete list of options, execute the shell with the --help option, as shown in Listing 4-1.

Listing 4-1. Getting Help for MySQL Shell

```
$ mysqlsh --help
MySQL Shell 8.0.11

Copyright (c) 2016, 2018, Oracle and/or its affiliates. All rights reserved.

Oracle is a registered trademark of Oracle Corporation and/or its
affiliates. Other names may be trademarks of their respective
owners.

Usage: mysqlsh [OPTIONS] [URI]
       mysqlsh [OPTIONS] [URI] -f <path> [script args...]
       mysqlsh [OPTIONS] [URI] --dba [command]
       mysqlsh [OPTIONS] [URI] --cluster

  -?, --help                Display this help and exit.
  -e, --execute=<cmd>       Execute command and quit.
  -f, --file=file           Process file.
  --uri=value               Connect to Uniform Resource Identifier. Format:
                            [user[:pass]@]host[:port][/db]
  -h, --host=name           Connect to host.
  -P, --port=#              Port number to use for connection.
  -S, --socket=sock         Socket name to use in UNIX, pipe name to use in
                            Windows (only classic sessions).
  -u, --dbuser=name         User for the connection to the server.
  --user=name               see above
  -p, --password[=name]     Password to use when connecting to server.
  --dbpassword[=name]       see above
  -p                        Request password prompt to set the password
  -D, --schema=name         Schema to use.
  --database=name           see above
  --recreate-schema         Drop and recreate the specified schema.Schema
                            will be deleted if it exists!
  -mx, --mysqlx             Uses connection data to create Creating an X
                            protocol session.
  -mc, --mysql              Uses connection data to create a Classic Session.
  -ma                       Uses the connection data to create the session
                            withautomatic protocol detection.
...
```

Tip   On Windows, MySQL Shell appears as an application, but you can add `C:\ Program Files\MySQL\MySQL Shell 8.0\bin` to your path and execute it from a command window.

Sessions and Modes

As with the original client and indeed most MySQL client applications, you will need to connect to a MySQL server so that you can run commands. MySQL Shell supports several ways to connect to a MySQL server and a variety of options for interacting with the server (called a *session*). Within a session, you can change the way the shell accepts commands (called *modes*) to include SQL, JavaScript, or Python commands.

Given all the different and new concepts of working with servers, those new to using the shell may find the difference subtle and even at times confusing. Indeed, the online reference manual and various blogs and other reports sometimes use *mode* and *session* interchangeably, but as you will see, they are different (however subtle). The following sections clarify each of the major concepts including sessions, modes, and connections so that you can get accustomed to the new methods faster. I introduce the concepts first with simple examples and then discuss making connections in detailed examples. Let's begin by looking at the session objects available.

Session Objects

The first thing to understand about sessions s that a *session* is a connection to a single server. The second thing to understand is that each session can be started with one of two session objects. Sessions are connections to servers (with all parameters defined), and a session object is what the shell uses to interact with a server in one of several ways. More specifically, a MySQL Shell session object defines how you interact with the server, including what modes are supported and even how the shell communicates with the server. The shell supports two session objects as follows:

- *Session*: An X Protocol session is used for application development and supports the JavaScript, Python, and SQL modes. Typically used to develop scripts or execute scripts. To start the shell with this option, use the `--mx` (`--mysqlx`) option.

- *Classic session*: Uses the older server communication protocol with limited support for the DevAPI. Use this mode with older servers that do not have the X Plugin or do not support the X Protocol. Typically used for SQL mode with older servers. To start the shell with this option, use the `--mc` (`--mysqlc`) option.

Note   A classic session is available only in MySQL Shell. It is not part of the X DevAPI. Only the session connection via the X Protocol is available via the X DevAPI.

You can specify the session object (protocol) to use when you use the `\connect` shell command by specifying `-mc` for classic session, `-mx` for X Protocol session, or `-ma` for automatic protocol selection. The following shows each of these in turn. Note that `<URI>` specifies a Uniform Resource Identifier.

- `\connect -mx <URI>`: Use the X Protocol (session).

- `\connect -mc <URI>`: Use the classic protocol (classic session).

- `\connect -ma <URI>`: Use automatic protocol selection.

Recall that sessions are loosely synonymous with a connection. However, a session is a bit more than just a connection because all the settings used to establish the connection, including the session object, are included as well as the protocol to use to communicate with the server. Thus, we sometimes encounter the term, *protocol* for describing a session. You will see more examples of using sessions in later sections.

Modes Supported

The shell supports three modes (also called *language support* or simply the *active language*): SQL, JavaScript, and Python. Recall that we can initiate any one of these modes by using a shell command. You can switch modes (languages) as often as you want without disconnection each time. The following lists the three modes and how to switch to each.

- `\sql`: Switch to the SQL language.

- `\js`: Switch to the JavaScript language (default mode).

- `\py`: Switch to the Python language.

Now that you understand sessions, session objects, and modes, you can look at how to make connections to MySQL servers.

Connections

Making connections in the shell is one area that may take some getting used to doing differently than the original MySQL client, which required the use of several options on the command line. You can use a specially formatted URI string or connect to a server by using individual options by name (like the old client). SSL connections are also supported. Connections can be made via startup options, shell commands, and in scripts. However, all connections are expected to use a password. Unless you state otherwise, the shell will prompt for a password if one is not given.

Note   If you want to use a connection without a password (not recommended), you must use the --password option or, if using a URI, include an extra colon to take the place of the password.

Rather than discuss all the available ways to connect and all the options to do so, the following sections present one example of each method of making a connection.

Using a URI

A URI is a special string that uses the format <dbuser>[:<dbpassword>]@host[:<por>t] [/<schema>/], where <> indicates string values for the various parameters. Notice the password, port, and schema are optional, but the user and host are required. The schema in this case is the default schema (database) that you want to use when connecting. The default port for the X Protocol is 33060. To connect to a server by using a URI on the command line when starting the shell, specify it with the --uri option as follows:

```
$ mysqlsh --uri root:secret@localhost:33060
```

The shell assumes that all connections require a password and will prompt for a password if one is not provided. Listing 4-2 shows the same connection made without the password. Notice how the shell prompts for the password.

Listing 4-2. Connecting with a URI

```
$ mysqlsh --uri root@localhost:33060/world_x
Creating a session to 'root@localhost:33060/world_x'
Enter password:
Fetching schema names for autocompletion... Press ^C to stop.
Your MySQL connection id is 13 (X protocol)
Server version: 8.0.11 MySQL Community Server (GPL)
Default schema `world_x` accessible through db.
MySQL Shell 8.0.11

Copyright (c) 2016, 2018, Oracle and/or its affiliates. All rights reserved.

Oracle is a registered trademark of Oracle Corporation and/or its
affiliates. Other names may be trademarks of their respective
owners.

Type '\help' or '\?' for help; '\quit' to exit.

 MySQL  localhost:33060+  world_x  JS >
```

Notice that we also specified the default schema (world_x) with the /schema option in the URI. The world_x database is a sample database you can download from https:// dev.mysql.com/doc/index-other.html. You will install this database during the tutorial on MySQL Shell in a later section.

Using Individual Options

You can also specify connections on the shell command line by using individual options. The available connection options are those shown in Table 4-1. For backward compatibility (and to make the transition to the MySQL Shell easier, the shell also supports --user in place of --dbuser, --password in place of --dbpassword, and --database in place of --schema. Listing 4-3 shows how to connect to a MySQL server by using individual options. Notice that I changed the mode (language) to Python with the --py option.

Listing 4-3. Connecting by Using Individual Options

```
$ mysqlsh --dbuser root --host localhost --port 33060 --schema world_x
--py -mx
Creating an X protocol session to 'root@localhost:33060/world_x'
```

```
Enter password:
Fetching schema names for autocompletion... Press ^C to stop.
Your MySQL connection id is 14 (X protocol)
Server version: 8.0.11 MySQL Community Server (GPL)
Default schema `world_x` accessible through db.
MySQL Shell 8.0.11

Copyright (c) 2016, 2018, Oracle and/or its affiliates. All rights reserved.

Oracle is a registered trademark of Oracle Corporation and/or its
affiliates. Other names may be trademarks of their respective
owners.

Type '\help' or '\?' for help; '\quit' to exit.

 MySQL  localhost:33060+  world_x  Py >
```

Using Connections in Scripts

If you plan to use the shell to create scripts or simply as a prototyping tool, you will also
want to use sessions in your scripts. In this case, we will create a variable to contain
the session after it is fetched. A session created in this manner is called a *global session*
because after it is created, it is available to any of the modes. However, depending on
the session object we're using (recall, this is classic or X Protocol), we will use a different
method of the mysqlx object to create an X or classic session. We use the getSession()
method for an X Protocol session object, and the getClassicSession() method for a
classic session object.

The following demonstrates getting an X Protocol session object in JavaScript. Notice
that I specify the password in a URI as the method parameter:

```
 MySQL  JS > var js_session = mysqlx.getSession('root@localhost:33060', 'secret')
 MySQL  JS > print(js_session)
<Session:root@localhost:33060>
The following demonstrates getting a Classic session object in JavaScript.
 MySQL  JS > var js_session = mysql.getClassicSession('root@localhost:3306',
'secret')
 MySQL  JS > print(js_session)
<ClassicSession:root@localhost:3306>
```

Using SSL Connections

You can also create SSL connections for secure connections to your servers. To use SSL, you must configure your server to use SSL. To use SSL on the same machine where MySQL is running, you can use the `--ssl-mode=REQUIRED` option. You can also specify the SSL options as shown in Table 4-1. You can specify them on the command line by using the command-line options or as an extension to the `\connect` shell command. The following shows how to connect to a server via SSL and command-line options:

```
$ mysqlsh -uroot -h127.0.0.1 --port=33060 --ssl-mode=REQUIRED
```

Tip   See the "Using Encrypted Connections" section in the MySQL Shell reference manual for more details about encrypted connections (`https://dev.mysql.com/doc/refman/8.0/en/encrypted-connections.html`).

Now that you know how to connect to our servers, let's review how to set up and install the shell and, more important, how to ensure that the X Plugin is set up correctly.

Installing the MySQL Shell

As of the current release of MySQL, MySQL Shell is released as a separate product from the server. On all platforms except Windows, you install it separately. This section demonstrates the steps needed to install MySQL Shell on Windows. To install on other platforms, visit `http://dev.mysql.com/downloads/shell/` and select the latest version and package for your platform and install the shell.

Note   The server provisioning script in the shell requires Python 2.7. If you are installing the shell on another platform, you must ensure that you have Python 2.7 installed on all servers that you want to use in InnoDB Cluster.

Installing MySQL Shell with the MySQL Installer follows the same pattern as installing MySQL Server. However, because the installer is already on the system, we simply launch it again and add the MySQL products we want (such as MySQL Shell). When you launch the installer, you will be presented with a welcome panel that contains a list of the installed products. Figure 4-2 shows the welcome panel for the MySQL Installer after installation of the server.

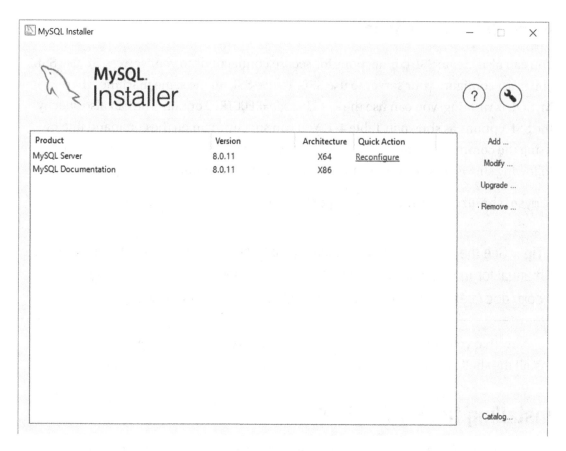

Figure 4-2. *Installer Welcome Panel – Post Installation (MySQL Installer)*

Notice we have the option of adding (*Add...*) new products, modifying (*Modify...*) the installation or configuration of an installed product, upgrading (*Upgrade...*) an installed product with a newer version from the catalog (installer), or removing installed products (*Remove...*). Notice there is also a button named *Catalog...*, which allows you to update the catalog of products in the installer. This allows you to update the products with newer versions. We will see how to do this in a later step.

For this tutorial, we want to install MySQL Shell, so click Add to proceed. You will then be presented with a product selection panel, shown in Figure 4-3. Navigate the tree on the left to find MySQL Shell, select it, and then click the green arrow to add it to the list on the right. When it is added, click the Next button to proceed.

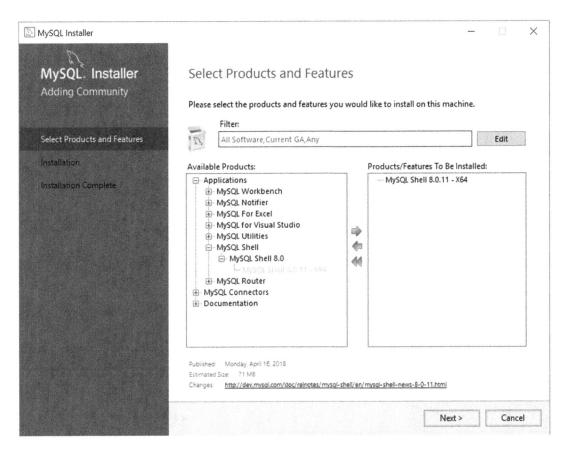

Figure 4-3. *Select Products and Features (MySQL Installer)*

The next screen is an installation summary that permits you to confirm that you have the correct products listed for installation. This panel also indicates the status so you can observe the progress of the installation. Figure 4-4 shows the Installation panel. When you are ready to begin installation of the products selected, click Execute.

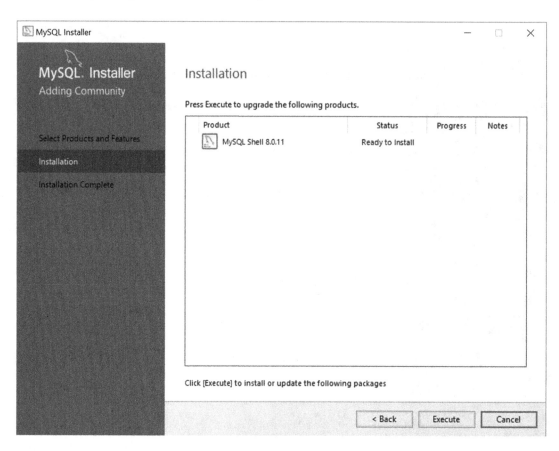

Figure 4-4. *Installation Dialog – staging (MySQL Installer)*

After installation begins, you will see the progress of each product, as shown in Figure 4-5.

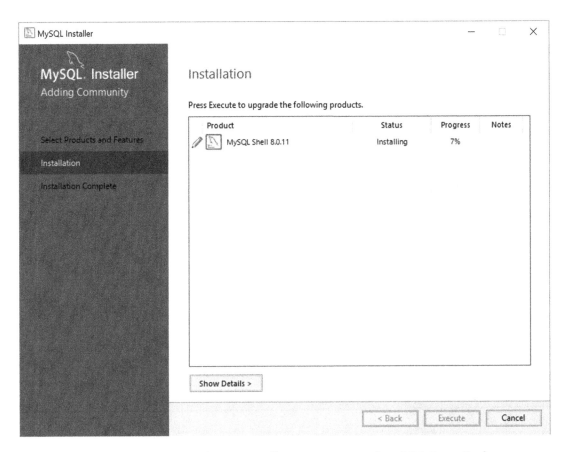

Figure 4-5. *Installation Dialog – installation progress (MySQL Installer)*

After all products are installed, the Installation panel will show the status of all installations as complete and change the buttons at the bottom to show Next, as shown in Figure 4-6. When you're ready, click Next.

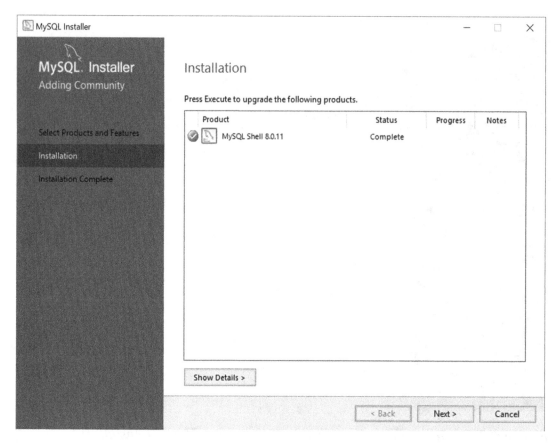

Figure 4-6. *Installation Dialog – installation complete (MySQL Installer)*

After you have verified there are no errors, click the Next button to proceed to the final panel, shown in Figure 4-7. You can click the Finish button to complete the installation and close the installer.

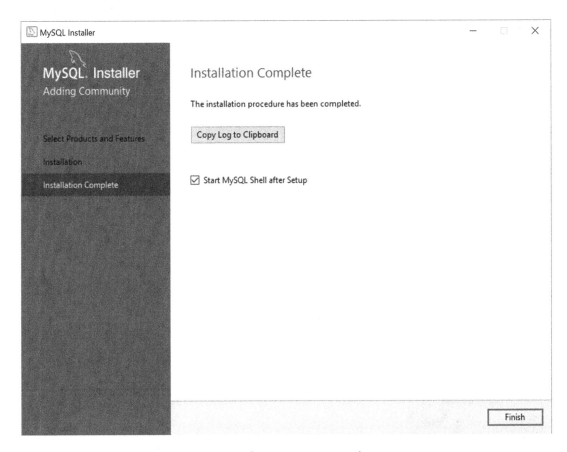

Figure 4-7. *Installation Complete (MySQL Installer)*

One of the really nice additions that the MySQL Installer provides is the ability to update its catalog of products to install. If newer packages are available, the MySQL Installer gives you the option to update them. Recall from the welcome panel that we can do this manually if we choose. However, at the end of an installation, the installer will prompt you to do the update, as shown in Figure 4-8. If you want to connect to the Internet and update the catalog, click Execute. If you do not, you can tick the Do Not Update at This Time check box and continue. Let's see how the catalog updates.

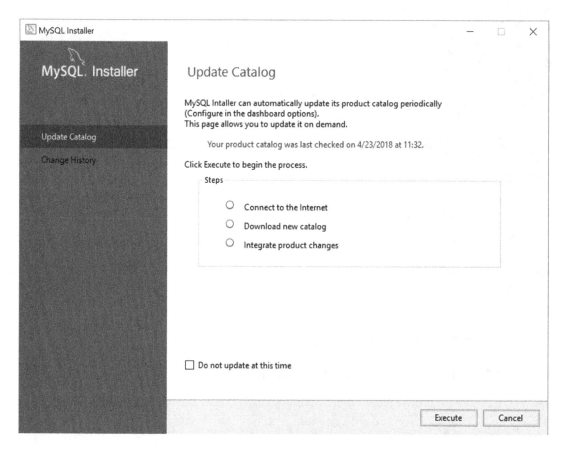

Figure 4-8. *Update Catalog - Initialize (MySQL Installer)*

The installer will connect to the Internet, download the catalog changes, and then integrate them into the installer for the next installation operation. Note that this is not the same as upgrading an existing installation; it merely updates the installer catalog. After the update is complete, click Next to finish the upgrade.

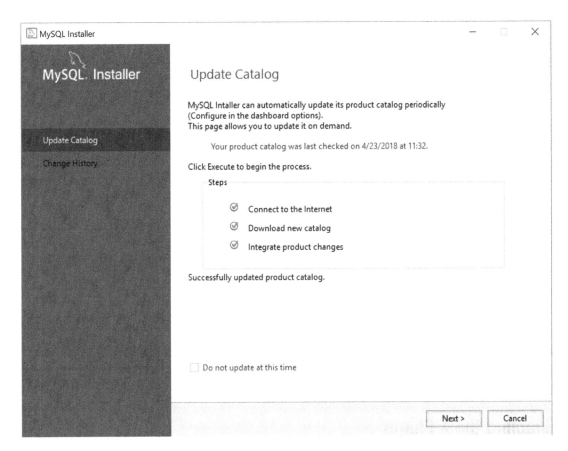

Figure 4-9. *Update Catalog - Complete (MySQL Installer)*

When all operations are complete, the installer will return to the welcome panel showing a list of all the products installed, as shown in Figure 4-10. You can close the installer when you're finished or add, modify, upgrade, or remove other products.

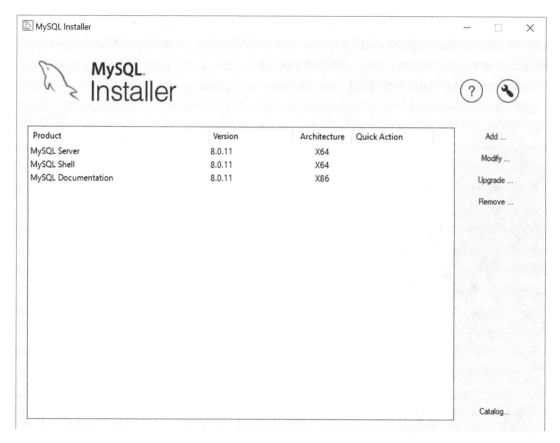

Figure 4-10. *Installer Welcome Panel – Post Installation (MySQL Installer)*

Now that MySQL Shell is installed, we need to configure the X Plugin.

Enabling the X Plugin

If you installed MySQL on your system, you already have the X Plugin installed. If you have version 8.0.11 or later, the X Plugin is already installed and enabled. However, older installation packages do not set up or enable the X Plugin by default. Thus, you may need to enable the plugin to connect to your server with the shell. Although you can still use the shell to connect using a classic session object, you won't be able to use the X Protocol session object until the X Plugin is enabled. If you need to enable the X Plugin, you can choose from at least two other methods: you can use the new MySQL Shell or you can use the old client. The following demonstrates each option.

> **Tip**   If you have trouble connecting to a MySQL server on a fresh installation of MySQL, be sure to enable the X Plugin as shown in this section.

Enable the X Plugin by Using MySQL Shell

To enable the X Plugin via MySQL Shell, start a classic session by using individual options for the user and host as well as specifying the --mysql and --dba enableXProtocol options, as shown here. We use a classic session object because we do not have the X Protocol enabled yet.

```
$ mysqlsh -uroot -hlocalhost --mysql --dba enableXProtocol
Enter password: ****
Fetching schema names for autocompletion... Press ^C to stop.
Your MySQL connection id is 13
Server version: 8.0.11 MySQL Community Server - GPL
No default schema selected; type \use <schema> to set one.
enableXProtocol: Installing plugin mysqlx...
enableXProtocol: done
```

Enable the X Plugin by Using the MySQL Client

To enable the X Plugin via the old MySQL client, you must connect to the server and install the plugin manually. There is no new magical command option to turn it on for you. This involves using the INSTALL PLUGIN SQL command, shown in Listing 4-4.

Listing 4-4. Enabling the X Plugin Using the MySQL Client

```
$ mysql -uroot -p
Enter password:
Welcome to the MySQL monitor.  Commands end with ; or \g.
Your MySQL connection id is 343
Server version: 8.0.11 MySQL Community Server (GPL)

Copyright (c) 2000, 2018, Oracle and/or its affiliates. All rights reserved.
```

Oracle is a registered trademark of Oracle Corporation and/or its affiliates. Other names may be trademarks of their respective owners.

Type 'help;' or '\h' for help. Type '\c' to clear the current input statement.

```
mysql> INSTALL PLUGIN mysqlx SONAME 'mysqlx.so';
Query OK, 0 rows affected (0.00 sec)

mysql> SHOW PLUGINS \G
*************************** 1. row ***************************
   Name: keyring_file
 Status: ACTIVE
   Type: KEYRING
Library: keyring_file.so
License: GPL
...
*************************** 43. row ***************************
   Name: mysqlx
 Status: ACTIVE
   Type: DAEMON
Library: mysqlx.so
License: GPL
43 rows in set (0.00 sec)
```

Notice that I use the SHOW PLUGINS SQL command to list the plugins installed before and after the command. I omit some of the lengthy output for clarity.

Interestingly, you can also uninstall a plugin by using the UNINSTALL PLUGIN SQL command as follows. This may be helpful if you need to diagnose connections by using the X Protocol or want to test scripts with MySQL Shell by using only the classic session object.

```
mysql> UNINSTALL PLUGIN mysqlx;
Query OK, 0 rows affected (0.80 sec)
```

Now, let's see MySQL Shell in action by way of a demonstration of its basic features.

Tutorial

The following sections demonstrate how to use MySQL Shell. The example uses the `world_x` database and is designed to present an overview rather than a deep dive. You will see MySQL Shell in use with InnoDB Cluster in Chapter 5. If you do not know anything about the MySQL Document Store or JSON data, do not despair; the tutorial is meant to demonstrate working with MySQL Shell, and because the shell is intended for use with JSON documents, we will do so. However, in Chapter 5 you will see the AdminAPI in use for configuring InnoDB Cluster.

The objective in this tutorial is to insert new data in the `world_x` database and then execute a search to retrieve rows that meet the criteria that it contains the new data. I will use a relational table to illustrate the concepts because that is easier for those of us familiar with "normal" database operations.

Before we begin our journey, let's take a moment to install the sample database we will need, the `world_x` sample MySQL database from Oracle.

Installing the Sample Database

Oracle provides several sample databases for you to use in testing and developing your applications. Sample databases can be downloaded from `http://dev.mysql.com/doc/index-other.html`. The sample database we want to use is named `world_x` to indicate it contains JSON documents and is intended for testing with the X DevAPI, the shell, and so forth. Go ahead and navigate to that page and download the database. The sample database contains several relational tables (`country`, `city`, and `countrylanguage`) as well as a collection (`countryinfo`).

After you've downloaded the file, uncompress it and note the location of the files. You will need that when you import it. Next, start MySQL Shell and make a connection to your server. Use the `\sql` shell command to switch to SQL mode and then the `\source` shell command to read the `world_x.sql` file and process all its statements.

We will also use the `SHOW DATABASES` command to list all of the databases on the server (to ensure that the new database was added). We use the `USE` command to select the default database and the `SHOW TABLES` command to see the tables in the `world_x` database. Finally, we will also see the schema (layout) of the `city` table by using the `EXPLAIN` command. If you run these commands on your own, you may get a different list of databases with the `SHOW DATABASES` command. That's OK because you may have fewer (or more) databases than the machine used in the tutorial.

Listing 4-5 shows an excerpt of the commands and the responses you should see. I highlight the commands and a row in the output to show that this world database does indeed permit storing of JSON documents in a table.

Listing 4-5. Installing the world_x Database (SQL Mode)

```
MySQL  JS > \connect root@localhost:33060
Creating a session to 'root@localhost:33060'
Enter password:
Your MySQL connection id is 9 (X protocol)
Server version: 8.0.11 MySQL Community Server (GPL)
No default schema selected; type \use <schema> to set one.
 MySQL  localhost:33060+ ssl  JS > \sql
Switching to SQL mode... Commands end with ;
 MySQL  localhost:33060+ ssl  SQL > \source /Users/cbell/Downloads/
world_x-db/world_x.sql
...
Query OK, 0 rows affected (0.00 sec)

MySQL  localhost:33060+ ssl  SQL > SHOW DATABASES;
+--------------------+
| Database           |
+--------------------+
| animals            |
| information_schema |
| mysql              |
| performance_schema |
| sys                |
| test               |
| world_x            |
+--------------------+
7 rows in set (0.00 sec)
 MySQL  localhost:33060+ ssl  SQL > USE world_x;
Query OK, 0 rows affected (0.00 sec)
 MySQL  localhost:33060+ ssl  SQL > SHOW TABLES;
```

```
+-------------------+
| Tables_in_world_x |
+-------------------+
| city              |
| country           |
| countryinfo       |
| countrylanguage   |
+-------------------+
4 rows in set (0.00 sec)
MySQL  localhost:33060+ ssl  SQL > EXPLAIN city;
+-------------+----------+------+-----+---------+----------------+
| Field       | Type     | Null | Key | Default | Extra          |
+-------------+----------+------+-----+---------+----------------+
| ID          | int(11)  | NO   | PRI | NULL    | auto_increment |
| Name        | char(35) | NO   |     |         |                |
| CountryCode | char(3)  | NO   |     |         |                |
| District    | char(20) | NO   |     |         |                |
| Info        | json     | YES  |     | NULL    |                |
+-------------+----------+------+-----+---------+----------------+
5 rows in set (0.00 sec)
```

Notice that the \source shell command is a way to load a file and execute the commands in a batch. This is a popular method of replaying frequently used command sequences, and it does work for JavaScript and Python commands too.

Tip   If the path to the file has spaces in it, you should include the path within double quotes.

You can also install the sample database by using the --recreate-schema option on the command line as follows. Note that this will delete and re-create the database if it already exists. This is another example of running the SQL commands as a batch.

```
$ mysqlsh -uroot -hlocalhost --sql --recreate-schema --schema=world_x <
~/Downloads/world_x-db/world_x.sql
Enter password:
Recreating schema world_x...
```

Of course, you could install the sample database with the old client by using the similar source command, but where's the fun in that?

Now, let's see how to insert data.

Inserting Data

We want to insert two rows into the `city` table by adding a JSON document in each and then read from the table only those rows that have the extra data. More specifically, we are going to be adding a list of places of interest to the table so that we can ask questions later about which cities have places of interest. Think of it as a way to add your own comments about places you've visited in those cities that you found interesting and would recommend to others.

Because this exercise is an example, you will also see how to delete the data we added so that we return the database to its original state. It also helps to do this if you plan to follow along with these examples so that completing one doesn't affect trying out the next.

Next, let's insert some data. We will insert two rows into the table: one for each city I've visited recently (Charlotte, North Carolina and Daytona, Florida). In this step, we will use the INSERT SQL command to insert data. Recall from earlier, we need to format our JSON document carefully so that we don't encounter errors. Specifically, we want to add structured data including the name, country code, and district, but we also want to add a JSON document that contains the population and a list (array) of places of interest. The following shows each of the commands we would use to insert the rows:

```
INSERT INTO world_x.city (Name, CountryCode, District, Info) VALUES
('Charlotte', 'USA', 'North Carolina', '{"Population": 792862, "Places_
of_interest": [{"name": "NASCAR Hall of Fame"}, {"name": "Charlotte Motor
Speedway"}]}');
```

```
INSERT INTO world_x.city (Name, CountryCode, District, Info) VALUES
('Daytona', 'USA', 'Florida', '{"Population": 590280, "Places_of_interest":
[{"name": "Daytona Beach"}, {"name": "Motorsports Hall of Fame of
America"}, {"name": "Daytona Motor Speedway"}]}');
```

Caution   Do not use spaces in key names in JSON documents. The SQL functions cannot correctly identify keys with spaces in them.

Although that seems a bit messy (and it is), if you read the statements carefully, you will see that the JSON document is encoded as a string. For example, a well-formatted version of the JSON document for the first insert is shown next. Clearly, that's a lot easier to read. You could enter the statement by using formatting like this, but the results will be shown without the extra formatting.

Notice that we retain the population key per the other rows in the table (select some and see), and we also add an array named Places_of_interest to list those places we may want to visit.

```
{
  "Population": 792862,
  "Places_of_interest": [
    {
      "name": "NASCAR Hall of Fame"
    },
    {
      "name": "Charlotte Motor Speedway"
    }
  ]
}
```

Note that I truncate the table-formatting rows (the dashed lines) from the examples for brevity.

Selecting the Data

Now, let's see how the data looks if we use a SELECT SQL statement. In this case, we'll select just the two rows by city name because they are unique in the table. The following is an excerpt of the results:

```
MySQL  localhost:33060+ ssl  SQL > SELECT * FROM city WHERE Name in
('Charlotte', 'Daytona') \G
*********************** 1. row ***************************
        ID: 3818
      Name: Charlotte
CountryCode: USA
  District: North Carolina
```

```
       Info: {"Population": 540828}
*************************** 2. row ***************************
        ID: 4080
      Name: Charlotte
CountryCode: USA
   District: North Carolina
       Info: {"Population": 792862, "Places_of_interest": [{"name": "NASCAR
       Hall of Fame"}, {"name": "Charlotte Motor Speedway"}]]
*************************** 3. row ***************************
        ID: 4081
      Name: Daytona
CountryCode: USA
   District: Florida
       Info: {"Population": 590280, "Places_of_interest": [{"name":
       "Daytona Beach"}, {"name": "Motorsports Hall of Fame of America"},
       {"name": "Daytona Motor Speedway"}]]
```

That's interesting, but it doesn't answer the question we want to ask: which cities have places of interest? To do that, we need to use a few special functions designed for the JSON data type. All the functions begin with the name JSON_*. Let's see each of these in turn, starting with a way to search for rows that have a specific key in the JSON document. In this case, we select all of the data for rows that have places of interest.

To determine whether a JSON document has a specific key, we use the JSON_CONTAINS_PATH() function. Recall that a path is a resolution of the keys in the document. In this case, we want to know whether the JSON document contains a path for Places_of_interest. Because the function returns a 0 for no match and 1 for at least one match, we check to see whether it is equal to 1. You can omit the equality, but it is best to be pedantic when experimenting with new features and commands. We also use the all option to tell the function to return all the matches (values) as opposed to one, which returns only the first occurrence. You can also use the slightly more correct IS NOT NULL comparison.

```
MySQL  localhost:33060+ ssl  SQL > SELECT * FROM city WHERE JSON_CONTAINS_
PATH(info, 'all', '$.Places_of_interest') = 1 \G
*************************** 1. row ***************************
        ID: 4080
      Name: Charlotte
```

```
CountryCode: USA
   District: North Carolina
        Info: {"Population": 792862, "Places_of_interest": [{"name": "NASCAR
        Hall of Fame"}, {"name": "Charlotte Motor Speedway"}]]}
************************** 2. row **************************
         ID: 4081
       Name: Daytona
CountryCode: USA
   District: Florida
        Info: {"Population": 590280, "Places_of_interest": [{"name":
        "Daytona Beach"}, {"name": "Motorsports Hall of Fame of America"},
        {"name": "Daytona Motor Speedway"}]]}
2 rows in set (0.00 sec)
```

Now, let's say we want to see only those places of interest and not the entire JSON document. In this case, we need to use the JSON_EXTRACT() function to extract the values from the document. Specifically, we want to search the info column for all values in the array Places_of_interest. Although that seems complicated, it isn't too bad, as you can see here:

```
MySQL  localhost:33060+ ssl  SQL > SELECT Name, District, JSON_
EXTRACT(info, '$.Places_of_interest') as Sights FROM city WHERE JSON_
EXTRACT(info, '$.Places_of_interest') IS NOT NULL \G
************************** 1. row **************************
    Name: Charlotte
District: North Carolina
  Sights: [{"name": "NASCAR Hall of Fame"}, {"name": "Charlotte Motor
  Speedway"}]
************************** 2. row **************************
    Name: Daytona
District: Florida
  Sights: [{"name": "Daytona Beach"}, {"name": "Motorsports Hall of Fame of
  America"}, {"name": "Daytona Motor Speedway"}]
2 rows in set (0.00 sec)
```

Now, what if we wanted to retrieve only the values for the Places_of_interest array? In this case, we can use a special format of the JSON access to get these values from the array. The following demonstrates the technique. Notice the portion highlighted in bold:

```
MySQL  localhost:33060+ ssl  SQL > SELECT Name, District, JSON_
EXTRACT(info, '$.Places_of_interest[*].name') as Sights FROM city WHERE
JSON_EXTRACT(info, '$.Places_of_interest') IS NOT NULL \G
*************************** 1. row ***************************
    Name: Charlotte
District: North Carolina
  Sights: ["NASCAR Hall of Fame", "Charlotte Motor Speedway"]
*************************** 2. row ***************************
    Name: Daytona
District: Florida
  Sights: ["Daytona Beach", "Motorsports Hall of Fame of America", "Daytona
  Motor Speedway"]
2 rows in set (0.00 sec)
```

OK, now that's a lot easier to read, isn't it? It's also a messy SQL command. And if all of that seems a bit painful, you're right, it is. Working with JSON data in SQL works with the help of the JSON functions, but it requires an extra step and can use confusing syntax. See the online MySQL reference manual for full explanations of each of the JSON_* functions.

If you've used the old MySQL client much to query data with wide rows, chances are you've used the \G option to display the results in a vertical format, which makes reading the data easier. With the shell, we can display data by using the --json option. Although the option is easier to read, it tends to be a bit verbose. Listing 4-6 shows the query with the shell using the --json option.

Listing 4-6. Using the JSON Option (MySQL Shell)

```
$ mysqlsh root:root@localhost --json --sql
mysqlsh: [Warning] Using a password on the command line interface can be
insecure.
{
    "info": "Creating a session to 'root@localhost'"
}
```

```
{
    "info": "Fetching schema names for autocompletion... Press ^C to stop."
}
{

    "info": "Your MySQL connection id is 17 (X protocol) Server version:
    8.0.11 MySQL Community Server - GPL No default schema selected; type
    \\use <schema> to set one."

}
{

    "info": "MySQL Shell 8.0.11 Copyright (c) 2016, 2018, Oracle and/or its
    affiliates. All rights reserved. Oracle is a registered trademark of
    Oracle Corporation and/or its affiliates. Other names may be trademarks
    of their respective owners."

}

{

    "info": "Type '\\help' or '\\?' for help; '\\quit' to exit."

}
MySQL  localhost:33060+ ssl  SQL > SELECT * FROM world_x.city WHERE Name in
('Charlotte', 'Daytona');
{
    "executionTime": "0.0060 sec",
    "warningCount": 0,
    "warnings": [],
    "rows": [
        {
            "ID": 3818,
            "Name": "Charlotte",
            "CountryCode": "USA",
            "District": "North Carolina",
            "Info": "{\"Population\": 540828}"
        },
        {
            "ID": 4080,
            "Name": "Charlotte",
            "CountryCode": "USA",
```

```
                    "District": "North Carolina",
                    "Info": "{\"Population\": 792862, \"Places_of_interest\":
                    [{\"name\": \"NASCAR Hall of Fame\"}, {\"name\": \"Charlotte
                    Motor Speedway\"}]}"
                },
                {
                    "ID": 4081,
                    "Name": "Daytona",
                    "CountryCode": "USA",
                    "District": "Florida",
                    "Info": "{\"Population\": 590280, \"Places_of_interest\":
                    [{\"name\": \"Daytona Beach\"}, {\"name\": \"Motorsports
                    Hall of Fame of America\"}, {\"name\": \"Daytona Motor
                    Speedway\"}]}"
                }
        ],
        "hasData": true,
        "affectedRowCount": 0,
        "autoIncrementValue": 0
}

 MySQL  localhost:33060+ ssl  SQL > \q
Bye!
```

Notice that the output is more verbose, and even the messages from the shell are in JSON format, but it does make for reading JSON data much nicer.

Finally, we can remove the rows with the DELETE SQL command:

```
MySQL  localhost:33060+ ssl  SQL > DELETE FROM city WHERE Name in
('Charlotte', 'Daytona');
Query OK, 3 rows affected (0.00 sec)
```

Summary

MySQL Shell is a huge leap forward in technology for MySQL clients. It is designed not only to work with SQL in MySQL in a smarter way, but also to enable prototyping of JavaScript and Python. You can work with any language you want and switch between them easily without having to restart the application or drop the connection. How cool is that?

If that wasn't enough, the added benefit of the X DevAPI and built-in objects enable using the shell as a front end to the Document Store, so you don't have to write separate applications to manage your data. You simply choose the mode (language) that fits your needs, switch to that language, and perform the tasks. As you learned in Chapter 1, the shell also forms the front end to the newest features, including InnoDB Cluster, giving you a one-stop client for all your MySQL administrative, programming, and high-availability needs.

In this chapter, you learned how to use MySQL Shell. You reviewed the startup options, shell commands, connections, sessions, and even learned how to do a bit of interactive SQL. Although this chapter doesn't provide exhaustive coverage of all the features of MySQL Shell, it provides a broad tutorial for how to use it for the most common tasks.

In the next chapter, you will explore an overview of setting up an experimental InnoDB Cluster by using MySQL Shell and the AdminAPI.

## CHAPTER 5

High Availability in a Sandbox

Now that you have learned more about what InnoDB Cluster is and the components that make up the feature, including Group Replication and MySQL Shell, you have enough knowledge to be able to set up a small experimental InnoDB Cluster. You will do so using the new AdminAPI via MySQL Shell.

What follows is a demonstration of deploying three servers and configuring them as a cluster via Group Replication using the X AdminAPI in the new MySQL Shell. Although that sounds like a lot of effort, it really isn't. In fact, it's really easy.

Let's begin with an overview of the AdminAPI.

Note   You also must have MySQL Server and MySQL Shell, at a minimum, installed on our target machine. If you have not already done so, please refer to Chapters 2 and 4, respectively, for installing the server and shell.

Getting Started with the AdminAPI

The key component that permits us to set up our experimental InnoDB Cluster is called a *sandbox*. The AdminAPI has several methods to work with MySQL servers in a sandbox on a local machine. However, the AdminAPI also has classes with methods for working with InnoDB Clusters that use MySQL servers on remote machines. This chapter provides an overview of the classes and methods available in the AdminAPI. We will use some of the methods discussed in this section in a demonstration of InnoDB Cluster in the next section.

© Charles Bell 2018
C. Bell, *Introducing InnoDB Cluster*, https://doi.org/10.1007/978-1-4842-3885-1_5

WHAT'S A SANDBOX?

A *sandbox* is a term describing the organization of data and metadata (configuration files, and so forth) in a way that it does not affect (replace) any existing data or installations of a product. In the case of the MySQL AdminAPI, the sandbox it implements ensures that any configuration of the servers in an InnoDB Cluster will not affect any existing installation of MySQL on the machine.

Recall from Chapter 2 that the AdminAPI has two major classes: dba and cluster. Let's look at the details of each.

Note   The following is a condensed version of the documentation available online that provides an overview rather than specific use examples.

The dba Class

The dba class enables you to administer InnoDB clusters by using the AdminAPI. The dba class enables you to administer the cluster—for example, creating a new cluster, working with a sandbox configuration (a way to experiment with InnoDB Cluster using several MySQL instances on the same machine), checking the status of instances and the cluster.

Because this class is the setup and configuration arm of the API, it has methods for working with the sandbox as well as methods for working with remote servers. Table 5-1 shows the methods available for working with instances in a sandbox (those with sandbox in the name).

Table 5-1. *Sandbox Methods (dba Class)*

Returns	Function	Description
None	`delete_sandbox_instance (int port, dict options)`	Deletes an existing MySQL Server instance on localhost
Instance	`deploy_sandbox_instance (int port, dict options)`	Creates a new MySQL Server instance on localhost
None	`kill_sandbox_instance (int port, dict options)`	Kills a running MySQL Server instance on localhost
None	`start_sandbox_instance (int port, dict options)`	Starts an existing MySQL Server instance on localhost
None	`stop_sandbox_instance (int port, dict options)`	Stops a running MySQL Server instance on localhost

Notice that there are methods for deploying an instance in the sandbox as well as deleting an instance or killing an instance (`delete` removes it, `kill` stops the instance but leaves the data and metadata), and starting and stopping an instance (`kill` issues an uncontrolled shutdown). We will use most of these methods in the demonstration of the InnoDB Cluster in a sandbox in a later section.

Notice also that these methods take a port number and a dictionary of options. The options that you can use for these and other methods in the AdminAPI depend on the method itself, as each method permits one or more options. Table 5-2 shows the options available for the methods in Table 5-1.

Table 5-2. *Options for the Sandbox Methods (dba Class)*

Function	Option	Description
delete_sandbox_ instance	sandboxDir	The path where the new instance will be deployed
deploy_sandbox_ instance	portx	The port where the new instance will listen for X Protocol connections
	sandboxDir	The path where the new instance will be deployed
	password	The password for the MySQL root user on the new instance
	allowRootFrom	Create the remote root account, restricted to the given address pattern (for example, %)
	ignoreSslError	Ignore errors when adding SSL support for the new instance, by default: true
kill_sandbox_ instance	sandboxDir	The path where the new instance will be deployed
start_sandbox_ instance	sandboxDir	The path where the new instance will be deployed
stop_sandbox_ instance	password	The password for the MySQL root user on the new instance
	sandboxDir	The path where the new instance will be deployed

The options are specified in a dictionary in the form of a simple JSON document. For example, if you wanted to stop an instance on port 13004 and specify the sandbox directory and password, you would call the method as follows:

```
stop_sandbox_instance(13004, {'sandboxDir':'/home/cbell/data1',
'password':'secret'})
```

Table 5-3 shows the remaining methods in the class used for setup and configuration of MySQL instances and clusters.

Table 5-3. *Instance and Cluster Methods (dba Class)*

Returns	Function	Description
JSON	`check_instance_configuration(InstanceDef instance, dict options)`	Validates an instance for MySQL InnoDB Cluster usage
None	`configure_local_instance(InstanceDef instance, dict options)`	Validates and configures a local instance for MySQL InnoDB Cluster usage
None	`configure_instance(InstanceDef instance, dict options)`	Validates and configures an instance for MySQL InnoDB Cluster usage
Cluster	`create_cluster(str name, dict options)`	Creates a MySQL InnoDB cluster
None	`drop_metadata_schema(dict options)`	Drops the metadata schema
Cluster	`get_cluster(str name, dict options)`	Retrieves a cluster from the metadata store
None	`reboot_cluster_from_complete_outage(str clusterName, dict options)`	Brings a cluster back online when all members are offline

There are considerably more options for these methods. In fact, some methods permit a long list of options. Rather than list each of the options for each of the methods, the following list summarizes the options in three categories. You will see some of these in action during the demonstration. More specific options are required for certain methods.

- *General*: Common options for some methods.

  - verifyMyCnf: Optional path to the MySQL configuration file for the instance. If this option is given, the configuration file will be verified for the expected option values, in addition to the global MySQL system variables.

  - outputMycnfPath: Alternative output path to write the MySQL configuration file of the instance.

  - password: The password to be used on the connection.

- clusterAdmin: The name of the InnoDB cluster administrator user to be created. The supported format is the standard MySQL account name format.

- clusterAdminPassword: The password for the InnoDB cluster administrator account.

- clearReadOnly: Boolean value used to confirm that super_read_only must be disabled.

- interactive: Boolean value used to disable the wizards in the command execution (prompts are not provided to the user, and confirmation prompts are not shown).

- *URI or dictionary*: Options for secure connections.

  - ssl-mode: The SSL mode to be used in the connection.

  - ssl-ca: The path to the X509 certificate authority in PEM format.

  - ssl-capath: The path to the directory that contains the X509 certificate authorities in PEM format.

  - ssl-cert: The path to the X509 certificate in PEM format.

  - ssl-key: The path to the X509 key in PEM format.

  - ssl-crl: The path to the file that contains certificate revocation lists.

  - ssl-crlpath: The path of the directory that contains certificate revocation list files.

  - ssl-cipher: SSL cipher to use.

  - tls-version: List of protocols permitted for secure connections.

  - auth-method: Authentication method.

  - get-server-public-key: Request public key from the server required for password exchange based on RSA key pairs. Use when connecting to MySQL 8.0 servers with classic MySQL sessions with SSL mode disabled.

  - server-public-key-path: The path name to a file containing a client-side copy of the public key required by the server for password exchange based on RSA key pairs.

- *Connection dictionary*: Connection parameters.

  - scheme: The protocol to be used on the connection.

  - user: The MySQL username to be used on the connection.

  - dbUser: Alias for user.

  - password: The password to be used on the connection.

  - dbPassword: Same as password.

  - host: The hostname or IP address to be used on a TCP connection.

  - port: The port to be used in a TCP connection.

  - socket: The socket file name to be used on a connection through UNIX sockets.

  - schema: The schema to be selected after the connection is done.

The class also has a single property named verbose, which permits developers to set the level of verbosity for output of debug and related statements during provisioning of servers (deploying servers in the sandbox). Setting this is property is not recommended for production use. The verbose settings are as follows:

- 0: Disables mysqlprovision verbosity

- 1: Enables mysqlprovision verbosity

- >1: A value of 2 or more enables mysqlprovision debug verbosity.

The cluster Class

The cluster class is a handle (think *object instance*) to an InnoDB cluster. This class enables you to work with the cluster to add instances, remove instances, get the status (health) of the cluster, and more.

Because this class is used to work directly with instances and the cluster, most of the methods are designed to work with a specific instance of the cluster retrieved via the dba class. Table 5-4 lists the methods in the cluster class.

Table 5-4. *Methods for the Cluster Class*

Returns	Function	Description
None	add_instance(InstanceDef instance, dict options)	Adds an instance to the cluster
dict	check_instance_state(Instance Def instance, str password)	Verifies the instance GTID state in relation to the cluster
str	describe()	Describes the structure of the cluster
None	disconnect()	Disconnects all internal sessions used by the cluster object
None	dissolve(Dictionary options)	Dissolves the cluster
None	force_quorum_using_partition_ of(InstanceDef instance, str password)	Restores the cluster from quorum loss
str	get_name()	Retrieves the name of the cluster
None	rejoin_instance(InstanceDef instance, dict options)	Rejoins an instance to the cluster
None	remove_instance(InstanceDef instance, dict options)	Removes an instance from the cluster
None	rescan()	Rescans the cluster
str	status()	Describes the status of the cluster

Notice that we have methods for adding, removing, and rejoining an instance. We will use these often in managing the instances in the cluster. There are also several methods for obtaining information and status, and forcing updates to the metadata, such as get_name(), status(), and rescan().

Notice also that like the dba class, some of the methods accept a dictionary of options. Such options are again unique to the method, but in general use the same options described in the previous section for connecting to an instance. And as mentioned, some permit options specific to the method.

The class has one property; the name of the cluster. The property is named simply name, and can be set programmatically but is normally set when the cluster is created using the dba class.

> **Tip**   See `https://dev.mysql.com/doc/dev/mysqlsh-api-python/8.0/group___admin_a_p_i.html` to learn more about the AdminAPI.

Now that you've had a brief overview of the classes and methods in the AdminAPI, let's see it in action!

Demonstration

This section presents a short demonstration of creating an InnoDB Cluster by using the sandbox deployment method via MySQL Shell and the AdminAPI. We will create an InnoDB Cluster with four instances running on our local machine. We will see not only how to set up the cluster for use but also how the cluster handles failover and, finally, how to set up DevOps scripts for quick setup and shutdown of the experimental cluster.

Setup and Configuration

To prepare for using the sandbox, you merely need to decide on a few parameters and prepare an area on your system for working with the data for the cluster. One parameter is required: we must decide on what port numbers we want to use for the experimental cluster. In this case, we will use ports 3311–3314 for the server listening ports.

We can also specify a directory to contain the sandbox data. Although this is not required, it is recommended if you want to reinitialize the cluster later. There is no need to specify a directory otherwise, because the Admin API uses a predetermined path for the sandbox. For example, on Windows it is in the user directory named `MySQL\mysql-sandboxes`. This folder forms the root for storing all data and metadata for the sandbox. For example, when you deploy an instance to the sandbox using port 3312, you will see a folder with that name as follows:

`C:\Users\olias\MySQL\mysql-sandboxes\3312`

If you plan to reuse the cluster at a later date, you may want to specify a specific folder by using the `sandboxDir` option. For example, you can specify the dictionary as `{'sandboxDir':'c://idc_sandbox'}` and the AdminAPI. However, the folder must exist, or you will get an error when you call the `deploy_sandbox_instance()` method. Listing 5-1 shows a custom sandbox directory on Windows with a single instance deployed on port 3311.

Listing 5-1. Creating a Directory for the Sandbox

```
C:\idc_sandbox>dir
 Volume in drive C is Local Disk
 Volume Serial Number is AAFC-6767

 Directory of C:\idc_sandbox

04/23/2018  04:18 PM    <DIR>          .
04/23/2018  04:18 PM    <DIR>          ..
04/23/2018  04:18 PM    <DIR>          3311
               0 File(s)              0 bytes
               3 Dir(s)  172,731,768,832 bytes free

C:\idc_sandbox>dir 3311
 Volume in drive C is Local Disk
 Volume Serial Number is AAFC-6767

 Directory of C:\idc_sandbox\3311

04/23/2018  04:19 PM    <DIR>          .
04/23/2018  04:19 PM    <DIR>          ..
04/23/2018  04:19 PM                 6 3311.pid
04/23/2018  04:18 PM               726 my.cnf
04/23/2018  04:18 PM    <DIR>          mysql-files
04/23/2018  04:18 PM    <DIR>          sandboxdata
04/23/2018  04:18 PM               147 start.bat
04/23/2018  04:18 PM               207 stop.bat
               4 File(s)          1,086 bytes
               4 Dir(s)  172,557,893,632 bytes free
```

Note   To reuse the instance data, you must start the instance. Attempting to redeploy it by using the same port will generate an error because the directory is not empty.

The following demonstration uses MySQL Shell in Python mode. The commands shown will also work in JavaScript mode, but some of the method names may have slightly different spellings (such as the use of underscore and initial capitals). This was done intentionally to allow the AdminAPI to conform to language-specific naming conventions and practices.[1]

Several steps are required to create a sandbox deployment of InnoDB Cluster:

1. *Create and deploy instances in the sandbox*: set up and configure our MySQL servers.

2. *Create the cluster*: create an object instance of the cluster class.

3. *Add the instances to the cluster*: add the sandbox instances to the cluster.

4. *Check the status of the cluster*: check the cluster health.

You will also see a demonstration of how failover works within the cluster by killing one of the instances. Let's get started!

Create and Deploy Instances in the Sandbox

Let's begin by starting the shell and deploying four servers by using the AdminAPI. In this case, we will use the ports 3311–3314 and the `deploy_sandbox_instance()` method in the `dba` object to create new instances for each server. All of these will run on our localhost, which for this example is Windows; adjust the paths accordingly for use on other systems. Listing 5-2 demonstrates how to deploy four servers. The commands used are highlighted in bold to help identify the commands from the messages. Notice that I start the shell in Python mode.

Tip   It is not necessary to import the dba class. MySQL Shell makes it available whenever you switch to Python mode by using the \py command (or --py command-line option) or JavaScript mode by using the \js command (or --js command-line option).

> [1]JavaScript experts and Pythonistas alike will appreciate this feature.

Listing 5-2. Creating Local Server Instances

```
C:\idc_sandbox>mysqlsh --py
MySQL Shell 8.0.11
```

Copyright (c) 2016, 2018, Oracle and/or its affiliates. All rights reserved.

Oracle is a registered trademark of Oracle Corporation and/or its affiliates. Other names may be trademarks of their respective owners.

Type '\help' or '\?' for help; '\quit' to exit.

 MySQL Py > **dba.deploy_sandbox_instance(3311, {'sandboxDir':'c://idc_ sandbox'})**
A new MySQL sandbox instance will be created on this host in c://idc_sandbox\3311

Warning: Sandbox instances are only suitable for deploying and running on your local machine for testing purposes and are not accessible from external networks.

Please enter a MySQL root password for the new instance: ****
Deploying new MySQL instance...

Instance localhost:3311 successfully deployed and started.
Use shell.connect('root@localhost:3311'); to connect to the instance.

 MySQL Py > **dba.deploy_sandbox_instance(3312, {'sandboxDir':'c://idc_ sandbox'})**
A new MySQL sandbox instance will be created on this host in c://idc_sandbox\3312

Warning: Sandbox instances are only suitable for deploying and running on your local machine for testing purposes and are not accessible from external networks.

Please enter a MySQL root password for the new instance: ****
Deploying new MySQL instance...

Instance localhost:3312 successfully deployed and started.
Use shell.connect('root@localhost:3312'); to connect to the instance.

**MySQL Py > dba.deploy_sandbox_instance(3313, {'sandboxDir':'c://idc_
sandbox'})**

A new MySQL sandbox instance will be created on this host in
c://idc_sandbox\3313

Warning: Sandbox instances are only suitable for deploying and
running on your local machine for testing purposes and are not
accessible from external networks.

Please enter a MySQL root password for the new instance: ****
Deploying new MySQL instance...

Instance localhost:3313 successfully deployed and started.
Use shell.connect('root@localhost:3313'); to connect to the instance.

**MySQL Py > dba.deploy_sandbox_instance(3314, {'sandboxDir':'c://idc_
sandbox'})**

A new MySQL sandbox instance will be created on this host in
c://idc_sandbox\3314

Warning: Sandbox instances are only suitable for deploying and
running on your local machine for testing purposes and are not
accessible from external networks.

Please enter a MySQL root password for the new instance: ****
Deploying new MySQL instance...

Instance localhost:3314 successfully deployed and started.
Use shell.connect('root@localhost:3314'); to connect to the instance.

MySQL Py >

Notice that the deploy_sandbox_instance() method displays the location of the sandbox data and metadata (for example, c://idc_sandbox\3314) and prompts for a password for the instance. Be sure to use a password that you will remember if you intend to restart or reuse the cluster. It is OK to use the same password for all instances. After you run all of the commands, you will have four instances running on the local machine.

Tip   JavaScript is case sensitive, so make sure you use correct spelling for variables, objects, and methods. The variable named abc is not the same as the variable named Abc.

Create the Cluster

The next thing we need to do is set up a new cluster. We do this with the create_cluster() method in the dba object, which creates an object instance to the cluster class. But first, we must connect to the server that we want to make our primary server. Note that this is a continuation of our shell session and demonstrates how to create a new cluster.

We will also set up the cluster in single-master mode. There will be one instance with the primary role (read/write), and all other instances will be read-only. To do this, we must set the multiMaster option to False. Notice how this is done in Listing 5-3.

Listing 5-3. Creating a Cluster in InnoDB Cluster

```
MySQL  Py > \connect root@localhost:3311
Creating a session to 'root@localhost:3311'
Enter password: ****
Fetching schema names for autocompletion... Press ^C to stop.
Your MySQL connection id is 12
Server version: 8.0.11 MySQL Community Server - GPL
No default schema selected; type \use <schema> to set one.

 MySQL  localhost:3311 ssl  Py > my_cluster = dba.create_
 cluster('MyCluster', {'multiMaster':False})
A new InnoDB cluster will be created on instance 'root@localhost:3311'.
ster', {'multiMaster':False})

Validating instance at localhost:3311...
Instance detected as a sandbox.
Please note that sandbox instances are only suitable for deploying test
clusters for use within the same host.
```

```
This instance reports its own address as DESKTOP-JBLO81L
```

```
Instance configuration is suitable.
Creating InnoDB cluster 'MyCluster' on 'root@localhost:3311'...
Adding Seed Instance...
```

```
Cluster successfully created. Use Cluster.add_instance() to add MySQL
instances.
At least 3 instances are needed for the cluster to be able to withstand up to
one server failure.
```

```
 MySQL  localhost:3311 ssl  Py >
```

Notice that we name the cluster MyCluster and use a variable named my_cluster to store the object returned from the create_cluster() method. Notice also that the server we connected to first has become the primary and that the AdminAPI has detected that we are running in a sandbox.

Note   If you exit the shell, you can retrieve a running cluster with the get_cluster() method.

Add the Instances to the Cluster

Next, we add the other two server instances to complete the cluster. We are now using the cluster class instance saved in the variable my_cluster and using add_instance(). We will add the three remaining instances to the cluster. These servers automatically become secondary servers in the group. Listing 5-4 shows how to add the instances to the cluster.

Listing 5-4. Adding Instances to the Cluster

```
 MySQL  localhost:3311 ssl  Py > my_cluster.add_instance('root@
localhost:3312')
```
A new instance will be added to the InnoDB cluster. Depending on the amount of data on the cluster this might take from a few seconds to several hours.

Please provide the password for 'root@localhost:3312': ****
Adding instance to the cluster ...

Validating instance at localhost:3312...
Instance detected as a sandbox.
Please note that sandbox instances are only suitable for deploying test
clusters for use within the same host.

This instance reports its own address as DESKTOP-JBLO81L

Instance configuration is suitable.
The instance 'root@localhost:3312' was successfully added to the cluster.

**MySQL localhost:3311 ssl Py > my_cluster.add_instance('root@
localhost:3313')**
A new instance will be added to the InnoDB cluster. Depending on the amount of
data on the cluster this might take from a few seconds to several hours.

Please provide the password for 'root@localhost:3313': ****
Adding instance to the cluster ...

Validating instance at localhost:3313...
Instance detected as a sandbox.
Please note that sandbox instances are only suitable for deploying test
clusters for use within the same host.

This instance reports its own address as DESKTOP-JBLO81L

Instance configuration is suitable.
The instance 'root@localhost:3313' was successfully added to the cluster.

**MySQL localhost:3311 ssl Py > my_cluster.add_instance('root@
localhost:3314')**
A new instance will be added to the InnoDB cluster. Depending on the amount of
data on the cluster this might take from a few seconds to several hours.

Please provide the password for 'root@localhost:3314': ****
Adding instance to the cluster ...

```
Validating instance at localhost:3314...
Instance detected as a sandbox.
Please note that sandbox instances are only suitable for deploying test
clusters for use within the same host.

This instance reports its own address as DESKTOP-JBL081L

Instance configuration is suitable.
The instance 'root@localhost:3314' was successfully added to the cluster.

 MySQL  localhost:3311 ssl  Py >
```

Notice that the add_instance() method takes a string with the URI connection information. In this case, it is simply the username, at sign (@), hostname, and port in the form <user>@<host>:<port>. Notice also that the method prompts for the password for the instance.

At this point, you've seen how InnoDB Cluster can set up servers and add them to the group. Take a moment and reflect on Chapter 3 and the Group Replication tutorial. What you do not see behind the scenes is all of the Group Replication mechanisms—you get them for free! How cool is that?

Clearly, using the shell to set up and manage a cluster is a lot easier than setting up and managing a standard Group Replication. Specifically, you don't have to manually configure replication! Better still, should a server fail, you don't have to worry about reconfiguring your application or the topology to ensure the solution remains viable. InnoDB Cluster does this automatically for you.

Check the Status of the Cluster

After the cluster is created and instances are added, we can get the status of the cluster by using the status() method of our my_cluster object, as shown in Listing 5-5. In this example, you'll also see how to retrieve the cluster from a running instance of one of the servers by connecting with the \connect command and using the get_cluster() method from the dba class. You can also connect to the server instance by using the command line (mysqlsh root@localhost:3313). Note that you do not have to connect to the first (or primary) server instance to retrieve the cluster. You can connect to any server to retrieve the cluster.

Listing 5-5. Getting the Status of the Cluster

```
C:\idc_sandbox>mysqlsh --py
MySQL Shell 8.0.11

Copyright (c) 2016, 2018, Oracle and/or its affiliates. All rights reserved.

Oracle is a registered trademark of Oracle Corporation and/or its
affiliates. Other names may be trademarks of their respective
owners.

Type '\help' or '\?' for help; '\quit' to exit.

 MySQL  Py > \connect root@localhost:3311
Creating a session to 'root@localhost:3311'
Enter password: ****
Fetching schema names for autocompletion... Press ^C to stop.
Your MySQL connection id is 55
Server version: 8.0.11 MySQL Community Server - GPL
No default schema selected; type \use <schema> to set one.

 MySQL  localhost:3311 ssl  Py > my_cluster = dba.get_cluster('MyCluster')
 MySQL  localhost:3311 ssl  Py > my_cluster.status()
{
    "clusterName": "MyCluster",
    "defaultReplicaSet": {
        "name": "default",
        "primary": "localhost:3311",
        "ssl": "REQUIRED",
        "status": "OK",
        "statusText": "Cluster is ONLINE and can tolerate up to ONE failure.",
        "topology": {
            "localhost:3311": {
                "address": "localhost:3311",
                "mode": "R/W",
                "readReplicas": {},
                "role": "HA",
                "status": "ONLINE"
            },
```

```
        "localhost:3312": {
            "address": "localhost:3312",
            "mode": "R/O",
            "readReplicas": {},
            "role": "HA",
            "status": "ONLINE"
        },
        "localhost:3313": {
            "address": "localhost:3313",
            "mode": "R/O",
            "readReplicas": {},
            "role": "HA",
            "status": "ONLINE"
        },
        "localhost:3314": {
            "address": "localhost:3314",
            "mode": "R/O",
            "readReplicas": {},
            "role": "HA",
            "status": "ONLINE"
        }
    }
  },
  "groupInformationSourceMember": "mysql://root@localhost:3311"
}

MySQL  localhost:3311 ssl  Py >
```

Notice that the output is in the form of a JSON document and contains the metadata about the cluster, including all of the instances, their roles, and status. You want to ensure that all instances are online.

Failover

Now, let's re-create the failover scenario from Chapter 3. In this case, we will purposefully kill one of the instances. Let's kill the one running on port 3311. We can do this in a variety of ways, including using the operating system to terminate the `mysqld` process, using the `shutdown` SQL command from the shell or MySQL client, or the `dba` class. Listing 5-6 shows how to kill the instance and the results of the status after the instance stops.

Listing 5-6. Failover Demonstration

```
MySQL  localhost:3311 ssl  Py > dba.kill_sandbox_instance(3311,
{'sandboxDir':'c://idc_sandbox'})
The MySQL sandbox instance on this host in
c://idc_sandbox\3311 will be killed

Killing MySQL instance...

Instance localhost:3311 successfully killed.

 MySQL  localhost:3311 ssl  Py > my_cluster.status()
Traceback (most recent call last):
  File "<string>", line 1, in <module>
SystemError: RuntimeError: Cluster.status: Unable to detect target instance
state. Please check account privileges.

MySQL  localhost:3311 ssl  Py > \connect root@localhost:3312
Creating a session to 'root@localhost:3312'
Enter password: ****
Fetching schema names for autocompletion... Press ^C to stop.
Closing old connection...
Your MySQL connection id is 44
Server version: 8.0.11 MySQL Community Server - GPL
No default schema selected; type \use <schema> to set one.

MySQL  localhost:3312 ssl  Py > my_cluster = dba.get_cluster('MyCluster')
 MySQL  localhost:3312 ssl  Py > my_cluster.status()
{
    "clusterName": "MyCluster",
    "defaultReplicaSet": {
```

```
"name": "default",
"primary": "localhost:3312",
"ssl": "REQUIRED",
"status": "OK_PARTIAL",
"statusText": "Cluster is ONLINE and can tolerate up to ONE
failure. 1 member is not active",
"topology": {
    "localhost:3311": {
        "address": "localhost:3311",
        "mode": "R/O",
        "readReplicas": {},
        "role": "HA",
        "status": "(MISSING)"
    },
    "localhost:3312": {
        "address": "localhost:3312",
        "mode": "R/W",
        "readReplicas": {},
        "role": "HA",
        "status": "ONLINE"
    },
    "localhost:3313": {
        "address": "localhost:3313",
        "mode": "R/O",
        "readReplicas": {},
        "role": "HA",
        "status": "ONLINE"
    },
    "localhost:3314": {
        "address": "localhost:3314",
        "mode": "R/O",
        "readReplicas": {},
        "role": "HA",
        "status": "ONLINE"
    }
```

```
        }
    },
    "groupInformationSourceMember": "mysql://root@localhost:3312"
}

 MySQL  localhost:3312 ssl  Py >
```

Notice that we killed the server running on port 3311. However, when we went to check the status again, we got an error. This is because we were already connected to that server. We need to connect to another server and retrieve the cluster again to refresh the data. Then we can get the status, and when we do, we see the server instance on port 3311 is listed as missing and the server on port 3312 has taken over the read/write capability.

At this point, we can try to recover the server instance on port 3311 or remove it from the cluster. Listing 5-7 demonstrates how to remove it from the cluster. Notice that we use the force option set to True to remove the instance because we cannot connect to it (it is down).

Listing 5-7. Removing the Downed Instance from the Cluster

```
MySQL  localhost:3312 ssl  Py > my_cluster.remove_instance
('root@localhost:3311', {'force':True})
The instance will be removed from the InnoDB cluster. Depending on the
instance being the Seed or not, the Metadata session might become invalid.
If so, please start a new session to the Metadata Storage R/W instance.

The instance 'root@localhost:3311' was successfully removed from the
cluster.

 MySQL  localhost:3312 ssl  Py > my_cluster.status()
{
    "clusterName": "MyCluster",
    "defaultReplicaSet": {
        "name": "default",
        "primary": "localhost:3312",
        "ssl": "REQUIRED",
        "status": "OK",
        "statusText": "Cluster is ONLINE and can tolerate up to ONE failure.",
        "topology": {
```

```
        "localhost:3312": {
            "address": "localhost:3312",
            "mode": "R/W",
            "readReplicas": {},
            "role": "HA",
            "status": "ONLINE"
        },
        "localhost:3313": {
            "address": "localhost:3313",
            "mode": "R/O",
            "readReplicas": {},
            "role": "HA",
            "status": "ONLINE"
        },
        "localhost:3314": {
            "address": "localhost:3314",
            "mode": "R/O",
            "readReplicas": {},
            "role": "HA",
            "status": "ONLINE"
        }
    }
},
"groupInformationSourceMember": "mysql://root@localhost:3312"
}

MySQL  localhost:3312 ssl  Py >
```

DevOps Scripts

Now, let's make DevOps scripts we can use to set up and shut down an InnoDB Cluster. Fortunately, we don't need to invent much here because we will be using the same commands we used in the demonstration. The only difference is we will add print statements for better feedback and substitute the shell commands with methods from the shell class, which is part of the MySQL API.

The first script sets up an InnoDB Cluster in a sandbox. The steps we follow are the same ones we used previously. Listing 5-8 shows the complete script written in Python. Feel free to study the script to ensure that you see how the Python commands match the preceding demonstration. If you like the script, you can create a file named setup_idc_sandbox.py and save it on your system.

Listing 5-8. DevOps Script to Set Up the InnoDB Cluster (Sandbox)

```python
# Introducing InnoDB Cluster
#
# This Python script is designed to set up an InnoDB Cluster in a sandbox.
#
# Note: Change the cluster directory to match your preferred directory setup.
#
# The steps include:
# 1) create the sandbox directory
# 2) deploy instances
# 3) create the cluster
# 4) add instances to the cluster
# 5) show the cluster status
#
# Dr. Charles Bell, 2018
#
import os
import time

# Method to deploy sandbox instance
def deploy_instance(port):
    try:
        dba.deploy_sandbox_instance(port, {'sandboxDir':'c://idc_sandbox',
        'password':'root'})
    except:
        print("ERROR: cannot setup the instance in the sandbox.")
    time.sleep(1)
```

```python
# Add instance to cluster
def add_instance(cluster, port):
    try:
        cluster.add_instance('root:root@localhost:{0}'.format(port))
    except:
        print("ERROR: cannot add instance to cluster.")
    time.sleep(1)

print("##### STEP 1 of 5 : CREATE SANDBOX DIRECTORY #####")
os.mkdir('c://idc_sandbox')

print("##### STEP 2 of 5 : DEPLOY INSTANCES #####")
deploy_instance(3311)
deploy_instance(3312)
deploy_instance(3313)
deploy_instance(3314)

print("##### STEP 3 of 5 : CREATE CLUSTER #####")
shell.connect('root:root@localhost:3311')
my_cluster = dba.create_cluster('MyCluster', {'multiMaster':False})
time.sleep(1)

print("##### STEP 4 of 5 : ADD INSTANCES TO CLUSTER #####")
add_instance(my_cluster, 3312)
add_instance(my_cluster, 3313)
add_instance(my_cluster, 3314)

print("##### STEP 5 of 5 : SHOW CLUSTER STATUS #####")
shell.connect('root:root@localhost:3311')
time.sleep(1)
my_cluster = dba.get_cluster('MyCluster')
time.sleep(1)
status = my_cluster.status()
print(status)
```

To execute the script, we use the -f option for the shell, providing the name of the script. This tells the shell to load the script and execute it:

```
mysqlsh -f setup_idc_sandbox.py
```

Listing 5-9 shows an excerpt of the output for running the script. Repetitious sections have been omitted for brevity.

Listing 5-9. Setup Script Output

```
##### STEP 1 of 5 : CREATE SANDBOX DIRECTORY #####
##### STEP 2 of 5 : DEPLOY INSTANCES #####
Deploying new MySQL instance...

Instance localhost:3311 successfully deployed and started.
Use shell.connect('root@localhost:3311'); to connect to the instance.
...
##### STEP 3 of 5 : CREATE CLUSTER #####
A new InnoDB cluster will be created on instance 'root@localhost:3311'.

Validating instance at localhost:3311...
Instance detected as a sandbox.
Please note that sandbox instances are only suitable for deploying test
clusters for use within the same host.

This instance reports its own address as DESKTOP-JBLO81L

Instance configuration is suitable.
Creating InnoDB cluster 'MyCluster' on 'root@localhost:3311'...
Adding Seed Instance...

Cluster successfully created. Use Cluster.add_instance() to add MySQL
instances.
At least 3 instances are needed for the cluster to be able to withstand up to
one server failure.

##### STEP 4 of 5 : ADD INSTANCES TO CLUSTER #####
A new instance will be added to the InnoDB cluster. Depending on the amount of
data on the cluster this might take from a few seconds to several hours.

Adding instance to the cluster ...

Validating instance at localhost:3312...
Instance detected as a sandbox.
Please note that sandbox instances are only suitable for deploying test
clusters for use within the same host.
```

This instance reports its own address as DESKTOP-JBL081L

Instance configuration is suitable.
The instance 'root@localhost:3312' was successfully added to the cluster.
...
STEP 5 of 5 : SHOW CLUSTER STATUS
{"clusterName": "MyCluster", "defaultReplicaSet": {"name": "default",
"primary": "localhost:3311", "ssl": "REQUIRED", "status": "OK",
"statusText": "Cluster is ONLINE and can tolerate up to ONE failure.",
"topology": {"localhost:3311": {"address": "localhost:3311", "mode": "R/W",
"readReplicas": {}, "role": "HA", "status": "ONLINE"}, "localhost:3312":
{"address": "localhost:3312", "mode": "R/O", "readReplicas": {},
"role": "HA", "status": "ONLINE"}, "localhost:3313": {"address":
"localhost:3313", "mode": "R/O", "readReplicas": {}, "role": "HA",
"status": "ONLINE"}, "localhost:3314": {"address": "localhost:3314",
"mode": "R/O", "readReplicas": {}, "role": "HA", "status": "ONLINE"}}},
"groupInformationSourceMember": "mysql://root@localhost:3311"}

Now, let's create a script to shut down the cluster. In this case, we will write a script that shuts down all instances and removes the sandbox directory. We do this by first attempting to remove the instances from the cluster; then we kill the instances and, finally, delete the directory. Listing 5-10 shows the completed shutdown script. If you like the script, you can create a file named shutdown_idc_sandbox.py and save it on your system.

Listing 5-10. DevOps Script to Shut Down InnoDB Cluster (Sandbox)

```
# Introducing InnoDB Cluster
#
# This Python script is designed to perform an orderly shutdown of an
InnoDB Cluster.
#
# Note: Change the cluster directory to match your preferred directory setup.
#
# The steps include:
# 1) connect to one of the instances
# 2) retrieve the cluster
# 3) remove the instances from the cluster
# 4) kill all instances
```

```
# 5) delete the sandbox directory
#
# Dr. Charles Bell, 2018
#
import shutil
import time

# Method to remove instance
def remove_instance(cluster, port):
    try:
        cluster.remove_instance('root@localhost:{0}'.format(port),
        {'password':'root', 'force':True})
    except:
        pass
    time.sleep(1)

# Method to kill the instance
def kill_instance(port):
    try:
        dba.kill_sandbox_instance(port, {'sandboxDir':'c://idc_sandbox'})
    except:
        pass
    time.sleep(1)

my_cluster = None
try:
    print("##### STEP 1 of 5 : CONNECT TO ONE INSTANCE (3314) #####")
    shell.connect('root:root@localhost:3314')
    print("##### STEP 2 of 5 : GET THE CLUSTER #####")
    my_cluster = dba.get_cluster('MyCluster')
    time.sleep(1)
except:
    print("ERROR: cannot connect to or remove instances from cluster.")
if my_cluster:
    print("##### STEP 3 of 5 : REMOVE INSTANCES FROM THE CLUSTER #####")
    remove_instance(my_cluster, 3311)
    remove_instance(my_cluster, 3312)
```

```
    remove_instance(my_cluster, 3313)
    remove_instance(my_cluster, 3314)
print("##### STEP 4 of 5 : KILL THE INSTANCES #####")
kill_instance(3311)
kill_instance(3312)
kill_instance(3313)
kill_instance(3314)
print("##### STEP 5 of 5 : REMOVE THE SANDBOX DIRECTORY #####")
try:
    shutil.rmtree('c://idc_sandbox')
except:
    print("Cannot remove directory!")
```

We run the script the same way as the setup script with the following command:

```
mysqlsh -f shutdown_idc_sandbox.py
```

Listing 5-11 shows an excerpt of the output for running the script. Repetitious sections have been omitted for brevity.

Listing 5-11. Shutdown Script Output

```
##### STEP 1 of 5 : CONNECT TO ONE INSTANCE (3314) #####
##### STEP 2 of 5 : GET THE CLUSTER #####
##### STEP 3 of 5 : REMOVE INSTANCES FROM THE CLUSTER #####
The instance will be removed from the InnoDB cluster. Depending on the
instance being the Seed or not, the Metadata session might become invalid.
If so, please start a new session to the Metadata Storage R/W instance.

The instance 'root@localhost:3311' was successfully removed from the cluster.

##### STEP 4 of 5 : KILL THE INSTANCES #####
The MySQL sandbox instance on this host in
c://idc_sandbox\3311 will be killed

Killing MySQL instance...
```

```
Instance localhost:3311 successfully killed.
...
##### STEP 5 of 5 : REMOVE THE SANDBOX DIRECTORY #####
```

This concludes the demonstration of using InnoDB Cluster in a sandbox.

Summary

What may have sounded like hype that MySQL Shell is a game changer for MySQL should, by now, start to look more like the truth. We touched on a small part of MySQL Shell in the preceding chapter, and in this chapter you saw a little bit more. In this case, we took a look at the AdminAPI for use in creating an InnoDB Cluster in a sandbox.

If you read this chapter or another work that covers setting up InnoDB Cluster, you may not see or appreciate the huge step forward in user friendliness that MySQL Shell and AdminAPI provide. On the other hand, if you have worked with MySQL Replication, or especially Group Replication, and learned to endure the specific commands and actions needed to get it all working, you will see the raw power that MySQL Shell and AdminAPI bring.

In short, InnoDB Cluster makes working with Group Replication a simple matter of learning a few API classes and methods. The best part is that it opens the door for DevOps and automation of the InnoDB Cluster—something that up until now required expensive, custom tools. Yes, InnoDB Cluster is easier to manage and easier to automate.

However, you're not finished learning about InnoDB Cluster. In the next chapter, you will look at the final piece of InnoDB Cluster: MySQL Router. You will see what MySQL Router is and how it can be used. A demonstration of using MySQL Router is presented in Chapter 7.

CHAPTER 6

MySQL Router

Now that you understand how InnoDB Cluster works and have seen a short demonstration of how to quickly configure a test cluster using the AdminAPI via MySQL Shell, there is one more part of InnoDB Cluster you need in order to make your applications truly highly available.

Consider for a moment what an application will do if we connect to the cluster and the machine we're connected to goes offline. We know that the cluster can recover from such a loss (assuming the number of servers in the group is sufficient (see Chapter 3)), but what do we do about our applications? If the server goes offline, we have no way of knowing which (or if) another server has taken over.

Some developers may be tempted to build into their applications the ability to retry connections or retry a predetermined, different connection should the connection to the current server fail. Although this could get you what you need, it is fragile and requires embedding or providing all the hostnames, ports, and more about the servers in the cluster to the application. Clearly, there must be a better way. Oracle has answered that call with MySQL Router.

This chapter discusses MySQL Router, including how to set up and configure the router. The chapter concludes with recommendations on modifying your applications to get the most out of the router.

Overview

MySQL Router is a transparent connection routing service for MySQL InnoDB Cluster that offers load balancing, application connection failover, and client routing. The connection routing features of the router mean we can code our application to connect to the router and let MySQL Router handle routing the connections to the correct servers by using one of the supported routing strategies. The router becomes an intermediary service between your application and the cluster.

© Charles Bell 2018
C. Bell, *Introducing InnoDB Cluster*, https://doi.org/10.1007/978-1-4842-3885-1_6

Other connection routing applications and servers may inspect packets to (or in addition to) routing to the correct server, but MySQL Router (hence, Router) does no such inspection. Your communication packets are not opened, examined, or changed; they are simply forwarded to the correct server based on one of several options.

Although this simplicity means the router is lightweight, requiring few resources, the router's configuration has some challenges. More specifically, simple setup and configuration of a single write cluster is easy. In fact, the MySQL Installer has an automated configuration step to make installing the router on Windows a click-through affair. However, for more sophisticated configurations, you may want to plan on spending some time configuring and testing your applications with the possible strategies and other options. You will see more about configuring the router in a later section.

For those wanting to enhance their diagnostics or debugging efforts, the router also supports logging of messages that include statements about how connections are routed, status, errors and warnings, and more. This is just one several critical features that are fully customizable.

The router can be used in several use cases, including providing high availability and even scalability to MySQL servers. In this case, high availability is achieved through the automatic failover feature that automatically routes the client connection should the designated (selected) server in the cluster fail.

When used with MySQL InnoDB Cluster (through the underlying Group Replication) to replicate databases across multiple servers while performing automatic failover in the event of a server failure, the router acts as a proxy to hide the multiple MySQL instances on your network and map the data requests to one of the cluster instances. Provided there are enough online replicas and reliable network communication is possible, your applications that use the router will be able to contact one of the remaining servers. The router makes this possible by having applications connect to MySQL Router instead of directly to a specific MySQL server. Figure 6-1 shows a logical view of where the router sits in relation to your application and the InnoDB Cluster.

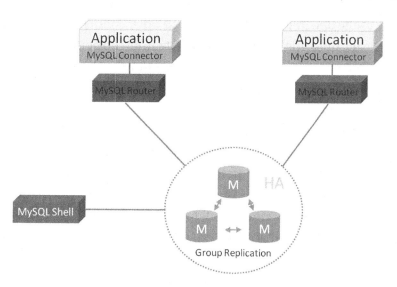

Figure 6-1. *Application Architecture with MySQL Router (courtesty of Oracle Corporation)*

Notice that we have two applications depicted, each connecting to an instance of MySQL Router. The router works by sitting between applications and MySQL servers. When an application connects to the router, the router chooses a suitable MySQL server from the pool of candidates and connects, forwarding all network traffic from the application to that server (and the returning responses from the server to the application).

Tip   You can run multiple instances of MySQL Router on one or more machines, providing a level of fault tolerance at the routing point. You do not need to isolate the router to a single machine. This is possible because the router has no affinity to its host.

Behind the scenes, the router stores a list of the servers from InnoDB Cluster along with their status. This list (or cache) of servers is read initially from a configuration file, and subsequent communication between the router and the cluster ensures that it gets updated when the topology changes. When servers are lost, they become marked as offline by the router, and the router skips them. Similarly, if new servers are added to the cluster, the router's cache is updated to include them.

191

To keep the cache updated, the router keeps an open connection to one of the servers in the cluster, querying the cluster metadata from the performance schema database. These tables (or views) are updated in real time by Group Replication whenever a cluster state change is detected—for example, if one of the MySQL servers had an unexpected shutdown.

Finally, the router enables developers to extend MySQL Router by using plugins for custom use cases. If your application requires a different routing strategy or you want to build packet inspection into your solution, you can extend the router with a custom plugin. Although building custom plugins for the router is beyond the scope of this chapter, and there are no examples (yet) to study, be sure to check the MySQL developer web site (`https://dev.mysql.com`) and the MySQL Engineering blogs (`https://mysqlserverteam.com/`) for the latest information and examples.

Now that you know more about what the router is and where it should be placed in your infrastructure, let's see how to install and configure the router.

Installation

Installing MySQL Router is easy. Oracle provides installation packages for the router for all platforms supported by MySQL Server. The router is also included in the MySQL Installer for Windows.

In this section, you will learn how to install MySQL Router on Windows and see a demonstration of the sample configuration steps provided in the MySQL Installer. You will also see briefly how to install the router for other platforms. You will learn how to configure the router manually in a later section. Let's begin with a look at the MySQL Installer.

MySQL Installer (Windows)

If you have been following along with the previous chapters to install MySQL Server, MySQL Shell, and other components, the information in this section will be familiar. However, if this is your first encounter using the router on Windows, let's take the installation step-by-step.

Tip   If your environment is not homogenous and your application server is a Windows machine, you will want to use this section as a guide to set up the router on your Windows application server.

Installing MySQL Router with the MySQL Installer follows the same pattern as installing MySQL Shell. However, because the installer is already on the system, we simply launch it again and add the MySQL products we want (such as the router). When you launch the installer, you will be presented with a welcome panel that contains a list of the installed products. Figure 6-2 shows the welcome panel for the MySQL Installer after installation of MySQL Shell.

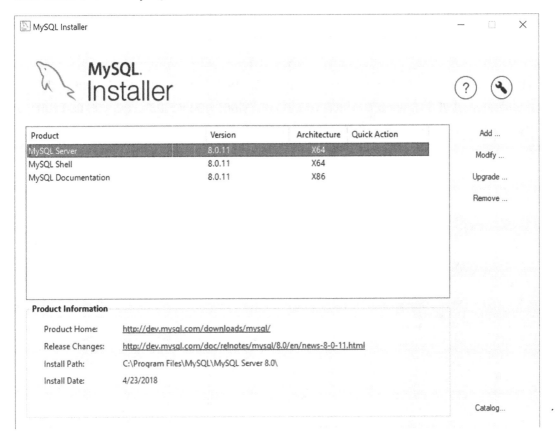

Figure 6-2. *Installer Welcome Panel – Post Installation (MySQL Installer)*

Notice we have the option of adding (*Add…*) new products, modifying (*Modify…*) the installation or configuration of an installed product, upgrading (*Upgrade…*) an installed product with a newer version from the catalog (installer), or removing installed products (*Remove…*). Notice there is also a button named *Catalog…*, which allows you to update the catalog of products in the installer. This allows you to update the products with newer versions.

For this tutorial, we want to install MySQL Router and the Connector/Python database connector. We will use the database connector to test the router installation by writing a rudimentary connection example, which means we also need to install Python. If you do not have Python installed on your Windows machine, see `https://www.python.org/downloads/windows/` to download and install the latest version (version 2.7 or 3.6 or later).

Recall, we click Add to proceed. You will then be presented with the product selection panel, shown in Figure 6-3. Simply navigate the tree on the left to find MySQL Router, select it, and click the green arrow to add it to the list on the right. Repeat the steps to select the Connector/Python version that matches your Python installation. When both are added, click the Next button to proceed.

Tip   The MySQL Installer will gray out any versions that do not match your Python installation. If you're unsure which version of Python you've installed, you can run `python --version` from a command prompt.

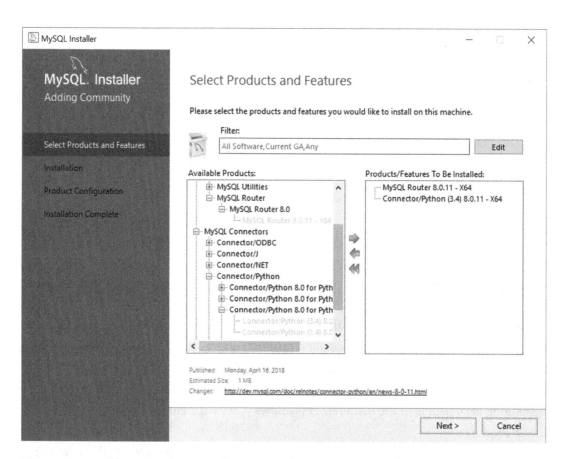

Figure 6-3. *Select Products and Features (MySQL Installer)*

The next panel, shown in Figure 6-4, is an installation summary that permits you to confirm that you have the correct products listed for installation. The panel also indicates the status so you can observe the progress of the installation. When you are ready to begin installation of the products selected, click Execute.

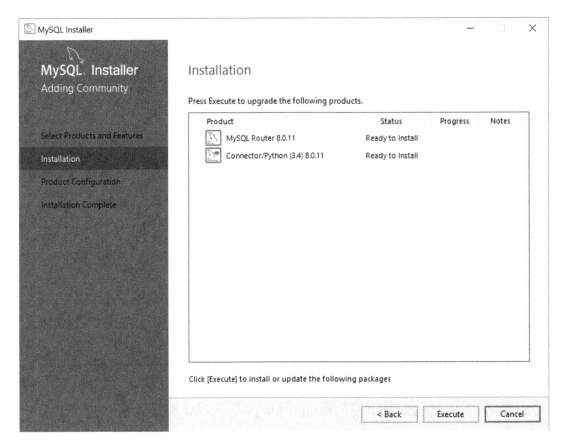

Figure 6-4. *Installation Dialog – staging (MySQL Installer)*

After installation begins, you will see the progress of each product, as shown in Figure 6-5.

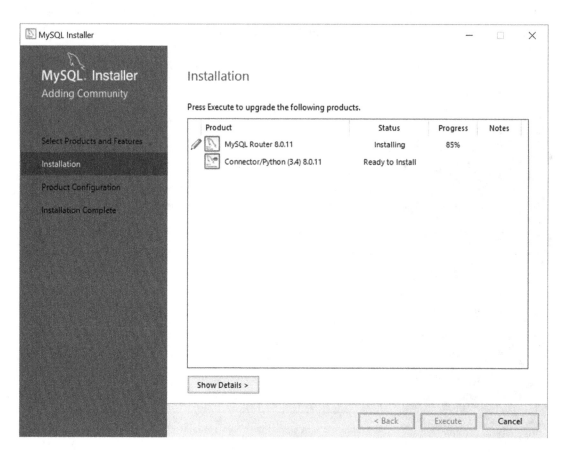

Figure 6-5. *Installation Dialog – installation progress (MySQL Installer)*

After all products are installed, the installation panel will show the status of all installations as complete and change the buttons at the bottom to show Next, as shown in Figure 6-6. When you're ready, click Next.

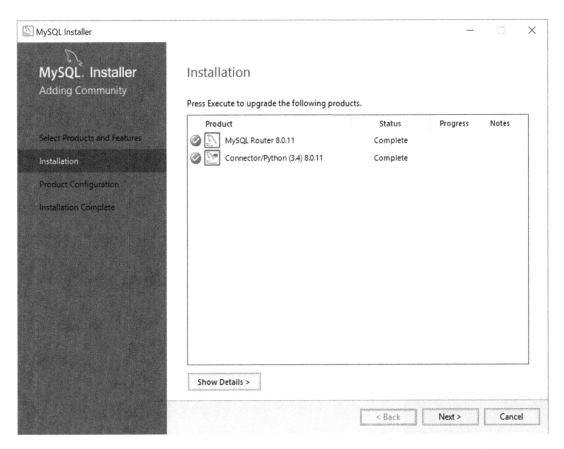

Figure 6-6. *Installation Dialog – installation complete (MySQL Installer)*

The next step in the installation is to configure any products that have post-installation options. MySQL Server is one such product that permits you to set several configuration items to complete installation. Figure 6-7 shows the Product Configuration panel. Click Next when you're ready to begin the configuration.

For this step, we will be configuring the router for use with a sandbox installation. If you have not already configured InnoDB Cluster to run in a sandbox, see Chapter 5 for details. You must have the InnoDB Cluster running before configuring the router using the MySQL Installer.

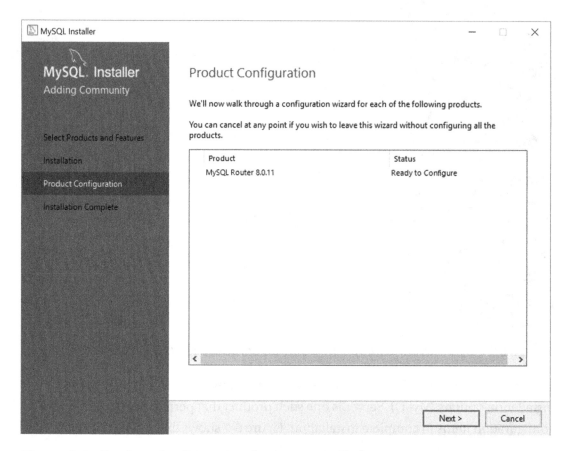

Figure 6-7. *Product Configuration (MySQL Installer)*

This step begins the MySQL Router configuration. Notice that in Figure 6-8 the installer is asking for the connection information to one of the servers in the cluster. Recall from Chapter 5, we used port 3311 for the primary. Thus, we enter 3311 in the Port text box and provide the root password in the Password text box. We will use the defaults for the classic protocol ports. When you're ready, click Next.

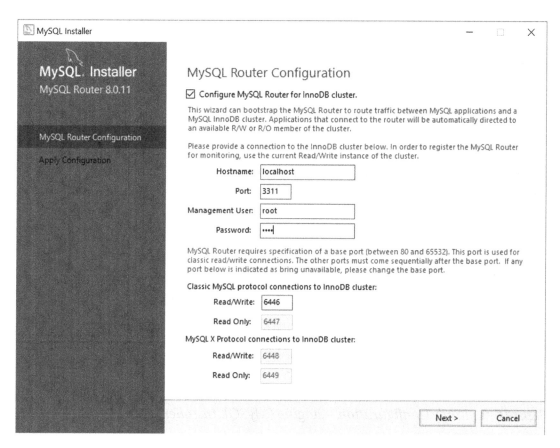

Figure 6-8. *MySQL Router Configuration (MySQL Installer)*

At this point, the installer will show you a summary of the steps to execute and permit you to start the process or go back and make changes, as shown in Figure 6-9. Click the Execute button when you're ready to proceed.

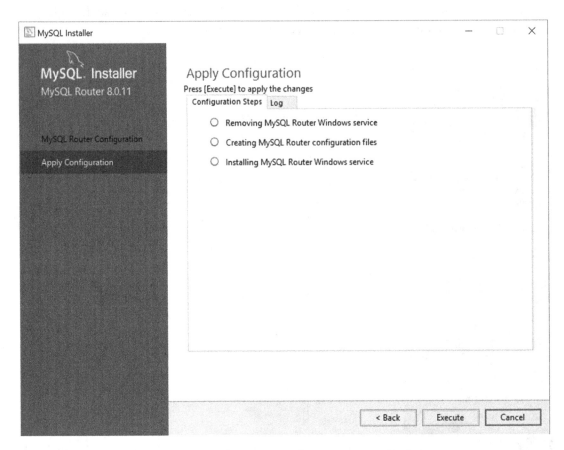

Figure 6-9. Apply Configuration – staging (MySQL Installer)

While the configuration process is running, the panel will change to gray out the Execute and Back buttons and show green check marks on the dots next to each step, as shown in Figure 6-10. If errors occur, the panel will show a red X and may display an error message if the error prohibits continuing.

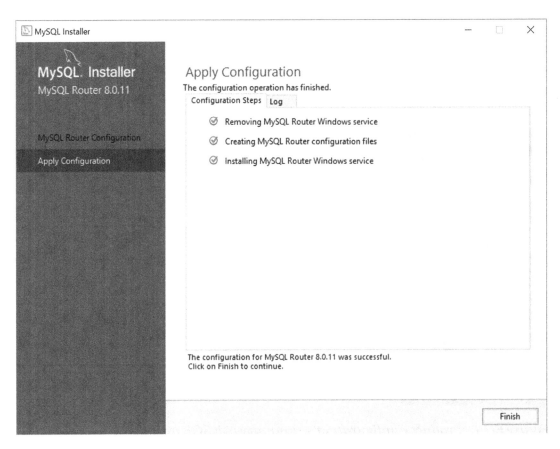

Figure 6-10. *Apply Configuration – complete (MySQL Installer)*

When the product configurations are complete, the panel will change to show a summary of the products configured, as shown in Figure 6-11. When you're ready, click the Next button to proceed.

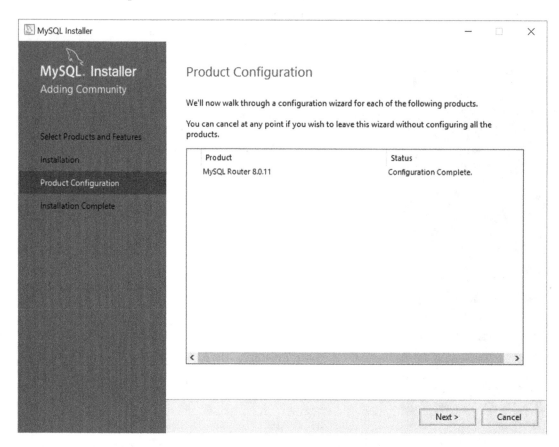

Figure 6-11. *Product Configuration – summary (MySQL Installer)*

After you have verified there are no errors, click the Next button to proceed to the final panel, shown in Figure 6-12. You can click the Finish button to complete the installation.

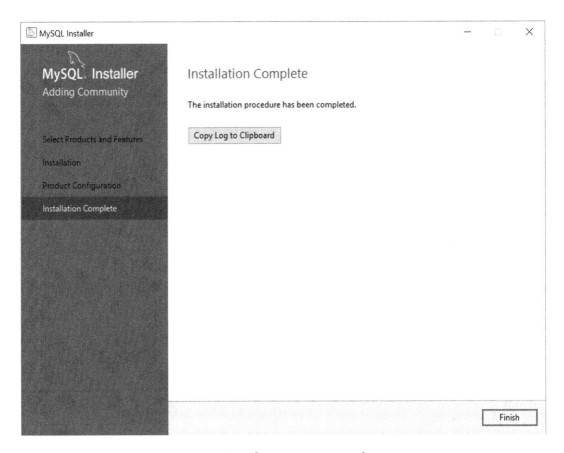

Figure 6-12. *Installation Complete (MySQL Installer)*

When all operations are complete, the installer will return to the welcome panel displaying a list of all the products installed, as shown in Figure 6-13. You can close the installer when you're finished or add, modify, upgrade, or remove other products. You can also reconfigure any of the products installed by clicking the Reconfigure link.

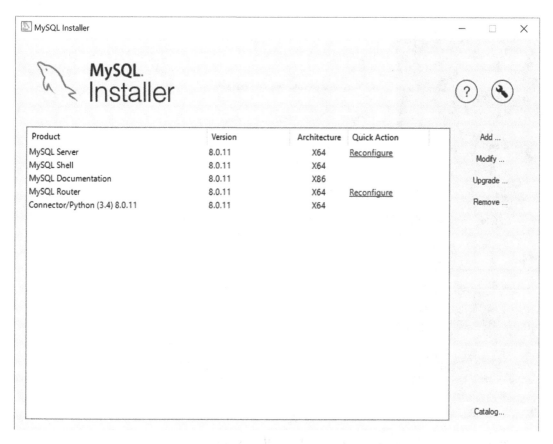

Figure 6-13. *Installer Welcome Panel – Post Installation (MySQL Installer)*

PROBLEMS CONFIGURING THE ROUTER

If you get to this point and can install MySQL Router, but the configuration steps fail, it is most likely due to having the wrong password for the root user. It can also be caused by using the wrong port for a server in the InnoDB Cluster (typically, this is the primary in a single-primary setup). If you correct this information and still cannot get the configuration to complete, try connecting to your InnoDB Cluster as demonstrated in Chapter 5. When you can successfully connect to your cluster, the configuration of the router should succeed. If you want to run the configuration again, simply restart the MySQL Installer and click the Reconfigure link to rerun the configuration.

Now that we have the router installed on Windows and configured for our InnoDB Cluster, let's test the router by using a simple Python script.

Listing 6-1 shows a simple Python script for connecting to InnoDB Cluster via the router. Recall that we installed the router on our Windows machine and thus this script (for conformity, if not practice) should be executed on the same machine. Take a moment to examine the code. It should be clear what is happening even if you've never used Connector/Python or written Python.

Listing 6-1. Router Connection Test

```
#
# Introducing MySQL InnoDB Cluster
#
# This example shows how to use the MySQL Router to connect to
# the cluster. Notice how connecting via the router port 6446
# results in a seamless transport to one of the cluster servers,
# in this case, the server with the primary role.
#
# Dr. Charles Bell, 2018
#
import mysql.connector

# Simple function to display results from a cursor
def show_results(cur_obj):
  for row in cur:
    print(row)

my_cfg = {
  'user':'root',
  'passwd':'secret',
  'host':'127.0.0.1',
  'port':6446    # <<<< Router port (R/W)
}

# Connecting to the server
conn = mysql.connector.connect(**my_cfg)
```

```
print("Listing the databases on the server.")
query = "SHOW DATABASES"
cur = conn.cursor()
cur.execute(query)
show_results(cur)

print("\nRetrieve the port for the server to which we're connecting.")
query = "SELECT @@port"
cur = conn.cursor()
cur.execute(query)
show_results(cur)

# Close the cursor and connection
cur.close()
conn.close()
```

The first part of the code imports the connector and defines a dictionary of connection terms—in this case, the user, password, host, and port for the router. We are using the port number 6446, as shown during the configuration of the router in the MySQL Installer (refer to Figure 6-8).

Next, the code opens a connection to then run two queries; one to get a list of the databases and display them (using a function defined as show_results()), and another to select the current port of the server. This second query result may surprise you.

To execute the code, save this file named router_connect_test.py (the extension identifies it as a Python script). Then, run the code using the following command:

```
python ./router_connect_test.py
```

After it runs, you will see output like the following:

```
Listing the databases on the server.
('information_schema',)
('mysql',)
('mysql_innodb_cluster_metadata',)
('performance_schema',)
('sys',)

Retrieve the port for the server to which we're connecting.
(3311,)
```

Wait! Why did the output show port 3311? Shouldn't it show port 6446? After all, that's the port we used in the code. Recall, the router simply routes communication to the appropriate server; it is not a server connection itself. Thus, the router successfully routed our connection to the machine on port 3311. This machine is the primary (listed as read/write in the cluster).

So, how do we connect to the read-only servers in the cluster? All we need to do is to modify the program to connect to the read-only servers (on port 6447). When we rerun the script, we will see the following output:

```
Listing the databases on the server.
('information_schema',)
('mysql',)
('mysql_innodb_cluster_metadata',)
('performance_schema',)
('sys',)

Retrieve the port for the server to which we're connecting.
(3312,)
```

Now we see we're connecting to a server other than one on port 3311. Recall from the sandbox setup, the machines on ports 3312, 3313, and 3314 are all read-only.

Although this example is quite primitive, it illustrates how the router redirects connections to other MySQL servers. This example also helps reinforce the concept that we must connect our applications to the router itself rather than to the machines in the cluster, and allow the router to do all the heavy connection routing for us. As you can see, the MySQL Router is quite sophisticated and knows from its initial (and later cached) configuration which servers are requested based on the port used. In this case, we use 6446 for read/write connections and 6447 for read-only connections. Yes, it is that easy. No more elaborate hard-coded ports!

Other Platforms

As mentioned, if you are not using Windows, you can still use MySQL Router; nothing in the router requires using Windows. However, setting up the router on other platforms is a bit more manual in nature.

Installing MySQL Router on other platforms is best done by using the platform-specific repository as described in Chapter 2. This section demonstrates installing the shell by using the MySQL APT Repository on Ubuntu. The prerequisite is only that you have installed the repository.

After the repository is installed and you've updated your system with `sudo apt-get update`, you can simply issue the `sudo apt-get install mysql-router` command as demonstrated in Listing 6-2.

Listing 6-2. Installing the MySQL Router (Ubuntu)

```
$ sudo apt-get install mysql-router
Reading package lists... Done
Building dependency tree
Reading state information... Done
The following packages were automatically installed and are no longer
required:
  libevent-core-2.0-5 libllvm4.0 libqmi-glib1 snap-confine
Use 'sudo apt autoremove' to remove them.
The following NEW packages will be installed:
  mysql-router
0 upgraded, 1 newly installed, 0 to remove and 38 not upgraded.
Need to get 2,388 kB of archives.
After this operation, 15.3 MB of additional disk space will be used.
Get:1 http://repo.mysql.com/apt/ubuntu xenial/mysql-tools amd64 mysql-
router amd64 8.0.11-1ubuntu16.04 [2,388 kB]
Fetched 2,388 kB in 20s (115 kB/s)
Selecting previously unselected package mysql-router.
(Reading database ... 309484 files and directories currently installed.)
Preparing to unpack .../mysql-router_8.0.11-1ubuntu16.04_amd64.deb ...
Unpacking mysql-router (8.0.11-1ubuntu16.04) ...
Processing triggers for libc-bin (2.23-0ubuntu10) ...
/sbin/ldconfig.real: /usr/lib/libmysqlcppconn.so.7 is not a symbolic link

Processing triggers for systemd (229-4ubuntu21.2) ...
Processing triggers for ureadahead (0.100.0-19) ...
```

```
Setting up mysql-router (8.0.11-1ubuntu16.04) ...
Processing triggers for libc-bin (2.23-0ubuntu10) ...
/sbin/ldconfig.real: /usr/lib/libmysqlcppconn.so.7 is not a symbolic link

Processing triggers for systemd (229-4ubuntu21.2) ...
Processing triggers for ureadahead (0.100.0-19) ...
```

Now that the router is installed, recall that we also want install Connector/Python to allow us to test the router as we did in the previous section. We use the sudo apt-get install mysql-connector-python command as shown in Listing 6-3 to install Connector/Python.

Listing 6-3. Installing the MySQL Connector/Python (Ubuntu)

```
$ sudo apt-get install mysql-connector-python
[sudo] password for cbell:
Reading package lists... Done
Building dependency tree
Reading state information... Done
The following packages were automatically installed and are no longer
required:
  libevent-core-2.0-5 libllvm4.0 libqmi-glib1 snap-confine
Use 'sudo apt autoremove' to remove them.
The following NEW packages will be installed:
  mysql-connector-python
0 upgraded, 1 newly installed, 0 to remove and 38 not upgraded.
Need to get 174 kB of archives.
After this operation, 1,339 kB of additional disk space will be used.
Get:1 http://repo.mysql.com/apt/ubuntu xenial/mysql-tools amd64 mysql-
connector-python all 8.0.11-1ubuntu16.04 [174 kB]
Fetched 174 kB in 6s (25.7 kB/s)
Selecting previously unselected package mysql-connector-python.
(Reading database ... 309396 files and directories currently installed.)
Preparing to unpack .../mysql-connector-python_8.0.11-1ubuntu16.04_all.deb ...
Unpacking mysql-connector-python (8.0.11-1ubuntu16.04) ...
Setting up mysql-connector-python (8.0.11-1ubuntu16.04) ...
```

As mentioned, installing MySQL Router in this manner does not run the custom configuration step as demonstrated on Windows. To use the router on other platforms or for custom installations, we must manually configure the router to match our cluster.

Configuration

Configuring MySQL Router is not difficult, but the number of configuration items may make it seem so. This section presents a brief example of how to configure MySQL Router for use with an InnoDB Cluster running in a sandbox; this section demonstrates the manual steps needed to make the router work. We will also use the same simple Python script shown in the previous section to test the router setup.

Setting Up InnoDB Cluster in a Sandbox

Let's take a moment to review how we set up InnoDB Cluster in a sandbox. This can be helpful at this point if you have not tried the examples from the preceding chapter or you are not using the router on Windows or haven't set up the router before. Recall from Chapter 5, we have two scripts that use Python commands via MySQL Shell to set up and shut down a sample cluster.

In this case, we will use the same script as shown in Chapter 5 to set up a cluster running with a single write (primary) and three read-only (secondary) servers. However, because the script was written for Windows, we must alter it slightly to change the default directory for the cluster data. Listing 6-4 shows the modified version of the setup_idc_sandbox.py file with the changes shown in bold.

Listing 6-4. Setup InnoDB Cluster Script (Ubuntu)

```
# Introducing InnoDB Cluster
#
# This Python script is designed to set up an InnoDB Cluster in a sandbox.
#
# Note: Change the cluster directory to match your preferred directory setup.
#
# The steps include:
# 1) create the sandbox directory
# 2) deploy instances
```

```
# 3) create the cluster
# 4) add instances to the cluster
# 5) show the cluster status
#
# Dr. Charles Bell, 2018
#
import os
import time

# Method to deploy sandbox instance
def deploy_instance(port):
    try:
        dba.deploy_sandbox_instance(port, {'sandboxDir':'/home/cbell/idc_
        sandbox', 'password':'secret'})
    except:
        print("ERROR: cannot setup the instance in the sandbox.")
    time.sleep(1)

# Add instance to cluster
def add_instance(cluster, port):
    try:
        cluster.add_instance('root:secret@localhost:{0}'.format(port))
    except:
        print("ERROR: cannot add instance to cluster.")
    time.sleep(1)

print("##### STEP 1 of 5 : CREATE SANDBOX DIRECTORY #####")
os.mkdir('/home/cbell/idc_sandbox')

print("##### STEP 2 of 5 : DEPLOY INSTANCES #####")
deploy_instance(3311)
deploy_instance(3312)
deploy_instance(3313)
deploy_instance(3314)

print("##### STEP 3 of 5 : CREATE CLUSTER #####")
shell.connect('root:secret@localhost:3311')
my_cluster = dba.create_cluster('MyCluster', {'multiMaster':False})
time.sleep(1)
```

```
print("##### STEP 4 of 5 : ADD INSTANCES TO CLUSTER #####")
add_instance(my_cluster, 3312)
add_instance(my_cluster, 3313)
add_instance(my_cluster, 3314)

print("##### STEP 5 of 5 : SHOW CLUSTER STATUS #####")
shell.connect('root:secret@localhost:3311')
time.sleep(1)
my_cluster = dba.get_cluster('MyCluster')
time.sleep(1)
status = my_cluster.status()
print(status)
```

Note   You must also change the password in the script and the paths to match your configuration.

Listing 6-5 shows an excerpt of this script running on Ubuntu. Recall, because the script is using the AdminAPI, we must use MySQL Shell to execute it.

Listing 6-5. Setting Up the InnoDB Cluster in a Sandbox

```
$ mysqlsh -f setup_idc_sandbox.py
##### STEP 1 of 5 : CREATE SANDBOX DIRECTORY #####
##### STEP 2 of 5 : DEPLOY INSTANCES #####
Deploying new MySQL instance...

Instance localhost:3311 successfully deployed and started.
Use shell.connect('root@localhost:3311'); to connect to the instance.
...
##### STEP 3 of 5 : CREATE CLUSTER #####
A new InnoDB cluster will be created on instance 'root@localhost:3311'.
...
##### STEP 4 of 5 : ADD INSTANCES TO CLUSTER #####
A new instance will be added to the InnoDB cluster. Depending on the amount of
data on the cluster this might take from a few seconds to several hours.
```

Adding instance to the cluster ...

Validating instance at localhost:3312...
Instance detected as a sandbox.
...
STEP 5 of 5 : SHOW CLUSTER STATUS
{"clusterName": "MyCluster", "defaultReplicaSet": {"name": "default",
"primary": "localhost:3311", "ssl": "REQUIRED", "status": "OK",
"statusText": "Cluster is ONLINE and can tolerate up to ONE failure.",
"topology": {"localhost:3311": {"address": "localhost:3311", "mode": "R/W",
"readReplicas": {}, "role": "HA", "status": "ONLINE"}, "localhost:3312":
{"address": "localhost:3312", "mode": "R/O", "readReplicas": {},
"role": "HA", "status": "ONLINE"}, "localhost:3313": {"address":
"localhost:3313", "mode": "R/O", "readReplicas": {}, "role": "HA",
"status": "ONLINE"}, "localhost:3314": {"address": "localhost:3314",
"mode": "R/O", "readReplicas": {}, "role": "HA", "status": "ONLINE"}}},
"groupInformationSourceMember": "mysql://root@localhost:3311"}

Modifying the Configuration File

MySQL Router stores its initial configuration in a file. This file sets the parameters for the way the router will work with the cluster, including the protocols for failover, routing information, ports to advertise (listen on) for the application, as well as connection metadata for the cluster itself, and much more.

Tip   See the online MySQL Router documentation (https://dev.mysql.com/doc/mysql-router/8.0/en/) for a complete explanation of all the options and configuration items for MySQL Router.

Although the router does not have any platform affinity (it runs well on all platforms), the location of the configuration files may vary. For Windows, the configuration file is in the C:\ProgramData\MySQL\MySQL Router folder named mysqlrouter.conf. On Linux, the configuration file is in the /etc/mysqlrouter/ folder named mysqlrouter.conf.

You can instantly find the location of the file as well as a host of other information by running the command mysqlrouter --help, which not only documents all the options, but also displays the location of files. Listing 6-6 shows an excerpt of the output.

Listing 6-6. MySQL Router Help (Ubuntu)

```
$ mysqlrouter --help
MySQL Router v8.0.11 on Linux (64-bit) (GPL community edition)
Copyright (c) 2015, 2018, Oracle and/or its affiliates. All rights
reserved.
...
Configuration read from the following files in the given order (enclosed
in parentheses means not available for reading):
  /etc/mysqlrouter/mysqlrouter.conf
  (/home/cbell/.mysqlrouter.conf)
Plugins Path:
  /usr/lib/x86_64-linux-gnu/mysqlrouter
Default Log Directory:
  /var/log/mysqlrouter
Default Persistent Data Directory:
  /var/lib/mysqlrouter
Default Runtime State Directory:
  /run/mysqlrouter
...
```

Now that we know the cluster is running and MySQL Router is installed, let's look at the router's default configuration file. Listing 6-7 shows the configuration file from a typical Linux installation.

Listing 6-7. Default Router Configuration File

```
[DEFAULT]
logging_folder = /var/log/mysqlrouter/
plugin_folder = /usr/lib/x86_64-linux-gnu/mysqlrouter
runtime_folder = /var/run/mysqlrouter
config_folder = /etc/mysqlrouter
```

```
[logger]
level = INFO

# If no plugin is configured that starts a service, keepalive
# will make sure MySQL Router will not immediately exit. It is
# safe to remove after Router is configured.
[keepalive]
interval = 60
```

Notice the last few lines in the file. We will see those removed as we complete our configuration. Notice also that there is no information in the file about our cluster configuration. Two basic components are needed to complete the router configuration. First, we must set up the correct paths to ensure that the router has access to the proper password-encryption mechanisms. Second, we must configure all the routing parameters and strategies for each server in our initial configuration. Although you can do this yourself manually, a quick-start method is available using the --bootstrap option.

Configuring with the Bootstrap Option

The special bootstrap option will connect to your cluster, read the metadata, and then update the configuration file automatically. If you're using a sandbox installation, this is the quickest and surest way to set up the router. Even if you are not using a sandbox installation, you can use this method to quickly set the base configuration, which you can later change to match your needs.

Let's see how to use the bootstrap option. To use the option, we need other parameters. In short, we must provide the connection information and a user to use for securing the configuration file. We'll also add an optional parameter to supply a name for the configuration, which can be helpful if you're working with different clusters or configurations. The following are the parameters we need:

- --bootstrap <server_url>: Bootstraps and configures Router for operation with a MySQL InnoDB Cluster. You can also use the shortcut -B.

- --name (optional): Gives a symbolic name for the router instance.

- --user <username>: Runs mysqlrouter as the user with the name specified (not available on Windows). You can also use the shortcut -u.

In this example, we provide the connection information with the bootstrap option in the form of a URI such as <username>:<password>@<hostname>:<port>. We will use the local user to make it easier to run the router with the sandbox installation, which is also running under the current user. We use elevated privileges because the default locations of the router files are protected. Here is the command:

```
sudo mysqlrouter --bootstrap root:secret@localhost:3311 --name sandbox
--user cbell
```

When we run this command, the router will contact the server we specified and retrieve all the metadata for the cluster, creating the routes for us automatically. Listing 6-8 shows an example of the output from the command.

Listing 6-8. Configuration with the Bootstrap Option

```
$ sudo mysqlrouter --bootstrap root:secret@localhost:3311 --name sandbox
--user cbell

Bootstrapping system MySQL Router instance...
Module " not registered with logger - logging the following message as
'main' instead
MySQL Router 'sandbox' has now been configured for the InnoDB cluster
'MyCluster'.

The following connection information can be used to connect to the cluster.

Classic MySQL protocol connections to cluster 'MyCluster':
- Read/Write Connections: localhost:6446
- Read/Only Connections: localhost:6447
X protocol connections to cluster 'MyCluster':
- Read/Write Connections: localhost:64460
- Read/Only Connections: localhost:64470

Existing configurations backed up to '/etc/mysqlrouter/mysqlrouter.conf.bak'
```

Notice that the router has identified the read/write and read-only connections using the default ports of 6446 and 6447, respectively. We also see that the bootstrap step creates routes for using the X Protocol on ports 64460 and 64470, respectively. Before we test the router, let's learn more about what the bootstrap method has done for us. Specifically, we will look at the modified configuration file.

Using the Bootstrap Configuration File

The configuration file created by the bootstrap option contains all of the information needed to start using the router with your application and the cluster. It uses default values for all settings and values from the cluster to set up the queues and ports. Port defaults are 6446, 6447 for the classic protocol and 64460, 64470 for the X Protocol.

Listing 6-9 shows the resulting configuration file from the execution shown in Listing 6-8.

Listing 6-9. Bootstrap Configuration File

```
# File automatically generated during MySQL Router bootstrap
[DEFAULT]
name=sandbox
user=cbell
keyring_path=/var/lib/mysqlrouter/keyring
master_key_path=/etc/mysqlrouter/mysqlrouter.key
connect_timeout=30
read_timeout=30

[logger]
level = INFO

[metadata_cache:MyCluster]
router_id=10
bootstrap_server_addresses=mysql://localhost:3311,mysql://
localhost:3312,mysql://localhost:3313,mysql://localhost:3314
user=mysql_router10_r7dqvu1t52bj
metadata_cluster=MyCluster
ttl=5

[routing:MyCluster_default_rw]
bind_address=0.0.0.0
bind_port=6446
destinations=metadata-cache://MyCluster/default?role=PRIMARY
routing_strategy=round-robin
protocol=classic
```

```
[routing:MyCluster_default_ro]
bind_address=0.0.0.0
bind_port=6447
destinations=metadata-cache://MyCluster/default?role=SECONDARY
routing_strategy=round-robin
protocol=classic

[routing:MyCluster_default_x_rw]
bind_address=0.0.0.0
bind_port=64460
destinations=metadata-cache://MyCluster/default?role=PRIMARY
routing_strategy=round-robin
protocol=x

[routing:MyCluster_default_x_ro]
bind_address=0.0.0.0
bind_port=64470
destinations=metadata-cache://MyCluster/default?role=SECONDARY
routing_strategy=round-robin
protocol=x
```

Wow, that's very different from the short default configuration file we saw earlier. It may look complicated, but it really isn't. Let's look at each of the sections in the configuration file. More specifically, the file is formatted like so many other configuration files: square brackets are used to define sections, and within each section is one or more keywords (variables) with values assigned (sometimes called *key/ value pairs*).

[DEFAULT]

The default section is where all the general settings for the router instance are placed— all the parameters needed for the router to execute correctly. The following summarizes the variables and their uses as they appear in the example:

- name: The name provided for the cluster from the bootstrap option

- user: Username to use to access the configuration files and metadata for the router instance

- keyring_path: Path to the keyring security file

- `master_key_path`: Path to the keyring master key file

- `connect_timeout`: Number of seconds to time out when a connection is attempted

- `read_timeout`: Number of seconds to time out when waiting for a read request

As you can see, the bootstrap step has supplied defaults to all these variables except the name and user, which were specified on the command line.

[logger]

The logger section is not modified from the default file. In this case, it logs only informational messages. To learn more about the logging options, including how to customize what is logged, see the "Using the Logging Feature" section in the online reference manual (`https://dev.mysql.com/doc/mysql-router/8.0/en/mysql-router-server-logging.html`).

[metadata_cache:MyCluster]

This section defines the initial metadata for the cluster. This example uses the following variables:

- `router_id`: Like the `server_id`, this is a unique value for the router instance, and each router instance should have its own ID value.

- `bootstrap_server_addresses`: The list of servers in the initial queue.

- `user`: Autogenerated user for connecting to the server by using the keyring service.

- `metadata_cluster`: The name of the cluster.

- `ttl`: Time to live (in seconds) for information in the metadata cache.

The two critical variables in this section that you should learn more about are `bootstrap_server_addresses` and `user`. The `bootstrap_server_addresses` variable requires a comma-separated list of the `host:port` values for each server in the cluster. Because the bootstrap operation connects to the cluster, it retrieves the information for us. Here, the list includes all the servers in the cluster. The `user` variable here is an autogenerated user for use with the keyring protocol. You need not change this.

If you are building your configuration file manually, `bootstrap_server_addresses` is the most critical value to get correct. Be sure to include all known servers in the cluster. Remember, the router will automatically update its cache as the cluster topology changes, but it needs a firm starting point, and this variable provides that data.

[routing:<name>]

This section is the connection routing section and is used to define the connection routes that the router provides for applications. The routes are organized by types such as read/write and read-only. The section is repeated once for each type of route we want to define. In this case, we have four routes: one for read/write using the legacy (classic) protocol, another for read-only, one for read/write using the X Protocol, and one for read-only using the X Protocol. With each section, we specify the following variables. Each section name must start with `routing:` followed by a unique name tag. In this case, the bootstrap operation chooses names that describe the read/write state for each connection and the protocol used.

- `bind_address`: The address that the router is bound to, also uses `bind_port` if a port is not defined

- `bind_port`: Default port used by `bind_address`

- `destinations`: Routing destinations as a comma-separated list of MySQL servers

- `routing_strategy`: Routing strategy (optional), how the router chooses destination MySQL servers

- `protocol`: The protocol to use for the connection with the value `classic` (also called legacy) or simply `x` for X Protocol

The `bind_address` and `bind_port` variables are specific to the server used to define the connection. Similarly, `protocol` gives us the choice of protocol to use for the connection. Therefore, we see two connection routes for the read/write and read-only routes: one for classic and another for the X Protocol. Also, the port specified is the port the router is listening on for the connection route, not the port for the server to which it directs routes. This is perhaps the most import concept to grasp for configuring connection routes.

The `destinations` variable is the most interesting here. This variable provides host information for establishing connections. It accepts either a comma-separated list of destination addresses or a metadata-cache link to the cluster. The bootstrap operation generates the metadata cache option. The string is defined as the following:

```
destinations=metadata-cache://mycluster/default?role=PRIMARY
```

The role can be `PRIMARY`, `SECONDARY`, or `PRIMARY_AND_SECONDARY`. This determines the type of instances available to the connection.

Finally, `routing_strategy` can be used to change how the router chooses the next server in the queue. The default is `round-robin` but may be one of the following values:

- `first-available`: The new connection is routed to the first available server from the destinations list. In case of failure, the next available server is used. This cycle continues until all servers are unavailable.

- `next-available`: Like `first-available`, in that the new connection is routed to the first available server from the destinations list. Unlike `first-available`, if a server is marked as unreachable, it gets discarded and is never used again as a destination.

- `round-robin`: For load-balancing, each new connection is made to the next available server in a round-robin fashion.

- `round-robin-with-fallback`: For load-balancing, each new connection is made to the next available secondary server in a round-robin fashion. If a secondary server is not available, servers from the primary list are used in round-robin fashion.

Take a moment to look through the file again and see how each of the connection routes is configured. Once you get used to the terminology, it won't seem as strange.

WAIT, WHERE ARE THE CONNECTIONS TO THE OTHER SERVERS?

If you're wondering why there are no connection routes for the other servers in the cluster, you must remember that the router is designed to query the metadata in the cluster and choose a server automatically. There is no need to indicate a specific connection route for each server. Instead, we define the routes for each of the types of servers: read/write, read-only, and so forth.

Now that you understand more about how to configure the router, let's start and test it.

Starting the Router

Finally, we can start the router with the following command:

```
$ mysqlrouter &
```

This launches the router, which will read the configuration file. Notice that we're not using elevated privileges. This is because we provided a user option during the bootstrap step that permits the user to read the file. This can be important for securing your installation, which you will explore in a later chapter.

Now that we have the router configured, let's test it with the sample Python connection script.

Testing the New Configuration

To test the router, we will use the Python script from Listing 6-1 (named `router_connect_test.py`). Recall, this is a script that contains calls to the AdminAPI in Python. We must run this script from MySQL Shell. Fortunately, it does not require any changes to run on Ubuntu. However, if you were following along with the examples previously, you should change the connection dictionary to connect to the read/write port 6446 as shown here:

```
my_cfg = {
  'user':'root',
  'passwd':'secret',
  'host':'127.0.0.1',
  'port':6446   # <<<< Router port (R/W)
}
```

Recall, we use the `python ./router_connect_test.py` command to tell the shell to load the Python script and execute it. When you do, you should see output like the following:

```
$ python ./router_connect_test.py
Listing the databases on the server.
(u'information_schema',)
(u'mysql',)
(u'mysql_innodb_cluster_metadata',)
(u'performance_schema',)
(u'sys',)
```

Retrieve the port for the server to which we're connecting.
(3311,)

Here we see that we are indeed connecting to our InnoDB Cluster via the router and that the port reported is 3311, which is the port of the primary (read/write) server. Cool!

This concludes demonstrating how to install and configure the router manually. For most installations, this is all you need to make the router work for your application. However, if you need more advanced routes or specific options, you can see the online reference manual for all the options available, which is highly recommended if you plan to configure your cluster for more than a single-primary mode or you want to deploy multiple instances of the router on multiple application servers. For example, if you want to run the router with SSL connections, see the options that start with `--ssl*`.

Tip   To learn more about configuring the router, including setting up different routing strategies, see the online reference manual at `https://dev.mysql.com/doc/mysql-router/8.0/en/mysql-router-configuration.html`.

The next section covers some aspects of using the router with your applications, including tips and recommendations for modifying your applications to make the most of the router.

Using the Router with Your Applications

At this point, we have a basic working router instance that routes connections to our InnoDB Cluster. You have seen how we use the ports listed in the router configuration in our application to connect to the cluster. Specifically, we have the following ports available, which map to a connection route defined in the router configuration file:

- 6446: Classic protocol connections for read/write operations (for example, `PRIMARY`)

- 6447: Classic protocol connections for read-only operations (for example, `SECONDARY`)

- 64460: X Protocol connections for read/write operations (for example, `PRIMARY`)

- 64470: X Protocol connections for read-only operations (for example, `SECONDARY`)

That's great, right? But what does all that mean for our applications? Let's take a step back and consider the conditions and ramifications for using the router in our applications.

First, it is important to understand that the MySQL Router does not require specific libraries or interfaces. It is self-contained and does not have any prerequisites or dependencies such as needing an instance of the server to work. That is great news when planning your application deployment. You can deploy the router on your application servers without fear of dependency clashes or even performance hits.

Second, when using the router with your applications, you should always connect to the ports defined in the connection routes and never connect directly to the cluster servers themselves. Furthermore, you should build in a retry mechanism for your connections. This is necessary because when the router detects that a server has gone offline, it may drop the connection and reestablish it with the next server. More specifically, because MySQL Router redirects connections when the connection is attempted and does not read packets or perform an analysis, then if a MySQL server fails, the router returns the connection error to the application. Thus, your applications should be written to test for connection errors and, if encountered, retry the connection. Fortunately, developers often build this mechanism into their applications, so you may not have to do much more than change the connection to that of the router.

Let's consider some use cases for implementing the router in your applications. There are certainly dozens of ways to use the router, and the following lists only some of the more common use cases:

- I want my application to connect to a service, so it gets a connection to, by default, the current primary of a group replication cluster.

- I want to set up multiple services, so MySQL Router listens on a different port for each highly available replica set (cluster).

- I want to be able to run a connection routing service on port 3306 so it is more transparent to a user or application.

- I want to configure a mode for each connection routing service, so I can specify whether a primary or secondary is returned.

Finally, let's discuss the workflow of the router so you can understand how it fits in planning your applications. The following is by no means the only workflow, but it is typical of most use cases:

1. The application connects to MySQL Router to, for example, port 6446.

2. The router checks for an available MySQL server.

3. The router opens a connection to a suitable MySQL server.

4. The router forwards packets back and forth, between the application and the MySQL server.

5. The router disconnects the application if the connected MySQL server fails.

6. The application can then retry connecting to Router, and Router chooses a different and available MySQL server.

We will consider more implications of using MySQL Router in our applications as we explore using InnoDB Cluster in a typical deployment scenario in the next chapter.

Summary

We now have a complete high-availability story. Although MySQL InnoDB Cluster provides high availability for our data, it does not help us (directly) for achieving high availability at the application level. Yes, you can write your applications to query the cluster and get information that can help your applications "heal" should a server go offline, but practice shows this is a brittle solution that relies far too much on known parameters. Should anything change in the cluster configuration, the application(s) can fail or require reworking to get restarted.

That's not ideal for most organizations. What we need is the ability to quickly and easily make our applications resilient to changes in the cluster. More specifically, the application should not stop if a server in the cluster goes offline or is taken offline or its role changes. This is where MySQL Router shines.

MySQL Router takes the burden of connection routing out of the application and places it in its own lightweight, easily configured instance. Now, applications can be built to rely on the router for all connection routing, including failover events or normal high-availability recovery events.

And because the router is small and lightweight, you can even build redundancy into the router by having more than one instance running with separate connection routing. What's not to like about MySQL Router? Not much. It is the missing piece that so many high-availability solutions seem to be left without.

The next chapter covers deploying MySQL InnoDB Cluster on a set of machines and configuring the router with a simple application to show how you can complete your high-availability goals for your own applications.

## CHAPTER 7

Example MySQL High Availability Deployment

The journey thus far into InnoDB Cluster has been one of discovery and experimentation. To make InnoDB Cluster truly useful and meaningful to your infrastructure, we must deploy it to real machines using real data. Although a walk-through of a live, working production system could be beneficial, that would be jumping too far ahead for those exploring InnoDB Cluster and MySQL high availability for the first time. We can't go from a simulated environment such as a sandbox to a product deployment. No administrator would do that. We must start from a development deployment that we can use to experiment and test our application. Only after careful testing can we then roll it out to our production environment.

In this chapter we'll explore a development environment using separate servers to demonstrate a generalized high-availability deployment of MySQL.[1] We will install MySQL on several machines, establish an InnoDB Cluster among them, and deploy a single application server to host a simple application via MySQL Router. And we will do it all using MySQL Shell. Let's get started!

Establishing the Servers

This section provides an overview of establishing the servers you need to simulate a small InnoDB Cluster deployment. The first thing we must do is set up and configure several servers. You can use whatever operating system and hardware you want, provided they are supported by MySQL. Oracle has labored long and hard to make MySQL run on almost all the modern platforms and latest versions. Assuming you use one of those, you should not

---

[1]Experience has shown that each installation of high-availability MySQL tends to become specific to the environment, goals, and application requirements. What is presented here is an example of a general installation that you can use to build upon.

227

have any problems installing MySQL. However, if you want to follow this walk-through, we will be establishing five servers for installing MySQL products on each. All servers will also need to have MySQL Shell installed. We'll use the following:

- *MySQL server*: We need four servers running MySQL 8.0.11 or later.

- *Application server*: We need one server running our sample application and MySQL Router 8.0.11 or later.

Another thing to consider is the hardware you want to use for this demonstration. You could use typical commodity hardware or choose a less conventional, but more economical, alternative using Raspberry Pi computers. We will briefly discuss each option in this section, but the walk-through uses the Raspberry Pi.

Raspberry Pi computers are small and inexpensive, but they run relatively well considering the slower speed of the processor and limited memory. It is unlikely that you would base your entire production infrastructure on Raspberry Pi computers. But using Raspberry Pi computers can be helpful in experimenting with new technologies, development installations, and similar non-mission-critical implementations.

WHY RASPBERRY PI?

If you're wondering why someone would choose to use Raspberry Pi computers in a development environment, consider for the moment the costs. A typical Raspberry Pi 3B (or 3B+) costs about $50 USD. Even when adding the required mass storage device and a case, you can easily assemble a reasonably fast and stable Raspberry Pi computer running MySQL 8.0.11 for under $100 USD.

Plus, you don't need a keyboard, mouse, and monitor for every Raspberry Pi. After you have one configured, you can restart it headless (without keyboard, mouse, and monitor) by using remote access (`ssh`, `scp`, `mysqlsh`). In fact, after all the servers are configured, you won't need the keyboard, mouse, and monitor. You can simply borrow them from another system or your spares.[2]

Perhaps even more intriguing is the fact that the Raspberry Pi is very small and ultraportable. In fact, you can establish an entire cluster of Raspberry Pi machines in less space than a typical mini tower server. Finally, the Raspberry Pi is easy to use because it runs a variant of Linux, making it most familiar to many developers and administrators.

---

[2]I haven't met too many experienced developers and administrators who couldn't lay their hands on several of each of these items at a moment's notice.

Installing MySQL on Commodity Hardware

If you choose to use more conventional PC or server hardware, you can do so, but it is recommended (but not required) that you use the same hardware for all the servers. This common practice makes repairs easier, allowing you to switch machines without having to adapt or make modifications for hardware differences.

Similarly, it is recommended that you use the same operating system for each of the servers. Once again, this isn't a requirement, but it makes things easier. That said, it is common practice to use one platform for MySQL servers and another platform for application servers. For example, you could use Ubuntu for the MySQL servers and Windows for the application server.

Regardless, it is fine if you want to run this walk-through on your own, using whatever machines you have available. It is common to experiment with a set of machines that vary in platform and operating system. For example, if you have several desktop computers running Ubuntu and Windows along with a laptop or two running macOS, you can still use all of these because MySQL runs on all these platforms.

The only issue with using a mix of older hardware may be if one of your platforms used a different endianness.[3] *Endianness* refers to the order of the bytes in memory or communications. Although this isn't a concern for most, if you are using any old Oracle Sun servers or similar platforms, you may want to omit them. That doesn't mean they won't work—on the contrary—but they may add a level of complexity you may not want (or need) to experience.

The steps necessary to install MySQL on commodity hardware for use with InnoDB Cluster are summarized next. Because you have already seen how to install MySQL, MySQL Shell, and other products, we defer the details of installation to the previous chapters. Here are the basic steps:

1. Install the operating system.

2. Configure the operating system for use as a server (networking, user accounts, and so forth).

3. Install MySQL Server.

---

[3]Wikipedia provides more information on endianness; see `https://en.wikipedia.org/wiki/Endianness`.

If you have any experience in setting up desktop or server hardware, this list should not be surprising. You also might have alternative processes you normally use to set up a new computer. Feel free to use your own judgment in setting up the servers and installing MySQL.

It would also be a good idea to install MySQL Shell on each server. If you have not downloaded and installed MySQL before, refer to the previous chapters for examples of installation and general configuration.

Tip   See the "Installing and Upgrading MySQL" section in the online reference manual (`https://dev.mysql.com/doc/refman/8.0/en/installing.html`) to learn more about installing MySQL on specific platforms.

Installing MySQL on Raspberry Pi

In this chapter, we will use Raspberry Pi computers rather than more expensive mainstream server hardware. If you would like to follow along and use more traditional server hardware, feel free to skim over the portions detailing setup on Raspberry Pi and compiling MySQL. However, the commands used on the Raspberry Pi are the same or similar to those you would use on typical Linux-based platforms.

The only thing that may give those without knowledge of using the Raspberry Pi pause is the lack of Raspberry Pi installation packages for MySQL 8.0.11. More specifically, there are no 32-bit ARM binaries. Although there is some demand for 64-bit binaries for ARM-based enterprise operating systems, there has been little commercial demand for the 32-bit Raspberry Pi operating systems. So, although we may see some support for ARM-based platforms (currently via third-party sources), finding 32-bit binaries is more challenging. Fortunately, because MySQL is open source, we can download the source code, compile, and install it ourselves. In fact, we will do just that in this walk-through. The following are the steps necessary to prepare a Raspberry Pi computer for use with InnoDB Cluster:

1. Download the Raspbian image (or NOOBS).

2. Prepare the USB drive (or SD card).

3. Configure Raspbian (networking, user account, and so forth).

4. Build MySQL.

5. Install MySQL manually.

6. Configure MySQL.

7. Build MySQL Shell.

8. Install MySQL Shell.

Note   We will be building and installing MySQL Shell on all machines, and MySQL Router on the application server.

WHAT ABOUT ARM64?

If you're using 64-bit platforms and want to use a 64-bit operating system on the Raspberry Pi, you can. Oracle has recently announced support for the Raspberry Pi 3 for Oracle Enterprise Linux 7.5 (`https://blogs.oracle.com/linux/announcing-the-general-availability-of-oracle-linux-7-for-arm`). More important, Oracle also includes a yum repository that contains MySQL Server 8.0.11 and its components. So, if you want to use a 64-bit operating system or you are more familiar with Oracle Linux, Red Hat, or Fedora, you will want to check out the custom build of Oracle Enterprise Linux for the Raspberry Pi 3.

I have written a complete tutorial of how to set up InnoDB Cluster on the Raspberry Pi 3 using Oracle Enterprise Linux. See my blog, "MySQL 8.0 InnoDB Cluster on ARM64 with Oracle Linux and the Raspberry Pi 3B" (`http://drcharlesbell.blogspot.com/2018/06/mysql-80-innodb-cluster-on-arm64-with.html`) for a detailed walk-through. Like this chapter, the tutorial will show you how to build the images for the cluster instances as well as how to set up an application server.

Those more familiar with Raspbian or those who are new to the Raspberry Pi may want to follow the tutorial in this chapter first and then follow the tutorial for ARM64. As you will see, the steps are similar, but the commands and setup procedures differ.

This list is like the process you would use to set up MySQL on commodity hardware, but the build and configuration steps are required to make MySQL work on Raspbian. It is important to note that these extra steps are not unique to Raspbian. In fact, building, installing, and configuring MySQL from source is a viable alternative to using installation packages. What makes it necessary on Raspbian (and other platforms) is that there are no installation packages for Raspbian. You can find instructions on building MySQL for various platforms in the "Installing MySQL from Source" section in the online reference manual (https://dev.mysql.com/doc/refman/8.0/en/source-installation.html).

If you choose to use the Raspberry Pi, the following section demonstrates how to set up each computer to run the latest version of the Raspberry Pi default operating system. We begin with a short tutorial on setting up the Raspberry Pi, which encompasses the first three steps of the process.

Raspberry Pi Setup Tutorial

The Raspberry Pi is a personal computer with a surprising amount of power and versatility. You may be tempted to consider it a toy or a severely limited platform, but that is far from the truth. With the addition of onboard peripherals like USB, Ethernet, and HDMI video, the Raspberry Pi has everything you need for a lightweight desktop computer. If you consider the addition of the General-Purpose Input Output (GPIO) header, the Raspberry Pi becomes more than a simple desktop computer and fulfills its role as a computing system designed to promote hardware experimentation.

The following sections present a short tutorial on getting started with your new Raspberry Pi, from a bare board to a fully operational platform.

Note Several excellent works cover this topic in much greater detail. If you find yourself stuck or wanting to know more about beginning to use the Raspberry Pi and more about the Raspbian operating system, see *Learn Raspberry Pi with Linux* by Peter Membrey and David Hows (Apress, 2012). If you want to know more about using the Raspberry Pi in hardware projects, an excellent resource is *Practical Raspberry Pi* by Brendan Horan (Apress, 2013).

Getting Started

The Raspberry computer comes without any accessories. At a minimum for this walk-through, you need a USB drive of at least 16GB (or an SD card), a USB power supply rated at 700mA or better with a male micro-USB connector, a keyboard, a mouse, and an HDMI monitor or a DVI monitor with an HDMI adapter. However, before you can plug these things in to your Raspberry Pi and bask in its brilliance, you need to create a boot image for your USB drive. Fortunately, most have a spare keyboard, mouse, and monitor laying around, and except for USB interfaces for the input devices, the monitor requires a normal-sized HDMI cable.

Further, it is recommended you use a USB drive such as the small SanDisk Cruzer Fit, which are small drives that are relatively fast and inexpensive (see `www.sandisk.com/home/usb-flash/cruzer-fit`). SD cards are more fragile and can become corrupt more easily, making them less suitable for intense use like that we will see with InnoDB Cluster. However, you can still use SD cards. Just be sure to shut down your devices properly and take care when handling the SD cards.

> **Tip**   For best results, use a USB thumb drive for the operating system and files.

Installing a Boot Image

The process of installing a boot image involves choosing an image, downloading it, and then copying it to your USB drive (or SD card). For this walk-through, we will use the Raspbian image from `raspberrypi.org`. We will download this file, extract it (if compressed), and copy the image to the USB drive. There are a variety of ways to do this, but we will use the Etcher application, which is available for most platforms. Let's get started!

Rather than install the same base image for all the servers, we will build one server, install MySQL, and configure it. Then, we will clone that drive and re-create it on the other servers. As you will see, this will save you a lot of time. The only catch is, we will have to make some minor modifications to each cloned server to complete the setup, but most of the heavy work will have been done.

Begin the image creation process by visiting `www.raspberrypi.org/downloads/raspbian/` and download the Raspbian Stretch with Desktop image. Although we would not typically use a graphical user interface for the operating system on a production server, it makes working with the Raspberry Pi a bit easier (and familiar to some). Download the `.zip` file (for example, `2018-04-18-raspbian-stretch.zip`), and when it's downloaded, unzip it. This will produce an image file (for example, `2018-04-18-raspbian-stretch.img`), which we will use with Etcher to write to the USB drive.

> **Tip**   See `www.raspberrypi.org/downloads/` if you want to learn about other operating systems that are available for the Raspberry Pi.

When we have the image downloaded, we need to copy it to the USB drive (or SD card). For this, we will use Etcher, which is formatter that works on Linux, macOS, and Windows. If you visit the Etcher site, `https://etcher.io/`, you can choose the platform and download its installer. You can then install Etcher on your system, following the normal installation procedures for your platform.

When you're ready, insert your USB drive into your computer and launch Etcher. The user interface is intuitive. We need to do three things: choose the image we want to write, choose the drive to write to, and start the image transfer. So, for this step, we select the image for Raspbian we downloaded previously and then select the USB drive we want to use. Figure 7-1 shows an example with these two steps completed.

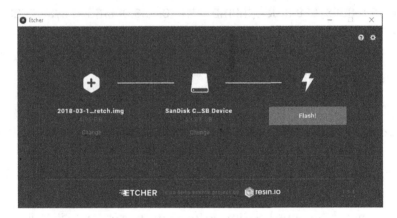

Figure 7-1. *Using Etcher to install Raspbian (USB drive)*

When you've checked to ensure that you've chosen the right image and drive, you can click Flash! to begin the image copy. When the copy is done, Etcher will verify the image. If all is well, Etcher will give you a message that the process succeeded. When that is done, you can close Etcher and remove the USB drive/SD card. It is now ready to be used in your Raspberry Pi.

Note   If you use Windows, your system may tell you that it has detected a drive that needs to be formatted after the copy. Ignore those messages! Do not format the drive or you will overwrite the image.

Initial Server Configuration

The next step is to insert the USB drive in the Raspberry Pi, power it on, and configure it for use with MySQL. This is where the keyboard, mouse, and monitor are needed. Connect them to the Raspberry Pi, insert the USB drive, and connect a power supply. The power supply is typically a USB 5V power supply such as a charger for your tablet or phone. Just make sure it is at least 700mA. The Raspberry Pi has no power switch, so when you plug in the power, the Raspberry Pi will boot.

What you should see on the screen after a minute or so are a series of Raspberry logos followed by a long list of boot messages. These are normal. Eventually, the system will automatically log in and boot into the graphical user interface, which is nice and simple to use. The first boot may be a bit slower, but subsequent boots will be a little faster.

MY RASPBERRY PI WON'T BOOT FROM USB!

If your Raspberry Pi won't boot from the USB drive, you must set a special write-once bit in the firmware. Most newer Raspberry Pi 3 computers will boot automatically from the USB drive. See `www.raspberrypi.org/documentation/hardware/raspberrypi/bootmodes/msd.md`. if your Raspberry Pi does not boot from USB.

In short, we must prepare an SD card image and modify it to allow for booting from USB and then enable USB boot mode with this command

`echo program_usb_boot_mode=1 | sudo tee -a /boot/config.txt.`

This adds `program_usb_boot_mode=1` to the end of `/boot/config.txt`. When that is done, reboot the Raspberry Pi with the SD card and then shut down. Remove the SD card and insert the USB drive. Power on the Raspberry Pi, and it should boot from the USB drive.

To configure the machine for use in this walk-through, the following tasks must be performed. Remember, we're doing this to one image and we'll copy it to the other servers later:

1. Change the root password.

2. Enable SSH.

3. Set the keyboard region/language.

4. Configure networking.

The following sections describe how to perform each of these tasks.

Change the Root Password

The root user account is named pi with a password of raspberry. Change that so prying eyes do not get into your computer and accidentally alter things. You'd be surprised how tempting a Raspberry Pi is to play with for someone who has never used one—especially someone who uses Linux. Choose a password that you will remember. Because we are cloning this drive for use for the other servers, changing the password here ensures that all the systems will use the same password. Cool.

Raspbian comes with a nice utility for making changes to the system, including changing the root user password, called the Raspberry Pi Configuration tool. You can access this by clicking the Raspberry Pi logo in the upper-left corner, choosing Preferences, and then clicking Raspberry Pi Configuration. Figure 7-2 shows an example of the tool.

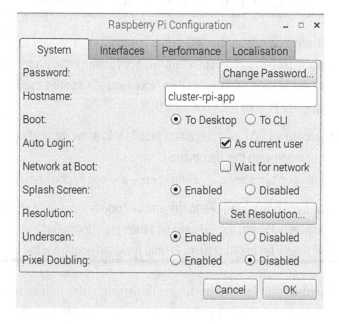

Figure 7-2. *Raspberry Pi Configuration tool*

To change the password, click Change Password and enter your new password. It is also strongly suggested that you turn off auto login by unticking the As Current User check box. But don't close the tool yet. We need to do two more things with this tool.

Enable SSH

When using the Raspberry Pi as a server (as with most servers), administrators find it easier to remotely log in to the server from their workstation rather than trudging down the long hallway to the secure room full or blinking lights to search through an endless array of server racks only to find a dumb terminal, connect it, and log in. You get the point—it is far easier to remotely log in.

Fortunately, we can do that with Raspbian. To configure Raspbian to allow remote logins through secure socket connections and the Secure Shell (SSH), we need to click the Interfaces tab in the Raspberry Pi Configuration tool and select the Enabled check box on the SSH line. Figure 7-3 shows how the interface should look after you've turned on SSH connections.

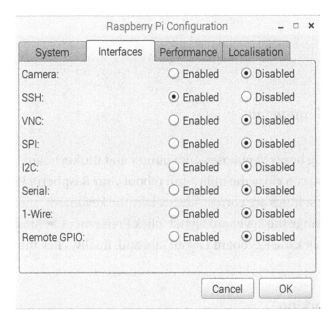

Figure 7-3. *Enabling SSH connections*

Set Keyboard Layout/Region

We need to do one more thing with the configuration tool: set the default keyboard layout. Raspbian comes with the keyboard layout set to English for Great Britain (the Raspberry Pi is built there). If you live somewhere else in the world and don't use that keyboard layout, you need to change it.

To change the keyboard layout, click the Localisation tab in the utility and then click the Set Keyboard button, as shown in Figure 7-4.

Figure 7-4. *Localisation tab*

Follow the dialog boxes to choose your country and the keyboard layout. When that is complete, you can close the utility and reboot your Raspberry Pi. After it reboots, ensure that all your settings are correct—especially the keyboard!

You can also change the keyboard layout: click Preferences ➤ Mouse and Keyboard Settings, and then click the Keyboard Layout tab, and, finally, click the Keyboard Layout button.

Configure Networking

The final task in setting up the Raspberry Pi operating system is enabling networking. You have two choices here. The Raspberry Pi 3 comes with both Wi-Fi and Ethernet connections. It is recommended that you use Ethernet connections and use a hub to tie in all the computers in the cluster. Although a hub is not needed if you decide to use Wi-Fi, using a hub with Ethernet connections symbolizes what is done for most cluster installations—installing them in an isolated subnet to ensure no loss of traffic due to competition or network load. For this walk-through, that isn't important, but a hub will make the connections a bit easier.

> **Note**   Although this section describes in detail how to set up the network for one of the MySQL servers, we will have to make small changes to the other servers after we've cloned the base server. For example, we will need to edit the specific IP and hostname for each server, which is easier than performing the same longer steps on each machine.

Whichever interface you choose, we must set up our servers to use static IP addresses. Check the Dynamic Host Configuration Protocol (DHCP)[4] server on your home (or work) network and choose five IP addresses from the range available. Most home routers have DHCP services running. Or, better, reserve a range of IP addresses for use. If you are not sure what this means, that's OK. You can just choose five IP addresses from the top (higher numbers) of the range and you should be safe.

For example, if your DHCP server uses the range 192.168.1.2–192.168.1.254, you can choose 192.168.1.240–192.168.1.244 and you should be fine. If, however, you encounter problems with other machines complaining about duplicate IP addresses, you may need to change the range you use.

> **Note**   If you are not the owner of the DHCP server (for example, you're using someone else's network), you may need to contact the system administrator and request the IP addresses.

For this demonstration, we will be changing the IP address of the Raspberry Pi computers to use 192.168.42.240–192.168.42.244 as follows:

- 192.168.42.240: The application server

- 192.168.42.241: First server in the InnoDB Cluster

- 192.168.42.242: Second server in the InnoDB Cluster

- 192.168.42.243: Third server in the InnoDB Cluster

- 192.168.42.244: Fourth server in the InnoDB Cluster

---

[4]DHCP is a network management protocol used on TCP/IP networks to manage IP addresses. See https://en.wikipedia.org/wiki/Dynamic_Host_Configuration_Protocol.

You also need to know the router IP address and at least one name server IP address. You can find this information at your router (typically, the same machine that runs the DHCP service). For example, the router IP address is likely the subnet address and the first number in range. For example, the 192.168.42.XXX network uses 192.168.42.1 as the router IP address.

Similarly, the domain name server (DNS) on the same network is also the 192.168.42.1 address. If you have other machines on the same network, you can also find this information by examining the networking settings. For example, you can run ifconfig on Linux and macOS machines to see all the network interfaces. On Windows, you can use ipconfig /all to see the network interfaces and their settings.

To set a static IP address, we must edit the dhcpcd.conf file. You can use the following command in a terminal window. This command uses elevated privileges through the superuser (sudo) command and the Nano editor to edit the file:

```
$ sudo nano /etc/dhcpcd.conf
```

You can open a terminal by clicking the small terminal icon in the upper-left portion of the toolbar, as shown in Figure 7-5 (indicated by the square box annotation).

Figure 7-5. *Locating the terminal application*

When you have the file open, scroll down to the bottom of the file (end) and add the following lines, substituting the base IP range for your network. For example, if your network uses 10.0.1.XXX, use 10.0.1 instead of 192.168.42.XXX. In this case, we're setting the static IP address to 192.168.42.241 for the first MySQL server. Use the router IP and name server IP addresses that you encountered when examining your router.

```
# Example static IP configuration:
interface eth0
static ip_address=192.168.42.241/24
static routers=192.168.42.1
static domain_name_servers=192.168.42.1
```

After you've added these lines, save the file by pressing Ctrl+X and then Y to save the file. Once saved, you can reboot the machine. When the machine reboots, you can check the settings by using the following command in a terminal window:

```
$ ip a
```

Examine the output to ensure that the eth0 interface is displaying the correct IP address as shown next. Notice that the report is showing an IP address of 192.168.42.241:

```
...
2: eth0: <BROADCAST,MULTICAST,UP,LOWER_UP> mtu 1500 qdisc pfifo_fast state
UP group default qlen 1000
    link/ether b8:27:eb:5e:7f:71 brd ff:ff:ff:ff:ff:ff
    inet 192.168.42.241/24 brd 192.168.42.255 scope global eth0
       valid_lft forever preferred_lft forever
    inet6 2001:5b0:4eca:9f28:cc4e:31cb:ecb0:226a/64 scope global mngtmpaddr
noprefixroute dynamic
       valid_lft 1175sec preferred_lft 1175sec
    inet6 fe80::a38:d8b:653b:81c/64 scope link
       valid_lft forever preferred_lft forever
...
```

Next, test the network connection to ensure that it works. If you can connect to the Internet or other computers on the network, you're finished. If you cannot, go back and check your settings and, if necessary, revert the changes by placing a # before each line you added to the file and reboot.

Tip   See `www.raspberrypi.org/learning/networking-lessons/rpi-static-ip-address/` for a full discussion of how to set a static IP address on Raspberry Pi for either Ethernet or Wi-Fi connections.

OK, we're not quite done with the network configuration. We also need to set a unique hostname for each server. We can use the Raspberry Pi Configuration tool to set the hostname. For this demonstration, we will use the hostname `cluster-rpi[1-4]`. For example, the third server setup has a hostname of `cluster-rpi3`. We will use the hostname `cluster-rpi-app` for the application server. To change the hostname, open the Raspberry Pi Configuration tool, locate the Hostname line on the first tab, and change the text in the text box to the right. Figure 7-6 shows an example of setting the hostname for the application server.

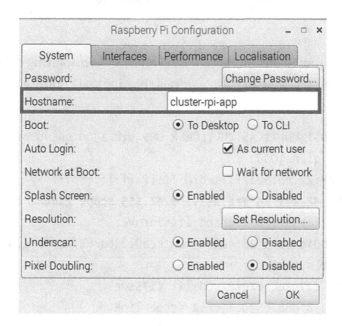

Figure 7-6. *Setting the hostname*

After you make the change, you will need to reboot the server, but there is one more change we need to make. We must also edit the `/etc/hosts` file to add the new IP addresses and hostnames for your cluster. This allows us to use the cluster without having to register the hostnames with our DNS server. That is possible if your home network has its own DNS, but that is unlikely. The lines you need to add are those at the bottom of the file (shown in bold):

```
127.0.0.1       localhost
::1             localhost ip6-localhost ip6-loopback
ff02::1         ip6-allnodes
ff02::2         ip6-allrouters
```

```
192.168.42.240  cluster-rpi-app
192.168.42.241  cluster-rpi1
192.168.42.242  cluster-rpi2
192.168.42.243  cluster-rpi3
192.168.42.244  cluster-rpi4
```

You can now reboot your server. We are now ready to build, install, and configure MySQL on Raspbian. It is strongly recommended that you use another machine to perform this task (such as the application server).

Tip   If you want to heed the advice to build MySQL on a separate Raspberry Pi computer, you should perform the preceding steps for another USB drive and machine. For example, you could build the application server and use that machine to build MySQL.

Building MySQL Server, Shell, and Router

Remember, there is no binary distribution for Raspbian for MySQL or its products. We must build MySQL Server, Shell, and Router and then install them manually on our Raspberry Pi computers. Fortunately, the process is straightforward, involving a few minor system configuration items to prepare our system and two commands: cmake and make. This section will walk you through all those steps with ample examples and every step documented.

The task of building MySQL from source code may seem daunting to those who have never programmed or for those who haven't written a program in a while, but do not despair. The hardest part of compiling MySQL on the Raspberry Pi is waiting for the process to complete. Compiling everything can take several hours. But that is a small price to pay for being able to use Raspberry Pi computers to experiment with InnoDB Cluster.

However, before we start modifying our system to begin building the code, let's discuss a deployment plan.

Deployment Plan

It is always a good idea to have a plan for deploying a high-availability solution. We have already discussed the general plan: having one application server and four servers in the cluster. Now let's discuss how best to build and deploy the MySQL products.

We will be using one machine to build MySQL Server, Shell, and Router. However, we do not need to install all three components on every machine in the cluster. Instead, we need to install MySQL Server and MySQL Shell on the four machines that will be members of the cluster. The application server needs only MySQL Shell and Router installed.

The way to do this is to use the application server as the build machine to build all three products. You can then copy the installation file (in the form of a TAR file, which stands for *tape archive*) to the base machine you prepared in the previous sections.

We will build all three products on the application server, but install only MySQL Shell and Router on that machine. MySQL Server and Shell are installed on our base MySQL server image discussed previously. It is that image that we will clone to form the machines in the cluster.

Let's dive into compiling MySQL on Raspbian, starting with the prerequisites.

Prerequisites

To prepare your Raspberry Pi to compile MySQL products, you need to take several steps. The first thing to consider is whether you want to build MySQL on the same server that you will clone later. If you build MySQL on the same server we just spent time configuring for use with InnoDB Cluster, you will be copying all the development code and applications needed to every machine, which is not necessary.

Therefore, the first prerequisite is to set up a new machine to be our build machine. As mentioned, this can be your application server. In addition, if you have an extra USB drive of at least 8GB (do not use an SD card for the build machine—it will be too slow), prepare it by copying the Raspbian image you downloaded earlier (see the previous "Installing a Boot Image" section on using Etcher). If you do not have an extra USB drive, you can use the drive designated for the application server, as we will not be cloning that system. If you have only one keyboard, mouse, and monitor, you will need to shut down the application server before booting the first MySQL server.

After you have the application server prepared at least as far as the steps in the previous "Raspberry Pi Setup Tutorial" section (be sure to use the right IP address and hostname—192.168.42.240, `cluster-rpi-app`), we will install the following software:

- *Curses 5* (`libncurses5-dev`): Terminal output library

- *Bison*: A language processor

- *OpenSSL* (`libssl-dev`): SSL libraries

- *CMake*: Make configuration tool

To install all these libraries at the same time, use the following command in a terminal window:

```
$ sudo apt-get install libncurses5-dev bison libssl-dev cmake
```

This downloads the necessary files and installs them. Notice that we must use elevated privileges to install the library.

WHAT IS SUDO?

On most Linux platforms, you must use elevated privileges to install software and modify system files. The `sudo` command (for *superuser do*, see `https://linuxacademy.com/blog/linux/linux-commands-for-beginners-sudo/`) allows you to temporarily gain those privileges for a normal user account. You will see this often to configure Raspbian and similar Linux systems.

We must do one more thing. We must increase the swap file size. This is necessary to allow the system sufficient memory to compile and link some of the larger source code files. It is recommended to set the swap file size to 2048. To do so, open a terminal window and enter the following command to edit the swap file configuration file:

```
$ sudo nano /etc/dphys-swapfile
```

Locate the following line in the file and change the value to 2048. No other lines in the file need to change:

```
CONF_SWAPSIZE=2048
```

To enable the new swap size, either reboot the machine or enter the following commands:

```
$ sudo /etc/init.d/dphys-swapfile stop
$ sudo /etc/init.d/dphys-swapfile start
```

These reset the swap file to the new size by stopping the system process and restarting it. Now we're ready to build MySQL Server, Shell, and Router.

Building MySQL Server

OK, this is the trickiest part of using the Raspberry Pi with MySQL 8.0.11. Because there are no Oracle binaries that we can download and use (some third-parties may eventually build some), we must compile MySQL ourselves. This is possible because MySQL is open source and, as you saw in the previous section, we can download the source code. Cool.

Building MySQL on Raspberry Pi requires just three steps. We first run the preprocessor called CMake, then build the code with make, and finally build an installation package with the make package command. Let's see the details of each step, beginning with CMake.

CMake (cmake.org) is another open source product used to build, test, and package software. Recall, we installed CMake in the previous section. There are many variations of options you can use to build software and many that apply to MySQL. In fact, you can spend a lot of time customizing the CMake command options to build for almost any platform. Because we downloaded the MySQL source code for generic Linux with the Boost libraries, we have everything we need.

The command options we need to use with CMake are minimal and include the following:

- You should set -DWITH_UNIT_TESTS=OFF to save compile time (unit tests are not needed).

- You should set PREFIX to the installation path to make it easy to install.

- We must build with the release code (debug requires too much memory for the Raspberry Pi).

- We must add additional compiling and build flags to ensure that the code builds properly on ARM32.

Each of these will be explained in a bit more detail, but let's get started with downloading the source code.

Preparing the Source Code

Now that we have our machine set up to build MySQL, the only prerequisite is that we must download the MySQL Server source code. Go to `https://dev.mysql.com/downloads/mysql/`. From the Select Operating System drop-down box, select Source Code. Then click the Generic Linux (Architecture Independent), Compressed TAR Archive Includes Boost Headers download link at the bottom of the list, as shown in Figure 7-7. This file contains another library that we need (Boost) as well as the server source code. It is the easiest of the downloads to start from to build.

Figure 7-7. *Downloading the MySQL Server source code*

Running CMake (Preparing to Compile)

The first thing we're going to do is extract the TAR file that we downloaded. You can do so with the following commands:

```
$ cd /home/pi
$ mkdir source
$ cd source
$ cp ~/Downloads/mysql- boost-8.0.11.tar.gz .
$ tar -xvf mysql-boost-8.0.11.tar.gz
```

This creates a folder named `mysql-8.0.11`. It is recommended that you unpack this file in a folder in the root user's home folder—for example, `/home/pi/source`. The unpacking process will take a few minutes because it contains a lot of code.

Tip   If you want to save space on your boot drive, you can format and use a second USB drive to download and compile the code. Just make sure to format the drive with the ext4 file system.

Next, we will make a directory to store all the compiled code by using the following commands. This helps prevent accidents when compiling and preserves the source code:

```
$ cd mysql-8.0.11
$ mkdir build
$ cd build
```

Now we can run the CMake command. Listing 7-1 shows the complete command you need to use from within the build folder. Notice that the command has many options specified, including (in order of appearance), using UNIX makefiles, setting the build to release code (rather than debug), ignoring All-in-one (AIO) checking, setting the Boost folder (included in the TAR file we downloaded), turning off the unit tests, and setting some arcane options for compiling on ARM32.

Listing 7-1. Running the CMake Command (ARM32)

```
$ cmake -G "Unix Makefiles" -DCMAKE_BUILD_TYPE=release -DBUILD_
CONFIG=mysql_release -DDEBUG_EXTNAME=OFF -DIGNORE_AIO_CHECK=1 -DWITH_
BOOST=/home/pi/source/mysql-8.0.11/boost -DWITH_UNIT_TESTS=OFF
-DCMAKE_C_LINK_FLAGS="-Wl,--no-keep-memory,--icf=safe" -DCMAKE_CXX_LINK_
FLAGS="-Wl,--no-keep-memory,--icf=safe" -DCMAKE_C_FLAGS_RELEASE="-fPIC"
-DCMAKE_CXX_FLAGS_RELEASE="-fPIC" -DCMAKE_INSTALL_PREFIX="/usr/local/mysql"
..
-- Running cmake version 3.7.2
-- Found Git: /usr/bin/git (found version "2.11.0")
-- Configuring with MAX_INDEXES = 64U
-- The C compiler identification is GNU 6.3.0
-- The CXX compiler identification is GNU 6.3.0
-- Check for working C compiler: /usr/bin/cc
...
-- COMPILE_DEFINITIONS:
_GNU_SOURCE;_FILE_OFFSET_BITS=64;BOOST_GEOMETRY_SQRT_CHECK_FINITENESS;HAVE_
CONFIG_H;RAPIDJSON_NO_SIZETYPEDEFINE;__STDC_LIMIT_MACROS;__STDC_
FORMAT_MACROS;_USE_MATH_DEFINES;HAVE_LIBEVENT1;UNISTR_FROM_STRING_
EXPLICIT=explicit;UNISTR_FROM_CHAR_EXPLICIT=explicit
-- CMAKE_C_FLAGS:  -Wall -Wextra -Wformat-security -Wvla -Wundef -Wwrite-strings
```

```
-- CMAKE_CXX_FLAGS:  -Wall -Wextra -Wformat-security -Wvla -Wundef
-Woverloaded-virtual -Wno-missing-field-initializers -Wlogical-op
-- CMAKE_C_LINK_FLAGS: -Wl,--no-keep-memory,--icf=safe -fuse-ld=gold
-Wl,--gc-sections
-- CMAKE_CXX_LINK_FLAGS: -Wl,--no-keep-memory,--icf=safe -fuse-ld=gold
-Wl,--gc-sections
-- CMAKE_C_FLAGS_RELEASE: -fPIC   -DDBUG_OFF
-- CMAKE_CXX_FLAGS_RELEASE: -fPIC -std=c++11   -DDBUG_OFF
-- Configuring done
-- Generating done
-- Build files have been written to: /home/pi/source/mysql-8.0.11/build
```

Don't worry if this command looks strange. You don't need to understand all the special settings we've used for the compile and link phases. However, if you do want to learn more about these options, you can see the documentation on the GNU compiler (http://gcc.gnu.org/onlinedocs/gcc/Option-Summary.html) and linker (https://gcc.gnu.org/onlinedocs/gcc/Link-Options.html) options.

The command could take a few minutes to run. Be sure there are no errors and that the last lines indicate that the build files have been written to the build folder. Pay special attention to the LINK_FLAGS messages at the end. The options in the CMake command do not include spaces. If you accidentally add spaces, the comma-separated list will show them in the CMake output. Be sure there are no spaces. If there are spaces, you may get an error stating --icf=safe (or other) options are invalid. If that happens, run the command again without the spaces.

If you've gotten this far without errors, you can almost relax. The next step, compiling the code, is easy but can take a while to run on a Raspberry Pi 3B+ (at least two to three hours).

Running make (Compiling)

The next step is to compile the code. This is done simply with the make command. This command allows us to specify the number of parallel threads we want to use. For the Raspberry Pi 3 and a total of four CPU cores, it is safe to use three cores for compiling. If you have a watcher for CPU usage running, you will see those three, and possibly at times all four, cores running at 100%. If your Raspberry Pi 3B is mounted in a case, make sure you have adequate ventilation or a fan blowing over the board. This isn't strictly necessary for the Raspberry Pi 3B+ (the newest board), but it can't hurt either.

Listing 7-2 shows the compilation step of the MySQL server code using the command make -j3. The listing is an excerpt of the messages you will likely see (there will be thousands of lines), but the important ones to note are the last several. These ensure that the code has compiled without errors.

Tip You may see minor warnings flow past when the code is compiling, which you can ignore. However, you should not see any compilation errors. If you do, go back and check your CMake command and rerun it if necessary. If all else fails, delete the build directory and start over.

Listing 7-2. Compiling MySQL Server

```
$ make -j3
[  0%] Built target INFO_SRC
[  0%] Built target INFO_BIN
[  0%] Building C object extra/zlib/CMakeFiles/zlib.dir/adler32.o
[  0%] Generating common.h
[  0%] Generating help.c
[  0%] Generating help.h
[  0%] Generating vi.h
[  0%] Generating emacs.h
[  0%] Building C object extra/zlib/CMakeFiles/zlib.dir/compress.o
[  0%] Generating fcns.c
[  0%] Generating fcns.h
...
...
[100%] Linking CXX static library ../archive_output_directory/libsql_main.a
[100%] Built target sql_main
Scanning dependencies of target mysqld
[100%] Building CXX object sql/CMakeFiles/mysqld.dir/main.cc.o
[100%] Linking CXX executable ../runtime_output_directory/mysqld
[100%] Built target mysqld
```

When the compilation is complete, the next step is to build a package (TAR file) we can use to install MySQL on our servers.

Making the Package

The last thing we need to do is build the installation package. In this case, we will build a compressed TAR file that we will be able to copy to our initial server and install. We do this with the make package command, as shown in Listing 7-3.

Listing 7-3. Building the TAR Package

```
$ make package
[  0%] Built target abi_check
[  0%] Built target INFO_SRC
[  0%] Built target INFO_BIN
[  0%] Built target zlib
[  1%] Built target edit
[  8%] Built target icuuc
[ 16%] Built target icui18n
[ 16%] Built target icustubdata
...
Run CPack packaging tool...
CPack: Create package using TGZ
CPack: Install projects
CPack: - Run preinstall target for: MySQL
CPack: - Install project: MySQL
CPack: Create package
CPack: - package: /home/pi/source/mysql-8.0.11/build/mysql-8.0.11-linux-
armv7l.tar.gz generated.
```

That's it! We've built MySQL on the Raspberry Pi! That wasn't so bad, was it? Now let's see how to install and test MySQL on our server.

Installing MySQL Server

Recall, we built MySQL on our application server. Thus, we need to copy the TAR file to a removable drive and boot up the first MySQL server we built previously. If you have only one keyboard, mouse, and monitor, you will need to shut down the application server before booting the first MySQL server. Go ahead and do that now after you copy the file.

After the server if booted, log in and change to the /usr/local directory and create a new folder named mysql. Then, change to the new folder and copy the TAR file to that folder. Finally, unpack the file by using the following commands. There are a lot of files, so it could take a few minutes to unpack.

```
$ cd /usr/local/
$ mkdir mysql
$ cd mysql
$ sudo cp ~/source/mysql-8.0.11/build/mysql-8.0.11-linux-armv7l.tar.gz .
$ sudo tar -xvf mysql-8.0.11-linux-armv7l.tar.gz --strip-components=1
```

Notice that the last command uses an option to strip one component (the first folder—mysql-8.0.11-linux-armv7l) from the extracted file directories. This ensures that the MySQL files get copied to /usr/local/mysql.

However, we need to run one more command. Because we are space conscious, we do not need the MySQL test files, so we can delete them with the following command. When we're done with the TAR file, we can delete that too, as shown here:

```
$ sudo rm -rf mysql-test
$ sudo rm mysql-8.0.11-linux-armv7l.tar.gz
```

Installing from the TAR file requires more steps than installing from a typical platform-specific package. This is because installation packages typically take care of several required configuration steps—all of which are detailed in the online reference manual section, "Installing MySQL on Unix/Linux Using Generic Binaries" (https://dev.mysql.com/doc/refman/8.0/en/binary-installation.html).

Configuring MySQL Server

Now that we have the files copied, we can finish the setup. The process is not tedious but does involve several commands run from a terminal, so patience is needed to ensure that all the commands are entered correctly.

We begin by creating a new group named mysql, adding a user named mysql, creating a folder for MySQL to use, and granting access to the folder to the mysql user. The following shows the commands needed; run these from a terminal (these commands have no output):

```
$ sudo groupadd mysql
$ sudo useradd -r -g mysql -s /bin/false mysql
$ cd /usr/local/mysql
$ sudo mkdir mysql-files
$ sudo chown mysql:mysql mysql-files
$ sudo chmod 750 mysql-files
```

The next step before starting the server for the first time is to set up secure connections by using the mysql_ssl_rsa_setup tool and ensuring that all the data files are accessible for the mysql user. Finally, we also need to prepare the data directory. The following shows the commands needed; run these in a terminal window, from the /usr/local/mysql folder:

```
$ sudo ./bin/mysql_ssl_rsa_setup --datadir=data
$ sudo chown mysql:mysql data
$ sudo chmod 750 data
```

We can initialize the data directory easily with the --initialize option, as shown in the next code line. Notice we run the command with elevated privileges and specify the user to use (mysql). The following shows an example of the output with the successful messages highlighted in bold. If you see errors, consult the online reference manual to resolve them. Notice that the output contains the initial root user password. You will need that for the next step.

```
$ sudo bin/mysqld --initialize --user=mysql
...
2018-05-23T18:37:53.120312Z 0 [System] [MY-013169] [Server] /usr/local/
mysql/bin/mysqld (mysqld 8.0.11) initializing of server in progress as
process 15340
2018-05-23T18:38:26.383044Z 5 [Note] [MY-010454] [Server] A temporary
password is generated for root@localhost: pPX4Ll8/grR2
2018-05-23T18:38:52.713071Z 0 [System] [MY-013170] [Server] /usr/local/
mysql/bin/mysqld (mysqld 8.0.11) initializing of server has completed
```

OK, we are now ready to start MySQL for the first time. Use the `mysqld_safe` command to start MySQL from the command line. We use this command instead of the `/etc/init.d/mysql` start command so we can check the output for errors. If there are no errors, you should see output like this:

```
$ sudo ./bin/mysqld_safe --user=mysql &
$ Logging to '/usr/local/mysql/data/raspberrypi.err'.
2018-05-23T18:42:34.968096Z mysqld_safe Starting mysqld daemon with
databases from /usr/local/mysql/data
```

Now we can test our MySQL server with the older client. Be sure to use the password displayed when you initialized the data directory. Listing 7-4 shows an example of using the `mysql` client to connect to the server for the first time. We will first display the version and then change the root user password. Notice that we also shut down the server with the `shutdown` SQL command.

Listing 7-4. Connecting to MySQL for the First Time

```
$ ./bin/mysql -uroot -p
Enter password:
Welcome to the MySQL monitor.  Commands end with ; or \g.
Your MySQL connection id is 8
Server version: 8.0.11

Copyright (c) 2000, 2018, Oracle and/or its affiliates. All rights
reserved.

Oracle is a registered trademark of Oracle Corporation and/or its
affiliates. Other names may be trademarks of their respective
owners.

Type 'help;' or '\h' for help. Type '\c' to clear the current input
statement.

mysql> SET PASSWORD = 'root';
Query OK, 0 rows affected (0.06 sec)
```

```
mysql> SELECT @@version;
+-----------+
| @@version |
+-----------+
| 8.0.11    |
+-----------+
1 row in set (0.00 sec)

mysql> shutdown;
Query OK, 0 rows affected (0.00 sec)

mysql> \q
```

Next, we must add the path to the MySQL binaries. We can do this easily by editing our Bash resource file with the command nano ~/.bashrc. When the file opens, add the following line to the bottom of the file:

```
export PATH=${PATH}:/usr/local/mysql/bin
```

The next time you open a terminal, you can execute the MySQL applications and tools without specifying the path.

One final step is needed: we must copy the startup and shutdown script (service) to allow us to automatically start MySQL at boot. To do so, copy the mysql.server file from the support-files folder from the build to the /etc/init.d/mysql file, as shown next. We will also test the server connection again and then shut it down with the /etc/init.d/mysql script. Note that you may be prompted for a password when using this script.

```
$ /etc/init.d/mysql start
[ ok ] Starting mysql (via systemctl): mysql.service.
$ mysql -uroot -p -e "select @@version"
Enter password:
+-----------+
| @@version |
+-----------+
| 8.0.11    |
+-----------+
$ /etc/init.d/mysql stop
[ ok ] Stopping mysql (via systemctl): mysql.service.
```

That's it! We've installed MySQL server and tested that it works. It would also be a good idea to install MySQL Shell on each server.

Building MySQL Shell

Building MySQL Shell on Raspberry Pi is like building MySQL Server, but the prerequisites are a bit different, requiring downloading and compiling the Protobuf library. Installation is a bit easier because no post-installation configuration is needed. You will explore how to build and install MySQL Shell on Raspberry Pi in this section.

Preparing the Source Code

The first thing we need to do is download the MySQL Shell source code. Go to `https://dev.mysql.com/downloads/shell/`. In the Select Operating System drop-down box, select Source Code. Then click the Generic Linux (Architecture Independent), Compressed TAR Archive download link at the bottom of the list, as shown in Figure 7-8. You can leave that file for now, as we will need it in the next section.

Generic Linux (Architecture Independent), Compressed TAR Archive	8.0.11	16.4M	Download
(mysql-shell-8.0.11-src.tar.gz)		MD5: 1e639e95c6ef9d1912b38e419616d876	Signature	

Figure 7-8. *Downloading the MySQL Shell source code*

Next, we also need to download the Protobuf 2.6.1 source code. We will need to download the source code, compile it, and install it for use with MySQL Shell. Go to `https://github.com/google/protobuf/releases/tag/v2.6.1` and download the `protobuf-2.6.1.tar.gz` file by clicking it. Copy or place it in your `/home/pi/source` folder and unpack it by using the following commands:

```
$ cd /home/source
$ cp ~/Downloads/protobuf-2.6.1.tar.gz .
$ tar -xvf protobuf-2.6.1.tar.gz
```

Next, change into the folder that we unpacked and run the `configure` command:.

```
$ cd protobuf-2.6.1
$ ./configure
checking whether to enable maintainer-specific portions of Makefiles... yes
checking build system type... armv7l-unknown-linux-gnueabihf
```

```
...
config.status: creating build-aux/config.h
config.status: executing depfiles commands
config.status: executing libtool commands
```

This ensures that the code is configured for the Raspberry Pi platform (as CMake did for the server code).

Next, we run the make command with elevated privileges, as shown next. An excerpt of the typical output follows. Hundreds of lines may be generated, but there will not be a "done" or "complete" message at the end. If you do not see any errors, the code is compiled properly.

```
$ make
make  all-recursive
make[1]: Entering directory '/home/pi/source/protobuf-2.6.1'
Making all in .
make[2]: Entering directory '/home/pi/source/protobuf-2.6.1'
make[2]: Leaving directory '/home/pi/source/protobuf-2.6.1'
Making all in src
...
```

Finally, we install the library with the make install command with elevated privileges, as shown next. An excerpt of the typical output follows. Hundreds of lines may be generated, but there will not be a "done" or "complete" message at the end. If you do not see any errors, the code is installed properly.

```
$ sudo make install
Making install in .
make[1]: Entering directory '/home/pi/source/protobuf-2.6.1'
make[2]: Entering directory '/home/pi/source/protobuf-2.6.1'
...
```

There is one final step: we need to tell the library loader that we have a new library installed. If you attempt to compile MySQL Shell now, you may encounter an error stating that the Protobuf library doesn't exist. It does; it just hasn't been loaded into the cache. The following command ensures that the library is loaded:

```
$ sudo ldconfig
```

Now we're ready to build MySQL Shell.

Note   You must build MySQL Shell on a system that has a compiled MySQL Server source code tree.

Running CMake (Preparing to Compile)

The first thing we're going to do is extract the TAR file that we downloaded. You can do so with the following commands:

```
$ cd /home/pi/source
$ cp ~/Downloads/mysql-shell-8.0.11-src.tar.gz .
$ tar -xvf mysql-shell-8.0.11-src.tar.gz
```

This creates a folder named mysql-shell-8.0.11-src. It is recommended that you unpack this file in a folder in the root user's home folder—or example, /home/pi/source. The unpacking process will take a few minutes because the file contains a lot of code.

Note   Unlike the server (and router) source code, we will build MySQL Shell from the root of the source tree.

Next, we can run the CMake command. As in the MySQL Server code, we need to specify some options. We need a reference to the server source code directory, the server source code build directory, and the location of the Protobuf source code. Finally, we will specify that we want to build with Python and set the installation prefix. Listing 7-5 shows the CMake command followed by a sample of the output. Notice the lines marked in bold.

Listing 7-5. Running CMake for MySQL Shell

```
$ cmake -DMYSQL_SOURCE_DIR=/home/pi/source/mysql-8.0.11 -DMYSQL_BUILD_DIR=
/home/pi/source/mysql-8.0.11/build -DWITH_PROTOBUF=/home/pi/source/ -DHAVE_
PYTHON=1 -DCMAKE_INSTALL_PREFIX=/usr/local/mysql .
DHAVE_PYTHON=1 .
-- MySQL Shell 8.0.11
```

```
CMake Warning at CMakeLists.txt:110 (message):
  V8 is unavailable: building without JavaScript support.
-- Python 2.7.13
-- PYTHON_INCLUDE_DIR: /usr/include/python2.7
-- PYTHON_LIRARIES: /usr/lib/arm-linux-gnueabihf/libpython2.7.so
PROTOBUF_INCLUDE_DIRS: /usr/local/include
PROTOBUF_LIBRARIES: /usr/local/lib/libprotobuf.so;-lpthread
-- /home/pi/source/mysql-8.0.11/build/scripts/mysql_config --libs: -L/usr/
local/mysql/lib -lmysqlclient -lpthread -lm -lrt -lssl -lcrypto -ldl
-- /home/pi/source/mysql-8.0.11/build/archive_output_directory/
libmysqlclient.a
-- Found MySQL client Libraries
...
-- Performing Test HAVE_IMPLICIT_DEPENDENT_NAME_TYPING
-- Performing Test HAVE_IMPLICIT_DEPENDENT_NAME_TYPING - Failed
-- Library mysqlshdk-static depends on OSLIBS -lpthread
-- Configuring done
-- Generating done
-- Build files have been written to: /home/pi/source/mysql-shell-8.0.11-src
```

Notice the warning that we're building without JavaScript support. This is because the V8 libraries are missing. Compiling and installing these libraries is a bit of work on Raspbian and not strictly necessary for this demonstration, so we will build MySQL Shell with only SQL and Python support.

Running make (Compiling)

The next step is to compile the code. As with the server code, we will use the make -j3 command to compile. You may see some warnings, but as for the server code, unless there are errors, you can ignore the warnings. The following shows a brief excerpt of compiling the shell code:

```
$ make -j3
Scanning dependencies of target utils
Scanning dependencies of target db
Scanning dependencies of target shellcore
...
```

```
[ 98%] Linking CXX executable ../bin/mysqlsh
[ 99%] Linking CXX executable ../bin/mysqlshrec
[100%] Built target mysqlsh
```

Making the Package

The last thing we need to do is build the installation package. In this case, we will build a compressed TAR file that we will be able to copy to our initial server and install. We will use the same make package command that we used with the server code. The following shows a brief excerpt of building the package for the shell:

```
$ make package
[  0%] Creating mysqlprovision.zip
[  0%] Built target mysqlprovision
[ 10%] Built target shellcore
...
CPack: - package: /home/pi/source/mysql-shell-8.0.11-src/mysql-
shell-8.0.11-.tar.gz generated.
CPack: Create package using DEB
CPack: Install projects
CPack: - Run preinstall target for: mysqlsh
CPack: - Install project: mysqlsh
CPack: Create package
CPack: - package: /home/pi/source/mysql-shell-8.0.11-src/mysql-
shell-8.0.11-.deb generated.
```

The command builds a Debian installer (DEB) file as well as a TAR file. To be consistent, we will use the TAR file. Besides, installing the shell is trivial.

Installing MySQL Shell

Installing MySQL Shell with the TAR file is a simple matter of copying the TAR file to the /usr/local/mysql folder and unpacking it. You should install MySQL Shell on all the machines in the cluster—which at this point means installing it on the application server and the base MySQL server we built earlier. The following shows the commands needed to install the shell. The last command removes the TAR file, because we do not need that after we've installed it:

```
$ cd /usr/local/mysql
$ sudo cp /home/pi/source/mysql-shell-8.0.11-src/mysql-shell-8.0.11-.tar.gz .
$ sudo tar -xvf mysql-shell-8.0.11-.tar.gz --strip-components=3
$ sudo rm mysql-shell-8.0.11-.tar.gz
```

OK, now we can test the MySQL Shell installation. The first thing we do if we haven't already done so is to start the server by using the following command:

```
$ /etc/init.d/mysql start
```

If you have set your path, you can start the shell with the `mysqlsh` command. Listing 7-6 shows an example of using the shell to connect to our server and run a simple command and then exit. We can also shut down the server at the end of the session.

Listing 7-6. Testing the MySQL Shell on Raspberry Pi

```
$ mysqlsh
MySQL Shell 8.0.11
...
 MySQL  Py > \connect root@localhost:3306
Creating a session to 'root@localhost:3306'
Enter password: ****
Fetching schema names for autocompletion... Press ^C to stop.
Your MySQL connection id is 9
Server version: 8.0.11 MySQL Community Server (GPL)
No default schema selected; type \use <schema> to set one.

 MySQL  localhost:3306 ssl  Py > \sql
Switching to SQL mode... Commands end with ;

 MySQL  localhost:3306 ssl  SQL > SELECT @@version;
+-----------+
| @@version |
+-----------+
| 8.0.11    |
+-----------+
1 row in set (0.0012 sec)
```

```
MySQL  localhost:3306 ssl  SQL > SHUTDOWN;
```

```
MySQL  localhost:3306 ssl  SQL > \q
Bye!
```

If you get an error starting the shell that reads, `/usr/local/mysql/bin/mysqlsh:` `error while loading shared libraries: libprotobuf.so.9: cannot open shared` `object file: No such file or directory`, be sure to run the following command first:

```
$ sudo ldconfig
```

This will fix the error by ensuring that the Protobuf library is loaded in the cache.

Building MySQL Router

Building MySQL Router on Raspberry Pi is also like building MySQL Server, but the prerequisite is simply downloading the source code. Installation is a bit easier because we'll use an automated base installation script. You will explore how to build and install MySQL Router on Raspberry Pi in this section.

Note   You need only install MySQL Router on the application server. If you've been using a different server to build the server and shell, be sure to install only the router on the application server.

Preparing the Source Code

The first thing we need to do is download the MySQL Router source code. Go to `https://dev.mysql.com/downloads/router/`. From the Select Operating System drop-down box, select Source Code. Then click the Generic Linux (Architecture Independent), Compressed TAR Archive download link at the bottom of the list, as shown in Figure 7-9. You can leave that file for now, as we will need it in the next section.

Figure 7-9. *Downloading the MySQL Router source code*

Running CMake (Preparing to Compile)

The first thing we're going to do is extract the TAR file that we downloaded. You can do so with the following commands:

```
$ cd /home/pi/source
$ cp ~/Downloads/mysql-router-8.0.11.tar.gz .
$ tar -xvf mysql-router-8.0.11.tar.gz
```

This creates a folder named mysql-router-8.0.11. It is recommended that you unpack this file in a folder in the root user's home folder—for example, /home/pi/ source. The unpacking process will take a few minutes because the file contains a lot of code.

Next, we can run the CMake command. As with the MySQL server code, we will run the command from a build directory. Unlike for the server, there are no CMake options we need to specify. Listing 7-7 shows the commands to run CMake for the router and an excerpt of the sample output. As you can see, it follows a familiar pattern.

Listing 7-7. Running CMake for MySQL Router

```
$ cd /home/pi/source/mysql-router-8.0.11
$ mkdir build
$ cd build
$ cmake ..
-- The C compiler identification is GNU 6.3.0
-- The CXX compiler identification is GNU 6.3.0
-- Check for working C compiler: /usr/bin/cc
-- Check for working C compiler: /usr/bin/cc -- works
-- Detecting C compiler ABI info
-- Detecting C compiler ABI info - done
-- Detecting C compile features
-- Detecting C compile features - done
...
-- Loading module 'x_protocol'
-- Performing Test CXX_HAVE_SIGN_COMPARE
-- Performing Test CXX_HAVE_SIGN_COMPARE - Success
-- Performing Test CXX_HAVE_PEDANTIC
-- Performing Test CXX_HAVE_PEDANTIC - Success
```

```
-- Performing Test CXX_HAVE_CONVERSION
-- Performing Test CXX_HAVE_CONVERSION - Success
-- Configuring done
-- Generating done
-- Build files have been written to: /home/pi/source/mysql-router-8.0.11/build
```

Running make (Compiling)

The next step is to compile the code. As with the server code, we will use the make -j3 command to compile the code. You may see some warnings, but as with the server code, unless there are errors, you can ignore the warnings. The following shows a brief excerpt of compiling the router code. Compiling the router may take a while because it uses a newer version of Protobuf that is already part of the source code tree.

```
$ make -j3
Scanning dependencies of target router_taocrypt
Scanning dependencies of target libprotobuf-lite
Scanning dependencies of target libprotobuf_3_0
[  0%] Building CXX object ext/yassl/CMakeFiles/router_yassl.dir/src/
handshake.cpp.o
...
[100%] Linking CXX shared library ../../stage/lib/mysqlrouter/routing.so
[100%] Built target routing
```

Making the Package

The last thing we need to do is build the installation package. In this case, we will build a compressed TAR file that we will be able to copy to our initial server and install. We will use the same make package command that we used with the server code. Listing 7-8 shows a brief excerpt of building the package for the router.

Listing 7-8. Building the Package for MySQL Router

```
$ make package
...
Run CPack packaging tool...
CPack: Create package using STGZ
CPack: Install projects
```

```
CPack: - Run preinstall target for: MySQLRouter
CPack: - Install project: MySQLRouter
CPack: Create package
```
CPack: - package: /home/pi/source/mysql-router-8.0.11/build/mysql-router-8.0.11-Linux.sh generated.
```
CPack: Create package using TGZ
CPack: Install projects
CPack: - Run preinstall target for: MySQLRouter
CPack: - Install project: MySQLRouter
CPack: Create package
```
CPack: - package: /home/pi/source/mysql-router-8.0.11/build/mysql-router-8.0.11-Linux.tar.gz generated.
```
CPack: Create package using TZ
CPack: Install projects
CPack: - Run preinstall target for: MySQLRouter
CPack: - Install project: MySQLRouter
CPack: Create package
CPack: - package: /home/pi/source/mysql-router-8.0.11/build/mysql-router-8.0.11-Linux.tar.Z generated.
```

The package builds a special file named mysql-router-8.0.11-Linux.sh, which we will use to install MySQL Router on the application server.

Installing MySQL Router

The router is unique of the three MySQL products in that it has a special setup script that prepares the machine to run the router with default settings. More specifically, the router configuration will use ports 6446, 6447 for read/write and read-only using the legacy client protocol, and ports 64460, 64470 for read/write and read-only using the X Protocol.

You could use the familiar copy-and-unpack method we used for the server and shell. However, the installation does all of that for us, so we don't have to do that manually. If you'd rather use the copy-and-unpack method, here are the steps:

```
$ cd /usr/local/mysql
$ sudo cp /home/pi/source/mysql-router-8.0.11/build/mysql-router-8.0.11-Linux.tar.gz .
$ sudo tar -xvf mysql-router-8.0.11-Linux.tar.gz --strip-component=1
```

```
$ sudo rm mysql-router-8.0.11-Linux.tar.gz
```

Let's see how to use the setup script. Recall, we are installing only the router on the application server. So, if you used that server and the build machine, you can install it after you build the package. You can run the script directly from the source build folder, but you must use elevated privileges. Here is the command you can use to start the script:

```
$ sudo ./mysql-router-8.0.11-Linux.sh --prefix=/usr/local/mysql
```

When the script starts, it will generate perfunctory greetings and license data, which you are expected to read. You can skip through this data by pressing the spacebar repeatedly or shortcut the process by pressing the Q key.[5] The script will ask whether you accept the license (press Y) and where you want to install the router (reply by pressing N to change the target to /usr/local/mysql). Listing 7-9 shows a transcript of running the installer.

Listing 7-9. Installing MySQL Router via the Install Script

```
Licensing Information User Manual
MySQL Router 8.0
...
Do you accept the license? [yN]:
y
By default the mysql-router will be installed in:
   "/usr/local/mysql/mysql-router-8.0.11-Linux"
Do you want to include the subdirectory mysql-router-8.0.11-Linux?
Saying no will install in: "/usr/local/mysql" [Yn]:
n

Using target directory: /usr/local/mysql
Extracting, please wait...

Unpacking finished successfully
```

The router is installed, but we cannot configure and test it until InnoDB Cluster is set up and configured.

---

[5]I suppose we should discourage that, eh? Always read the license!

> **Note**   If you install the router manually without MySQL or built MySQL on a machine other than the application server, you may need the `libmysqlclient.so` library. Copy that file from the build machine and place it in the `/usr/local/mysql/lib` folder on the application server.

Before we get into that, let's clone the base MySQL server drive and make copies so we have four instances.

Cloning the MySQL Server Image

In this step, we will take the USB drive that we used to install MySQL Server and Shell and copy (clone) it to the other three USB drives. There are a variety of ways to do this, including a small number of tools available for Windows (few of which are free/open source). However, because we have a perfectly working application server running Linux, we'll use that. This section demonstrates how to clone the USB drive on the Raspberry Pi. You can use the same technique on other forms of Linux as well as macOS!

The first step is to ensure that we've booted our application server with the correct image. It can become quite confusing quickly if you have got a bunch of USB drives lying around—especially if you haven't marked them! It may be a good idea to make a mark on the USB drive for the application server so that you know which one it is.

Next, we need to determine the system path for the device. If you are using a desktop distribution of Linux or macOS, detecting the drive is easy: just right-click the drive and look at the properties. Or, as we must do with the Raspberry Pi, we use the fdisk utility to list the drives.

> **Tip**   Run `sudo fdisk -l` before you insert the USB drive you want to clone. Then insert the USB drive and run the command again. The one that shows up on the second pass is your target drive.

To list the devices, use the command sudo fdisk -l. You will see a list of all the drives and their statistics. If you run this before you insert the drive you want to clone and then run it again after you've inserted the drive, you can be sure of which drive you want to clone because the second pass will contain a new drive. The following shows an excerpt of running the command on the Raspberry Pi. Here, I found the new device is on /dev/sdc:

```
$ sudo fdisk -l
[sudo] password for cbell:
...
Device     Boot Start      End    Sectors  Size Id Type
/dev/sdc1          8192    93802    85611 41.8M  c W95 FAT32 (LBA)
/dev/sdc2         98304 123174911 123076608 58.7G 83 Linux
```

After you locate the device, create the image with the following command. Note that this can take a while, depending on the size of the drive. We use compression to keep the file size minimal.

```
$ sudo dd if=/dev/sdc | bzip2 > idc_clone_rpi.bz2
```

You will get no feedback during the operation, sadly. However, you can roughly check the progress by listing the size of the file as follows. Although you cannot get an exact percentage of completion, subsequent checks of this file size will assure you that the command is still running. Sorry—it's the best we can do on Linux using built-in tools. Other tools are available for Linux, but if you're going to clone the USB on a Raspberry Pi, these commands will work.

```
$ ls -lsa idc_clone_rpi.bz2
1993436 -rw-rw-r-- 1 cbell cbell 2041274368 May  9 10:00 idc_clone_rpi.bz2
```

Here is the output when the image has been created and compressed:

```
$ sudo dd if=/dev/sdc | bzip2 > idc_clone_rpi.bz2
123174912+0 records in
123174912+0 records out
63065554944 bytes (63 GB, 59 GiB) copied, 3478.5 s, 18.1 MB/s
```

After the image has been created, you can remove it and insert the next drive and then copy the image to a new USB drive with the following. Be sure to check the device list first!

```
$ bzcat idc_clone_rpi.bz2 | sudo dd of=/dev/sdc
```

Once again, you will get no feedback during the operation, but when you're finished, you can remove the drive and place it in your Raspberry Pi and boot it to verify the image.

You can also use the Etcher application we used previously to clone the image after it has been created. Just copy the `idb_clone_rpi.bz2` image to your desktop and use Etcher to copy it to the other drives.

After you've created or cloned all the USB drives, you need to make a few small changes to each drive (image). Let's do that now.

Final Configuration of the MySQL Server Instances

Now that we have four identical copies of the MySQL server, we need to make each unique. We will therefore need to boot each machine in turn with the keyboard, mouse, and monitor connected and make the changes. We need to change several things on each machine, including the following. Fortunately, the process we did earlier installing and configuring the base MySQL server has saved us a lot of time, so these changes are small. But remember, you must run these four steps on each MySQL server drive/image:

- Unique `server_id` and hostname reported

- Unique UUID

- Static IP address

- Unique hostname

To ensure that the server has a unique `server_id`, you should now edit the configuration file on each machine and choose a unique server ID (`server_id`). For example, this demonstration uses the range 1-4. Edit the configuration file with the `sudo nano /etc/my.cnf` command and set the value as shown next.. The file may not exist, and that's OK; just enter the following lines:

```
[mysqld]
server-id=1
report-host=cluster-rpi1
```

There are two items here. First is the server ID, which we discussed. The second is used by Group Replication to report the hostname to the InnoDB Cluster. This ensures that the server will have a unique hostname in the cluster. You should include this line too to make it easier to refer to the servers by hostname when we configure the cluster.

Next, we must use unique UUIDs. The UUID is stored in a file named `auto.conf` and used by the server to uniquely identify it in the server (as part of Group Replication). However, because we cloned the image, all servers have the same UUID, which is a gotcha for the cloned images. If you built each machine separately, it will be OK, because `auto.cnf` will get generated on each installation. We can force the server to regenerate the UUID by removing the `auto.conf` file. The following shows a transcript of displaying the contents of the file, removing it, starting the server, and then displaying the new contents. As you can see, this will do the trick nicely:

```
$ sudo more /usr/local/mysql/data/auto.cnf
[auto]
server-uuid=4127c169-520f-11e8-a834-b827ebcb9200
$ sudo rm /usr/local/mysql/data/auto.cnf
$ sudo /etc/init.d/mysql restart
[ ok ] Restarting mysql.server (via systemctl): mysql.server.service.
$ sudo more /usr/local/mysql/data/auto.cnf
[auto]
server-uuid=bb1e15c5-53d1-11e8-982c-b827eb6ea7ce
```

Next, we must ensure that each machine has its own unique static IP address. Recall that in the example, we used IP addresses in the range 192.168.42.241–192.168.42.244 for the MySQL servers. To set the correct IP address, once again we must edit the `dhcpcd.conf` file and set the IP address. The following shows an example of the lines added for the first MySQL server:

```
# Example static IP configuration:
interface eth0
static ip_address=192.168.42.241/24
static routers=192.168.42.1
static domain_name_servers=192.168.42.1
```

Finally, we must set the unique hostname. We do this by using the Raspberry Pi Configuration tool as we did in an earlier section. The instructions are repeated here for convenience.

Recall, we will use the hostname `cluster-rpi[1-4]`. For example, the third server setup has a hostname of `cluster-rpi3`. We will use the hostname `cluster-rpi-app` for the application server. To change the hostname, open the Raspberry Pi Configuration tool, locate the Hostname line on the first tab, and then change the text in the text box to the right. Figure 7-10 shows an example of setting the hostname for the application server.

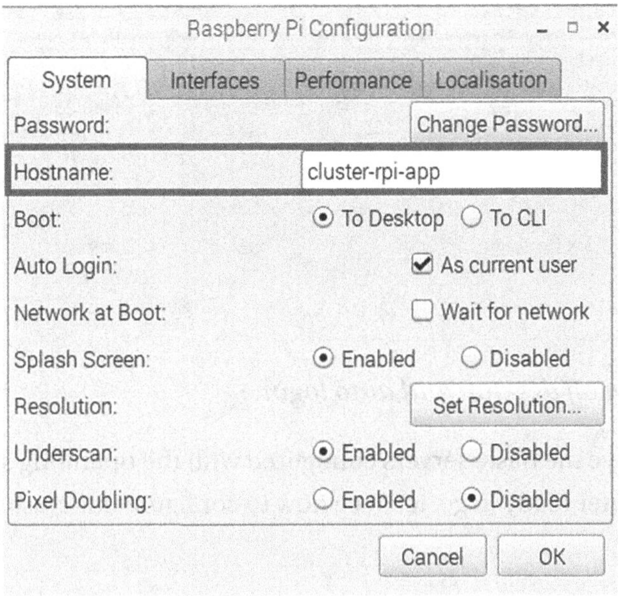

Figure 7-10. *Setting the hostname*

Remember, you must perform these steps on all four machines. If you do not customize these three items, you may have problems getting the cluster to start.

You may want to do one optional step. You may want to make the servers boot without the desktop (command-line interface) and not automatically log in. You can do this by using the Raspberry Pi Configuration tool. Just open the tool and locate the Boot and Auto Login lines, as shown in Figure 7-11. To turn off the desktop, select the To CLI radio button. To turn off automatic login, uncheck the As Current User check box.

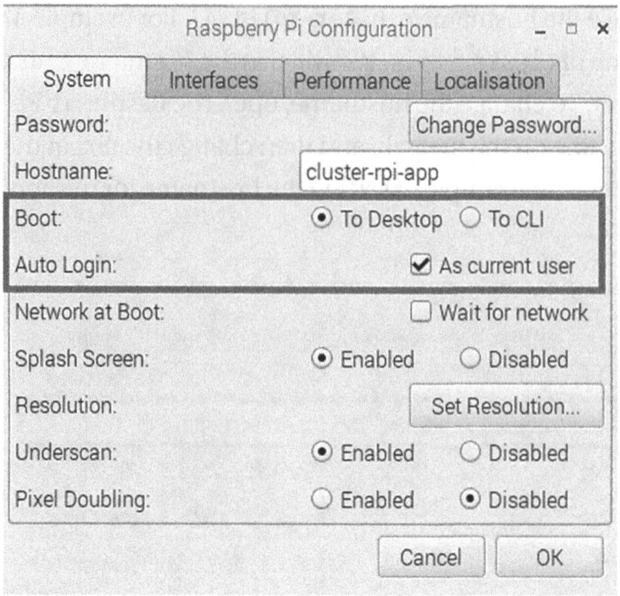

Figure 7-11. *Turn off desktop and auto login*

Now that we have the basic servers configured with the operating system, and the application and router ready to go, let's see how to configure our cluster.

Setting Up the Cluster

Now we can get into the fun part of setting up InnoDB Cluster on our small set of Raspberry Pi computers. The first thing you may want to consider is the physical layout of your test system. Recall, there is no need for a keyboard, mouse, and monitor for each of the computers. After we've powered them on and wait for them to boot, we can access them remotely. But we will still have five small Raspberry Pi computers in their own cases,[6] each connected to its own power supply and the Ethernet hub, which can make for a jumble of wires.

It is recommended that you place the Raspberry Pi computers, power supplies, and Ethernet hub in an arrangement that makes working with them easier. For example, you could bundle the wires so that they are not lying around like so much spaghetti and

---

[6]You are using a case, right? Using a Raspberry Pi without a case is not safe because anything that conducts electricity can fall on the boards, possibly causing damage. It is highly recommended that each Raspberry Pi has its own case.

then tie them with ties. Or you could find a way to mount the Raspberry Pi cases, power supplies, and Ethernet hub to a board or something to make it easier and portable. For example, you could invest in building a Pi Stack.

GOT PI STACK?

If you want to make your set of Raspberry Pi servers portable, you can build yourself a Pi Stack. There are several ways to do this, including using sets of acrylic mounting plates that are stackable. Rather than use those, I chose to use an existing 3D-printed Raspberry Pi case and add my own stacking hardware.

My Pi Stack sets all five computers, one atop the other, in a stack with brackets for mounting an Ethernet hub and power module. The following shows my Pi Stack printed in, yes, translucent purple.

If you have your own 3D printer or access to one, you can find my components on Thingiverse at www.thingiverse.com/thing:2893284.

Be sure all the servers are started and ready. For Raspberry Pi computers, you should give them about 3–5 minutes to boot up if you are not using a monitor to watch the boot sequence.

After you've situated your Raspberry Pi computers and peripherals, you should perform a critical preparation step to set up the cluster. As you may recall from Chapter 5, there is a command we can use to prepare a machine for use in the cluster. That command was unique for the sandbox installation; however, we have another method in the dba class that we can use to prepare a remote machine. This method is named dba.configure_local_instance() and takes as a parameter the connection of a local machine. Yes, this means we must run MySQL Shell on the local machine. That's why we install the shell on all machines.

Begin by powering on all the MySQL servers (you can leave the application server powered off for now). Then, from a desktop machine (or the application server if you have it powered on with a keyboard, mouse, and monitor) open a terminal and enter the following command:

```
$ ssh pi@192.168.42.241
```

This establishes a remote connection to the first MySQL server. If you have problems connecting to the machine, ensure that your desktop computer is connected to the same network and that the static IP address and hosts file on the MySQL server are set and the machine can access the network.

After the machine is connected, use MySQL Shell to run the configure local instance. We will reference the server by using localhost as the hostname and the port 3306. After we issue the method to configure the local instance, we will be prompted to provide the password for the root user. Next, we will be asked to choose how the user for administration of the cluster will be created. It is recommended for ease of working with the cluster to choose option (1), which uses the same root user, modifying it for proper access to the cluster. See the online reference manual (https://dev.mysql.com/doc/dev/mysqlsh-api-python/8.0/classmysqlsh_1_1dba_1_1_cluster.html) for more information about the other options.

Next, we will be prompted to provide the host for the user account (root) to use when logging in. For this demonstration, we will use the wildcard (%) again for ease of working with the cluster. However, for production deployments, you may want to specify a user/host combination to further secure access.

The method will then check the server to see if anything needs to be fixed, and if so, will ask whether you want to have them fixed automatically (we do, because that's part the beauty of this method).

Finally, we are given the option to restart the instance when the operation is complete so that the changes take effect. Be sure to reply yes to that prompt.

Wow, a lot goes on in this method. But again, that's what makes using the shell with InnoDB Cluster via the AdminAPI so nice—it saves us a lot of time fiddling with the small details when all we want is for it to "just work." Listing 7-10 shows a transcript of running the method on one of the servers.

Listing 7-10. Configuring the Local Instance for Use with InnoDB Cluster

```
$ mysqlsh
MySQL Shell 8.0.11

Copyright (c) 2016, 2018, Oracle and/or its affiliates. All rights reserved.

Oracle is a registered trademark of Oracle Corporation and/or its
affiliates. Other names may be trademarks of their respective
owners.

Type '\help' or '\?' for help; '\quit' to exit.

MySQL  Py > dba.configure_local_instance('localhost:3306')
Please provide the password for 'root@localhost:3306': ****
Configuring local MySQL instance listening at port 3306 for use in an
InnoDB cluster...

This instance reports its own address as cluster-rpi3

WARNING: User 'root' can only connect from localhost.
If you need to manage this instance while connected from other hosts, new
account(s) with the proper source address specification must be created.

1) Create remotely usable account for 'root' with same grants and password
2) Create a new admin account for InnoDB cluster with minimal required
grants
3) Ignore and continue
4) Cancel
```

```
Please select an option [1]: 1
Please provide a source address filter for the account (e.g: 192.168.% or %
etc) or leave empty and press Enter to cancel.
Account Host: %

Some configuration options need to be fixed:
```

Variable	Current Value	Required Value	Note
binlog_checksum	CRC32	NONE	Update the server variable
enforce_gtid_consistency	OFF	ON	Update read-only variable and restart the server
gtid_mode	OFF	ON	Update read-only variable and restart the server

```
Do you want to perform the required configuration changes? [y/n]: y
Do you want to restart the instance after configuring it? [y/n]: y

Cluster admin user 'root'@'%' created.
Configuring instance...
The instance 'localhost:3306' was configured for cluster usage.
Restarting MySQL...
MySQL server at localhost:3306 was restarted.
```

Now we have all the settings correct for this server. Be sure to perform the same step on the other three servers. If you're not sure whether the operation succeeded or you lose track of which server you've done, you can use the dba.check_instance_configuration() method to test the server for proper settings. If you see the status ok, you're finished, and the server is ready. Listing 7-11 shows an example of using this method.

Listing 7-11. Checking the Instance Configuration

```
MySQL  Py > dba.check_instance_configuration('root@localhost:3306')
Please provide the password for 'root@localhost:3306': ****
Validating local MySQL instance listening at port 3306 for use in an InnoDB
cluster...

This instance reports its own address as cluster-rpi1

Checking whether existing tables comply with Group Replication
requirements...
No incompatible tables detected

Checking instance configuration...
Instance configuration is compatible with InnoDB cluster

The instance 'localhost:3306' is valid for InnoDB cluster usage.
{
    "status": "ok"
}
```

Once we've run the command on all the servers, we're ready to configure the cluster.

Configuring the Cluster

Now we are ready to configure our server. If you haven't powered on the application server, now is a good time to do that. Be sure to connect the keyboard, mouse, and monitor. This will allow you to use the application server to remotely connect into the other machines in the cluster.

The process to configure the cluster by using remote machines is the same as that for the sandbox example in Chapter 5. Namely, we will create the server on one machine and then add the other machines to the cluster. We finish with configuring the router on the application server.

Note   Make sure all the servers are started and ready. For Raspberry Pi computers, you should give them about 3–5 minutes to boot up if you are not using a monitor to watch the boot sequence.

Let's begin by opening a remote connection to the first server (cluster-rpi1). Recall, we use SSH to connect to the remote machine. Simply open a terminal and enter one of the following commands. The first command can be used on the application server. If you are not running the command on the application server, you may need to use the second command. The only difference is that the first uses the hostname, and the second uses the IP address. Enter the password for the pi user when prompted.

```
$ ssh pi@cluster-rpi1
$ ssh pi@192.168.42.241
```

First, we connect using the shell and create the cluster. Use the name RPI_Cluster for the name of the cluster. Because we're working with hostnames we assigned ourselves and placed in the hosts file, we do not have to use IP addresses to ensure that we can connect. Recall, we can connect to the server by using the --uri option when we start the shell and use the dba.create_cluster(<name>) method to create the cluster. Listing 7-12 shows an example of using the MySQL Shell to create the cluster.

Listing 7-12. Creating the Cluster

```
$ mysqlsh --uri root@cluster-rpi1:3306
Creating a session to 'root@ cluster-rpi1:3306'
Enter password: ****
Fetching schema names for autocompletion... Press ^C to stop.
Your MySQL connection id is 19
Server version: 8.0.11 MySQL Community Server (GPL)
No default schema selected; type \use <schema> to set one.
MySQL Shell 8.0.11

Copyright (c) 2016, 2018, Oracle and/or its affiliates. All rights reserved.

Oracle is a registered trademark of Oracle Corporation and/or its
affiliates. Other names may be trademarks of their respective
owners.

Type '\help' or '\?' for help; '\quit' to exit.

 MySQL  cluster-rpi1:3306 ssl  Py > cluster = dba.create_cluster('RPI_Cluster')
A new InnoDB cluster will be created on instance 'root@cluster-rpi1:3306'.
```

Validating instance at cluster-rpi1:3306...

This instance reports its own address as cluster-rpi1

Instance configuration is suitable.
Creating InnoDB cluster 'RPI_Cluster' on 'root@cluster-rpi1:3306'...
Adding Seed Instance...

Cluster successfully created. Use Cluster.add_instance() to add MySQL
instances.
At least 3 instances are needed for the cluster to be able to withstand up to
one server failure.

Next, we add the instances starting with cluster-rpi2 (192.168.42.242). But first, let's check the cluster status. Listing 7-13 shows an example of the output expected when we run the cluster.status() method. Recall, if you have exited the shell, you will have to retrieve the cluster with the command cluster = dba.get_cluster().

Listing 7-13. Checking the Status of the Cluster

```
MySQL  cluster-rpi1:33060+ ssl  Py > cluster.status()
{
    "clusterName": "RPI_Cluster",
    "defaultReplicaSet": {
        "name": "default",
        "primary": "cluster-rpi1:3306",
        "ssl": "REQUIRED",
        "status": "OK_NO_TOLERANCE",
        "statusText": "Cluster is NOT tolerant to any failures.",
        "topology": {
            "cluster-rpi1:3306": {
                "address": "cluster-rpi1:3306",
                "mode": "R/W",
                "readReplicas": {},
                "role": "HA",
                "status": "ONLINE"
            }
        }
```

```
    },
    "groupInformationSourceMember": "mysql://root@cluster-rpi1:3306"
}
```

Next, let's add each server instance starting with cluster-rpi2. Listing 7-14 shows the command to add the instance to the cluster. Notice that we can do this remotely while logged into the cluster-rpi1 machine.

Listing 7-14. Adding an Instance to the Cluster

```
 MySQL  cluster-rpi1:33060+ ssl  Py > cluster.add_instance('root@cluster-
 rpi2:3306')
A new instance will be added to the InnoDB cluster. Depending on the amount
of data on the cluster this might take from a few seconds to several hours.

Please provide the password for 'root@cluster-rpi2:3306': ****
Adding instance to the cluster ...

Validating instance at cluster-rpi2:3306...

This instance reports its own address as cluster-rpi2

Instance configuration is suitable.
The instance 'root@cluster-rpi2:3306' was successfully added to the
cluster.
```

If we check the status again, we will see the new instance added, but we may see the status as RECOVERING for a little while. This is because Group Replication is negotiating with the new primary. Listing 7-15 shows the status after adding the first instance.

Listing 7-15. Cluster Status After the First Instance Is Added

```
 MySQL  cluster-rpi1:33060+ ssl  Py > cluster.status()
{
    "clusterName": "RPI_Cluster",
    "defaultReplicaSet": {
        "name": "default",
        "primary": "cluster-rpi1:3306",
```

```
    "ssl": "REQUIRED",
    "status": "OK_NO_TOLERANCE",
    "statusText": "Cluster is NOT tolerant to any failures. 1 member is
    not active",
    "topology": {
        "cluster-rpi1:3306": {
            "address": "cluster-rpi1:3306",
            "mode": "R/W",
            "readReplicas": {},
            "role": "HA",
            "status": "ONLINE"
        },
        "cluster-rpi2:3306": {
            "address": "cluster-rpi2:3306",
            "mode": "R/O",
            "readReplicas": {},
            "role": "HA",
            "status": "RECOVERING"
        }
    }
},
"groupInformationSourceMember": "mysql://root@cluster-rpi1:3306"
}
```

Notice that the state of the new server is RECOVERING. This is normal. On the
Raspberry Pi, this process can take a while, but eventually you will see the status change
to ONLINE, as shown in Listing 7-16.

Listing 7-16. Cluster Status After the First Instance Is Reconciled

```
MySQL   cluster-rpi1:33060+ ssl  Py > cluster.status()
{
    "clusterName": "RPI_Cluster",
    "defaultReplicaSet": {
        "name": "default",
        "primary": "cluster-rpi1:3306",
        "ssl": "REQUIRED",
```

```
    "status": "OK_NO_TOLERANCE",
    "statusText": "Cluster is NOT tolerant to any failures.",
    "topology": {
        "cluster-rpi1:3306": {
            "address": "cluster-rpi1:3306",
            "mode": "R/W",
            "readReplicas": {},
            "role": "HA",
            "status": "ONLINE"
        },
        "cluster-rpi2:3306": {
            "address": "cluster-rpi2:3306",
            "mode": "R/O",
            "readReplicas": {},
            "role": "HA",
            "status": "ONLINE"
        }
    }
},
    "groupInformationSourceMember": "mysql://root@cluster-rpi1:3306"
}
```

Now, let's add the other two instances. Listing 7-17 shows the commands to add cluster-rpi3 and cluster-rpi4.

Listing 7-17. Adding the Remaining Instances to the Cluster

```
 MySQL  cluster-rpi1:33060+ ssl  Py > cluster.add_instance('root@cluster-
 rpi3:3306')
A new instance will be added to the InnoDB cluster. Depending on the amount
of data on the cluster this might take from a few seconds to several hours.

Please provide the password for 'root@cluster-rpi3:3306': ****
Adding instance to the cluster ...

Validating instance at cluster-rpi3:3306...
```

This instance reports its own address as cluster-rpi3

Instance configuration is suitable.
The instance 'root@cluster-rpi3:3306' was successfully added to the
cluster.

```
 MySQL  cluster-rpi1:33060+ ssl  Py > cluster.add_instance('root@cluster-
 rpi4:3306')
```
A new instance will be added to the InnoDB cluster. Depending on the amount
of
data on the cluster this might take from a few seconds to several hours.

Please provide the password for 'root@cluster-rpi4:3306': ****
Adding instance to the cluster ...

Validating instance at cluster-rpi4:3306...

This instance reports its own address as cluster-rpi4

Instance configuration is suitable.
The instance 'root@cluster-rpi4:3306' was successfully added to the
cluster.

And, after a bit, we should see the status all clear and the status of the cluster as
ONLINE and ready, as shown in Listing 7-18.

Listing 7-18. Cluster Status After All Instances Are Added and Reconciled

```
 MySQL  cluster-rpi1:33060+ ssl  Py > cluster.status()
{
    "clusterName": "RPI_Cluster",
    "defaultReplicaSet": {
        "name": "default",
        "primary": "cluster-rpi1:3306",
        "ssl": "REQUIRED",
        "status": "OK_PARTIAL",
        "statusText": "Cluster is ONLINE and can tolerate up to ONE
        failure. 1 member is not active",
        "topology": {
            "cluster-rpi1:3306": {
```

```
                "address": "cluster-rpi1:3306",
                "mode": "R/W",
                "readReplicas": {},
                "role": "HA",
                "status": "ONLINE"
            },
            "cluster-rpi2:3306": {
                "address": "cluster-rpi2:3306",
                "mode": "R/O",
                "readReplicas": {},
                "role": "HA",
                "status": "ONLINE"
            },
            "cluster-rpi3:3306": {
                "address": "cluster-rpi3:3306",
                "mode": "R/O",
                "readReplicas": {},
                "role": "HA",
                "status": "RECOVERING"
            },
            "cluster-rpi4:3306": {
                "address": "cluster-rpi4:3306",
                "mode": "R/O",
                "readReplicas": {},
                "role": "HA",
                "status": "ONLINE"
            }
        }
    },
    "groupInformationSourceMember": "mysql://root@cluster-rpi1:3306"
}
```

Now, we're ready to bootstrap the router.

Bootstrapping the Router

Although not strictly part of configuring the cluster, the next step in the process is to bootstrap (configure) MySQL Router for use with applications that access the cluster. If you are not already logged in to the application server, you should do so now.

Recall, bootstrapping the router requires providing the --boostrap option, the user account using the --user option, and the URL to connect to one of the servers in the cluster. Listing 7-19 shows the command to bootstrap the router on the application server along with an example transcript of the execution.

Listing 7-19. Bootstrapping MySQL Router on the Application Server

```
$ sudo /usr/local/mysql/bin/mysqlrouter --bootstrap root@cluster-rpi4:3306
--user=pi
Please enter MySQL password for root:

Bootstrapping system MySQL Router instance...
Module " not registered with logger - logging the following message as
'main' instead
MySQL Router  has now been configured for the InnoDB cluster 'RPI_Cluster'.

The following connection information can be used to connect to the cluster.

Classic MySQL protocol connections to cluster 'RPI_Cluster':
- Read/Write Connections: localhost:6446
- Read/Only Connections: localhost:6447
X protocol connections to cluster 'RPI_Cluster':
- Read/Write Connections: localhost:64460
- Read/Only Connections: localhost:64470
```

Here's what the bootstrap operation has done to create the configuration file. It's almost what we need; if you manually installed the router, we may need to add the plugin_folder path, as shown in Listing 7-20.

Listing 7-20. Example MySQL Router Configuration File

```
$ sudo more /usr/local/mysql/lib/mysql-router/mysqlrouter.conf
# File automatically generated during MySQL Router bootstrap
[DEFAULT]
user=pi
plugin_folder=/usr/local/mysql/lib/mysqlrouter
logging_folder=/usr/local/mysql/lib/mysql-router/log
runtime_folder=/usr/local/mysql/lib/mysql-router/run
data_folder=/usr/local/mysql/lib/mysql-router/data
keyring_path=/usr/local/mysql/lib/mysql-router/data/keyring
master_key_path=/usr/local/mysql/lib/mysql-router/mysqlrouter.key
connect_timeout=30
read_timeout=30

[logger]
level = INFO

[metadata_cache:RPI_Cluster]
router_id=2
bootstrap_server_addresses=mysql://cluster-rpi1:3306,mysql://cluster-
rpi2:3306,mysql://cluster-rpi4:3306,mysql://cluster-rpi3:3306
user=mysql_router2_ty03b9q0tzzg
metadata_cluster=RPI_Cluster
ttl=5

[routing:RPI_Cluster_default_rw]
bind_address=0.0.0.0
bind_port=6446
destinations=metadata-cache://RPI_Cluster/default?role=PRIMARY
routing_strategy=round-robin
protocol=classic

[routing:RPI_Cluster_default_ro]
bind_address=0.0.0.0
bind_port=6447
destinations=metadata-cache://RPI_Cluster/default?role=SECONDARY
routing_strategy=round-robin
protocol=classic
```

```
[routing:RPI_Cluster_default_x_rw]
bind_address=0.0.0.0
bind_port=64460
destinations=metadata-cache://RPI_Cluster/default?role=PRIMARY
routing_strategy=round-robin
protocol=x

[routing:RPI_Cluster_default_x_ro]
bind_address=0.0.0.0
bind_port=64470
destinations=metadata-cache://RPI_Cluster/default?role=SECONDARY
routing_strategy=round-robin
protocol=x
```

Now, we run the router by using the following command:

```
$ sudo /usr/local/mysql/bin/mysqlrouter -c /usr/local/mysql/lib/mysql-
router/mysqlrouter.conf --user=pi &
```

If you want to look at the log, you can find it here:

```
$ sudo more /usr/local/mysql/lib/mysql-router/log/mysqlrouter.log
```

That's it! Our cluster is configured and ready for use. Although we don't have an application to test the cluster (but you will see one in the next chapter), we can use a simple Python application to test the cluster via the router.

Testing the Cluster

To test the cluster, you can manually connect to one of the servers via the router with the following command. In this case, we can log in via the port 6446 and then perform a query to return the variable report_host, which will show the host to which we are connected. The following shows what this may look like when run via MySQL Shell in batch mode:

```
$ mysqlsh root@cluster-rpi-app:6446 --sql -e "SHOW VARIABLES LIKE
'report_host'"
Enter password: ****
+---------------+-------------+
| Variable_name | Value       |
+---------------+-------------+
| report_host   | cluster-rp1 |
+---------------+-------------+
```

This shows us the router is forwarding our request to one of the servers in the cluster (the read/write server because we used port 6446), but where is the fun in that?

Let's use Python to test the cluster. In the next chapter, you will see a sample high availability application that is written in Python. To run that application— and better still, to test the router—we will need to download and install the Connector/Python database connector on the application server.

To download Connector/Python, visit `https://dev.mysql.com/downloads/connector/python/`From the Select Operating System drop-down box, select Platform Independent and then select the file named Platform Independent (Architecture Independent), Compressed TAR Archive, as shown in Figure 7-12.

Figure 7-12. *Download MySQL Connector/Python*

After the file is downloaded, you can extract the package and then run the Python setup command shown here; notice that this command requires elevated privileges:

```
$ tar -xvf mysql-connector-python-8.0.11.tar.gz
...
$ sudo python3 ./setup.py install
running install
Not Installing MySQL C Extension
running build
running build_py
creating build/lib
```

```
creating build/lib/mysql
copying lib/mysql/__init__.py -> build/lib/mysql
creating build/lib/mysql/connector
...
Copying lib/mysql_connector_python.egg-info to /usr/local/lib/python3.5/
dist-packages/mysql_connector_python-8.0.11.egg-info
```

Now that we have Connector/Python installed, we can run a test. We'll run it from the application server because that is where we will run our test application. Listing 7-21 shows a simple Python script to connect to the application server via the router and run a simple SQL statement.

Listing 7-21. Simple Python Script for Testing the Cluster

```python
import mysql.connector
conn_dict = {
'user':'root',
'passwd':'root',
'port':6446,
'host':'cluster-rpi-app',
}
conn = mysql.connector.connect(**conn_dict)
cur = conn.cursor()
res = cur.execute("SHOW DATABASES")
for row in cur:
  print(row)
cur.close()
conn.close()
```

You can either create a file and place the script commands in the file and execute it via MySQL Shell or you can use the Python console. Listing 7-22 shows an example of using the Python console. We start the Python console simply by using the command python from a terminal. You can run this script on any machine you want (for example, the application server), but it may be best to run it from your desktop computer. In that case, be sure to use the IP address of the application server as shown in the listing.

Listing 7-22. Testing the Cluster via the Python Console

```
C:\Users\cbell> python
Python 3.4.4 (v3.4.4:737efcadf5a6, Dec 20 2015, 20:20:57) [MSC v.1600 64
bit (AMD64)] on win32
Type "help", "copyright", "credits" or "license" for more information.
>>> import mysql.connector
>>> conn_dict = {
... 'user':'root',
... 'passwd':'root',
... 'port':3306,
... 'host':'localhost',
... }
>>> conn = mysql.connector.connect(**conn_dict)
>>> cur = conn.cursor()
>>> res = cur.execute("SHOW DATABASES")
>>> for row in cur:
...     print(row)
...
('information_schema',)
('mysql',)
('performance_schema',)
('sys',)
('world_x',)
>>> cur.close()
True
>>> conn.close()
>>> quit()
```

OK, now we know the cluster works and the router is configured correctly. We can move on to see how a small, high-availability application may be developed to use the cluster.

Shutting Down and Restarting the Cluster

Ordinarily, an InnoDB Cluster (or any high-availability system) would never be completely shut down. In fact, keeping the system running, always, is the goal. However, for our development cluster running on a set of Raspberry Pi computers, we likely won't want to allow the machines to run for an extended period. We not only want to power down the cluster, but also may want to power it back on later. This section explains one method to safely power down the cluster and then power it back on.

Shutting Down the Cluster

Simply put, the InnoDB Cluster is not designed to be powered on and off at will. Rather, powering down all the servers will cause the cluster to be in a complete loss of the cluster continuity. Although this would be very bad for a production system, for our development cluster (or any one similar), we may indeed want to power it down when not using it.

So, what do you do? The AdminAPI contains methods in the dba module to recover a cluster from complete loss. This will only work, however, if you perform a controlled shutdown of the servers in the cluster. The following outlines a process that you can use to power down your cluster:

1. Get the cluster status and note the read/write server.

2. Connect to each of the read-only servers and shut them down.

3. Shut down the read/write server.

Recall, we can connect to any machine in the cluster, fetch the cluster, and use the status() method to find the read/write server. Connecting to the read-only servers to shut them down should be done via MySQL Shell or the MySQL client issuing the shutdown SQL command:

```
$ mysqlsh --uri root@192.168.42.242:3306 --sql -e "SHUTDOWN"
```

Repeat this command for the other read-only servers and then for the read/write server. Make note of which server is the read/write server. At this point, you can shut down each of the Raspberry Pi computers with the following command:

```
$ sudo shutdown -h now
```

Restarting the Cluster

You may expect the cluster to reestablish itself simply by restarting all the servers in the cluster, but it doesn't work that way. When restarting the cluster from scratch, we must use a special method in the AdminAPI. This method works for clusters that have not suffered any errors—those that have been shut down successfully. This is known as *recovering* the cluster from total outage. However, this works only if all servers have been rebooted, MySQL has started on all of them, and they can access the network (and each other).

Caution   Make sure all servers are powered on and MySQL is running and accessible via the network before attempting to restart the cluster.

The following demonstrates recovering the cluster from total outage. Specifically, the servers have all been restarted (powered off and restarted), and you need to restart the cluster from the last known good position. We will use the dba.reboot_cluster_from_complete_outage() method to reboot the cluster. First, log into the read/write server as noted when you shut down the servers and run the command as shown here:

```
MySQL  localhost:33060+ ssl  Py > cluster = dba.reboot_cluster_from_
complete_outage('RPI_Cluster')
Reconfiguring the cluster 'RPI_Cluster' from complete outage...

The instance '192.168.42.244:3306' was part of the cluster configuration.
Would you like to rejoin it to the cluster? [y/N]: y

The instance '192.168.42.243:3306' was part of the cluster configuration.
Would you like to rejoin it to the cluster? [y/N]: y

The instance '192.168.42.242:3306' was part of the cluster configuration.
Would you like to rejoin it to the cluster? [y/N]: y

The cluster was successfully rebooted.
```

The command reads the cluster metadata and attempts to reconnect (rejoin) all the servers. If this works, you will see messages indicating the cluster was rebooted. If you encounter errors, make sure all the servers are running and can access the network, correct any issues, and retry the command. If it still doesn't work, see the "Last Resort" section in Chapter 9 for how to reset the cluster.

Summary

Building a high-availability MySQL solution has been made considerably easier with the MySQL 8.0.11 release. The many tools and resources available make installing and configuring InnoDB Cluster and its components a simple affair. Recall from earlier chapters, this all happens while suppressing the complexity of Group Replication. Clearly, MySQL has come a long way from a simple Internet back-end database store.

This chapter presented a development deployment using several, separate MySQL machines. We used Raspberry Pi computers to keep costs down and to help make any mistakes or accidental configurations nearly cost-free. After all, who wants to tell the IT manager that they must rebuild the developer database server because we were testing something? Maybe some would get away with that, but few of us are brave enough to tempt fate (and accept the consequences).

As you have seen, deploying InnoDB Cluster to a set of servers is not much more difficult than using the sandbox method. It merely means we have some remote connections to make and some minor settings to change to ensure that our servers are communicating properly.

Furthermore, now that we have a development environment with which to test our applications that we want to build into a high-availability MySQL solution, we can look at the rest of the pieces of knowledge needed to help us plan for deploying InnoDB Cluster into production.

In the next chapter, you will see how to build a basic high-availability application that uses the router and stores data in the cluster.

CHAPTER 8

Example Application

Now that you've learned how to set up InnoDB Cluster on a small set of test servers, complete with an application server and the router, you are ready to complete our walk-through with an example application. Rather than conclude the tutorial with the simple Python script from Chapter 7, your enlightenment can be complete by developing a simple yet fully functional high-availability application. This application will be written so that write requests are directed through the router to the current read/write server, and read requests directed also through the router to the read-only server queue.

Although this may not seem much different from what a normal application may do, the difference is significant when you consider that the application must be written to tolerate failures as they occur in the cluster. Remember, the router will reroute our connections, but we must retry any open connections to get the current live connection (route).

In this chapter, you will see how to develop a high-availability web-based application. We will be using Python for the application because it's easy to learn and the code reads with a level of clarity better than other languages. But don't worry if you prefer another language. You can easily rewrite the code in this chapter in any of the languages that have MySQL database connectors.

Let's begin with an overview of what this example application will do and how it will work. Fortunately, all the source code is available for download from the Apress book web site, so you don't have to enter the code by hand.

Tip   See `www.apress.com/us/book/9781484238844` to download the complete source code for this chapter.

To get started, you must first understand how the sample application is designed and how it works. After all, the best examples should be something you can use in your own environment; the example must be complex enough and complete enough to be meaningful.

© Charles Bell 2018
C. Bell, *Introducing InnoDB Cluster*, https://doi.org/10.1007/978-1-4842-3885-1_8

Overview

The example application we will write in this chapter is a simple grocery or to-do list. It is deliberately small and limited in functionality because we want to focus on the basic mechanics of writing an application for InnoDB Cluster rather than spending time on tricky or cool ways to write user interfaces or application code. For example, it is a single-user application, whereas high-availability applications are multiuser. Removing the multiuser aspect keeps the application much simpler and easier to use for a wider audience. Finally, the error-handling code is rudimentary.[1]

This is important because we do not need a massively complex, fully featured, enterprise-grade application to test MySQL InnoDB Cluster, especially for those new to the technology (or MySQL). Keeping the application simple on purpose— user interface and functionality—means we can focus on the basic functionality of a high-availability application as it interacts with data in the database.

We have only the four basic data functions to consider; create, read, update, and delete (CRUD). We will be using MySQL Connector/Python to write the database code to implement each of these functions. In fact, we will develop a separate module for handling the database code, giving us one code module for the user interface (made up of several related files), and a single code module for the database code.

The application will present a list of items (to-do, shopping items, and so forth) as the default view (a read action). Users can then create new items to add to the list or click an item to update or delete it in a separate, detail view. Users can tick items as "done" or "purchased" and hide those items (or reveal them). All in all, it's a simple application to manage a list.

The user interface, on the other hand, complicates things a bit. We can mitigate that by using a user-interface design that is familiar. For this, we will use a web application. Unfortunately, writing a web application in pure Python is tedious and requires more knowledge of the way web applications work than what we can expect in a work of this size.

---

[1]Experienced developers know that error-handling code is often longer than the code required to implement the functionality of the application. Because this is an example used in controlled situations, error handling is omitted for brevity.

To overcome that challenge, we will use one of the popular Python web application frameworks. In this case, we will use Flask, complete with a primer, tutorial, and walk-through of the user-interface code. As you will see, Flask is also easy to learn, with only a moderate number of nuances and concepts. Flask was originally developed by Armin Ronacher and has proven to be one of the easiest and most stable web platforms for Python.

Because this is a simplified application, the user-interface code is minimal in design and implementation. Savvy developers may spot places where the code may need to be improved for enterprise-level service, but again, that isn't a concern for an experiment such as this. However, feel free to embellish and improve the application as you see fit. In fact, there will be suggestions for things you can do to expand the application if you choose to do so at the end of the chapter.

Let's get started by taking a short journey into learning Flask.

Getting Started with Flask

If you want to follow along and implement the sample project, you will need a few things installed on your computer to get going. This section will help you prepare your computer with the tools needed—what you need to install and how to configure your environment. You will also see a short primer on the user-interface tools.

Because we will be developing this application to run on the Raspberry Pi application server (`cluster-rpi-app`), we will be installing the tools we need on that system. If you haven't done so already, go ahead and set up your application server with a keyboard, mouse, and monitor and then boot and log in. All commands will be run from a terminal window unless otherwise specified.

Set Up Your Environment

The changes to your environment are not difficult, nor are they lengthy. We will be installing Flask and a few extensions that are needed for the application user interface. Flask is one of several web libraries you can use with Python. These web libraries make developing web applications with Python much easier than using raw HTML code and writing your own handlers and code for the requests. Plus, Flask is not difficult to learn.

Table 8-1 lists the libraries we need to install. The table lists the name of the library/ extension, a short description, and the URL for the product documentation.

Table 8-1. *Required Libraries*

Library	Description	Documentation
Flask	Python Web API	`http://flask.pocoo.org/docs/0.12/installation/`
Flask-Script	Scripting support for Flask	`https://flask-script.readthedocs.io/en/latest/`
Flask-Bootstrap	User-interface improvements and enhancements	`https://pythonhosted.org/Flask-Bootstrap/`
Flask-WTF	WTForms integration	`https://flask-wtf.readthedocs.io/en/latest/` `https://wtforms.readthedocs.io/en/latest/`

Of course, you should already have Python installed on your system because it comes with the Raspberry Pi operating system (recall, the *Pi* is short for *Python*).

To install the libraries, we can use the Python package manager, `pip3`, to install the libraries from the command line. The `pip3` utility is also included on the Raspberry Pi and is designed to install packages for use with Python version 3.

Note   If you have multiple versions of Python installed on your system, the `pip` command will install into whichever Python version environment is the default. To use `pip` to install to a specific version, use `pipN`, where N is the version. For example, `pip3` installs packages in the Python 3 environment.

The `pip` command is handy because it makes installing registered Python packages—those packages registered in the Python Package Index, abbreviated as PyPI[2] (`https://pypi.python.org/pypi`)—very easy. The `pip` command will download, unpack, and install using a single command. Let's discover how to install each of the packages we need.

---

[2]PyPI is also called the cheese shop, which is a reference to the Cheese Shop skit from *Monty Python's Flying Circus* (`https://en.wikipedia.org/wiki/Cheese_Shop_sketch`).

Listing 8-1 demonstrates how to install Flask and the supporting libraries by using the pip3 commands for each library (Flask, Flask-Script, Flask-Bootstrap, and Flask-WTF).

Listing 8-1. Installing Flask

```
$ sudo pip3 install Flask
Collecting Flask
  Downloading https://files.pythonhosted.org/packages/7f/e7/08578774ed4536
  d3242b14dacb4696386634607af824ea997202cd0edb4b/Flask-1.0.2-py2.py3-none-
  any.whl (91kB)
    100% |████████████████████████████████| 92kB 1.6MB/s
Requirement already satisfied: click>=5.1 in /usr/lib/python3/dist-packages
(from Flask)
Collecting Jinja2>=2.10 (from Flask)
  Downloading https://files.pythonhosted.org/packages/7f/ff/
  ae64bacdfc95f27a016a7bed8e8686763ba4d277a78ca76f32659220a731/Jinja2-2.10-
  py2.py3-none-any.whl (126kB)
    100% |████████████████████████████████| 133kB 1.3MB/s
Requirement already satisfied: itsdangerous>=0.24 in /usr/lib/python3/dist-
packages (from Flask)
Collecting Werkzeug>=0.14 (from Flask)
  Downloading https://files.pythonhosted.org/packages/20/c4/12e3e56473e5237
  5aa29c4764e70d1b8f3efa6682bef8d0aae04fe335243/Werkzeug-0.14.1-py2.py3-
  none-any.whl (322kB)
    100% |████████████████████████████████| 327kB 637kB/s
Requirement already satisfied: MarkupSafe>=0.23 in /usr/lib/python3/dist-
packages (from Jinja2>=2.10->Flask)
Installing collected packages: Jinja2, Werkzeug, Flask
  Found existing installation: Jinja2 2.8
    Not uninstalling jinja2 at /usr/lib/python3/dist-packages, outside
    environment /usr
  Found existing installation: Werkzeug 0.11.15
    Not uninstalling werkzeug at /usr/lib/python3/dist-packages, outside
    environment /usr
Successfully installed Flask-1.0.2 Jinja2-2.10 Werkzeug-0.14.1
```

$ sudo pip3 install Flask-Script
```
Collecting Flask-Script
  Downloading https://www.piwheels.org/simple/flask-script/Flask_Script-
  2.0.6-py3-none-any.whl
Collecting Flask (from Flask-Script)
  Downloading https://files.pythonhosted.org/packages/7f/e7/08578774ed4536
  d3242b14dacb4696386634607af824ea997202cd0edb4b/Flask-1.0.2-py2.py3-none-
  any.whl (91kB)
    100% |███████████████████████████████| 92kB 2.1MB/s
Collecting click>=5.1 (from Flask->Flask-Script)
  Downloading https://files.pythonhosted.org/packages/34/c1/8806f99713ddb99
  3c5366c362b2f908f18269f8d792aff1abfd700775a77/click-6.7-py2.py3-none-any.
  whl (71kB)
    100% |███████████████████████████████| 71kB 1.0MB/s
Installing collected packages: Flask-Script
Successfully installed Flask-Script-2.0.6
```

$ sudo pip3 install Flask-Bootstrap
```
Collecting Flask-Bootstrap
  Downloading https://www.piwheels.org/simple/flask-bootstrap/Flask_
  Bootstrap-3.3.7.1-py3-none-any.whl (461kB)
    100% |███████████████████████████████| 471kB 25kB/s
Collecting visitor (from Flask-Bootstrap)
  Downloading https://www.piwheels.org/simple/visitor/visitor-0.1.3-py3-
  none-any.whl
Collecting dominate (from Flask-Bootstrap)
  Downloading https://www.piwheels.org/simple/dominate/dominate-2.3.1-py3-
  none-any.whl
Requirement already satisfied: Flask>=0.8 in /usr/lib/python3/dist-packages
(from Flask-Bootstrap)
Installing collected packages: visitor, dominate, Flask-Bootstrap
Successfully installed Flask-Bootstrap-3.3.7.1 dominate-2.3.1 visitor-0.1.3
```

$ sudo pip3 install Flask-WTF
```
Collecting Flask-WTF
```

```
Downloading https://files.pythonhosted.org/packages/60/3a/58c629472d1053
9ae5167dc7c1fecfa95dd7d0b7864623931e3776438a24/Flask_WTF-0.14.2-py2.py3-
none-any.whl
Requirement already satisfied: Flask in /usr/lib/python3/dist-packages
(from Flask-WTF)
Collecting WTForms (from Flask-WTF)
Downloading https://www.piwheels.org/simple/wtforms/WTForms-2.1-py2.py3-
none-any.whl (140kB)
    100% |████████████████████████████████| 143kB 41kB/s
Installing collected packages: WTForms, Flask-WTF
Successfully installed Flask-WTF-0.14.2 WTForms-2.1
```

Notice the command downloads the necessary components, extracts them, and then runs the setup for each. In this case, Flask is composed of several components including Werkzeug, MarkupSafe, and Jinja2. You will learn more about some of these in the upcoming "Flask Primer" section.

You should also have the MySQL Connector/Python 8.0.11 or later database connector installed. If you did not install it as part of the walk-through for Chapter 7, see the "Testing the Cluster" section in that chapter and install the database connector.

Now that our computer is set up, let's take a crash course on Flask and its associated extensions.

Flask Primer

Flask is one of several web application libraries (sometimes called *frameworks* or *application programming interfaces*, or APIs) for use with Python. Flask is unique among the choices in that it is small and, after you are familiar with how it works, easy to use. After you write the initialization code, most of your work with Flask will be limited to creating web pages, redirecting responses, and writing your feature code.

Flask is considered a micro framework because it is small and lightweight, and it doesn't force you into a box, writing code specifically to interact with the framework. It provides everything you need, and nothing you don't, leaving the choice of what to use in your code up to you.

Flask is made up of two major components providing its basic functionality: a Web Server Gateway Interface (WSGI) that handles all the work hosting web pages, and a template library for easier web page development that reduces the need to learn HTML, removes repetitive constructs, and provides a scripting capability for HTML code. The WSGI component is named *Werkzeug*, which loosely translated from German means *work stuff* (http://werkzeug.pocoo.org/). The template component is named *Jinja2* and is modeled after Django (http://jinja.pocoo.org/docs/2.10/). Both were developed and are maintained by the originators of Flask. Finally, both components are installed when you install Flask.

Flask is also an extensible library, allowing other developers to create additions (extensions) to the basic library to add functionality. You saw how to install some of the extensions available for Flask in the previous section. We will be using the scripting, bootstrap, and WTForms extensions in this chapter. Having the ability to pick and choose the extensions you want means you can keep your application as small as necessary, adding only what you need.

One of the components that you may consider "missing" from Flask is the ability to interact with other services like database systems. This was a purposeful design, and functionality like this can be achieved through extensions. In fact, several database extensions are available for Flask, including those that allow you to work with MySQL. However, because we want to use the application with InnoDB Cluster, we must use the Oracle-provided connector, MySQL Connector/Python.

Flask, together with the extensions described previously, provides all the wiring and plumbing you need to make a web application in Python. It removes almost all the burdens required to write web applications, such as interpreting client response packets, routing, HTML form handling, and more. If you've ever written a web application in Python, you will appreciate the ability to create robust web pages without the complexity of writing HTML and style sheets. Once you're familiar with how to use Flask, it will allow you to focus on the code for your application rather than spending a lot of time writing the user interface.

Now, let's get started learning Flask! If you take your time and try the sample application, your first Flask application will work on the first try. The hardest part of learning Flask is already past—installing Flask and its extensions. The rest is learning the concepts of writing applications in Flask. Before we do that, let's learn more about the terminology in Flask as well as how to set up the base code we will use to initialize the application instance that we will be using in this chapter.

Tip   If you want to explore Flask further, consider reading the online documentation, user guide, and examples at `http://flask.pocoo.org/docs/0.12/`.

Terminology

Flask is designed to reduce a lot of the tedium of writing web applications. In Flask parlance, a web page is rendered using two parts of your code: a *view*, which is defined in the HTML file(s), and a *route*, which processes the requests from a client. Recall, we can see one of two requests: a GET request that requests loading of a web page (read from the client's perspective), and a POST request that sends data from the client via the web page to the server (write from the client's perspective). Both requests are handled in Flask by using functions you define.

These functions then render the web page to send back to the client to satisfy the request. Flask calls the functions *view functions* (or *views* for short). The way Flask knows which method to call is by using decorators that identify the URL path (called a *route* in Flask). You can decorate a function with one or more routes, making it possible to provide multiple ways to reach the view. The decorator used is `@app.route(<path>)`. The following shows an example of multiple routes for a view function:

```
@app.route('/list_item', methods=['GET', 'POST'])
@app.route('/list_item/<string:item_selected>', methods=['GET', 'POST'])
def list_view(isbn_selected=None):
    notes = None
    form = ListForm()
...
    if request.method == 'POST':
        pass
    return render_template("list.html", form=form)
```

Notice that there are multiple decorators. The first is `list`, which allows us to use a URL like `localhost:5000/list_item`, which causes Flask to route execution to the `list_view()` function. The second is `list_item/<item_selected>`, which demonstrates how to use variables to pass information to the view. In this case, if the user (the application) uses the URL `localhost:5000/list_item/9`, Flask places the value, 9, in the `item_selected` variable. In this way, we can pass information dynamically to our views.

Notice also that the routes specify the methods allowed for each route. In this application, we can have a GET or POST for either route. If you leave these off the decorator, the default is GET only, making the web page read-only.

Finally, notice that at the end of the function, we return with a call to the render_ template() function (imported from the Flask module) which tells Flask to return (refresh) the web page with data we've acquired or assigned. The web page, book.html is called a *form* in Flask. It is this concept that we will use to retrieve information from the database and send it to the user. We can return a simple HTML string (or an entire file) or what is called a form. Because we are using the Flask-WTF and WTForms extensions, we can return a template rendered as a form class. We will discuss forms, form classes, and other routes and views for the chapter project in a later section. As you will see, templates are another powerful feature, making it easy to create web pages.

WHAT'S A DECORATOR?

In Python, we can specify special handling parameters by using decorators. *Decorators* are simply a way to change the behavior of functions. For example, you can use decorators to add stronger type checking, define macros, and invoke functions before and after execution. Using decorators in Flask for routing is one of the best examples of using decorators correctly. To learn more about decorators, see www.python.org/dev/peps/pep-0318.

Flask builds a list of all the routes in the application, making it easy for the application to route execution to the correct function when requested. But what happens when a route is requested but doesn't exist in the application? By default, you will get a generic error message like Not Found. The requested URL was not found on the server. You will see how to add our own custom error-handling routes in a later section.

Now that you know more about the terminology used in Flask and how it is structured to work with web pages, let's look at the construction of a typical Flask application with the extensions we need.

Initialization and the Application Instance

Flask and its extensions provide the entry point for your web application. Instead of writing all that onerous code yourself, Flask does it for you! The Flask extensions we will be using in this chapter include Flask-Script, Flask-Bootstrap, Flask-WTF, and WTForms. The following sections briefly describe each.

Flask-Script

Flask-Script enables scripting in Flask applications by adding a command-line parser (manifested as `manager`) that you can use to link to functions you've written. This is enabled by decorating the function with `@manager.command`. The best way to understand what this does for us is through an example.

The following is a basic, raw Flask application that does nothing. It's not even a "hello, world" example because nothing is shown and there are no web pages hosted—it's just the raw Flask application:

```
from flask import Flask      # import the Flask framework
app = Flask(__name__)        # initialize the application
if __name__ == "__main__":   # guard for running the code
    app.run()                # launch the application
```

Notice the `app.run()` call. This is called the *server startup* and is executed when we load the script by using the Python interpreter. When we run this code, all we see is this default message from Flask:

```
$ python3 ./flask-ex.py --help
 * Running on http://127.0.0.1:5000/ (Press CTRL+C to quit)
```

Notice that we don't have any way to see help, as there are no such options. The code launches by using defaults for the web server (which we can change in code if we desire). For example, we can change the port that the server is listening on.

With Flask-Script, we add not only a help option, but also options to control the server. The following code shows how easy it is to add the statements to enable Flask-Script. The new statements are highlighted in bold:

```
from flask import Flask            # import the Flask framework
from flask_script import Manager   # import the flask script manager class

app = Flask(__name__)              # initialize the application
manager = Manager(app)             # initialize the script manager class

# Sample method linked as a command-line option
@manager.command
def hello_world():
    """Print 'Hello, world!'"""
    print("Hello, world!")
```

```
if __name__ == "__main__":        # guard for running the code
    manager.run()                 # launch the application via manager class
```

When this code is run, we can see that additional options are available. Notice that the documentation string (immediately following the method definition) is shown as the help text for the command added:

```
$ python ./flask-script-ex.py --help
usage: flask-script-ex.py [-?] {hello_world,shell,runserver} ...

positional arguments:
  {hello_world,shell,runserver}
    hello_world         Print 'Hello, world!'
    shell               Runs a Python shell inside Flask application
                        context.
    runserver           Runs the Flask development server i.e. app.run()

optional arguments:
  -?, --help            show this help message and exit
```

We can see the command-line arguments (commands) we added, hello_world, but we can also see two new ones supplied by Flask-Script: shell and runserver. You must choose one of these commands when launching the server. The shell command allows you to use the code in a Python interpreter or similar tool, and runserver executes the code starting the web server.

Not only can we get help about the commands and options, but Flask-Script also provides more control over the server from the command line. In fact, we can see all the options for each command by appending the --help option:

```
$ python ./flask-script-ex.py runserver --help
usage: flask-script-ex.py runserver [-?] [-h HOST] [-p PORT] [--threaded]
                                    [--processes PROCESSES]
                                    [--passthrough-errors] [-d] [-D] [-r] [-R]
                                    [--ssl-crt SSL_CRT] [--ssl-key SSL_KEY]

Runs the Flask development server i.e. app.run()
```

```
optional arguments:
  -?, --help              show this help message and exit
  -h HOST, --host HOST
  -p PORT, --port PORT
  --threaded
  --processes PROCESSES
  --passthrough-errors
  -d, --debug             enable the Werkzeug debugger (DO NOT use in
                          production
                          code)
  -D, --no-debug          disable the Werkzeug debugger
  -r, --reload            monitor Python files for changes (not 100% safe for
                          production use)
  -R, --no-reload         do not monitor Python files for changes
  --ssl-crt SSL_CRT       Path to ssl certificate
  --ssl-key SSL_KEY       Path to ssl key
```

Here we can control all manner of things about the server, including the port, host, and even how it executes.

Finally, we can execute the method we've decorated as a command-line option:

```
$ python ./flask-script-ex.py hello_world
Hello, world!
```

Flask-Script provides some powerful features with only a few lines of code. You have to love that!

Flask-Bootstrap

Flask-Bootstrap was originally developed by Twitter for making uniform, nice-looking web clients. Fortunately, Twitter made it a Flask extension so everyone can take advantage of its features. Flask-Bootstrap is a framework on its own and provides even more command-line control as well as user-interface components for clean, attractive web pages. It is also compatible with the newest web browsers.

The framework does its magic behind the scenes as a client library of Cascading Style Sheets (CSS) and scripts that are invoked from the HTML templates (commonly referred to as either *HTML files* or *template files*) in Flask. You will learn more about templates in a later section. Because the application is client-side, we won't see much by initializing it in the main application. Regardless, the following shows how to add Flask-Bootstrap to our application code. Here, we have a skeleton with Flask-Script and Flask-Bootstrap initialized and configured:

```
from flask import Flask            # import the Flask framework
from flask_script import Manager # import the flask script manager class
from flask_bootstrap import Bootstrap  # import the flask bootstrap
                                       extension

app = Flask(__name__)              # initialize the application
manager = Manager(app)            # initialize the script manager class
bootstrap = Bootstrap(app)        # initialize the bootstrap extension

if __name__ == "__main__":        # guard for running the code
    manager.run()                 # launch the application via manager class
```

WTForms

WTForms is a component we need in order to support the Flask-WTF extension. It provides much of the functionality that the Flask-WTF component provides (because the Flask-WTF component is a Flask-specific wrapper for WTForms). We need only install it as a prerequisite for Flask-WTF, and we will discuss it in the context of Flask-WTF.

Note   Some package installations of Flask-WTF may include WTForms.

Flask-WTF

The *Flask-WTF* extension is an interesting component providing several useful additions—most notably for our purposes, integration with WTForms (a framework-agnostic component) that permits the creation of form classes, and additional web security in the form of cross-site request forgery (CSRF) protection. These two features allow you to take your web application to a higher level of sophistication.

Form Classes

Form classes provide a hierarchy of classes that make defining web pages more logical. With Flask-WTF, you can define your form with two pieces of code: a special class derived from the Form class (imported from the Flask framework) that you use to define fields using one or more additional classes that provide programmatic access to data, and an HTML file (or template) for rendering the web page. In this way, we see an abstraction layer (form classes) over the HTML files. You will learn more about the HTML files in the next section.

Using form classes, you can define one or more fields such as TextField for text, StringField for a string, and more. Better still, you can define validators that allow you to programmatically describe the data. For example, you can define a minimum and maximum number of characters for a text field. If the number of characters submitted is outside the range, an error message is generated. And, yes, you can define error message! See http://wtforms.readthedocs.io/en/latest/validators.html for a complete list of validators. The following are some of the validators available:

- DataRequired: Determines whether the input field is empty

- Email: Ensures that the field follows e-mail ID conventions

- IPAddress: Validates IP addresses

- Length: Ensures that the length of text is in a given range

- NumberRange: Ensures that text is numeric and within a given range

- URL: Validates URLs

To form classes, we must import the class and any field classes we want to use in the preamble of the application. The following shows an example of importing the form class and form field classes. In this example, we also import validators that we will use for validating the data automatically:

```
from flask_wtf import FlaskForm
from wtforms import (HiddenField, TextField, TextAreaField, SelectField,
                     SelectMultipleField, IntegerField, SubmitField)
from wtforms.validators import Required, Length
```

To define a form class, we must derive a new class from FlaskForm. From there, we can construct the class however we want, but it is intended to allow you to define the fields. The FlaskForm parent class includes all the necessary code that Flask needs to instantiate and use the form class.

Let's look at a simple, hypothetical example. The following shows the form class for a web page that displays first and last name for an author. In this example, there is a table named authors, which we can link to this code via the view function. The authors table contains three fields: an auto increment field (authorid), the first name of the author (firstname), and the last name of the author (lastname). Because the author ID field is not something users need to see, we make that field hidden, and the other fields derivatives of the TextField() class. Notice how these are defined in the listing with names (labels) as the first parameter:

```
class AuthorForm(FlaskForm):
    authorid = HiddenField('AuthorId')
    firstname = TextField('First name', validators=[
            Required(message=REQUIRED.format("Firstname")),
            Length(min=1, max=64, message=RANGE.format("Firstname", 1, 64))
        ])
    lastname = TextField( 'Last name', validators=[
            Required(message=REQUIRED.format("Lastname")),
            Length(min=1, max=64, message=RANGE.format("Lastname", 1, 64))
        ])
    create_button = SubmitField('Add')
    del_button = SubmitField('Delete')
```

Notice also that we have defined an array of validators in the form of function calls imported from the WTForms component for the fields. In each case, we use strings for the messages to make the code easier to read and more uniform. These strings include the following:

```
REQUIRED = "{0} field is required."
RANGE = "{0} range is {1} to {2} characters."
```

We use the Required() validator that indicates the field must have a value. We augment the default error message with the name of the field to make it easier for the user to understand. We also use a Length() validator function that defines the minimum and maximum length of the field data. Once again, we augment the default error message. Validators are applied only on POST operations (when a submit event has occurred).

Next, we have two SubmitField() instances: one for a create (add) button, and another for a delete button. As you may surmise, in HTML parlance, these fields are rendered as <input> fields with a type of submit.

Finally, to use a form class, we instantiate the class in a view function. The following shows a stub for the author view function. We instantiate the form class named AuthorForm() and assign it to a variable named form, which is passed to the render_ template() function:

```
@app.route('/author', methods=['GET', 'POST'])
@app.route('/author/<int:author_id>', methods=['GET', 'POST'])
def author(author_id=None):
    form = AuthorForm()
    if request.method == 'POST':
        pass
    return render_template("author.html", form=form)
```

Several field classes are available for use. Table 8-2 shows a sample of the most commonly used field classes (also called *HTML fields*). You can also derive from these fields to create custom field classes and provide text for the label that you can display next to the field (or as the button text, for example). You will see an example of this in a later section.

Table 8-2. *WTForms Field Classes*

Field Class	Description
BooleanField	A check box with True and False values
DateField	Accepts date values
DateTimeField	Accepts date-time values
DecimalField	Accepts decimal values
FileField	File upload field
FloatField	Accepts a floating-point value
HiddenField	Hidden text field
IntegerField	Accepts integer values
PasswordField	A password (masked) text field
RadioField	A list of radio buttons
SelectField	A drop-down list (choose one)
SelectMultipleField	A drop-down list of choices (choose one or more)
StringField	Accepts simple text
SubmitField	Form submit button
TextAreaField	Multiline text field

Cross-Site Request Forgery (CSRF) Protection

Cross-site request forgery (CSRF) protection is a technique that permits developers to sign web pages with an encrypted key, making it much more difficult for hackers to spoof a GET or POST request. This is accomplished by first placing a special key in the application code and then referencing the key in each of our HTML files. The following shows an example of the preamble of an application. All we need to do is assign the SECRET_KEY index of the app.config array with a phrase. This should be a phrase that is not easily guessed.

```
from flask import Flask           # import the Flask framework
from flask_script import Manager # import the flask script manager class
from flask_bootstrap import Bootstrap  # import the flask bootstrap
                                                extension

app = Flask(__name__)             # initialize the application
app.config['SECRET_KEY'] = "He says, he's already got one!"
manager = Manager(app)            # initialize the script manager class
bootstrap = Bootstrap(app)        # initialize the bootstrap extension

if __name__ == "__main__":        # guard for running the code
    manager.run()                 # launch the application via manager class
```

To activate the CSRF in our web pages, we merely add the form.csrf_token to the
HTML file. This is a special hidden field that Flask uses to validate the requests. You will
learn more about where to place this in a later section. But first, let's see a cool feature of
Flask called *flash*.

Message Flashing

Flask has many cool features. The creators of Flask and the creators of the Flask
extensions seem to have thought of everything—even error messaging. Consider a
typical web application. How do you communicate errors to the user? Do you redirect
to a new page,[3] issue a pop-up,[4] or perhaps display the error on the page? Flask has a
solution for this called *message flashing*.

Message flashing is accomplished using the flash() method from the Flask
framework. We import it in the preamble of our code, and when we want to display a
message, we call the flash() function, passing in the error message we want to see.
Flask will present the error in a nicely formatted box presented at the top of the form.
It doesn't replace the form and isn't a pop-up, but it does allow the user to dismiss the
message. You can use flash messaging to communicate errors, warnings, and even state
changes to the user.

---

[3]I find redirecting particularly annoying when entering data, because it is often lost when you
return to the page. Please don't use this method.
[4]If you have locked down your browser for better security, allowing pop-ups can be problematic.

Figure 8-1 shows an example of a flash message. In this example, two flash messages demonstrate that you can display multiple messages at the same time. Notice the small X to the right of the message used to dismiss the image.

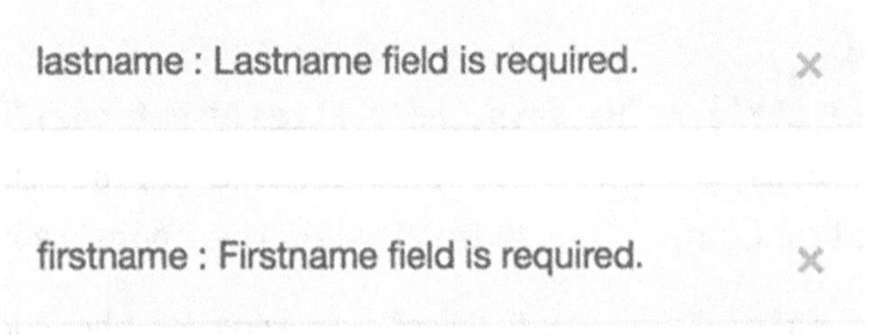

lastname : Lastname field is required.   ×

firstname : Firstname field is required.   ×

Figure 8-1. *Example flash messages*

You will see a mechanism to build flash messaging into all our web pages in the next section.

HTML Files and Templates

Let's review our tour so far. You have discovered how to initialize an application with the various components, and learned how Flask uses routes via the decorators to create a set of URLs for the application; these routes are directed to a view function, which instantiates the form class. The next piece of the puzzle is linking the HTML web page to the form class.

Recall, this is done via the render_template() function, where we pass in the name of an HTML file for processing. The reason *template* is in the name is that we can use the Jinja2 template component to make writing web pages easier. More specifically, the HTML file contains both HTML tags and Jinja2 template constructs.

Note   All HTML files (templates) must be stored in the templates folder in the same location as the main application code. For example, if your code is in a file named my-flask-app.py, there should be a templates folder in the same folder as my-flask-app.py. If you place the templates anywhere else, Flask won't be able to find the HTML files.

Templates, together with form classes, are where the user interface is designed. In short, templates are used to contain the presentation logic, and HTML files are used to contain the presentation data. Some readers likely will need to spend some time experimenting with how to use templates. The following sections give you a brief overview of Jinja2 templates and demonstrate how to use them in our HTML files. See the online documentation noted for more details.

Jinja2 Templates Overview

Jinja2 templates, hence *templates*, are used to contain any presentation logic such as looping through data arrays, making decisions on what to display, and even choosing formatting and presentation settings. If you are familiar with other web development environments, you may have seen this encapsulated in scripts or enabled through embedded scripting such as JavaScript.

Recall, we rendered our web pages in our main code. This function tells Flask to read the file specified and convert the template constructs (render them) into HTML. Flask will expand and compile the template constructs into HTML that the web server can present to the client.

You can use several template constructs to control the flow of execution, loops, and even comments. Whenever you want to use a template construct (think *scripting language*), you enclose it with the {% %} prefix and suffix. This is done so that the Flask framework recognizes the construct as a template operation rather than HTML.

However, it is not unusual (and quite normal) to see the template constructs intermixed with HTML tags. In fact, that is exactly how you should do it. After all, the files you will create are named .html. They just happen to contain template constructs. Does that mean you can use only templates when working with Flask? No, certainly not. If you want, you can render a pure HTML file!

At first, looking at templates can be quite daunting. But it isn't that difficult. Just look at all the lines with the {% and %} as the "code" portions.[5] You may also see comments in the form of a {# #} prefix and suffix.

Caution   All template constructs require a space after the {% and before the %}.

---

[5]Few will use the word "code" to describe the template constructs, and although that term is not accurate, considering them code-like components is OK if that helps you learn how to use Jinja2 templates.

If you look at the template, you will see the constructs and tags formatted by using indentation of two spaces. Indentation, and whitespace in general, doesn't matter outside the tags and constructs. However, most developers will use some form of indentation to make the file easier to read. In fact, most coding guidelines require indentation.

One of the cool features of templates beyond the constructs (think *code*) is the ability to create a hierarchy of templates. This allows you to create a "base" template that your other templates can use. For example, you can create a boilerplate of template constructs and HTML tags so that all your web pages look the same.

Recall from our look at Flask-Bootstrap, Bootstrap provides several nice formatting features. One of those features creates a pleasant-looking navigation bar. Naturally, we would want this to appear on all our web pages. We can do this by defining it in the base template and extending it in our other template (HTML) files. Let's look at a base template for the library application. Listing 8-2 shows the base template for the example application in this chapter. Line numbers have been added for ease of discussion.

Listing 8-2. Sample Base Template

```
01 {% extends "bootstrap/base.html" %}
02 {% block title %}ShoppingList{% endblock %}
03 {% block navbar %}
04 <div class="navbar navbar-inverse" role="navigation">
05    <div class="container">
06       <div class="navbar-header">
07          <button type="button" class="navbar-toggle"
             data-toggle="collapse" data-target=".navbar-collapse">
08             <span class="sr-only">Toggle navigation</span>
09             <span class="icon-bar"></span>
10             <span class="icon-bar"></span>
11             <span class="icon-bar"></span>
12          </button>
13          <a class="navbar-brand" href="/">Shopping List</a>
14       </div>
15       <div class="navbar-collapse collapse">
16          <ul class="nav navbar-nav">
17             <li><a href="/">List</a></li>
```

```
18              </ul>
19          </div>
20      </div>
21 </div>
22 {% endblock %}
23
24 {% block content %}
25 <div class="container">
26      {% for message in get_flashed_messages() %}
27      <div class="alert alert-warning">
28          <button type="button" class="close"
                 data-dismiss="alert">&times;</button>
29          {{ message }}
30      </div>
31      {% endfor %}
32
33      {% block page_content %}{% endblock %}
34 </div>
35 {% endblock %}
```

Wow, there is a lot going on here! Notice the first line. This tells us that we're inheriting (extending) another template named bootstrap/base.html. This is provided for you free when you install Flask-Bootstrap, and it is this template that contains support for the Bootstrap navigation bar feature. This is a common method of building a set of HTML files for a Flask application, as you will see later in this section.

Let's start our tour with a bird's-eye view. Notice that there are two "blocks" designated with {% block <> %} and {% endblock %} (lines 2, 3, 22, 24, 33, and 35). These are for logical sections, where we can apply formatting to the tags and constructs inside the block. In coding terms, this would be like a code block. The first block defines the title for the page—in this case, Shopping List, which is the executable name for the library application.

The second block defines the navigation bar (think *menu*) for the application. In that section, lines 5–21 define simple HTML <div> tags forming the items on the navigation bar. Of note is line 13, which specifies text to be used as the name of the application, which appears to the left of the navigation bar and acts like a "home" link. Lines 15–19 define the navigation bar items (submit buttons), but in this application there is only one form. Notice also the collapse keyword. This indicates it is possible to collapse the navigation bar.

The last block in lines 24–35 defines the template construct and HTML tags for the flash messages. Let's take a deeper look at this code (repeated here for convenience):

```
24 {% block content %}
25 <div class="container">
26     {% for message in get_flashed_messages() %}
27     <div class="alert alert-warning">
28         <button type="button" class="close"
           data-dismiss="alert">&times;</button>
29         {{ message }}
30     </div>
31     {% endfor %}
32
33     {% block page_content %}{% endblock %}
34 </div>
35 {% endblock %}
```

Here, we see another <div> tag that contains a button. This is the button we use to dismiss the flash message. Notice that this tag is placed inside a for loop as designated with {% for ... %} and ended with {% endfor %}. In this case, we are looping over the messages returned from the get_flashed_messages() function, which is collected by the flash() function in our application code. This tells us several things: we can use loops in our templates, the template allows displaying of multiple images (which you saw earlier), and templates can call functions! This is an example of the power of templates.

Note   Templates are not required to be formatted in any manner. Whitespace doesn't do anything outside the HTML tags or template constructs.

Finally, notice the variable we defined in the for loop in line 26. This variable, message, is defined local to the block in which it appears (in this case, the for loop), and can be referenced at any point by enclosing it in {{ }}. For example, in line 29 we use {{ message }} inside the <div> tag, which means this text will appear on the client rendered in place by Flask. The use of variables will become more important when we discuss how to build user interfaces with templates.

Template Language Constructs

The Jinja2 template features are many, and a complete discussion of all features is beyond the scope of this book. However, it is handy to have a quick reference for the major constructs of Jinja2. The following are some of the commonly used constructs, including some from the previous section (for completeness). Each is presented with a short example of the way the construct would appear in a template. Feel free to refer to this section when exploring the library application later in the chapter or when writing your own Flask applications.

Comments

You can embed your own comments in your templates. You may want to do this to ensure that you sufficiently explain what you are doing and as a reminder in case you reuse the code later.[6] The following is an example of using comments in templates. Recall, comments begin with {# and end with #} and can span multiple lines.

```
{# This is a line comment written by Dr. Charles Bell on 25 May 2018. #}

{#
   Introducing MySQL InnoDB Cluster

   This template defines the base template used for all of the HTML forms
   and responses in the MyLibrary application. It also defines the menu for
   the basic operations.

   Dr. Charles Bell, 2018
#}
```

Include

If your template files grow, and you find that portions are reusable such as a `<div>` tag, you can save the tag and template constructs in a separate file and include it in other templates by using the `{% include %}` construct. The `{% include %}` construct takes as

---

[6]The older you get, the more often you read code and say, "Who wrote this?" Sadly, it's often your own code! A few comments here and there will go a long way toward remembering what you were doing (and why).

a parameter the name of the file you want to include. Like templates, these must reside in the `templates` folder. In this way, we avoid repetition and the hassle and error-prone task of maintaining repetitive code.

```
{# Include the utilities common tags for a list. #}
{% include 'utilities.html' %}
```

Macros

Another form of reducing repetitive code is to create a macro for use in your templates (think *functions*). In this case, we use the {% `macro` ... %} and {% `endmacro` %} constructs to define a macro that we can call (use) later in our code. The following shows an example of defining a simple macro and later using it inside a loop. Notice how we pass variables to the macro for operating on the data.

```
{# Macro definition #}
{% macro bold_me(data) %}
    <b>{{ data }}</b>
{% endmacro %}

{# Invoke the macro #}
{% for value in data %}
    {{ bold_me(value) }}
{% endfor %}
```

Import

One of the best ways to use macros is to place them in a separate code file, therefore further enhancing reusability. To use a macro from a separate file, we use the {% `import` ... %} construct, supplying the name of the file from which to import. The following shows an example of importing the macro defined previously in a separate file. Like the include, this file must be in the `templates` folder. Notice that we can use an alias and refer to the macros by using dot notation.

```
{% import 'utilities.html' as utils %}
...
{{ utils.bold_me(value) }}
```

Extend (Inherit)

We can use a hierarchy of templates by inheriting (extending) them. You saw this earlier when we examined a base template. In this case, we use the {% extend ... %} construct, supplying the name of the template we want to extend. The following shows an example from the previous base template.

```
{% extends "base.html" %}
```

Blocks

Blocks are used to isolate execution and scope (for variables). We use blocks whenever we want to isolate a set of template constructs (think *code block*). The {% block ... %} construct is used with the {% endblock %} construct to define the block. The constructs allow you to name the block. The following is an example.

```
{% block if_true %}
...
{% endblock if_true %}
```

Loops

Loops are a way to execute the same block multiple times. We do this with the {% for <variable> in <data_array> %} construct. In this case, the loop will iterate over the array, replacing the value in <variable> with the value in each index of the array. This construct is great for looping through an array to create a table, show a list of data, and similar presentation activities. The following shows a for loop used in constructing a table. Notice that we use two for loops: one to loop over the columns in an array named columns, and another to loop over the rows in an array named rows.

```
<table border="1" cellpadding="1" cellspacing="1">
  <tr>
    <td style="width:80px"><b>Action</b></td>
    {% for col in columns %}
      {{ col|safe }}
    {% endfor %}
  </tr>
  {% for row in rows %}
```

```
    <tr>
      <td><a href="{{ '/%s/%s'%(kind,row[0]) }}">Modify</a></td>
      {% for col in row[1:] %}
        <td> {{ col }} </td>
      {% endfor %}
    </tr>
  {% endfor %}
</table>
```

You may be wondering at this point how the data in columns and rows gets to the template. Recall the render_template() function. If you want to pass data to the template, you simply list it in the parameters when you render the template. In this case, we would pass the columns and rows as follows. In this case, row_data and col_data are variables defined in the view function and passed to the rows and columns variables in the template through assignment. Cool, eh?

```
render_template("list.html", form=form, rows=row_data, columns=col_data)
```

Conditionals

Conditionals, or if statements (called *tests* in the Jinja2 documentation), allow you to make decisions in your template. We use the {% if <condition> %} construct, which is concluded with the {% endif %} construct. If you want an "else," you can use the {% else %} construct. Further, you may chain conditions with the {% elif <condition> %}. You typically use variables or form elements in the conditions and can use the common comparators (for a list of tests, see http://jinja.pocoo.org/docs/2.10/templates/#builtin-tests).

For example, you may want to change the label of a submit field depending on a certain event. You may want to define one submit button for adding or updating data; when the web page is used to add a new data item, the text should read "Add," but when you update the data by using the same web page, we want the text to read "Update." This is one of the keys to reusing the template for both GET and POST requests (read and write). The following shows an example of a conditional used in this manner.

```
{% if form.create_button.label.text == "Update" %}
  {{ form.new_note.label }}
  {{ form.new_note(rows='2',cols='100') }}
{% endif %}
```

```
{% if form.del_button %}
  {{ form.del_button }}
{% endif %}
```

This example has two conditions. The first demonstrates how to check the text of a label on the form. Notice here that we reference the element on the form with `form.create_button`, which is the name of the field class we defined in the form class, which was instantiated prior to rendering the template (you will see how to do this in a later section). The form variable is passed to the template in the `render_template("book.html", form=form)` call. In this case, we display the new_note field and its label only if the button text was set to `Update`.

The second example shows a simple test that if the `delete_button` on the form is active (not hidden or deleted), we display it. This is an example of how to display optional submit fields.

Variables and Variable Filters

Variables are a way to save data values for later processing. The most common use of variables is referencing data passed to the template from the view function (via the `render_template()` function). We can also use variables in our templates to save data such as counters, `for` loop data values, and more. Recall that we reference a variable by enclosing it in curly braces `{{ variable }}`, or in the case of the `for` loop, it is defined in the `for` loop construct. Note that when referenced inside HTML tags, the spaces inside the construct are ignored.

You can also use a filter in your template to change the values in variables. Variable filters are a way to programmatically change values for use in your presentation logic. You can change the case, remove whitespace, and even strip HTML tags or use the raw text directly. In this last case, we use the `safe` filter, which tells the template to use the text even if it has HTML tags. This is a little tricky because it could open a path for exploitation, but if you use the special security feature of WTForms (shown in the next section), it is normally OK to do this, but do so sparingly. Table 8-3 shows the commonly used variable filters.

Table 8-3. *Variable Filters*

Filter	Description
capitalize	Converts the first character of the text to uppercase
lower	Converts the text to lowercase characters
safe	Renders the text without escaping special characters
striptags	Removes HTML tags from text
title	Capitalizes each word in the string
trim	Removes leading and trailing whitespace
upper	Converts the text to uppercase

Tip   For a more in-depth look at Jinja2 template constructs, see `http://jinja.pocoo.org/`.

Now that you have an overview of how templates work and have defined a base template for the library application, let's look at how to use the base template to form the HTML files for our web pages. As you will see, it involves three concepts we've been discussing; these concepts will conclude our discussion about the way Flask works when building web pages and sending them to the client. You will look at getting data from the client in a later section.

HTML Files Using Templates

Now you are ready to see how to manifest the field classes we defined in our form classes. Let's begin with a walk-through of how to present data for the item detail view (data) in the example application. We begin with the form class and the field class defined to the view function, which renders the template and finally the template itself.

Recall, the form class is where we define one or more form fields. We will use these field class instances to access the data in our view functions and in the template. Listing 8-3 shows the form class for the item detail view.

Listing 8-3. Item Form Class

```
class ItemForm(FlaskForm):
    row_id = HiddenField('Id')
    description = TextField('Description', validators=[
            Required(message=REQUIRED.format("Description")),
            Length(min=1, max=64, message=RANGE.format("Description", 1, 64))
        ])
    note = TextField( 'Note')
    create_button = SubmitField('Add')
```

The form class creates three fields: one for a hidden field (id), one for the description of the item (description), and another to allow the user to make notes about the item (notes). We also have a submit field (create_button) used to submit (post) the form.

We pass the form data to the template when it is rendered after instantiating it in the view function. Listing 8-4 shows the view function for the list item data. Here, we instantiate the list view form class first and then pass it to the template. The code for interfacing with the database code module has been omitted for brevity.

Listing 8-4. Item View Function

```
@app.route('/item', methods=['GET', 'POST'])
def item_view(row_id=None):
    operation = request.args.get("operation", "Add")
    row_id = request.args.get("row_id")
    # Get data from the form if present
    form_row_id = form.row_id.data
    form_description = form.description.data
    form_note = form.note.data
    form.create_button.label.text = operation
    # If the route with the variable is called, retrieve the data item
    # and populate the form.
    if row_id:
        # Read data here
    if request.method == 'POST':
        # First, determine if we must create, update, or delete when form
        posts.
```

```
        if form.create_button.data:
            if form.create_button.label.text == "Update":
                operation = "Update"
            elif form.create_button.label.text == "Delete":
                operation = "Delete"
        if form.validate_on_submit():
            # Get the data from the form here
            if operation == "Add":
                # Add a new item here
            elif operation == "Update":
                # Update the data here
            else:
                # Delete the item here
            return redirect('/')
        else:
            flash_errors(form)
    return render_template("item.html", form=form)
```

Here we see the routes we've defined for the view. We also have set the methods for requests to include both GET and POST. Notice that we can check whether the request is a POST (submission of data). It is in this condition that we can retrieve data from the form class instance and save it to the database. You'll look at that a bit more when we add database capabilities.

Finally, notice that we instantiate an instance of the publisher form class (form) and later pass that as a parameter to the render_template("item.html", form=form) call. In this case, we now render the item.html template stored in the templates folder.

OK, now we have our form class and view function. The focus now is on what happens when we render the HTML template file. Listing 8-5 shows the HTML file (template) for the list item data.

Listing 8-5. Item HTML File

```
{% extends "base.html" %}
{% block title %}Shopping List{% endblock %}
{% block page_content %}
  <form method=post> {{ form.csrf_token }}
    <fieldset>
```

```
    <legend>Item View</legend>
    {{ form.hidden_tag() }}
    <div style=font-size:20pz; font-weight:bold; margin-left:150px;s>
        {{ form.description.label }} <br>
        {{ form.description(size=75) }} <br>
        {{ form.note.label }} <br>
        {{ form.note(size=75) }} <br><br>
        {{ form.create_button }}
    </div>
    </fieldset>
  </form>
{% endblock %}
```

The template begins with extending (inheriting) the `base.html` template file that we discussed earlier. We see a block defining the title and another block defining the page content. In that block, we see how to define the fields on the page, referencing the field class instances from the form class instance (`form`). Indeed, we reference the label of the field as well as the data. The label is defined when you declare the field class, and the data is where the values are stored. When we want to populate a form (`GET`), we set the data element to the value; and when we want to read the data (`POST`), we reference the data element.

Notice also that we add the CSRF token for security, render the hidden fields with the `form.hidden_tag()` function, and include the submit field (`create_button`).

Whew! That's how Flask works to present a web page. Once you're used to it, it is a nifty way to separate several layers of functionality and make it easy to get data from the user or present it to the user. If you're thinking you've seen only a small portion of the example application, you are correct. Those pieces of the example application are presented to give you a glimpse of what is to come. You will see the complete application code later in this chapter.

Now, let's look at how to build custom error handlers into our application and later how to redirect control in our application to the correct view functions.

Error Handlers

I mentioned that it is possible to create your own error-handling mechanisms for errors in your application. You should consider making two such error mechanisms: one for the 404 (Not Found) error, and another for 500 (application errors). To define each, we first make a view function decorated with @app.errorhandler(num), a view function, and an HTML file. Let's look at each example.

Not Found (404) Errors

To handle 404 (Not Found) errors, we create a view function with the special error-handler routing function, which renders the HTML file. Flask will automatically direct all Not Found error conditions to this view. The following shows the view function for the 404 Not Found error handler. As you can see, it is simple:

```
@app.errorhandler(404)
def page_not_found(e):
    return render_template('404.html'), 404
```

The associated error handler HTML code is in the file named 404.html, as shown here:

```
{% extends "base.html" %}
{% block title %}MyLibrary ERROR: Page Not Found{% endblock %}
{% block page_content %}
<div class="page-header">
    <h1>Page not found.</h1>
</div>
{% endblock %}
```

We inherit from the base.html file so the resulting web page looks the same as any other in the application, complete with the menu from the bootstrap component. We can also define the text for the error message and a title. Feel free to embellish your own error handlers to make things more interesting for your users.[7]

---

[7]An example of great custom error handlers can be found on GitHub. They have a custom background and style sheet that puts the boring 404 errors of other web sites to shame.

Application (500) Errors

To handle 500 (application) errors, we follow the same pattern as before. The following is the error handler for the application errors:

```
@app.errorhandler(500)
def internal_server_error(e):
    return render_template('500.html'), 500
```

The associated error handler HTML code is in the file named 500.html, shown here:

```
{% extends "base.html" %}
{% block title %}MyLibrary ERROR{% endblock %}
{% block page_content %}
<div class="page-header">
    <h1>OOPS! Application error.</h1>
</div>
{% endblock %}
```

We inherit from the base.html file, so the resulting web page looks the same as any other in the application, complete with the menu from the bootstrap component.

Creating these basic error handlers is highly recommended for all Flask applications. You may find the application error handler most helpful when developing your application. You can even augment the code to provide debug information to be displayed in the web page.

Redirects

At this point, you may be wondering how a Flask application can programmatically direct execution from one view to another. The answer is another simple construct in Flask: redirects. We use the redirect() function (imported from the Flask module) with a URL to redirect control to another view. For example, suppose you have an application that, depending on which button the user clicks (submitting the form via POST), you want to display a different web page. The following demonstrates how to use the redirect() function to do this:

```
if kind == 'book' or not kind:
    if request.method == 'POST':
        return redirect('book')
```

```
        return render_template("list.html", form=form, rows=rows,
                                columns=columns, kind=kind)
elif kind == 'author':
    if request.method == 'POST':
        return redirect('author')
    return render_template("list.html", form=form, rows=rows,
                            columns=columns, kind=kind)
elif kind == 'publisher':
    if request.method == 'POST':
        return redirect('publisher')
    return render_template("list.html", form=form, rows=rows,
                            columns=columns, kind=kind)
```

Here, we have three redirects after a POST request. In each case, we are using one of the routes defined in our application to tell Flask to call the associated view function. In this way, we can create a menu or a series of submit fields to allow the user to move from one page to another.

The redirect() function requires a valid route, and for most cases, it is simply the text you supplied in the decorator. However, if you need to form a complex URL path, you can use the url_for() function to validate the route before you redirect. The function also helps avoid broken links if you reorganize or change your routes. For example, you can use redirect(url_for("author")) to validate the route and form a URL for it.

Additional Features

There is much more to Flask than what you've seen in this crash course. The following are some topics not discussed that you may be interested in learning more about (these are just a few of them). If these interest you, consider looking them up in the online documentation.

- *Application and request context*: You can use variables to capture application context such as session, global, request, and more. For more information, see http://flask.pocoo.org/docs/0.12/appcontext/.

- *Cookies*: You can work with cookies if you need to. For more information, see http://flask.pocoo.org/docs/0.12/quickstart/#cookies.

- *Flask-Moment—localization of dates and times*: If you need to work with localization of date and time, see the Flask-Moment extension at `https://github.com/miguelgrinberg/Flask-Moment`.

Flask Review: Sample Application

Now that you've had a brief primer on Flask, let's see how all this works before we dive into the example application. This section reviews what you have learned in the form of a basic layout for a typical Flask web application. You will be using this as a guide for writing the example application later in this chapter. Don't worry too much about executing this code because it doesn't do much and is intended as a jumpstart for the chapter project. However, it does demonstrate how all the parts you've learned are pieced together to get the Flask web application running with no forms defined.

Listing 8-6 shows the sample application layout for a Flask application. Take a moment to read through it. You should find all the topics we've discussed thus far with placeholders for field classes, form classes, and view functions.

Listing 8-6. Sample Flask Application Template

```
#
# Introducing MySQL InnoDB Cluster - Template
#
# This file contains a template for building Flask applications. No form
# classes, routes, or view functions are defined, but placeholders for each
# are defined in the comments.
#
# Dr. Charles Bell, 2018
#
from flask import Flask, render_template, request, redirect, flash
from flask_script import Manager
from flask_bootstrap import Bootstrap
from flask_wtf import FlaskForm
from wtforms import (HiddenField, TextField, TextAreaField, SelectField,
                     SelectMultipleField, IntegerField, SubmitField)
from wtforms.validators import Required, Length

#
```

```
# Set up Flask, Bootstrap, and security.
#
app = Flask(__name__)
app.config['SECRET_KEY'] = "He says, he's already got one!"
manager = Manager(app)
bootstrap = Bootstrap(app)

#
# Utility functions
#
def flash_errors(form):
    for error in form.errors:
        flash("{0} : {1}".format(error, ",".join(form.errors[error])))

#
# Customized fields for skipping prevalidation
#
<custom field classes go here>

#
# Form classes - the forms for the application
#
<form classes go here>

#
# Routing functions - the following defines the routing functions for the
# menu including the index or "home", book, author, and publisher.
#
<routing functions (view functions) go here>

#
# Error handling routes
#
@app.errorhandler(404)
def page_not_found(e):
    return render_template('404.html'), 404
```

```
@app.errorhandler(500)
def internal_server_error(e):
    return render_template('500.html'), 500

#
# Main entry
#
if __name__ == '__main__':
    manager.run()
```

Notice that there is one thing in this template we haven't talked about yet: utility functions. These are your own functions to support your application. One such function you may want to consider including in all your Flask applications is a function to loop through the errors on a form and display them in a flash message. Recall that flash messages are displayed as pop-up boxes on the web page. The following presents the utility function for clarity. Notice that we use a for loop to loop through the errors array of the form instance, flashing each message. This permits you to display multiple messages on the web page.

```
def flash_errors(form):
    for error in form.errors:
        flash("{0} : {1}".format(error, ",".join(form.errors[error])))
```

Feel free to use this template when creating your own Flask applications. We will also be using it in a later section to define the user interface for the example application.

Tip   For more information about Flask and how to use it and its associated packages, an excellent reference on the topic is *Flask Web Development: Developing Web Applications with Python, Second Edition* by Miguel Grinberg (O'Reilly Media 2018).

Now that you've set up the Flask environment and discovered Flask and its extensions, let's look at the example application in more detail.

Example Application

Because we want to test our deployed InnoDB Cluster, we need an application that at least fits the profile of a typical application service. In this case, we will use a simple Python web application that uses Flask to serve simple data. We keep it as simple as possible for several reasons. First and foremost, this is not a book that examines every detail about writing high-availability applications. Rather, the application code is presented in a terse, rapid-start guide. If you need help getting the application to work, and the information presented in the previous section doesn't cover your specific situation, please refer to the URLs presented in the previous sections.

In this section, we present a step-by-step guide to creating the sample application. We'll start with creating the database on the cluster and creating a library (code module) to place the CRUD operations on the data. Then we'll move on to the user-interface code and the HTML files that make it all work. We conclude with a brief example execution to demonstrate how the application works.

Note   You don't need to understand all the nuances of this application. After you have established your own development environment, you can substitute your sample application for this one. The application connection parameters will be the same or similar in any case.

However, before you begin, you will need your cluster started and operational. If you shut it down, see the end of Chapter 7 for how to safely restart the cluster. If your cluster is offline and you do not want to start it, you can skip the following "Database" section, but you will need to return to it when the cluster is online and ready. You also must have the router installed, configured, and running on the application server to proceed.

Note   You must have the cluster running, with the router running on the application server, to develop and use the example application.

Database

The database we will use for the application is a simple, single table containing a limited number of columns. Once again, this isn't a book about database design, so we'll err on the side of simplicity. Savvy database developers will likely see ways to improve on the design. Unless those desires cause you some distress,[8] I recommend that you press on and see the application working before diving into "fixing" things.

Let's begin by creating the database on the cluster.

Creating the Database

For this step, we will use MySQL Shell and connect to our read/write server via the router. Recall, the router is running on the application server (`cluster-rpi-app`). The following command is an example you can use to connect to the read/write server via the router:

```
$ mysqlsh --sql root@cluster-rpi-app
```

You can use the application server to connect or you can use your desktop computer, so long as it is connected to the same network as your cluster. If you use your PC, you may need to access the application server via IP address (for example, 192.168.42.240). Also, recall that the router uses port 6446 for the read/write route (connection). Before we connect to the read/write server, let's look at the database design.

The data we will create is a simple shopping list. It has a column used to store a unique ID (auto-increment) a column to describe the item, another to add notes, and a column we can use to indicate whether the item was purchased (like ticking off the item on the list). We will name the database `shopping` and the table `list`. The following shows the SQL commands we need to create the database and the table:

```
CREATE DATABASE shopping;
CREATE TABLE shopping.list (
  id int AUTO_INCREMENT PRIMARY KEY,
  description char(200),
  notes char(100),
  ticked bool default FALSE
);
```

---

[8]Those who, like me, have a touch of OCD know exactly what this feels like.

OK, now we're ready to connect to the read/write server and create the database. Listing 8-7 shows a transcript of running the preceding SQL commands to create the database. The SQL commands are shown in bold.

Listing 8-7. Creating the Shopping List Database

```
$ mysqlsh --sql root@cluster-rpi-app:6446
Creating a session to 'root@ cluster-rpi-app:6446'
Enter password: ****
Fetching schema names for autocompletion... Press ^C to stop.
Error during auto-completion cache update: The user specified as a definer
('mysql.infoschema'@'localhost') does not exist
Your MySQL connection id is 10 (X protocol)
Server version: 8.0.11 MySQL Community Server - GPL
No default schema selected; type \use <schema> to set one.
MySQL Shell 8.0.11

Copyright (c) 2016, 2018, Oracle and/or its affiliates. All rights
reserved.

Oracle is a registered trademark of Oracle Corporation and/or its
affiliates. Other names may be trademarks of their respective
owners.

Type '\help' or '\?' for help; '\quit' to exit.


 MySQL  localhost:33060+ ssl  SQL > CREATE DATABASE shopping;
Query OK, 1 row affected (0.0391 sec)

 MySQL  localhost:33060+ ssl  SQL > CREATE TABLE shopping.list (
                        ...    id int AUTO_INCREMENT PRIMARY KEY,
                        ...    description char(200),
                        ...    notes char(100),
                        ...    ticked bool default FALSE
                        ... );
Query OK, 0 rows affected (0.0437 sec)
```

OK, now that we have the database created, let's add some data. Here, we will add some simple test data. The following shows sample SQL statements you can use to create some data to test the application:

```
INSERT INTO shopping.list VALUES (NULL, "Bagels", "Plain, of course.", NULL);
INSERT INTO shopping.list VALUES (NULL, "Jelly", "Grape, please!", NULL);
INSERT INTO shopping.list VALUES (NULL, "Milk", "2%", True);
INSERT INTO shopping.list VALUES (NULL, "Lunch meat", "Suprise me.", NULL);
INSERT INTO shopping.list VALUES (NULL, "Paper towels", "", NULL);
```

While we are still connected to the read/write server, we can run these SQL commands. The following shows a transcript of running the preceding SQL commands to add sample data to the database. The SQL commands are shown in bold:

```
MySQL  localhost:33060+ ssl  SQL > INSERT INTO shopping.list VALUES
(NULL, "Bagels", "Plain, of course.", NULL);
Query OK, 1 row affected (0.0570 sec)

 MySQL  localhost:33060+ ssl  SQL > INSERT INTO shopping.list VALUES
(NULL, "Jelly", "Grape, please!", NULL);
Query OK, 1 row affected (0.0056 sec)

 MySQL  localhost:33060+ ssl  SQL > INSERT INTO shopping.list VALUES
(NULL, "Milk", "2%", True);
Query OK, 1 row affected (0.0073 sec)

 MySQL  localhost:33060+ ssl  SQL > INSERT INTO shopping.list VALUES
(NULL, "Lunch meat", "Suprise me.", NULL);
Query OK, 1 row affected (0.0056 sec)

 MySQL  localhost:33060+ ssl  SQL > INSERT INTO shopping.list VALUES
(NULL, "Paper towels", "", NULL);
Query OK, 1 row affected (0.0055 sec)
```

While we're still connected, let's run a query to retrieve the data, just to check it. The following shows the results of running a SELECT SQL command to retrieve all the rows in the table:

```
MySQL  localhost:33060+ ssl  SQL > SELECT * FROM shopping.list;
+----+--------------+--------------------+--------+
| id | description  | notes              | ticked |
+----+--------------+--------------------+--------+
|  1 | Bagels       | Plain, of course.  |   NULL |
|  2 | Jelly        | Grape, please!     |   NULL |
|  3 | Milk         | 2%                 |      1 |
|  4 | Lunch meat   | Suprise me.        |   NULL |
|  5 | Paper towels |                    |   NULL |
+----+--------------+--------------------+--------+
5 rows in set (0.0009 sec)
```

Now that we have some sample data, let's write a code module to work with the database from Python.

Preparing the Directory Structure

Before we embark on implementing the example application, we need to make a few folders (directories). Recall from the "Flask Primer" section that we need folders to contain the .html files (form templates). We will also place the code for interfacing with MySQL in a folder named database. The following shows a suggested directory structure. You can name the root whatever you want. For example, you could name it shopping.

```
root folder (e.g. shopping)
  |
  +-- database
  |
  +-- templates
```

Creating the Database Library

It is common practice to create a separate code module containing the code to interact with a database (or any such data store). We will do this for the example application. In this case, we will create a file named shopping_lib.py and place it in a folder named database.

> **Note**   You also need to create an empty file named __init__.py. This is required for Python to locate the modules in the database directory.

Rather than present a detailed explanation of every line of code in the library, in this section we summarize the classes and methods, leaving the comprehension of the code itself as a later exercise. However, we will examine some critical parts of the code that deal with the high-availability aspects.

Let's begin with the classes. There are two classes: a general class named Library and another named ShoppingList. The Library class is used to create and manage connections via the router for reading and writing. The ShoppingList class implements the CRUD operations on the data in the database. We use the Library class to create a connection and pass that to the ShoppingList class to access the data. Let's look at the methods for each class.

Table 8-4 shows the methods for the Library class. There shouldn't be any surprises here, but we will discuss the connect() method and the connection criteria later in this section.

Table 8-4. *Methods for the Library Class*

Method	Returns	Description
__init__(self)		Constructor.
connect(self, read_write=False)		Make the connection via the router. Use the read/write port by default or read-only if read_write is set to True.
get_connection(self)	Connection class	Retrieve the current connection.
is_connected(self)	Boolean	Returns True if the connection is active.
disconnect(self)		Disconnect from the server.
sql(self, query_str, fetch=True, buffered=False)	Result set or cursor	Execute a query and return any results.
get_list(self, all=True)	Result set	Retrieve all the rows in the table or, if all is set to False, only those rows that have not been selected.

Table 8-5 shows the methods for the ShoppingList class. Again, there should be no surprises here, as these methods are typical for classes that implement CRUD operations. Also, each method is designed to connect to the database, execute the operation, and then disconnect. This helps ensure that we get a valid connection should a failover event occur between requests for CRUD operations.

Table 8-5. *Methods for the ShoppingList Class*

Method	Required Parameters	Description
def __init__(self, library)	library	Constructor. Requires an instance of the Library class.
create(self, description, note)	description	Create a row in the table.
read(self, rowid)	rowid	Return the row in the table with id = rowid. Returns None if no match is found.
update(self, rowid, description, note)	rowid, Description	Update the data for the row specified with id = rowid.
update_purchased(self, rowid, purchased=1)	rowid	Set the Purchased column for the row in the table with id = rowid. True is the default value, but if you pass False for purchased, it will clear the Purchased column for the row.
delete(self, rowid)	rowid	Delete the row in the table with id = rowid.

You may be wondering how we provide the connection information such as user ID, password, and hostname. Although it's not a recommended practice for production applications, we place the data in the library code. At the top of the code, we define constants for the read/write port and the read-only port. We also define a value to use for the maximum number of retries to reestablish a connection through the router. This is necessary because if a connection fails (there is a failover event in the cluster), we must retry the connection to reestablish it after the router reconnects:

```
RW_PORT = 6446
RO_PORT = 6447
MAX_RETRY = 6
```

We use a dictionary to store the user ID, password, and host. We set the default port to the read-only port. We can override this with the connect() method.

```
self.config = {
    'user': 'root',
    'password': '<secret>',
    'host': 'cluster-rpi-app',
    'port': RO_PORT,
    'database': None,
}
```

Let's look at the connect() method. The following shows the complete code for the method. Notice we have a parameter that, if not provided, ensures we always use the read-only connection. If we pass True, the method will connect to the read/write connection. This is an example of how you can use a single method to selectively choose the connection path—either to write data or read data.

```
def connect(self, read_write=False):
    attempts = 0
    while attempts < MAX_RETRY:
        self.config['port'] = (RO_PORT, RW_PORT)[read_write]
        try:
            self.db_conn = mysql.connector.connect(**self.config)
            break
        except mysql.connector.Error as err:
            print("Connection failed. Error = {0} Retrying.".format(err))
        attempts += 1
        time.sleep(1)
    if attempts >= MAX_RETRY:
        self.db_conn = None
        raise mysql.connector.Error("Connection timeout reached.")
```

Notice that the method also implements a loop for retrying the connection. We have mitigated the need for a lot of retries by making the CRUD methods in the ShoppingList class connect and disconnect before and after the operation. However, the retry loop is still needed here in the unlikely event that the cluster becomes unreachable.

Now, let's look at the complete code for the database library. Recall, we place this code in a file named `shopping_lib.py` placed in the `database` folder. The database library is written with the SQL strings declared at the top of the module, followed by the two classes. Listing 8-8 shows the complete code for the shopping list database library. Comments have been omitted for brevity.

Listing 8-8. Shopping List Database Library

```
import mysql.connector
import time

RW_PORT = 6446
RO_PORT = 6447
MAX_RETRY = 6  # Maximum times to attempt a reconnect should connection fail

ALL_ITEMS = """
    SELECT * FROM shopping.list
    ORDER BY description
"""
READ_ITEM = """
    SELECT * FROM shopping.list
    WHERE rowid = '{0}'
"""
UNCHECKED_ITEMS = """
    SELECT * FROM shopping.list
    WHERE purchased = 0
    ORDER BY description
"""
INSERT_ITEM = """
    INSERT INTO shopping.list (description, note) VALUES ('{0}','{1}')
"""
GET_LASTID = "SELECT @@last_insert_id"
UPDATE_ITEM = """
    UPDATE shopping.list
    SET description = '{1}', note = '{2}'
    WHERE rowid = '{0}'
"""
```

```python
UPDATE_PURCHASED = """
    UPDATE shopping.list
    SET purchased = {1}
    WHERE rowid = '{0}'
"""

DELETE_ITEM = """
    DELETE FROM shopping.list WHERE rowid = '{0}'
"""


class ShoppingList(object):
    def __init__(self, library):
        self.library = library

    def create(self, description, note):
        assert description, "You must supply a description for a new item."
        self.library.connect(True)
        query_str = INSERT_ITEM
        last_id = None
        try:
            self.library.sql(query_str.format(description, note))
            last_id = self.library.sql(GET_LASTID)
            self.library.sql("COMMIT")
        except Exception as err:
            print("ERROR: Cannot add item: {0}".format(err))
        self.library.disconnect()
        return last_id

    def read(self, rowid):
        assert rowid, "You must supply a rowid."
        self.library.connect()
        query_str = READ_ITEM.format(rowid)
        results = self.library.sql(query_str)
        self.library.disconnect()
        return results

    def update(self, rowid, description, note):
        assert rowid, "You must supply a rowid."
        assert description, "You must supply a description for a new item."
```

343

```python
        self.library.connect(True)
        query_str = UPDATE_ITEM
        try:
            self.library.sql(query_str.format(rowid, description, note))
            self.library.sql("COMMIT")
        except Exception as err:
            print("ERROR: Cannot update list item: {0}".format(err))
        self.library.disconnect()

    def update_purchased(self, rowid, Purchased=1):
        assert rowid, "You must supply a rowid."
        self.library.connect(True)
        query_str = UPDATE_PURCHASED
        try:
            self.library.sql(query_str.format(rowid, Purchased))
            self.library.sql("COMMIT")
        except Exception as err:
            print("ERROR: Cannot update list item: {0}".format(err))
        self.library.disconnect()

    def delete(self, rowid):
        assert rowid, "You must supply a rowid."
        self.library.connect(True)
        query_str = DELETE_ITEM.format(rowid)
        try:
            self.library.sql(query_str)
            self.library.sql("COMMIT")
        except Exception as err:
            print("ERROR: Cannot delete item: {0}".format(err))
        self.library.disconnect()

class Library(object):
    def __init__(self):
        self.config = {
            'user': 'root',
            'password': '<secret>',
            'host': 'cluster-rpi-app',
```

```python
            'port': RO_PORT,
            'database': None,
        }
        self.db_conn = None

    def connect(self, read_write=False):
        attempts = 0
        while attempts < MAX_RETRY:
            self.config['port'] = (RO_PORT, RW_PORT)[read_write]
            try:
                self.db_conn = mysql.connector.connect(**self.config)
                break
            except mysql.connector.Error as err:
                print("Connection failed. Error = {0} Retrying.".format(err))
            attempts += 1
            time.sleep(1)
        if attempts >= MAX_RETRY:
            self.db_conn = None
            raise mysql.connector.Error("Connection timeout reached.")

    def get_connection(self):
        return self.db_conn

    def is_connected(self):
        return (self.db_conn and (self.db_conn.is_connected()))

    def disconnect(self):
        try:
            self.db_conn.disconnect()
        except:
            pass

    def sql(self, query_str, fetch=True, buffered=False):
        # If we are fetching all, we need to use a buffered
        if fetch:
            cur = self.db_conn.cursor(buffered=True)
        else:
            cur = self.db_conn.cursor(raw=True)
```

```python
        try:
            cur.execute(query_str)
        except Exception as err:
            cur.close()
            print("Query error. Command: {0}:{1}".format(query_str, err))
            raise

        # Fetch rows (only if available or fetch = True).
        if cur.with_rows:
            if fetch:
                try:
                    results = cur.fetchall()
                except mysql.connector.Error as err:
                    print("Error fetching all query data: {0}".format(err))
                    raise
                finally:
                    cur.close()
                return results
            else:
                # Return cursor to fetch rows elsewhere (fetch = false).
                return cur
        else:
            return cur

    def get_list(self, all=True):
        self.connect()
        try:
            if all:
                results = self.sql(ALL_ITEMS)
            else:
                results = self.sql(UNCHECKED_ITEMS)
        except Exception as err:
            print("ERROR: {0}".format(err))
            raise
        self.disconnect()
        return results
```

OK, now let's look at the user interface for the application.

User Interface

Before we dive into the code, let's look at the rendering of the web forms. The default view is to show all the rows in the table regardless of whether the items were ticked as purchased. Figure 8-2 shows the main view of the application. The list represents the read operation of the data. We will also see read operations for the update and delete operations (we read the data and display it before the update or delete).

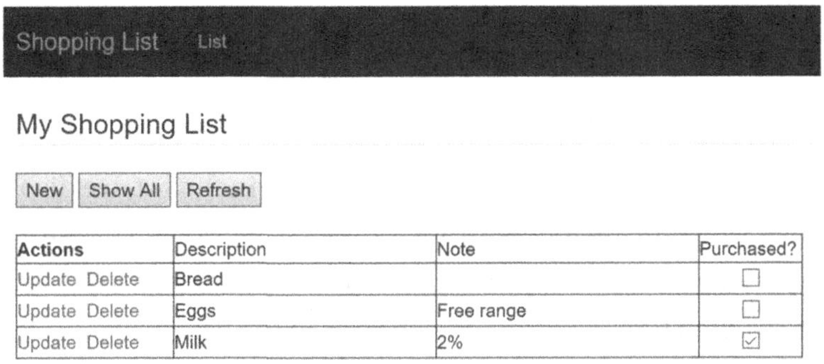

Figure 8-2. *Main Form - List (Default)*

This view has three buttons: New adds a new item to the list, Show All reveals all the rows in the table, and Refresh hides the rows in the table that have the Purchased column selected. In this view, if the user selects the Purchased column for several items and then clicks Refresh, the list will update to show only the unticked rows. Clicking the Show All button displays all rows. Notice also that we placed the update and delete operations as links beside each row in the list. This permits the user to choose a row to update or delete.

The item view form is reused for create, update, and delete operations. We reuse the same HTML file, changing only the label (and thus operation) of the submit button. Specifically, we use New for create, Update for updating the row, and Delete to delete the row.

When the user clicks the New button, we display the New version of the item view, shown in Figure 8-3. This form allows the user to add a description (required) and a note (optional) and then click Add to add the item to the list. After the item is added (created), the view returns to the list view.

Figure 8-3. *Item View (New)*

When the user clicks the Update link next to an item in the list, we display the Update version of the item view, shown in Figure 8-4. This form allows the user to change the description (required) and note (optional) and then click Update to change the data. After the item is updated (created), the view returns to the list view.

Figure 8-4. *Item View (Update)*

When the user clicks the Delete link next to an item in the list, we display the Delete version of the item view, shown in Figure 8-5. This form allows the user to view the data and then click Delete to delete the row. After the item is removed, the view returns to the list view.

Figure 8-5. *Item View (Update)*

In the following sections, you will discover the user-interface elements in the same order as the template discussed previously. The only exception is we do not have any custom field classes, so we will skip that section.

If you want to follow along with the code, open a file named shopping_list.py and include the following sections of code, starting at the top of the file. Save this file in the root of the application folder (for example, shopping).

Note   The following sections describe the code in general terms, but do not despair. If you are new to programming in Python, take your time and read through the code. Except for the imports section, the code is easy to read and understand.

Imports Section

At the top of the file is where we place all the import statements. This allows Python to find and include the libraries we need for the application. In this case, there is a long list of Flask-related imports. The following shows the imports we need for the example application:

```
from flask import Flask, render_template, request, redirect, flash
from flask_script import Manager
from flask_bootstrap import Bootstrap
from flask_wtf import FlaskForm
from wtforms import (HiddenField, TextField, SelectField,
                     SelectMultipleField, IntegerField, SubmitField)
from wtforms.validators import Required, Length
```

Next, we import the database library named Library() we created earlier and define a couple of strings to make the validator definitions easier:

```
from database.shopping_lib import Library, ShoppingList

REQUIRED = "{0} field is required."
RANGE = "{0} range is {1} to {2} characters."
```

Next comes the initialization portion. Here, we initialize the Flask components as we learned during the tutorial, including the Manager() and Bootstrap() libraries:

```
app = Flask(__name__)
app.config['SECRET_KEY'] = "He says, he's already got one!"
manager = Manager(app)
bootstrap = Bootstrap(app)
```

Finally, we can add a line of code to initialize the database library:

```
library = Library()
```

Utility Functions

The utilities function we need is the one described previously to collect the Flask flash errors. The following shows the flash_errors() function:

```
def flash_errors(form):
    for error in form.errors:
        flash("{0} : {1}".format(error, ",".join(form.errors[error])))
```

Form Classes

The form classes section is where we define the methods used to link the controls in the HTML file with the view functions that populate the data. Recall from the introduction to the user interface, we have two forms: the default list view and the item detail view. Let's look at the form class for the list view named ListForm(). Here, we see three fields added to the form: New, Show All, and Refresh.

```
class ListForm(FlaskForm):
    submit = SubmitField('New')
    show_all = SubmitField('Show All')
    hide_checked = SubmitField('Refresh')
```

Next, we see the form class for the item view named ItemForm(). Here, we have one hidden field, Id, a text field for the description and note. Finally, we have one submit field named Add. Recall, we will reuse this form for the create, update, and delete operations.

```
class ItemForm(FlaskForm):
    row_id = HiddenField('Id')
    description = TextField('Description', validators=[
            Required(message=REQUIRED.format("Description")),
            Length(min=1, max=64, message=RANGE.format("Description", 1, 64))
        ])
    note = TextField( 'Note')
    create_button = SubmitField('Add')
```

Routing Functions

The routing functions are where the flow control or execution paths of the user interface are realized. Recall, the routing functions are named such because we define the places in our code where Flask will redirect (route) execution based on the URL submitted.

Routing functions often become complicated quickly. This is because they are typically written to support two or more operations and both GET and POST operations. Thus, we often see code that seems to be a jumbled mess. However, if you look closely, you will see a guard (if statement) that redirects execution for the POST operation. The way to read code for routing functions is to assume that all the code is for GET operations (because a GET often precedes or follows a POST), with the POST operational code separated with the guard. Don't worry; this will be clearer after you read through the code.

There are two main routing functions. One is the default, where we display the general list. The other is the item view route, which displays the details of an item for create, update, and delete operations. Let's look at the list routing function first.

The list routing function is named shopping_list(). This code is a bit long because we're mixing several operations. In fact, we have all four of the CRUD operations, and you will see places in the code for each operation. The create, update, and delete operations are easy, because anytime the user clicks those buttons and links, we redirect (route) the code to the item routing function. However, if the Show All or Refresh buttons are clicked, we must do some more work—either displaying (reading) all rows, or only rows without the purchased column ticked. Listing 8-9 shows the complete code for the list view routing function.

Listing 8-9. List View Routing Function

```
#
# Shopping List
#
# This is the default page for "home" and listing rows in the database.
#
@app.route('/', methods=['GET', 'POST'])
def shopping_list(row_id=None):
    rows = []
    columns = []
    form = ListForm()
    if request.method == 'POST':
        if form.submit.data:
            return redirect('item')
        elif form.hide_checked.data:
            # returns list of all checkboxes
            checkboxes = request.form.getlist('checkboxes')
            # returns a list of values that were checked
            list_row_ids = request.form.getlist('row_ids')
            for list_row_id in list_row_ids:
                shopping_list_db = ShoppingList(library)
                purchased_value = (0, 1)[list_row_id in checkboxes]
                shopping_list_db.update_purchased(list_row_id, purchased_
                value)
                print(">>> Setting purchased = {1} for rowid =
                {0}.".format(list_row_id, purchased_value))
            rows = library.get_list(False)
        else:
            rows = library.get_list()
    else:
        # Default is to get all items
        rows = library.get_list()
    columns = (
        '<td style="width:200px">Description</td>',
        '<td style="width:200px">Note</td>',
```

```
        '<td style="width:80px">Purchased?</td>',
    )
    return render_template("list.html", form=form, rows=rows,
                                columns=columns)
```

One thing that may be of special note is the way the columns of the list are defined. Notice in the code, we use HTML code as strings in the columns list. This is a nice trick we can use when writing lists in Flask applications. Take a few moments to read through the code. Once again, it is not necessary to understand all the nuances; the example is used only to test the cluster, but if you want to learn more about writing Flask, this example can help you get there.

The other routing function named item_view() is for the item view where we allow users to create a new item or update or delete an existing item by displaying the data first. Because we have three operations to implement, the code for this function is a bit longer. Line numbers were added for clarity.

Let's discuss the read operation first. At the top of the function, we see code for establishing an instance of the database library class (ShoppingList). After that, we capture any data that is in the form already. If the URL includes the ID of a row in the table, we then read the data and display it in the form. We see this in lines 14–20.

In the next section of code, we check for the POST operation. Here, we are displaying the data and waiting for a submit operation. The POST section begins on line 21. The first thing we do is try to determine which of the database operations we are about to permit. We know this by checking the label of the submit button. Recall, we set the label in the view function to either add, update, or delete. The default is add, which we check in line 03 is saved to the variable named operation. We check the label of the submit button and save the result in the operation variable in the code in lines 23–27.

Following this, we see code for the add, update, and delete operations, which we will discuss later. Listing 8-10 shows the complete code for the item view function.

Listing 8-10. Item View Routing Function

```
01 @app.route('/item', methods=['GET', 'POST'])
02 def item_view(row_id=None):
03     operation = request.args.get("operation", "Add")
04     row_id = request.args.get("row_id")
05     shopping_list_db = ShoppingList(library)
06     form = ItemForm()
```

```
07      # Get data from the form if present
08      form_row_id = form.row_id.data
09      form_description = form.description.data
10      form_note = form.note.data
11      form.create_button.label.text = operation
12      # If the route with the variable is called, retrieve the data item
13      # and populate the form.
14      if row_id:
15          data = shopping_list_db.read(row_id)
16          if data == []:
17              flash("Item not found!")
18          form.row_id.data = row_id
19          form.description.data = data[0][1]
20          form.note.data = data[0][2]
21      if request.method == 'POST':
22          # First, determine if we must create, update, or delete when
            form posts.
23          if form.create_button.data:
24              if form.create_button.label.text == "Update":
25                  operation = "Update"
26              elif form.create_button.label.text == "Delete":
27                  operation = "Delete"
28          if form.validate_on_submit():
29              # Get the data from the form here
30              if operation == "Add":
31                  try:
32                      shopping_list_db.create(form_description, form_note)
33                      flash("Added.")
34                  except Exception as err:
35                      flash(err)
36              elif operation == "Update":
37                  try:
38                      print(">>> {0}".format(form.row_id.data))
39                      shopping_list_db.update(form_row_id, form_
                        description, form_note)
```

```
40                    flash("Updated.")
41                except Exception as err:
42                    flash(err)
43          else:
44              try:
45                  shopping_list_db.delete(form_row_id)
46                  flash("Deleted.")
47              except Exception as err:
48                  flash(err)
49          return redirect('/')
50      else:
51          flash_errors(form)
52  return render_template("item.html", form=form)
```

The add operation is shown in lines 30–35. Here, we retrieve the data from the form and save it to the database by using the shopping_list_db.create() method. Notice that we place the code in a try block, which allows us to capture any errors. This is a common practice and will help capture the error and display it by using the Flask flash mechanism.

The update operation is shown in lines 36–42. Here, we get the data from the form and update the row in the database by using the shopping_list_db.update() method.

The delete operation is shown in lines 44–48. We delete the row from the database by using the shopping_list.delete() method.

Wow, that is a lot of code for such a simple application, isn't it? Now you see why we kept the example application as small as possible. Even so, a typical web-based application (a Flask application) requires a bit more code than you might expect. We're almost done. Let's look at the rest of the code.

Error-Handling Functions

The next section has two additional routing functions used to handle errors. We have one for the Page Not Found error and another for general errors from the application. The following shows the code for both routes:

```
@app.errorhandler(404)
def page_not_found(e):
    return render_template('404.html'), 404
```

```
@app.errorhandler(500)
def internal_server_error(e):
    return render_template('500.html'), 500
```

Main Entry

Finally, we implement the main entry code, which is simply calling the run() method for the Flask manager class. We place a guard (if statement) before it to ensure that this executes only once, when the code is run as the main entry (not imported). The following shows the code for the main entry section:

```
if __name__ == '__main__':
    manager.run()
```

That's it for the application code. Now, let's complete the code by looking at the HTML files needed.

HTML Files

There are no mysteries in the HTML files for the example application. The following lists the HTML files we need for the application. We have already seen the contents of the error handling and the base HTML files. Recall, we place the HTML files in a folder named templates:

- 404.html: Not Found error

- 500.html: General application error

- base.html: Base template

- item.html: Item details

- list.html: Shopping list details

Because the files are basic Flask template code (Jinja2), we won't explore them in any detail. Rather, we present them to complete the walk-through of the code, leaving comprehension as a later exercise.

Let's look at the list.html file first. This file is used by the list_view() function to render the default view of the application. Listing 8-11 shows the code for the list HTML file (template).

Listing 8-11. List HTML Template

```
{% extends "base.html" %}
{% block title %}Shopping List Query Results{% endblock %}
{% block page_content %}
  <legend>My Shopping List</legend>
  <form method=post> {{ form.csrf_token }}
    <fieldset>
      {{ form.submit }} {{ form.show_all }} {{ form.hide_checked }}
      <br><br>
    </fieldset>
    <table border="1" cellpadding="1" cellspacing="1">
      <tr>
        <td style="width:120px"><b>Actions</b></td>
        {% for col in columns %}
          {{ col|safe }}
        {% endfor %}
      </tr>
      {% for row in rows %}
        <input type="hidden" name="row_ids" value="{{row[0]}}">
        <tr>
          <td>
            <a href="{{ '/item?operation=Update&row_id=%s'%(row[0])
            }}">Update</a>
            <label>  </label>
            <a href="{{ '/item?operation=Delete&row_id=%s'%(row[0])
            }}">Delete</a>
          </td>
          <td> {{ row[1] }} </td>
          <td> {{ row[2] }} </td>
          <td>
            <div align="center">
              {% if row[3] == 1 %}
                <input type="checkbox" name="checkboxes" value="{{row[0]}}"
                checked >
              {% else %}
```

357

```
                <input type="checkbox" name="checkboxes" value="{{row[0]}}" >
              {% endif %}
            </div>
          </td>
        </tr>
      {% endfor %}
    </table>
  </form>
  <br>
{% endblock %}
```

One thing to notice in the template is the way we define the links for the update and delete operations. This is a handy trick for adding links in a list view. Nice. In addition, notice that later in the code is an example of how to add and populate check boxes in the list—also nice to know.

The other HTML file is the item.html file. You saw this file in the "HTML Files Using Templates" section earlier in the chapter. Please refer to that section if you want to review the file again.

That's it! That is all the code and supporting files for the example application. Now, let's see how to run it and display some data.

Running the Example Application

To run the example application, you must have all the code in the correct locations on disk. Refer to the previous "Preparing the Directory Structure" section to ensure that you've created the proper directories. If you have trouble launching the application, and all the Flask libraries are installed correctly, you could have a file misplaced among the directories.

You also need to ensure that the cluster is up and running and that the database and sample data have been created. If you have been working along with this chapter, you should have these tasks complete.

When we run the example application, we will run it from a terminal as we did for the examples in the Flask primer. In this case, we pass in the option runserver and set the host to the IP address of the application server with the -h option. The following shows an example of how to start the application. Notice that you need to run this command in the root of the application folder (the same folder where shopping_list.py exists). To stop the web server, press Ctrl+C in the terminal where you started it.

```
$ python3 ./shopping_list.py runserver -h 192.168.42.240
```

To connect to the application, use your browser and enter http://<IP>:5000 (where <IP> is the IP address you choose) in the URL entry box. Note that the :5000 is the default port for the Flask web server. This will direct your browser to the Flask web server on the application server and display the initial form (list view), as shown in Figure 8-6. In this example, we used the IP address 192.168.42.123 for the application server.

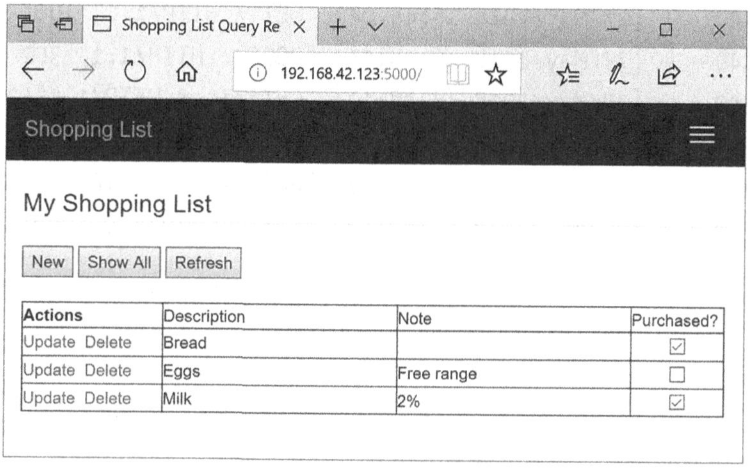

Figure 8-6. *Connecting to the application via the application server*

When you start the application from the terminal, you will see a series of output messages. You will see a message whenever a browser connects to the web server as well as diagnostic messages. The following shows an example of what you should see in the terminal (console). Notice that there are messages from Flask explaining what is happening with the web server, followed by additional messages.

```
$python3 ./shopping_list.py runserver -h 192.168.42.240
 * Serving Flask app "shopping_list" (lazy loading)
 * Environment: production
   WARNING: Do not use the development server in a production environment.
   Use a production WSGI server instead.
 * Debug mode: off
 * Running on http://192.168.42.240:5000/ (Press CTRL+C to quit)
```

```
192.168.42.240 - - [27/May/2018 16:46:34] "GET / HTTP/1.1" 200 -
>>> Setting purchased = 1 for rowid = 2.
>>> Setting purchased = 0 for rowid = 3.
>>> Setting purchased = 1 for rowid = 1.
192.168.42.240 - - [27/May/2018 16:47:47] "POST / HTTP/1.1" 200 -
192.168.42.240 - - [27/May/2018 16:47:49] "GET /item?operation=Update&row_
id=3 HTTP/1.1" 200 -
>>> 3
192.168.42.240 - - [27/May/2018 16:48:04] "POST /item?operation=Update&row_
id=3 HTTP/1.1" 302 -
192.168.42.240 - - [27/May/2018 16:48:04] "GET / HTTP/1.1" 200 -
192.168.42.240 - - [27/May/2018 16:48:12] "POST / HTTP/1.1" 302 -
192.168.42.240 - - [27/May/2018 16:48:12] "GET /item HTTP/1.1" 200 -
192.168.42.240 - - [27/May/2018 16:48:48] "GET /item HTTP/1.1" 200 -
192.168.42.240 - - [27/May/2018 16:48:57] "POST /item HTTP/1.1" 302 -
192.168.42.240 - - [27/May/2018 16:48:57] "GET / HTTP/1.1" 200 -
```

Notice also that we have several types of messages, including messages from the code itself. For example, Setting purchased was written to the log in the shopping_ list() routing function. Look into that code if you want to see how that is done.

OK, now that we have the application working, let's do some experimentation and see what happens when bad things happen to the servers in our cluster.

Testing the Cluster with the Application

So, let's put the new development cluster to the test. Let's test our application during a simulated failure. We will simulate two types of failures: in one, the read/write server (primary) goes offline; and in another, the current read-only server in use goes offline. Fortunately, the loss of any server in a cluster is a rare event. Even so, it is interesting to see how InnoDB Cluster and an application handles the events. We explore both scenarios in this section.

Scenario: Read/Write (Primary) Goes Offline

In this scenario, we disable the read/write server by disconnecting the Ethernet cable while the application is running; we disrupt the networking capabilities of the server. If you opted for using Wi-Fi instead of Ethernet and you want to run this scenario, you may have to power off the machine or kill the MySQL server process instead.

So, how do we know which server is the read/write server? Recall, we can simply use these commands via the MySQL Shell to find the read/write server, and that's the preferred method:

```
MySQL  cluster-rpi2:3306 ssl  Py > cluster = dba.get_cluster('RPI_Cluster')
MySQL  cluster-rpi2:3306 ssl  Py > cluster.status()
...
            "cluster-rpi4:3306": {
                "address": "cluster-rpi4:3306",
                "mode": "R/W",
                "readReplicas": {},
                "role": "HA",
                "status": "ONLINE"
            }
...
```

Here, we see in this example, `cluster-rpi4` is the read/write server. When ready, launch the application and then unplug the Ethernet cable.

Next, try adding a new item in the application. You may see a slight delay as the application retries the connection that failed via the router. When the router reconnects to the new read/write server, the application operation will complete. So, besides a slight delay, how can we know the cluster healed itself?

We can look at the cluster status via the shell, but it is clear when we examine the log for the router that the event has occurred. The following shows an example excerpt. Notice the event that shows the `cluster-rpi4` was lost and replaced with `cluster-rpi3` as the read/write server. Cool.

```
...
2018-05-14 21:28:28 metadata_cache INFO [72eff430] Metadata for cluster
'RPI_Cluster' has 1 replicasets:
2018-05-14 21:28:28 metadata_cache INFO [72eff430] 'default' (4 members,
single-master)
2018-05-14 21:28:28 metadata_cache INFO [72eff430]    cluster-rpi1:3306 /
33060 - role=HA mode=n/a
```

```
2018-05-14 21:28:28 metadata_cache INFO [72eff430]      cluster-rpi2:3306 /
33060 - role=HA mode=RO
2018-05-14 21:28:28 metadata_cache INFO [72eff430]      cluster-rpi4:3306 /
33060 - role=HA mode=RW
2018-05-14 21:28:28 metadata_cache INFO [72eff430] Replicaset 'default' has
a new Primary cluster-rpi4:3306
2018-05-14 21:28:28 metadata_cache INFO [72eff430]      cluster-rpi3:3306 /
33060 - role=HA mode=RO
2018-05-14 21:28:29 routing INFO [724ff430] Retrying connection for
'default' after possible failover
...
```

Now, plug the Ethernet cable back in and then open a connection to an active server with MySQL Shell and issue the cluster.rejoin_instance() method. Wait a bit and then check the status to see the cluster heal itself. The following shows the updated status of the cluster-rpi4 server. Notice that it has been returned to the cluster as a read-only server. Nice.

```
MySQL  cluster-rpi2:3306 ssl  Py > cluster.rejoin_instance
('root@cluster-rpi1:3306')
MySQL  cluster-rpi2:3306 ssl  Py > cluster.status()
...
            "cluster-rpi4:3306": {
                "address": "cluster-rpi4:3306",
                "mode": "R/O",
                "readReplicas": {},
                "role": "HA",
                "status": "ONLINE"
            },
...
```

Now, let's see what happens when we lose a read-only server.

Scenario: Read-Only (Secondary) Goes Offline

This example takes a bit more work. Here, we need to find which server the router is directing for reading. This can be tricky, depending on which machine is the next one in the list. To keep it simple, we've configured the router by using the default routing policies, so we should be able to predict which server is "next" in the read queue. We'll cheat a bit by adding a `print()` statement to the database code to report the hostname for the connection

The setup for this scenario requires that the cluster is started with all four servers running and joined to the cluster. We will be using the application server, so you can log into that machine now. If you have the router running, you can stop it because we will be truncating the log to make it easier to find the example messages.

Also, in this demonstration of the scenario, the read/write server is `cluster-rpi1`. However, it is possible your cluster may have elected a different machine for the read/write server, and you may see slightly different output in the demonstration.

OK, let's get started by first adding the following line of code (shown in bold) to the end of the `connect()` method in the `Library` class in the `database/shopping_lib.py`. This will print the hostname of the server to which we have connected. Make sure the indentation matches the `if` statement and not the last line of that method, as shown:

```
...
if attempts >= MAX_RETRY:
    self.db_conn = None
    raise mysql.connector.Error("Connection timeout reached.")
print(">>> Hostname =", self.sql("SHOW VARIABLES LIKE 'report_host'")
[0][1])
```

Next, let's truncate the router log. If you have the router running, you can stop it. If you started it from the command line, you can use the `ps a` command to find the process ID and then kill it with `sudo kill -9 <id>`. This will not damage the router. After it's stopped, remove the log file with this command:

```
$ sudo rm /usr/local/mysql/var/log/mysqlrouter/mysqlrouter.log
```

Next, we can start our application with the following command. Leave the terminal you use to run this command open, so you can see the messages displayed.

```
$ python ./shopping_list.py runserver -h 192.168.42.240
```

After the application launches, open a browser and connect via the URL
http://192.168.42.240:5000. You will see the application default page, as shown in
Figure 8-7.

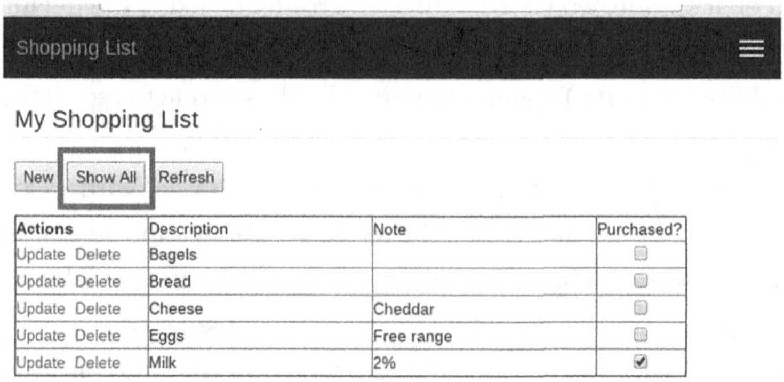

Figure 8-7. *Shopping List application*

Notice the Show All button. We will use this button to test the scenario. This button
will connect to the router via the read-only port (6447) and retrieve all rows from the
database. Because nothing is cached, this will connect every time we click the button.

If you now view the router log by using the following command, you will see
messages near the top, where the router connected to the cluster and established
its connection queues. For example, the following shows that the cluster in this
demonstration has the read/write server as cluster-rp1 and the read-only servers as
cluster-rpi2-4. You may need to press the spacebar a few times to find the data. Press
Q to exit the more utility.

```
$ sudo more /usr/local/mysql/var/log/mysqlrouter/mysqlrouter.log
...
2018-05-28 18:46:07 metadata_cache INFO [75c40430]    cluster-rpi1:3306 /
33060 - role=HA mode=RW
2018-05-28 18:46:07 metadata_cache INFO [75c40430]    cluster-rpi2:3306 /
33060 - role=HA mode=RO
2018-05-28 18:46:07 metadata_cache INFO [75c40430]    cluster-rpi3:3306 /
33060 - role=HA mode=RO
2018-05-28 18:46:07 metadata_cache INFO [75c40430]    cluster-rpi4:3306 /
33060 - role=HA mode=RO
```

Now, go ahead and click the Show All button three times now. Then inspect the terminal window where you launched the application. You should notice that the application reports the host to which it connected for each click of the button. For example, the following shows the results of starting the application and then clicking the button four times:

```
* Running on http://192.168.42.240:5000/ (Press CTRL+C to quit)
('>>> Hostname =', u'cluster-rpi2')
192.168.42.240 - - [28/May/2018 18:46:21] "POST / HTTP/1.1" 200 -
('>>> Hostname =', u'cluster-rpi3')
192.168.42.240 - - [28/May/2018 18:46:22] "POST / HTTP/1.1" 200 -
('>>> Hostname =', u'cluster-rpi4')
192.168.42.240 - - [28/May/2018 18:46:23] "POST / HTTP/1.1" 200 -
('>>> Hostname =', u'cluster-rpi2')
192.168.42.240 - - [28/May/2018 18:46:24] "POST / HTTP/1.1" 200 -
('>>> Hostname =', u'cluster-rpi3')
192.168.42.240 - - [28/May/2018 18:46:25] "POST / HTTP/1.1" 200 -
```

What we see here is something interesting. The router has directed the connection to cluster-rpi2 and then cluster-rpi3 and then cluster-rpi4. It then repeats the sequence. Why? Because the router, by default, uses a round-robin policy to spread the reads out among the read-only servers.

Now, let's get to the mad scientist portion of our demonstration. Go to your cluster and disconnect the Ethernet cable for cluster-rpi2. Wait about 30 seconds and examine the router log again. You should find a message stating that the router detected a change, and it marks the status of cluster-rpi2 as n/a because it is no longer available. If you look at the cluster status, you will see the machine is marked as MISSING. The following shows an example of what you should find in the router log:

```
2018-05-28 18:47:03 metadata_cache INFO [72eff430] Changes detected in
cluster 'RPI_Cluster' after metadata refresh
2018-05-28 18:47:03 metadata_cache INFO [72eff430] Metadata for cluster
'RPI_Cluster' has 1 replicasets:
2018-05-28 18:47:03 metadata_cache INFO [72eff430] 'default' (4 members,
single-master)
2018-05-28 18:47:03 metadata_cache INFO [72eff430]    cluster-rpi1:3306 /
33060 - role=HA mode=RW
```

```
2018-05-28 18:47:03 metadata_cache INFO [72eff430]    cluster-rpi2:3306 /
33060 - role=HA mode=n/a
2018-05-28 18:47:03 metadata_cache INFO [72eff430]    cluster-rpi3:3306 /
33060 - role=HA mode=RO
2018-05-28 18:47:03 metadata_cache INFO [72eff430]    cluster-rpi4:3306 /
33060 - role=HA mode=RO
```

Now try the application and click the Show All button a few times. You should see several connections displayed in the terminal where you're running the application, but you should notice cluster-rpi2 is not among them. The application will continue to run, but cluster-rpi2 will not be one of the machines you connect to for reading data. The following shows an example of the output:

```
('>>> Hostname =', u'cluster-rpi3')
192.168.42.240 - - [28/May/2018 18:47:10] "POST / HTTP/1.1" 200 -
('>>> Hostname =', u'cluster-rpi4')
192.168.42.240 - - [28/May/2018 18:47:17] "POST / HTTP/1.1" 200 -
```

Now, let's go one step further. Let's disconnect the Ethernet cable for cluster-rpi4. If you look in the router log, you will find another metadata refresh event like the following:

```
2018-05-28 18:47:36 metadata_cache INFO [72eff430] Changes detected in
cluster 'RPI_Cluster' after metadata refresh
2018-05-28 18:47:36 metadata_cache INFO [72eff430] Metadata for cluster
'RPI_Cluster' has 1 replicasets:
2018-05-28 18:47:36 metadata_cache INFO [72eff430] 'default' (4 members,
single-master)
2018-05-28 18:47:36 metadata_cache INFO [72eff430]    cluster-rpi1:3306 /
33060 - role=HA mode=RW
2018-05-28 18:47:36 metadata_cache INFO [72eff430] Replicaset 'default' has
a new Primary cluster-rpi1:3306 [4127c169-520f-11e8-a834-b827ebcb9200].
2018-05-28 18:47:36 metadata_cache INFO [72eff430]    cluster-rpi2:3306 /
33060 - role=HA mode=n/a
2018-05-28 18:47:36 metadata_cache INFO [72eff430]    cluster-rpi3:3306 /
33060 - role=HA mode=RO
2018-05-28 18:47:36 metadata_cache INFO [72eff430]    cluster-rpi4:3306 /
33060 - role=HA mode=n/a
```

366

At this point, if you click the Show All button a few times, you should still see the application refresh, but now it uses only `cluster-rpi3` to read. If you disconnect the Ethernet cable for `cluster-rpi4` and immediately try the application, you may encounter a situation where the application captures the connect error for the router. The following shows an example of the messages you will see for the application. Recall, the application will retry, so it will continue to run because, technically, we still have a viable read-only server. The following shows an example of the error message and recovery message you should see if this event occurs (with some messages removed for brevity):

```
('>>> Hostname =', u'cluster-rpi4')
192.168.42.240 - - [28/May/2018 18:46:59] "POST / HTTP/1.1" 200 -
Connection failed. Error = 2003: Can't connect to remote MySQL server for
client connected to '192.168.42.240:6447' Retrying.
('>>> Hostname =', u'cluster-rpi4')
192.168.42.240 - - [28/May/2018 18:47:20] "POST / HTTP/1.1" 200 -
----------------------------------------
Exception happened during processing of request from ('192.168.42.240',
37546)
..
error: [Errno 32] Broken pipe
----------------------------------------
('>>> Hostname =', u'cluster-rpi3')
192.168.42.240 - - [28/May/2018 18:47:20] "POST / HTTP/1.1" 200 -
```

If this looks like gobbledygook Python spew, it's OK. It is spew from Python, and this is the normal way Python communicates network errors. The important message is the last two lines, which show we were able to reconnect and retrieve data. This is one area that you could improve in the application, should you desire to expand it.

So now we have a cluster with only two machines left, which is not a desirable state. We need to rejoin the missing servers. Go ahead and connect the Ethernet cables for `cluster-rpi2` and `cluster-rpi4`. Give them a few moments to reconnect; then start MySQL Shell, connecting to `cluster-rpi1`. We should first get the cluster and then show the status to verify that the two servers are missing. Of special note in the status is that the cluster reports `OK_NO_TOLERANCE`, which means it cannot tolerate another server failing. We rejoin the servers with the `cluster.rejoin_instance()` method. Listing 8-12 shows an excerpt in which the missing servers are rejoined.

Listing 8-12. Rejoining Instances to the Cluster

```
MySQL  cluster-rpi1:3306 ssl  Py > cluster = dba.get_cluster()
MySQL  cluster-rpi1:3306 ssl  Py > cluster.status()
{
    "clusterName": "RPI_Cluster",
    "defaultReplicaSet": {
        "name": "default",
        "primary": "cluster-rpi1:3306",
        "ssl": "REQUIRED",
        "status": "OK_NO_TOLERANCE",
        "statusText": "Cluster is NOT tolerant to any failures. 2 members
        are not active",
        "topology": {
            "cluster-rpi1:3306": {
                "address": "cluster-rpi1:3306",
                "mode": "R/W",
                "readReplicas": {},
                "role": "HA",
                "status": "ONLINE"
            },
            "cluster-rpi2:3306": {
                "address": "cluster-rpi2:3306",
                "mode": "R/O",
                "readReplicas": {},
                "role": "HA",
                "status": "(MISSING)"
            },
            "cluster-rpi3:3306": {
                "address": "cluster-rpi3:3306",
                "mode": "R/O",
                "readReplicas": {},
                "role": "HA",
                "status": "ONLINE"
            },
```

```
            "cluster-rpi4:3306": {
                "address": "cluster-rpi4:3306",
                "mode": "R/O",
                "readReplicas": {},
                "role": "HA",
                "status": "(MISSING)"
            }
        }
    },
    "groupInformationSourceMember": "mysql://root@cluster-rpi1:3306"
}

 MySQL  cluster-rpi1:3306 ssl  Py > cluster.rejoin_instance('root@cluster-
 rpi2:3306')
Rejoining the instance to the InnoDB cluster. Depending on the original
...
The instance 'cluster-rpi2:3306' was successfully rejoined on the cluster.
 MySQL  cluster-rpi1:3306 ssl  Py > cluster.rejoin_instance('root@cluster-
 rpi4:3306')
Rejoining the instance to the InnoDB cluster. Depending on the original
...
The instance 'cluster-rpi4:3306' was successfully rejoined on the cluster.
 MySQL  cluster-rpi1:3306 ssl  Py > cluster.status()
{
    "clusterName": "RPI_Cluster",
    "defaultReplicaSet": {
        "name": "default",
        "primary": "cluster-rpi1:3306",
        "ssl": "REQUIRED",
        "status": "OK",
        "statusText": "Cluster is ONLINE and can tolerate up to ONE
        failure.",
        "topology": {
            "cluster-rpi1:3306": {
                "address": "cluster-rpi1:3306",
```

```
            "mode": "R/W",
            "readReplicas": {},
            "role": "HA",
            "status": "ONLINE"
        },
        "cluster-rpi2:3306": {
            "address": "cluster-rpi2:3306",
            "mode": "R/O",
            "readReplicas": {},
            "role": "HA",
            "status": "ONLINE"
        },
        "cluster-rpi3:3306": {
            "address": "cluster-rpi3:3306",
            "mode": "R/O",
            "readReplicas": {},
            "role": "HA",
            "status": "ONLINE"
        },
        "cluster-rpi4:3306": {
            "address": "cluster-rpi4:3306",
            "mode": "R/O",
            "readReplicas": {},
            "role": "HA",
            "status": "ONLINE"
        }
    }
},
"groupInformationSourceMember": "mysql://root@cluster-rpi1:3306"
}
```

OK, the cluster is back to normal. If we now click the button a few more times, we see the router has recovered the servers and is redirecting connections to them. The following is an example of what you should see in the terminal where you are running the application:

```
('>>> Hostname =', u'cluster-rpi2')
192.168.42.240 - - [28/May/2018 18:49:56] "POST / HTTP/1.1" 200 -
('>>> Hostname =', u'cluster-rpi3')
192.168.42.240 - - [28/May/2018 18:49:56] "POST / HTTP/1.1" 200 -
('>>> Hostname =', u'cluster-rpi4')
192.168.42.240 - - [28/May/2018 18:49:57] "POST / HTTP/1.1" 200 -
```

If you now look at the router log, you will see another metadata refresh event showing the healed cluster:

```
2018-05-28 18:49:44 metadata_cache INFO [72eff430]     cluster-rpi1:3306 /
33060 - role=HA mode=RW
2018-05-28 18:49:44 metadata_cache INFO [72eff430]     cluster-rpi2:3306 /
33060 - role=HA mode=RO
2018-05-28 18:49:44 metadata_cache INFO [72eff430]     cluster-rpi3:3306 /
33060 - role=HA mode=RO
2018-05-28 18:49:44 metadata_cache INFO [72eff430]     cluster-rpi4:3306 /
33060 - role=HA mode=RO
```

If you ever had any doubts about the router and how failover is handled for the read-only servers, this demonstration should put those to rest.

Note   If we were to disable the remaining read-only server, the application would stop. Although the router will allow reads on the read/write port (6446), the application is designed to connect only to the read-only port (6447). Thus, it is possible to build in a last-resort connection attempt to redirect reads to the read/write port. However, this is not a best practice because we general separate reads from writes.

Expanding the Example Application

Like an example that strives to communicate key aspects without overcomplicating things, the example high-availability application in this chapter is limited in practical features. However, if you like the application or see a way you can use it for further experimentation, you may want to explore a few things. The following is a short list of suggested improvements for the sample application that you may want to consider, listed in order of increasing complexity:

- Improve the error handling for the application.

- Although not a best practice, it is possible to redirect read-only connections to the read/write server (port via the router) if the read-only connection fails repeatedly.

- Add the ability to e-mail the list to others.

- Add functionality to handle more than one list.

- Convert the list to a document store, allowing you to store additional information about each item.

- Modify the application to allow multiple users to store their own lists.

- When developing the multiuser capability, allow users to make read-only access to others.

- Incorporate scanning capability to read the UPC labels on products to add items to a list or tick off items on a list.

Summary

Building high-availability applications requires solving all the same problems as a typical multiuser application. What makes a high-availability application more difficult is having to handle failures when servers go offline. Fortunately, InnoDB Cluster combined with MySQL Router makes this easier. In fact, the biggest challenge is structuring connections to the database (the cluster) so that they retry in case there is an error. Savvy enterprise application developers will tell you this is something they've always done.

In this chapter, we explored a simple high-availability web-based example application using Flask and Python. Although the application lacks the sophistication of a true multiuser application, the example is helpful for testing InnoDB Cluster and experimenting with the way InnoDB Cluster (and the router) recover from failover events.

You saw how to connect to the cluster via the router and how to isolate our database connections so that they retry if an error occurs. You also saw a technique for minimizing how long connections are held open: we open a connection only when we need to perform an operation, and then close it (disconnect) when the operation is complete. Finally, you saw an example of the log from the router, when the read/write server fails and the cluster recovers. You saw this demonstrated using the application.

The next chapter covers the various administrative tasks required to keep our InnoDB Cluster healthy and our high-availability capabilities at its peak. As you will see, not a lot needs done, but ease of administrative tasks does not mean we can be any less vigilant in our upkeep!

## CHAPTER 9

InnoDB Cluster Administration

As you have discovered, setting up InnoDB Cluster is not difficult, and except for learning how to use MySQL Shell and a few of the classes and methods in the AdminAPI, the steps for configuring InnoDB Cluster are equally easy. However, we all know from experience that setup and administration don't always compare in complexity.

Indeed, managing and maintaining MySQL Replication prior to InnoDB Cluster required learning a set of specific tasks and techniques for keeping everything running well. Fortunately, that is not the case for InnoDB Cluster. Administrative tasks were one of the key targeted areas during the evolution of what has become InnoDB Cluster along with the goal of easier to use with less complexity. As you will see, except from some rare and exceptional cases, the AdminAPI has met this goal.

In this chapter, you will look at the common tasks to administer an InnoDB Cluster. You can use this chapter as a reference as you explore InnoDB Cluster in your environment. As you will see, we have already visited some of the tasks through our walk-through of both the sandbox and live server deployment examples in Chapters 5, 7, and 8. This chapter summarizes those tasks for completeness, using brief examples. Tasks we have not discussed feature examples in more detail.

You will also look at how to make your InnoDB Cluster more secure by examining the administrative tasks for securing the cluster.

Overview

Administering an InnoDB Cluster requires using the AdminAPI via MySQL Shell. Although it is possible to work with InnoDB Cluster and Group Replication directly, it is not recommended. Administration of InnoDB Cluster should always be via the AdminAPI.

© Charles Bell 2018
C. Bell, *Introducing InnoDB Cluster*, https://doi.org/10.1007/978-1-4842-3885-1_9

> **Caution**   Always use the AdminAPI via MySQL Shell to administer an InnoDB Cluster. Working directly with Group Replication or the InnoDB Cluster metadata is not recommended.

You saw an overview of the AdminAPI in Chapter 5. There are two classes in the AdminAPI: the dba class, which is used to establish the cluster along with working with instances to prepare them for the cluster, and the cluster class, which is used to administer a cluster from checking status to resolving problems with instances.

Let's get started with a brief review of the tools and then look at the common tasks. Then we will discuss troubleshooting tasks, which are not used frequently, but only when something goes wrong.

Tools, Commands

The tool of choice for working with InnoDB Cluster is MySQL Shell, which has been featured prominently in this book. It is the only tool recommended for working with the cluster. However, it should be noted that you can write your own special scripts in either Java or Python to work with a cluster. Either method uses the AdminAPI to work with the cluster. Once again, you should not use any tools or utilities that do not use the AdminAPI. If you are an expert working with Group Replication, you may be tempted to work with the cluster by manipulating the Group Replication parameters and options, but that is not recommended. You should migrate to using MySQL Shell.

In this section, we examine the common administrative tasks for working with InnoDB Cluster. We group the tasks into the following categories:

- *General*: Basic administrative tasks for status and related checks

- *Instances*: Tasks for working with instances

Because this chapter is meant to be used as a reference, the examples are somewhat brief, showing just the basic commands you can use to complete the tasks. However, for those tasks that are used more frequently, detailed examples and output are shown. Also, the examples omit the connection step for MySQL Shell. For more information about connecting to servers using MySQL Shell, see Chapter 4.

General

The tasks in this category are those that are performed more frequently, including getting the cluster, checking status, and describing the cluster configuration.

Getting the Cluster

When working with MySQL Shell to administer InnoDB Cluster, we must first request an instance of the `cluster` class. Recall, you have seen this done several times throughout this book. To retrieve the `cluster` instance, we use the `dba.get_cluster()` method. The following shows an example of retrieving the cluster. Remember, we must connect to one of the servers in the cluster before we can retrieve it.

```
\connect root@cluster-rpi1:3306
cluster = dba.get_cluster()
```

You can also pass the name of the cluster as a parameter, but this is used for an additional error check (an error is raised if the server is not part of the cluster indicated). This helps when you have more than one cluster in your infrastructure.

Checking the Cluster Status

As with the last task, you've previously seen how to retrieve the cluster status report. Recall, we use the `cluster.status()` method. We must connect to one of the servers in the cluster, retrieve it, and then use the status method:

```
\connect root@cluster-rpi1:3306
cluster = dba.get_cluster()
cluster.status()
```

You can also chain the methods to retrieve the cluster and display the status:

```
dba.get_cluster().status()
```

This may be handy if you want to use MySQL Shell in batch mode to quickly retrieve the status.

Describing the Cluster

You can also get information about the cluster, such as the hostnames of the machines in the cluster along with the ports used by each MySQL instance. We use the `cluster.describe()` method as demonstrated in Listing 9-1.

Listing 9-1. Describing the Cluster

```
MySQL  cluster-rpi2:3306 ssl  Py > cluster = dba.get_cluster('RPI_Cluster')
MySQL  cluster-rpi2:3306 ssl  Py > cluster.describe()
{
    "clusterName": "RPI_Cluster",
    "defaultReplicaSet": {
        "name": "default",
        "topology": [
            {
                "address": "cluster-rpi1:3306",
                "label": "cluster-rpi1:3306",
                "role": "HA"
            },
            {
                "address": "cluster-rpi2:3306",
                "label": "cluster-rpi2:3306",
                "role": "HA"
            },
            {
                "address": "cluster-rpi3:3306",
                "label": "cluster-rpi3:3306",
                "role": "HA"
            },
            {
                "address": "cluster-rpi4:3306",
                "label": "cluster-rpi4:3306",
                "role": "HA"
            },
        ]
    }
}
```

Now, let's look at the tasks that work with instances.

Instances

The tasks in this category are those intended to be used on a single instance to join instances to a cluster, rejoin instances to a cluster, check the instance fitness for use with InnoDB Cluster, and similar tasks.

Check an Instance for Suitability for Use with InnoDB Cluster

You have seen the two methods you can use to prepare an instance for use with InnoDB Cluster. The first, dba.configure_local_instance(), is used to prepare the local machine for use in the cluster. The second, dba.check_instance_configuration(), can be used to test the server for proper settings. Unlike the first method, the check instance configuration method can be run remotely. The following are examples of each command:

```
\connect root@localhost:3306
dba.configure_local_instance()
dba.check_instance_configuration('root@cluster-rpi2:43306')
```

Check an Instance for Cluster Status

You can also check an instance for its current or last-known state by using the dba.check_instance_state() method. This method takes server connection information as a parameter and returns one of four states:

- OK new: The instance has not executed any GTID transactions, so it cannot conflict with the GTIDs executed by the cluster.

- OK recoverable: The instance has executed GTIDs that do not conflict with the executed GTIDs of the cluster seed instances.

- ERROR diverged: The instance has executed GTIDs that diverge from the executed GTIDs of the cluster seed instances.

- ERROR lost_transactions: The instance has more executed GTIDs than the executed GTIDs of the cluster seed instances.

Listing 9-2 shows an example of running this command.

Listing 9-2. Configuring the Local Instance

```
MySQL  Py > \connect root@localhost:3306
MySQL  Py > dba.configure_local_instance('localhost:3306')
Please provide the password for 'root@localhost:3306': ****
Configuring local MySQL instance listening at port 3306 for use in an
InnoDB cluster...

This instance reports its own address as cluster-rpi3

WARNING: User 'root' can only connect from localhost.
If you need to manage this instance while connected from other hosts, new
account(s) with the proper source address specification must be created.

1) Create remotely usable account for 'root' with same grants and password
2) Create a new admin account for InnoDB cluster with minimal required grants
3) Ignore and continue
4) Cancel

Please select an option [1]: 1
Please provide a source address filter for the account (e.g: 192.168.% or %
etc) or leave empty and press Enter to cancel.
Account Host: %

Some configuration options need to be fixed:
```

Variable	Current Value	Required Value	Note
binlog_checksum	CRC32	NONE	Update the server variable
enforce_gtid_consistency	OFF	ON	Update read-only variable and restart the server
gtid_mode	OFF	ON	Update read-only variable and restart the server

```
Do you want to perform the required configuration changes? [y/n]: y
Do you want to restart the instance after configuring it? [y/n]: y

Cluster admin user 'root'@'%' created.
Configuring instance...
The instance 'localhost:3306' was configured for cluster usage.
Restarting MySQL...
MySQL server at localhost:3306 was restarted.
```

Join an Instance to the Cluster

You have seen how to join an instance to the cluster several times during this book.
Recall, we use the cluster.add_instance() method, passing in the connection
information to connect to an instance to join the current cluster. An example of the
command to join an instance to a cluster is shown here; we must be connected to a
server in the cluster to use this method:

```
\connect root@cluster-rpi1:3306
cluster = dba.get_cluster()
cluster.add_instance('root@cluster-rpi3:3306')
```

Rejoin an Instance to the Cluster

If a server becomes disconnected from the cluster, we can rejoin it to the cluster with
the cluster.rejoin_instance() method. This takes connection information as the
parameter and attempts to reconnect the instance to the cluster. You saw this method
in action in Chapter 8. The following shows an example of rejoining an instance to the
cluster. It is always a good idea to check the status of the cluster after the operation.

```
\connect root@cluster-rpi1:3306
\connect root@cluster-rpi1:3306
cluster = dba.get_cluster()
cluster.rejoin_instance('root@cluster-rpi4:3306')
cluster.status()
```

Remove an Instance from the Cluster

If you need to perform maintenance on a physical machine or the MySQL instance running on the server, you should first remove it from the cluster. We can do this with the `cluster.remove_instance()` method:

```
\connect root@cluster-rpi1:3306
cluster = dba.get_cluster()
cluster.remove_instance('root@cluster-rpi2:3306')
cluster.status()
```

It is always a good idea to check the status of the cluster after the operation. You can add the server back to the cluster with the `cluster.rejoin_instance()` method if the InnoDB Cluster metadata is intact. If you had to remove the data or rebuild the server, you may need to use the `cluster.add_instance()` method instead.

Create a Whitelist of Instances

Say we want to specify a list of approved servers for use with the cluster (a permissive list called a *whitelist*[1]), which restricts connection to the cluster to only those machines on the list. We can create the whitelist explicitly by passing a special parameter to the `create_cluster()`, `add_instance()`, or `rejoin_instance()` method. For example, the following shows how to create a cluster that restricts connections to the servers on a specific subnet (192.168.42.X):

```
\connect root@cluster-rpi1:3306
cluster = dba.create_cluster('RPI_Cluster', {ipWhitelist: '192.168.42.0/24"})
```

Customize Cluster Metadata

As you may recall from the various examples in this book and this chapter, we normally do not add any customization to the cluster metadata beyond naming the cluster. This is because default values are set for options such as the group name, the local address, and the seed instances. However, we can specify values for these attributes by overriding them in the setup and configuration methods, including `dba.create_cluster()` and `cluster.add_instance()`.

---

[1]As opposed to a blacklist, which is a list of things you want to prohibit.

Setting the Group Name

To set the name of the replication group, use the groupName option for the dba.create_cluster() method. However, you must use a valid UUID. The following is an example:

```
dba.create_cluster('RPI_Cluster', {'groupName':'0cc3ebad-6759-11e8-966f-c49ded13bebf'})
```

You can see the value in the group_replication_group_name system variable by issuing the following SQL statement:

```
\sql;
SHOW VARIABLES LIKE 'group_replication_group_name';
```

Setting the Local Address

The *local address* is the address that an instance provides for connections from other instances. You can set the local address by using the localAddress option when calling the dba.create_cluster() and cluster.add_instance() methods. This sets the group_replication_local_address system variable on the instance.

You must provide a value by using the string format host:port. Note that the address must be one that all instances in the cluster can access (supported by DNS or hosts file entries). Furthermore, Oracle states in the online reference manual that this value must be used for only internal, instance-to-instance communication and not external access to/from the cluster. The following is an example of how to use the option:

```
dba.create_cluster('RPI_Cluster', {'localAddress':'192.168.42.241:3306'})
```

You can see the value in the group_replication_local_address system variable by issuing the following SQL statement:

```
\sql;
SHOW VARIABLES LIKE 'group_replication_local_address';
```

Setting the Group Seeds

The *group seeds* are a list of those instances that are used to connect when an instance joins the cluster. This allows the instance to get the correct metadata for use with the cluster. You can set the group seeds by using the groupSeeds option when calling the dba.create_cluster() and cluster.add_instance() methods.

The addresses are specified as a comma-separated list (string) using the format host1:port1,host2:port2, <etc>. The following is an example of how to use the option:

```
dba.create_cluster('RPI_Cluster',
{'groupSeeds':'192.168.42.241:3306,192.168.42.242:3306'})
```

You can see the value in the group_replication_group_seeds system variable by issuing the following SQL statement:

```
\sql;
SHOW VARIABLES LIKE ' group_replication_group_seeds ';
```

Now, let's look at the troubleshooting tasks.

Troubleshooting InnoDB Cluster

If you are struggling with getting the cluster to form and add instances, chances are something odd has happened to your machines or to MySQL on those machines. Say, for example, that you are unable to add an instance and have checked that the instance is valid via the dba.check_instance_configuration() method, but the cluster still won't accept the instance. In this case, the cluster may have gone away (the metadata is wrong, corrupt, or missing).

The tasks in the troubleshooting category are those tasks that you may encounter or need should something go wrong or fail. These are not tasks that you would perform routinely—quite the contrary, we hope to never need these tasks! In fact, some may be considered dangerous, so use them with caution.

Recover from Quorum Loss

It is possible under unusual conditions that an instance could lose its quorum (the ability to participate in the voting scheme for determining the primary in the event of loss). We can use the cluster.force_quorum_using_partition_of() method to reestablish the quorum. You will know this has occurred when the status of the instances is set to NO_QUORUM. The following shows an example of the command and output from the AdminAPI:

```
cluster.force_quorum_using_partition_of ("localhost:3310")

  Restoring replicaset 'default' from loss of quorum, by using the
  partition composed of [localhost:3310]
```

```
Please provide the password for 'root@localhost:3310': ******
Restoring the InnoDB cluster ...
```

The InnoDB cluster was successfully restored using the partition from the instance 'root@localhost:3310'.

Caution   Use this method with extreme care. You can encounter a split-brain scenario. To avoid this, ensure that all other members of the replica set are removed or joined back to the group that was restored.

Reboot from Complete Loss

Should you need to reboot a cluster after a complete outage or loss—such as when all the servers in the cluster have been shut down (or a similar event)—you can use the dba. reboot_cluster_from_complete_outage() method. Just make sure that all your cluster servers are online and that MySQL is started and working on all nodes. This task can be used for experimental or developmental clusters that have been shut down intentionally or from necessity. Listing 9-3 shows an example of rebooting a cluster from complete loss.

Listing 9-3. Rebooting the Cluster from Complete Loss

```
MySQL  Py > \connect root@cluster-rpi1:3306
Creating a session to 'root@cluster-rpi1:3306'
Enter password: ****
Fetching schema names for autocompletion... Press ^C to stop.
Your MySQL connection id is 15
Server version: 8.0.11 MySQL Community Server (GPL)
No default schema selected; type \use <schema> to set one.

 MySQL  cluster-rpi1:3306 ssl  Py > cluster = dba.reboot_cluster_from_
complete_outage('RPI_Cluster')
Reconfiguring the cluster 'RPI_Cluster' from complete outage...

The instance 'cluster-rpi2:3306' was part of the cluster configuration.
Would you like to rejoin it to the cluster? [y/N]: y
```

The instance 'cluster-rpi4:3306' was part of the cluster configuration. Would you like to rejoin it to the cluster? [y/N]: y

The instance 'cluster-rpi3:3306' was part of the cluster configuration. Would you like to rejoin it to the cluster? [y/N]: y

The cluster was successfully rebooted.

```
 MySQL  cluster-rpi1:3306 ssl  Py > cluster.status()
{
    "clusterName": "RPI_Cluster",
    "defaultReplicaSet": {
        "name": "default",
        "primary": "cluster-rpi1:3306",
        "ssl": "REQUIRED",
        "status": "OK",
        "statusText": "Cluster is ONLINE and can tolerate up to ONE
        failure.",
        "topology": {
            "cluster-rpi1:3306": {
                "address": "cluster-rpi1:3306",
                "mode": "R/W",
                "readReplicas": {},
                "role": "HA",
                "status": "ONLINE"
            },
            "cluster-rpi2:3306": {
                "address": "cluster-rpi2:3306",
                "mode": "R/O",
                "readReplicas": {},
                "role": "HA",
                "status": "ONLINE"
            },
            "cluster-rpi3:3306": {
                "address": "cluster-rpi3:3306",
                "mode": "R/O",
                "readReplicas": {},
```

```
                "role": "HA",
                "status": "ONLINE"
            },
            "cluster-rpi4:3306": {
                "address": "cluster-rpi4:3306",
                "mode": "R/O",
                "readReplicas": {},
                "role": "HA",
                "status": "ONLINE"
            }
        }
    },
    "groupInformationSourceMember": "mysql://root@cluster-rpi1:3306"
}
```

Note   You must specify the cluster name to use this method. Otherwise, you will get an error.

Rescan Cluster Metadata

Should you (or someone) make changes to the cluster without using the AdminAPI (such as manually adding or removing a machine from Group Replication), you may be able to repair the InnoDB Cluster metadata by using the cluster.rescan() method.

This method will attempt to repair the metadata and attempt to add the instances to the cluster. You will be prompted to approve each server found. Should a server not be allowed to join the cluster or encounter errors, the server is reported so that you can try to add the instance later. The following is an example of running this command:

```
 MySQL  cluster-rpi1:3306 ssl  Py > cluster.rescan()
Rescanning the cluster...

Result of the rescanning operation:
{
    "defaultReplicaSet": {
```

```
        "name": "default",
        "newlyDiscoveredInstances": [],
        "unavailableInstances": []
    }
}
```

Here, we don't see any instances that are new or unavailable. Had there been any, you would have seen them as follows:

```
 MySQL  cluster-rpi1:3306 ssl  Py > cluster.rescan()
Rescanning the cluster...
```

```
Result of the rescanning operation:
{
    "defaultReplicaSet": {
        "name": "default",
        "newlyDiscoveredInstances": [],
        "unavailableInstances": [
            {
                "host": "cluster-rpi4:3306",
                "label": "cluster-rpi4:3306",
                "member_id": "1fec2731-53d2-11e8-914c-b827ebcb9200"
            }
        ]
    }
}
```

Notice the instance cluster-rpi4:3306 is no longer part of the high availability setup. It is either offline or has left the high availability group. You can try to add it to the cluster again with the cluster.rejoin_instance('cluster-rpi4:3306') command, or you can remove it from the cluster configuration.

```
Would you like to remove it from the cluster metadata? [Y/n]: n
```

For this question, we typically do not want to remove the instance under normal circumstances—for example, when you need to take an instance offline for repairs. Therefore, we should reply N. If, on the other hand, the instance should be removed, you can do so by answering Y to the question.

The following is an example of using the `cluster.rejoin_instance()` method to rejoin an instance to the cluster:

```
MySQL  cluster-rpi1:3306 ssl  Py > cluster.rejoin_instance('root@cluster-
 rpi4:3306')
Rejoining the instance to the InnoDB cluster. Depending on the original
problem that made the instance unavailable, the rejoin operation might not
be successful and further manual steps will be needed to fix the underlying
problem.

Please monitor the output of the rejoin operation and take necessary action
if the instance cannot rejoin.

Please provide the password for 'root@cluster-rpi4:3306': ****
Rejoining instance to the cluster ...

The instance 'cluster-rpi4:3306' was successfully rejoined on the cluster.
```

Now, if we rescan the cluster, we should see that there are no longer any instances unavailable or new to the cluster, as shown here:

```
MySQL  cluster-rpi1:3306 ssl  Py > cluster.rescan()
Rescanning the cluster...

Result of the rescanning operation:
{
    "defaultReplicaSet": {
        "name": "default",
        "newlyDiscoveredInstances": [],
        "unavailableInstances": []
    }
}
```

Cluster Teardown

In the rare case that you need to completely remove all instances from a cluster and remove the cluster, you can use the `cluster.dissolve()` method. If you set the `force` option to `True`, the method will remove all instances and dissolve the cluster. Like similar methods, this is one to use as a last resort or for experimentation or development. The following is an example of using the method:

```
 MySQL  cluster-rpi1:3306 ssl  Py > cluster.dissolve({'force':True})
The cluster was successfully dissolved.
Replication was disabled but user data was left intact.

You can now rebuild your cluster.
```

If you performed this task to try to fix errors or rebuild the cluster, you can do so, because all the metadata and settings have been removed from the instance. Listing 9-4 shows how to reestablish the example cluster from Chapter 7.

Listing 9-4. Reestablishing the Cluster after Dissolving

```
 MySQL  cluster-rpi1:3306 ssl  Py > dba.create_cluster('RPI_Cluster')
A new InnoDB cluster will be created on instance 'root@cluster-rpi1:3306'.

The MySQL instance at 'cluster-rpi1:3306' currently has the super_read_only
system variable set to protect it from inadvertent updates from applications.
You must first unset it to be able to perform any changes to this instance.
For more information see: https://dev.mysql.com/doc/refman/en/server-
system-variables.html#sysvar_super_read_only.

Note: there are open sessions to 'cluster-rpi1:3306'.
You may want to kill these sessions to prevent them from performing
unexpected updates:

1 open session(s) of 'root@192.168.42.240'.

Do you want to disable super_read_only and continue? [y/N]: y

Validating instance at cluster-rpi1:3306...
```

This instance reports its own address as cluster-rpi1

Instance configuration is suitable.
Creating InnoDB cluster 'RPI_Cluster' on 'root@cluster-rpi1:3306'...
Adding Seed Instance...

Cluster successfully created. Use Cluster.add_instance() to add MySQL
instances. At least 3 instances are needed for the cluster to be able to
withstand up to one server failure.

<Cluster:RPI_Cluster>

```
 MySQL  cluster-rpi1:3306 ssl  Py > cluster = dba.get_cluster()
 MySQL  cluster-rpi1:3306 ssl  Py > cluster.add_instance('root@cluster-
 rpi2:3306')
```
A new instance will be added to the InnoDB cluster. Depending on the amount
of data on the cluster this might take from a few seconds to several hours.

Please provide the password for 'root@cluster-rpi2:3306': ****
Adding instance to the cluster ...

Validating instance at cluster-rpi2:3306...

This instance reports its own address as cluster-rpi2

Instance configuration is suitable.
The instance 'root@cluster-rpi2:3306' was successfully added to the
cluster.

```
 MySQL  cluster-rpi1:3306 ssl  Py > cluster.add_instance('root@cluster-
 rpi3:3306')
```
A new instance will be added to the InnoDB cluster. Depending on the amount
of data on the cluster this might take from a few seconds to several hours.

Please provide the password for 'root@cluster-rpi3:3306': ****
Adding instance to the cluster ...

Validating instance at cluster-rpi3:3306...

This instance reports its own address as cluster-rpi3

Instance configuration is suitable.
The instance 'root@cluster-rpi3:3306' was successfully added to the
cluster.

```
 MySQL  cluster-rpi1:3306 ssl  Py > cluster.add_instance('root@cluster-
 rpi4:3306')
```
A new instance will be added to the InnoDB cluster. Depending on the amount
of data on the cluster this might take from a few seconds to several hours.

Please provide the password for 'root@cluster-rpi4:3306': ****
Adding instance to the cluster ...

Validating instance at cluster-rpi4:3306...

This instance reports its own address as cluster-rpi4

Instance configuration is suitable.
The instance 'root@cluster-rpi4:3306' was successfully added to the
cluster.

```
 MySQL  cluster-rpi1:3306 ssl  Py > cluster.status()
{
    "clusterName": "RPI_Cluster",
    "defaultReplicaSet": {
        "name": "default",
        "primary": "cluster-rpi1:3306",
        "ssl": "REQUIRED",
        "status": "OK",
        "statusText": "Cluster is ONLINE and can tolerate up to ONE failure.",
        "topology": {
            "cluster-rpi1:3306": {
                "address": "cluster-rpi1:3306",
                "mode": "R/W",
                "readReplicas": {},
                "role": "HA",
                "status": "ONLINE"
            },
```

```
            "cluster-rpi2:3306": {
                "address": "cluster-rpi2:3306",
                "mode": "R/O",
                "readReplicas": {},
                "role": "HA",
                "status": "ONLINE"
            },
            "cluster-rpi3:3306": {
                "address": "cluster-rpi3:3306",
                "mode": "R/O",
                "readReplicas": {},
                "role": "HA",
                "status": "ONLINE"
            },
            "cluster-rpi4:3306": {
                "address": "cluster-rpi4:3306",
                "mode": "R/O",
                "readReplicas": {},
                "role": "HA",
                "status": "ONLINE"
            }
        }
    },
    "groupInformationSourceMember": "mysql://root@cluster-rpi1:3306"
}

 MySQL  cluster-rpi1:3306 ssl  Py > cluster.describe()
{
    "clusterName": "RPI_Cluster",
    "defaultReplicaSet": {
        "name": "default",
        "topology": [
            {
                "address": "cluster-rpi1:3306",
                "label": "cluster-rpi1:3306",
                "role": "HA"
            },
```

```
        {
            "address": "cluster-rpi2:3306",
            "label": "cluster-rpi2:3306",
            "role": "HA"
        },
        {

            "address": "cluster-rpi3:3306",
            "label": "cluster-rpi3:3306",
            "role": "HA"
        },
        {

            "address": "cluster-rpi4:3306",
            "label": "cluster-rpi4:3306",
            "role": "HA"
        }
    ]
  }
}
```

Recovering from Metadata Errors

If your servers were powered off—say, you shut them all down at the end of the day—you may encounter the following error (or one similar) when restarting work the next day. This is because InnoDB Cluster (and any high availability system) is not designed to be shut down and restarted. You can shut down some of the servers for maintenance, but you should always keep at least three servers running. Although InnoDB Cluster will continue to run, warnings and potentially errors will occur in the log until at least three servers have been added to the cluster. So, if you have only three instances and must take one offline for maintenance, you can. However, you should consider adding another instance to the cluster during the maintenance task to ensure that you have the minimum number of instances.

```
MySQL  localhost:33060+ ssl  Py > cluster = dba.get_cluster('RPI_Cluster')
Traceback (most recent call last):
  File "<string>", line 1, in <module>
SystemError: RuntimeError: Dba.get_cluster: This function is not available
through a session to a standalone instance (metadata exists, but GR is not
active)
```

The following demonstrates how to recover the cluster from total outage. Specifically, the servers have all been restarted (powered off and restarted), and you need to restart the cluster from the last-known-good position. We will use the dba.reboot_cluster_ from_complete_outage() method to reboot the cluster. First, log into one of the servers and run the command as follows:

```
MySQL  localhost:33060+ ssl  Py > cluster = dba.reboot_cluster_from_
complete_outage('RPI_Cluster')
Reconfiguring the cluster 'RPI_Cluster' from complete outage...

The instance '192.168.42.244:3306' was part of the cluster configuration.
Would you like to rejoin it to the cluster? [y/N]: y

The instance '192.168.42.243:3306' was part of the cluster configuration.
Would you like to rejoin it to the cluster? [y/N]: y

The instance '192.168.42.242:3306' was part of the cluster configuration.
Would you like to rejoin it to the cluster? [y/N]: y

The cluster was successfully rebooted.
```

If this works, you will see messages indicating that the cluster was rebooted.

Last Resort

If, after attempting to recover the cluster, you still have issues and want to start over from scratch, you can do so by issuing the following commands on each server. This is a rather radical step and will remove all metadata and restart Group Replication. However, you should use this as a last resort because it disrupts the normal flow of any transactions that occurred during the outage event (unlikely, but possible).

```
dba.drop_metadata_schema()
RESET SLAVE
RESET MASTER
```

The first command drops the InnoDB Cluster metadata, effectively removing the server from the cluster. The next two SQL commands reset replication on the server. Recall, we can run each of these commands via MySQL Shell connected to the machine, but we must use Python mode (\py) for the first command and SQL mode (\sql) for the last two commands.

Caution   This is a very dangerous task and recommended for use only as a last resort.

After these commands are entered on all the servers, you can start over by creating the cluster and adding the instances. Again, this is a last-resort technique and not recommended for any production system.

Now, let's look at some best practices for administering MySQL InnoDB Cluster.

Best Practices

Now that you have seen a list of the common maintenance tasks as well as some of the troubleshooting tasks you may need in order to repair your cluster, let's discuss a few key best practices for administering InnoDB Cluster. The practices listed in this section are neither complete nor the only practices you should consider for InnoDB Cluster. Rather, the practices listed here are meant to be reminders of the key practices you should employ. Further, these practices assume that you are also employing the typical best practices for any high-availability system.

We begin with a few things that may seem mundane to some but merit including for those new to InnoDB Cluster or high-availability solutions. The following sections contain those best practices that you should consider in addition to any best practices you have developed in your organization.

No Shutdown and Restart

High-availability systems are not designed to be shut down and restarted routinely. Indeed, there is no "shutdown" command in the AdminAPI. This statement refers to the entire cluster, not a single instance; you may need to take an instance offline for maintenance or repair, but the cluster should never be shut down (the only exceptions are experiments or development trials). You should plan your InnoDB Cluster installation so that you do not have to shut it down or restart it often.

Back Up Your Data Before Making Changes

One of the primary tools for any administrator of any system that has data with value[2] is the ability to save the data before making any changes. The tool of choice here is a backup-and-restore utility. Fortunately, MySQL comes with two such tools in the community edition: mysqlpump and mysqldump. These are logical backup tools that allow you to create a file with the SQL statements to restore data from one or more databases. The mysqlpump utility is the replacement for mysqldump and works a bit better, especially with larger databases, because mysqlpump can perform parallel dumps. However, either is OK for use in this demonstration.

As mentioned, these are logical backup utilities that make a copy of the data row by row rather than a binary backup that makes binary copies of the data. Thus, logical backups tend to be slower and take more space than binary backups. Binary backups also typically allow the server to be put in a short period of locking the data, allowing for backups to be taken while the server is online and accepting changes (sometimes called a *hot backup*). Logical backups typically require locking the database(s) for the duration of the backup. For this demonstration, we do not have a large dataset, nor do we have any concerns for an online backup operation and thus can use a logical backup without any issues.

---

[2]Isn't all data valuable to the owner?

ENTERPRISE-GRADE BACKUP FOR MYSQL

If you are planning to use MySQL in your enterprise, and especially if you plan to deploy InnoDB Cluster, you should consider the Enterprise Edition. Although it is a paid offering from Oracle, it includes a host of enterprise-grade tools including MySQL Enterprise Backup (MEB).

MEB is a full binary backup utility that permits all manner of backups required for providing backup and recovery of MySQL servers. MEB can perform full backups, incremental backups, encrypted backups, compressed backups, and much more. If you're interested in learning more about MEB, see the online MySQL Enterprise Backup reference manual at `https://dev.mysql.com/doc/mysql-enterprise-backup/8.0/en/`.

In this section, you will discover how to take a logical backup of our data before performing any maintenance operation. This is imperative to allow you to recover from a change that disables the data or in some way makes access to the data (or the data itself) compromised. A good systems administrator should always make a backup before any maintenance occurs. After the change has been verified as good, you can always delete the backup files if space is an issue.[3]

If you have the cluster active, let's first take a backup of the data we created to ensure that we don't lose it. Because we have only a small amount of data, we will use the simple, logical backup tool named `mysqlpump`. Let's work from the application server.

The following shows a command you can use to perform a logical backup of the example database and store it locally on the application server. We must provide the user connection information, host, and port. We also provide an option to generate the `DROP DATABASE` and `TABLE` commands placed at the top of the file, which helps to restore the data by deleting the data first. We also add an option to set the `GTID_PURGED` variable to `OFF` so we do not capture the GTID information. Recall, InnoDB Cluster uses Group Replication, but we are using InnoDB Cluster and the AdminAPI to manage the cluster, so we do not need the GTID information. We will name the file `backup_pre_changes.sql`. It's named as a `.sql` file because `mysqlpump` creates SQL statements for saving the schema and data.

```
$ mysqlpump -uroot -p -h localhost --port=3306 --add-drop-database --add-
drop-table --set-gtid-purged=OFF shopping > backup_pre_changes.sql
```

---

[3]I tend to save backup files for at least a month, just in case.

When you execute this command, nothing will appear to happen because we redirected all output to the file. This is because the utility prints the SQL commands to standard out. If you're curious, open the file and look at the SQL commands. Listing 9-5 is an example excerpt of what the file should contain.

Listing 9-5. Example Logical Backup (mysqlpump)

```
-- Dump created by MySQL pump utility, version: 8.0.11, Linux (armv7l)
-- Dump start time: Fri Jun  1 15:23:00 2018
-- Server version: 8.0.11

SET @OLD_UNIQUE_CHECKS=@@UNIQUE_CHECKS, UNIQUE_CHECKS=0;
SET @OLD_FOREIGN_KEY_CHECKS=@@FOREIGN_KEY_CHECKS, FOREIGN_KEY_CHECKS=0;
SET @OLD_SQL_MODE=@@SQL_MODE;
SET SQL_MODE="NO_AUTO_VALUE_ON_ZERO";
SET @@SESSION.SQL_LOG_BIN= 0;
SET @OLD_TIME_ZONE=@@TIME_ZONE;
SET TIME_ZONE='+00:00';
SET @OLD_CHARACTER_SET_CLIENT=@@CHARACTER_SET_CLIENT;
SET @OLD_CHARACTER_SET_RESULTS=@@CHARACTER_SET_RESULTS;
SET @OLD_COLLATION_CONNECTION=@@COLLATION_CONNECTION;
SET NAMES utf8mb4;
SET @@GLOBAL.GTID_PURGED=/*!80000 '+'*/ '16cce4a6-53d1-11e8-badc-
b827eb2bc4f3:1-2,
2d550a88-5453-11e8-9517-b827eb2bc4f3:1-27,
4127c169-520f-11e8-a834-b827ebcb9200:1-170,
4b2d0de2-5454-11e8-9517-b827eb2bc4f3:1-3,
de5cbffd-5455-11e8-85a7-b827eb2bc4f3:1-119:1000102,
f1cdcfd9-62a2-11e8-9e50-b827eb2bc4f3:1-37,
fc2bf2b7-53ca-11e8-a131-b827eb2bc4f3:1-2';
DROP DATABASE IF EXISTS `shopping`;
CREATE DATABASE /*!32312 IF NOT EXISTS*/ `shopping` /*!40100 DEFAULT
CHARACTER SET utf8mb4 COLLATE utf8mb4_0900_ai_ci */;
DROP TABLE IF EXISTS `shopping`.`list`;
CREATE TABLE `shopping`.`list` (
`rowid` int(11) NOT NULL AUTO_INCREMENT,
`description` char(64) DEFAULT NULL,
```

```
`note` char(64) DEFAULT NULL,
`purchased` int(11) DEFAULT '0',
PRIMARY KEY (`rowid`)
) ENGINE=InnoDB AUTO_INCREMENT=6 DEFAULT CHARSET=utf8mb4
COLLATE=utf8mb4_0900_ai_ci
;
INSERT INTO `shopping`.`list` VALUES (1,"Milk","2%",1),(2,"Bread","",0),(3,"
Eggs","Free range",0),(4,"Cheese","Cheddar",0),(5,"Bagels","",0);
Dump progress: 1/1 tables, 0/5 rows
mysqlpump: [WARNING] (3719) 'utf8' is currently an alias for the character
set UTF8MB3, which will be replaced by UTF8MB4 in a future release. Please
consider using UTF8MB4 in order to be unambiguous.
mysqlpump: [WARNING] (3719) 'utf8' is currently an alias for the character
set UTF8MB3, which will be replaced by UTF8MB4 in a future release. Please
consider using UTF8MB4 in order to be unambiguous.
SET TIME_ZONE=@OLD_TIME_ZONE;
SET CHARACTER_SET_CLIENT=@OLD_CHARACTER_SET_CLIENT;
SET CHARACTER_SET_RESULTS=@OLD_CHARACTER_SET_RESULTS;
SET COLLATION_CONNECTION=@OLD_COLLATION_CONNECTION;
SET FOREIGN_KEY_CHECKS=@OLD_FOREIGN_KEY_CHECKS;
SET UNIQUE_CHECKS=@OLD_UNIQUE_CHECKS;
SET SQL_MODE=@OLD_SQL_MODE;
-- Dump end time: Fri Jun  1 15:23:11 2018
Dump completed in 10798
```

Should you need to restore the data, you can use MySQL Shell to read the file by using the \source command in SQL mode, as shown in Listing 9-6. However, you should not need to do that unless you've accidentally deleted the data. Also, for restoring data in an InnoDB Cluster, you should run this command on the read/write server connection (6446).

Listing 9-6. Restoring a Logical Backup (mysqlsh)

```
pi@cluster-rpi1:~ $ mysqlsh root@cluster-rpi1:3306 --sql
Creating a session to 'root@cluster-rpi1:3306'
Enter password: ****
Fetching schema names for autocompletion... Press ^C to stop.
Your MySQL connection id is 93
```

```
Server version: 8.0.11 MySQL Community Server (GPL)
No default schema selected; type \use <schema> to set one.
MySQL Shell 8.0.11

Copyright (c) 2016, 2018, Oracle and/or its affiliates. All rights reserved.

Oracle is a registered trademark of Oracle Corporation and/or its
affiliates. Other names may be trademarks of their respective
owners.

Type '\help' or '\?' for help; '\quit' to exit.

 MySQL  cluster-rpi1:3306 ssl  SQL > \source shopping_logical_backup.sql
Query OK, 0 rows affected (0.0022 sec)
Query OK, 0 rows affected (0.0018 sec)
Query OK, 0 rows affected (0.0017 sec)
Query OK, 0 rows affected (0.0017 sec)
Query OK, 0 rows affected (0.0016 sec)
Query OK, 0 rows affected (0.0017 sec)
Query OK, 0 rows affected (0.0019 sec)
Query OK, 0 rows affected (0.0017 sec)
Query OK, 0 rows affected (0.0017 sec)
Query OK, 0 rows affected (0.0017 sec)
Query OK, 0 rows affected (0.0019 sec)
Query OK, 1 row affected (0.2923 sec)
Query OK, 1 row affected (0.0121 sec)
Query OK, 0 rows affected, 1 warning (0.0083 sec)
Note (code 1051): Unknown table 'shopping.list'
Query OK, 0 rows affected (0.1067 sec)
Query OK, 5 rows affected (0.0187 sec)

Records: 5  Duplicates: 0  Warnings: 0
Query OK, 0 rows affected (0.0013 sec)
Query OK, 0 rows affected (0.0017 sec)
Query OK, 0 rows affected (0.0018 sec)
Query OK, 0 rows affected (0.0017 sec)
Query OK, 0 rows affected (0.0018 sec)
Query OK, 0 rows affected (0.0017 sec)
Query OK, 0 rows affected (0.0015 sec)
```

> **Tip**   Always make a backup of your data prior to making major changes to your cluster.

Think Group, Not Independent Servers

One the biggest hurdles in learning how to deploy and manage InnoDB Cluster is thinking of the cluster as a group of like servers rather than as a set of individual servers. This is an especially important lesson for those coming from traditional MySQL master/ slave replication. In the past, it was common to think of the servers in the topology as individuals that you must work with separately. This is because we had machines that would process changes from a single master through relay logs, and these servers (slaves) were never communicating with each other.

However, InnoDB Cluster (thanks to its Group Replication roots) treats the machines in the cluster as a group, with one (or more) acting as read/write servers. In fact, managing which machines play which roles is automatic, so we need not know which server has which role. The addition of MySQL Router handles the changes for us as they occur in the cluster.

When working with InnoDB Cluster, we must think of the cluster as a high-availability component of our infrastructure rather than as a set of loosely coupled servers. This will allow you to consider InnoDB Cluster as a data store in and of itself, which is exactly what it is meant to become.

Although it is true that hardware maintenance is still on a machine-by-machine basis, working with InnoDB Cluster can be done from any machine in the cluster or from another machine not in the cluster. This makes things far easier than older forms of MySQL Replication, freeing the developer to focus on the application rather than the details of this high-availability data store.

Securing InnoDB Cluster

The last best practice should be the first thing anyone thinks about—security! Given the rising threats from both within and without an organization, improving security must be a primary goal for any project. InnoDB Cluster is no exception.

Developers should consider securing not only their applications, but also the data and services behind the scenes. Indeed, all solutions that use the Internet must develop better security practices. The unique aspects of a high-availability solutions make it especially difficult to plan and implement stringent security practices because of the multiple points of vulnerability. More specifically, each component may have different types of vulnerability, from physical access to devices, to remote attacks against the services.

The recent rash of massive data breaches proves that their security wasn't enough. We've seen everything from outright theft to exploitation of data stolen from well-known businesses like Target (more than 40 million credit card numbers may have been compromised) and government agencies like the United States Office of Personnel Management (more than 20 million Social Security numbers compromised). Interestingly, the source of the breach was traced back to third-party contractors and services. Clearly, no one is safe. We need a revolutionary step rather than refining the tried-and-true mechanisms.

Sadly, there is a limit to how far we can go in securing our solutions. As any information technology (IT) professional will tell you, applying the best, stringent password policies and tight security practices can force users to jeopardize the very strategy designed to protect them and their data. For example, consider password policies that require passwords to be 16 or more characters with at least four capital letters, six numerals, three special characters, and no English dictionary words; to expire every 60 days; and to not have more than seven characters in common with previous passwords. In this situation, some users will be forced to write down their passwords because they cannot remember a random mixture of letters, capitals, numerals, and special characters.

However, making passwords harder to guess or crack is only one strategy. Indeed, various philosophies exist about how to secure systems properly. Although an in-depth discussion of all techniques is beyond the scope of this book, considering how to improve security in InnoDB Cluster is important.

So, what do we do? Do we implement good practices to ensure that systems are not easily compromised, or do we risk lower security for ease of use? The bottom line is that you must choose the security solution that best meets the need to protect the data and services without forcing users to endure onerous practices and without making their lives difficult.

InnoDB Cluster is designed to work with the latest security improvements in MySQL, including the new authentication plugin (`https://dev.mysql.com/doc/refman/8.0/en/caching-sha2-pluggable-authentication.html`), making it more secure than any previous releases of MySQL. Still, we can do more to protect our data. Fortunately, MySQL makes this easy to do by enabling SSL connections to encrypt our communication between the cluster and the client (yes, even via the router).

There are two main aspects or tools for securing InnoDB Cluster. First, we should use SSL connections. Second, we can add a whitelist of servers for allowing only certain servers access to the cluster.

SSL Connections

By default, SSL connections are enabled for MySQL servers in the GA release of MySQL 8. If you are using MySQL 8.0.11 or later, your connections among the servers in your cluster are already configured with SSL. However, if you loaded a different authentication plugin or are using older, but compatible, MySQL 5.7 servers, you may want to consider enabling SSL connections.

Tip MySQL can be configured to use only security connections. A complete tutorial for setting up SSL in MySQL can be found in the "Using Encrypted Connections" section of the online reference manual for more details.

You can quickly determine whether your servers are using SSL by issuing the query shown in Listing 9-7 on any server. Notice that the HAVE_SSL variable is set to YES, and the SSL options are populated accordingly, with a minimal set of options.

Listing 9-7. Displaying the SSL Variables

```
SHOW VARIABLES LIKE '%ssl%';
+-----------------------------------------------------+----------------+
| Variable_name                                       | Value          |
+-----------------------------------------------------+----------------+
| group_replication_recovery_ssl_ca                   |                |
| group_replication_recovery_ssl_capath               |                |
| group_replication_recovery_ssl_cert                 |                |
| group_replication_recovery_ssl_cipher               |                |
| group_replication_recovery_ssl_crl                  |                |
```

```
| group_replication_recovery_ssl_crlpath               |                 |
| group_replication_recovery_ssl_key                   |                 |
| group_replication_recovery_ssl_verify_server_cert    | OFF             |
| group_replication_recovery_use_ssl                   | ON              |
| group_replication_ssl_mode                           | REQUIRED        |
| have_openssl                                         | YES             |
| have_ssl                                             | YES             |
| mysqlx_ssl_ca                                        |                 |
| mysqlx_ssl_capath                                    |                 |
| mysqlx_ssl_cert                                      |                 |
| mysqlx_ssl_cipher                                    |                 |
| mysqlx_ssl_crl                                       |                 |
| mysqlx_ssl_crlpath                                   |                 |
| mysqlx_ssl_key                                       |                 |
| ssl_ca                                               | ca.pem          |
| ssl_capath                                           |                 |
| ssl_cert                                             | server-cert.pem |
| ssl_cipher                                           |                 |
| ssl_crl                                              |                 |
| ssl_crlpath                                          |                 |
| ssl_fips_mode                                        | OFF             |
| ssl_key                                              | server-key.pem  |
+------------------------------------------------------+-----------------+
27 rows in set (0.0415 sec)
```

The way we tell InnoDB Cluster to use SSL is to pass an option to the cluster during the `dba.create_cluster()` method, much as we do to set other metadata. In this case, we must set the `memberSslMode` key to one of the following values. As you can see, the default is to use SSL on create, so creating the cluster as demonstrated in this book will ensure that the cluster is configured to SSL connections.

- AUTO: (Default) SSL encryption is automatically enabled if the server instance supports it, or disabled if the server does not support it.

- REQUIRED: SSL encryption is enabled for the seed instance in the cluster. If it cannot be enabled, an error is raised.

- DISABLED: Ensures that SSL encryption is disabled for the seed instance in the cluster.

Similarly, when we add instances with the `cluster.add_instance()` method or permit an instance to rejoin the cluster with the `cluster.rejoin_instance()` method, SSL encryption on the instance is enabled or disabled based on the setting found for the seed instance (the first instance where we created the cluster). However, you can use the same `memberSslMode` option with these methods to control SSL connections as follows. As you can see, the default is to use SSL for instances, just as it is for creating the cluster.

- AUTO: (Default) SSL encryption is automatically enabled or disabled based on the setting used by the seed instance (other members of the cluster) and the available SSL support provided by the instance itself.

- REQUIRED: Forces SSL encryption to be enabled for the instance in the cluster.

- DISABLED: Ensures that SSL encryption is disabled for the instance in the cluster.

For deployments of InnoDB Cluster that already have Group Replication configured, we can tell InnoDB Cluster to adopt the SSL settings from the existing group by using the `adoptFromGR` key when creating the cluster. When you do this, no SSL settings are changed on the adopted cluster.

Note   The `memberSslMode` key cannot be used with the `adoptFromGR` key.

Server Whitelist

As mentioned in the "Create a Whitelist of Instances" section previously, you can create a whitelist of servers that limits access to certain servers so that no other servers can connect to or join the cluster. This is an excellent option to use if you have a large infrastructure and want to isolate access to the cluster to a set of servers for compartmentalization or similar organizational goals.

Recall, we can create the whitelist explicitly by passing a special parameter to the `create_cluster()`, `add_instance()`, or `rejoin_instance()` method. Thus, using a whitelist must be considered before you configure your server. However, if you want to build a whitelist for an existing cluster, you may need to remove the instance and then add it back to the cluster, passing the metadata to add it to the whitelist.

> **Tip**   If you plan to use a whitelist, you should set the whitelist options when you create the cluster and add the instances.

Example: Requiring SSL Connections

The most secure form of these options is setting memberSslMode to REQUIRED. Let's see a short example of how to do this. While we're at it, we will also create a whitelist of servers to further secure the cluster. Recall, we do this by setting ipWhitelist to the subnet 192.168.42. Otherwise, we issue the normal commands for creating the cluster and adding instances, but we pass the following options to the methods. You will see a demonstration of using this option in this section.

```
{'memberSslMode': 'REQUIRED', 'ipWhitelist': '192.168.42.0/24'}
```

These options allow us to make our cluster more secure by always requiring SSL connections and limiting access to those servers on the specified subnet. If you have the cluster running (and you've done a backup), go ahead and dissolve the cluster as shown next. Be sure to take a backup before doing this so you don't accidentally lose any data.

```
MySQL  cluster-rpi1:3306 ssl  Py > cluster.dissolve({'force':True})
The cluster was successfully dissolved.
Replication was disabled but user data was left intact.
```

After the cluster is dissolved, you can shut down the MySQL instances for all servers. Recall, we can shut down MySQL by using the SHUTDOWN SQL command via MySQL Shell, as shown next. Remember to use the --sql option! Run this command on all machines in the cluster:

```
$ mysqlsh root@cluster-rpi1:3306 --sql -e "SHUTDOWN"
```

Next, if SSL is not configured on all the servers, we should set that up now. Once again, if you are using MySQL 8.0.11 or later, it's already done. If you are unsure, you can run the following command to determine whether SSL is enabled on each server:

```
SHOW VARIABLES LIKE 'have_ssl';
```

OK, now we're ready. We'll name this example cluster RPI_Cluster_SSL to indicate that it requires SSL connections. We issue the following commands to create the cluster and add all the instances:

```
cluster = dba.create_cluster('RPI_Cluster_SSL',
{'memberSslMode':'REQUIRED', 'ipWhitelist':'192.168.42.0/24'})
cluster.add_instance('root@cluster-rpi2:3306', {'memberSslMode':'REQUIRED',
'ipWhitelist':'192.168.42.0/24'})
cluster.add_instance('root@cluster-rpi3:3306', {'memberSslMode':'REQUIRED',
'ipWhitelist':'192.168.42.0/24'})
cluster.add_instance('root@cluster-rpi4:3306', {'memberSslMode':'REQUIRED',
'ipWhitelist':'192.168.42.0/24'})
```

Notice that the whitelist value is 192.168.42.0/24, which permits connections from 192.168.42.1 to 192.168.42.255. If you want more restrictions, you can use a wider mask. If you are not sure how to calculate this, you can use an online subnet calculator like the one found at www.subnet-calculator.com.

Let's see a demonstration. Listing 9-8 shows an example of setting up a cluster for which SSL is required, and a whitelist has been specified. Because you have seen these commands in action, we will skip detailed explanations of the commands and focus on the status report at the end of the listing.

Listing 9-8. Example Cluster Setup with SSL = Required and Whitelist Defined

```
MySQL  cluster-rpi1:3306 ssl  Py > cluster = dba.create_
cluster('RPI_Cluster_SSL', {'memberSslMode':'REQUIRED',
'ipWhitelist':'192.168.42.0/24'})
A new InnoDB cluster will be created on instance 'root@cluster-rpi1:3306'.

Validating instance at cluster-rpi1:3306...

This instance reports its own address as cluster-rpi1

Instance configuration is suitable.
Creating InnoDB cluster 'RPI_Cluster_SSL' on 'root@cluster-rpi1:3306'...
Adding Seed Instance...

Cluster successfully created. Use Cluster.add_instance() to add MySQL
instances.
```

At least 3 instances are needed for the cluster to be able to withstand up to one server failure.

 MySQL cluster-rpi1:3306 ssl Py > **cluster.add_instance('root@cluster-rpi2:3306', {'memberSslMode':'REQUIRED', 'ipWhitelist':'192.168.42.0/24'})**
A new instance will be added to the InnoDB cluster. Depending on the amount of data on the cluster this might take from a few seconds to several hours.

Please provide the password for 'root@cluster-rpi2:3306': ****
Adding instance to the cluster ...

Validating instance at cluster-rpi2:3306...

This instance reports its own address as cluster-rpi2

Instance configuration is suitable.
The instance 'root@cluster-rpi2:3306' was successfully added to the cluster.

 MySQL cluster-rpi1:3306 ssl Py > **cluster.add_instance('root@cluster-rpi3:3306', {'memberSslMode':'REQUIRED', 'ipWhitelist':'192.168.42.0/24'})**
A new instance will be added to the InnoDB cluster. Depending on the amount of data on the cluster this might take from a few seconds to several hours.

Please provide the password for 'root@cluster-rpi3:3306': ****
Adding instance to the cluster ...

Validating instance at cluster-rpi3:3306...

This instance reports its own address as cluster-rpi3

Instance configuration is suitable.
The instance 'root@cluster-rpi3:3306' was successfully added to the cluster.

 MySQL cluster-rpi1:3306 ssl Py > **cluster.add_instance('root@cluster-rpi4:3306', {'memberSslMode':'REQUIRED', 'ipWhitelist':'192.168.42.0/24'})**
A new instance will be added to the InnoDB cluster. Depending on the amount of data on the cluster this might take from a few seconds to several hours.

```
Please provide the password for 'root@cluster-rpi4:3306': ****
Adding instance to the cluster ...

Validating instance at cluster-rpi4:3306...

This instance reports its own address as cluster-rpi4

Instance configuration is suitable.
The instance 'root@cluster-rpi4:3306' was successfully added to the
cluster.

 MySQL  cluster-rpi1:3306 ssl  Py > cluster.status()
{
    "clusterName": "RPI_Cluster_SSL",
    "defaultReplicaSet": {
        "name": "default",
        "primary": "cluster-rpi1:3306",
        "ssl": "REQUIRED",
        "status": "OK",
        "statusText": "Cluster is ONLINE and can tolerate up to ONE failure.",
        "topology": {
            "cluster-rpi1:3306": {
                "address": "cluster-rpi1:3306",
                "mode": "R/W",
                "readReplicas": {},
                "role": "HA",
                "status": "ONLINE"
            },
            "cluster-rpi2:3306": {
                "address": "cluster-rpi2:3306",
                "mode": "R/O",
                "readReplicas": {},
                "role": "HA",
                "status": "ONLINE"
            },
            "cluster-rpi3:3306": {
                "address": "cluster-rpi3:3306",
                "mode": "R/O",
```

```json
            "readReplicas": {},
            "role": "HA",
            "status": "ONLINE"
        },
        "cluster-rpi4:3306": {
            "address": "cluster-rpi4:3306",
            "mode": "R/O",
            "readReplicas": {},
            "role": "HA",
            "status": "ONLINE"
        }
    }
},
    "groupInformationSourceMember": "mysql://root@cluster-rpi1:3306"
}
```

Notice in the status report, we see the SSL mode is required (which it is by default). We can confirm this by querying for the SSL options:

```
MySQL  cluster-rpi1:3306 ssl  mysql_innodb_cluster_metadata  SQL > SHOW
VARIABLES LIKE '%ssl%';
+-------------------------------------------------------+------------------+
| Variable_name                                         | Value            |
+-------------------------------------------------------+------------------+
| group_replication_recovery_ssl_ca                     |                  |
| group_replication_recovery_ssl_capath                 |                  |
| group_replication_recovery_ssl_cert                   |                  |
| group_replication_recovery_ssl_cipher                 |                  |
| group_replication_recovery_ssl_crl                    |                  |
| group_replication_recovery_ssl_crlpath                |                  |
| group_replication_recovery_ssl_key                    |                  |
| group_replication_recovery_ssl_verify_server_cert     | OFF              |
| group_replication_recovery_use_ssl                    | ON               |
| group_replication_ssl_mode                            | REQUIRED         |
| have_openssl                                          | YES              |
| have_ssl                                              | YES              |
```

```
| mysqlx_ssl_ca        |                  |
| mysqlx_ssl_capath    |                  |
| mysqlx_ssl_cert      |                  |
| mysqlx_ssl_cipher    |                  |
| mysqlx_ssl_crl       |                  |
| mysqlx_ssl_crlpath   |                  |
| mysqlx_ssl_key       |                  |
| ssl_ca               | ca.pem           |
| ssl_capath           |                  |
| ssl_cert             | server-cert.pem  |
| ssl_cipher           |                  |
| ssl_crl              |                  |
| ssl_crlpath          |                  |
| ssl_fips_mode        | OFF              |
| ssl_key              | server-key.pem   |
+-------------------------------------------------+------------------+
27 rows in set (0.0391 sec)
```

So, what about the whitelist? We can see the whitelist by examining the variables for Group Replication, as shown in Listing 9-9. We can see the whitelist as well as all the other variables for Group Replication, all of which InnoDB Cluster has set for us.

Listing 9-9. Displaying the Group Replication Variables

```
MySQL  cluster-rpi1:3306 ssl  mysql_innodb_cluster_metadata  Py > \sql
Switching to SQL mode... Commands end with ;

 MySQL  cluster-rpi1:3306 ssl  mysql_innodb_cluster_metadata  SQL > SHOW
VARIABLES LIKE '%ssl%';
+-------------------------------------------------+------------------+
| Variable_name                                   | Value            |
+-------------------------------------------------+------------------+
| group_replication_recovery_ssl_ca               |                  |
| group_replication_recovery_ssl_capath           |                  |
| group_replication_recovery_ssl_cert             |                  |
| group_replication_recovery_ssl_cipher           |                  |
| group_replication_recovery_ssl_crl              |                  |
```

```
| group_replication_recovery_ssl_crlpath              |                  |
| group_replication_recovery_ssl_key                  |                  |
| group_replication_recovery_ssl_verify_server_cert   | OFF              |
| group_replication_recovery_use_ssl                  | ON               |
| group_replication_ssl_mode                          | REQUIRED         |
| have_openssl                                        | YES              |
| have_ssl                                            | YES              |
| mysqlx_ssl_ca                                       |                  |
| mysqlx_ssl_capath                                   |                  |
| mysqlx_ssl_cert                                     |                  |
| mysqlx_ssl_cipher                                   |                  |
| mysqlx_ssl_crl                                      |                  |
| mysqlx_ssl_crlpath                                  |                  |
| mysqlx_ssl_key                                      |                  |
| ssl_ca                                              | ca.pem           |
| ssl_capath                                          |                  |
| ssl_cert                                            | server-cert.pem  |
| ssl_cipher                                          |                  |
| ssl_crl                                             |                  |
| ssl_crlpath                                         |                  |
| ssl_fips_mode                                       | OFF              |
| ssl_key                                             | server-key.pem   |
+-----------------------------------------------------+------------------+
27 rows in set (0.0391 sec)

 MySQL  cluster-rpi1:3306 ssl  mysql_innodb_cluster_metadata  SQL > SHOW
VARIABLES LIKE '%white%';

+-------------------------------+-----------------+
| Variable_name                 | Value           |
+-------------------------------+-----------------+
| group_replication_ip_whitelist | 192.168.42.0/24 |
+-------------------------------+-----------------+
1 row in set (0.0383 sec)
```

```
MySQL  cluster-rpi1:3306 ssl  SQL > SHOW VARIABLES LIKE 'group_
replication%';
```

Variable_name	Value
group_replication_allow_local_lower_version_join	OFF
group_replication_auto_increment_increment	7
group_replication_bootstrap_group	OFF
group_replication_communication_debug_options	GCS_DEBUG_NONE
group_replication_components_stop_timeout	31536000
group_replication_compression_threshold	1000000
group_replication_enforce_update_everywhere_checks	OFF
group_replication_flow_control_applier_threshold	25000
group_replication_flow_control_certifier_threshold	25000
group_replication_flow_control_hold_percent	10
group_replication_flow_control_max_quota	0
group_replication_flow_control_member_quota_percent	0
group_replication_flow_control_min_quota	0
group_replication_flow_control_min_recovery_quota	0
group_replication_flow_control_mode	QUOTA
group_replication_flow_control_period	1
group_replication_flow_control_release_percent	50
group_replication_force_members	
group_replication_group_name	a587a3ad-7002-11e8-8612-b827eb2bc4f3
group_replication_group_seeds	
group_replication_gtid_assignment_block_size	1000000
group_replication_ip_whitelist	192.168.42.0/24
group_replication_local_address	
group_replication_member_weight	50
group_replication_poll_spin_loops	0
group_replication_recovery_complete_at	TRANSACTIONS_APPLIED
group_replication_recovery_get_public_key	ON
group_replication_recovery_public_key_path	

```
| group_replication_recovery_reconnect_interval  | 60               |
| group_replication_recovery_retry_count         | 10               |
| group_replication_recovery_ssl_ca              |                  |
| group_replication_recovery_ssl_capath          |                  |
| group_replication_recovery_ssl_cert            |                  |
| group_replication_recovery_ssl_cipher          |                  |
| group_replication_recovery_ssl_crl             |                  |
| group_replication_recovery_ssl_crlpath         |                  |
| group_replication_recovery_ssl_key             |                  |
| group_replication_recovery_ssl_verify_server_cert | OFF           |
| group_replication_recovery_use_ssl             | OFF              |
| group_replication_single_primary_mode          | ON               |
| group_replication_ssl_mode                      | DISABLED         |
| group_replication_start_on_boot                 | OFF              |
| group_replication_transaction_size_limit        | 150000000        |
| group_replication_unreachable_majority_timeout  | 0                |
+------------------------------------------------+------------------+
44 rows in set (0.0340 sec)
```

Securing the Router

Now that we have the MySQL servers configured for SSL and the whitelist, you may be wondering what needs to be done for the router. How do we know we have SSL connections from the application to the router?

Because we are using MySQL 8.0.11 or later, we know we're using SSL connections by default, even with the setting to require SSL connections. Because we changed the name of the cluster, we have only one change to make: we have to edit the router configuration file to connect to the correct cluster. Open the router configuration file (for example, /usr/local/mysql/lib/mysql-router/mysqlrouter.conf) and change the cluster name as highlighted in Listing 9-10.

Listing 9-10. Change the Router Configuration File

```
# File automatically generated during MySQL Router bootstrap
[DEFAULT]
user=pi
logging_folder=/usr/local/mysql/lib/mysql-router/log
```

```
runtime_folder=/usr/local/mysql/lib/mysql-router/run
data_folder=/usr/local/mysql/lib/mysql-router/data
plugin_folder=/usr/local/mysql/lib/mysqlrouter
keyring_path=/usr/local/mysql/lib/mysql-router/data/keyring
master_key_path=/usr/local/mysql/lib/mysql-router/mysqlrouter.key
connect_timeout=30
read_timeout=30

[logger]
level = INFO
```

[metadata_cache:RPI_Cluster_SSL]
```
router_id=4
bootstrap_server_addresses=mysql://cluster-rpi1:3306,mysql://cluster-
rpi2:3306,mysql://cluster-rpi3:3306,mysql://c
luster-rpi4:3306
user=mysql_router4_gnl6peiy2z2v
```
metadata_cluster=RPI_Cluster_SSL
```
ttl=5
```

[routing:RPI_Cluster_SSL_default_rw]
```
bind_address=0.0.0.0
bind_port=6446
```
destinations=metadata-cache://RPI_Cluster_SSL/default?role=PRIMARY
```
routing_strategy=round-robin
protocol=classic
```

[routing:RPI_Cluster_SSL_default_ro]
```
bind_address=0.0.0.0
bind_port=6447
```
destinations=metadata-cache://RPI_Cluster_SSL/default?role=SECONDARY
```
routing_strategy=round-robin
protocol=classic
```

[routing:RPI_Cluster_SSL_default_x_rw]
```
bind_address=0.0.0.0
bind_port=64460
```

destinations=metadata-cache://RPI_Cluster_SSL/default?role=PRIMARY
routing_strategy=round-robin
protocol=x

[routing:RPI_Cluster_SSL_default_x_ro]
bind_address=0.0.0.0
bind_port=64470
destinations=metadata-cache://RPI_Cluster_SSL/default?role=SECONDARY
routing_strategy=round-robin
protocol=x

Notice that we changed all occurrences of RPI_Cluster to RPI_Cluster_SSL. You can do the search-and-replace or, if you want to create a new router configuration file, you can use the Bootstrap option and specify a new configuration file, as shown next. Notice the use of the --directory option to specify a new directory to store the configuration and the --name option to specify a new name for the configuration.

```
$ sudo /usr/local/mysql/bin/mysqlrouter --bootstrap root@cluster-rpi4:3306 \
    --directory=/usr/local/mysql/lib/mysql-router-ssl/mysqlrouter.conf
    --user=pi \
    --name=router_rpi_ssl
```

After we make these changes, we can restart the router by using the configuration file (either the modified one or a new one) and try our test code, as shown in Listing 9-11. You can save this file as router_connect_test.py.

Listing 9-11. Router Test Script

```
import mysql.connector

# Simple function to display results from a cursor
def show_results(cur_obj):
  for row in cur_obj:
    print(row)

my_cfg = {
  'user':'root',
  'passwd':'secret',
```

```
    'host':'127.0.0.1',
    'port':6446
}

# Connecting to the server
conn = mysql.connector.connect(**my_cfg)

print("Listing the databases on the server.")
query = "SHOW DATABASES"
cur = conn.cursor()
cur.execute(query)
show_results(cur)

print("\nRetrieve the port for the server to which we're connecting.")
query = "SELECT @@port"
cur = conn.cursor()
cur.execute(query)
show_results(cur)

# Close the cursor and connection
cur.close()
conn.close()
```

Now, we run the Python script and should see output like the following. You may be expecting the code to fail, but nothing has changed in our cluster regarding client connections. Because we're using MySQL 8.0.11, SSL connections are turned on by default.

```
$ python3 ./router_connect_test.py
('information_schema',)
('mysql',)
('mysql_innodb_cluster_metadata',)
('performance_schema',)
('shopping',)
('sys',)
```

That's it! We have just made our development InnoDB Cluster more secure by enabling SSL connections and using a whitelist.

Summary

The true test of a system is how well it can be maintained over time. A huge element of that success is the complexity of the tasks needed to complete routine tasks. The easier it is to perform maintenance tasks, the easier it is to keep the system healthy. Similarly, it's important to have clear tasks for how to recover from errors or conditions that result in the need to repair or troubleshoot. Fortunately, the AdminAPI has the tools we need to keep InnoDB Cluster running well.

In this chapter, you reviewed the most common administrative tasks, looked at a set of troubleshooting tasks, and discovered some best practices related to administering InnoDB Cluster.

The next chapter concludes our introduction to InnoDB Cluster by discussing considerations for deploying InnoDB Cluster as well as preparing to migrate to MySQL 8.0 for those working with earlier versions of MySQL.

CHAPTER 10

Planning Your Deployment

This book has covered a lot of material, including a brief overview of high availability in terms of what it means to you and how MySQL fulfills those requirements. We focused on MySQL InnoDB Cluster and all its components: the InnoDB storage engine, Group Replication, the AdminAPI, MySQL Shell, and MySQL Router. Not only that, but we also walked through developing high-availability applications as well as setting up InnoDB Cluster by using the sandbox and a set of MySQL servers running on separate machines.

You also saw a unique alternative platform to experiment with InnoDB Cluster: the Raspberry Pi. Recall, you learned that although the Raspberry Pi is limited by a relatively small memory and slow processor, MySQL runs rather well on the platform—well enough that we can experiment with InnoDB Cluster without spending a lot of money on a bunch of server hardware.

However, now it is time to learn more about how to adopt MySQL 8 and MySQL InnoDB Cluster in the enterprise. What follows in this chapter are considerations and techniques for planning your cluster deployment. Because many readers are likely to be new to MySQL 8, we also include information about how to plan for adopting MySQL 8 in your enterprise.

Let's begin by briefly discussing some strategies for planning your cluster deployments.

Planning Your Clusters

Systems administration and planning are inseparable—if you want to be successful—and no more inseparable than when planning high-availability solutions. We must plan for setting up, configuring, and deploying the solution in advance or face the perils of unexpected problems and delays. InnoDB Cluster is no exception to this policy, and you would do well to plan for the way you want to use it in your environment.

© Charles Bell 2018
C. Bell, *Introducing InnoDB Cluster*, https://doi.org/10.1007/978-1-4842-3885-1_10

The information in this section will provide you with insight into areas of planning specific to InnoDB Cluster. You should consider this section an additional resource to use along with your established policies, practices, and tools for planning systems. The following lists some of the key areas where deliberate planning is needed for InnoDB Cluster:

- Create a separate user for the InnoDB Cluster administrator

- Configure the hostname

- Consider what metadata options you want

- Use logging with MySQL Shell and the AdminAPI for debugging

- Consider the number of read/write servers

- Consider the number of read-only servers

- Plan the physical deployment

- Plan your upgrade from a Group Replication deployment

We have already discussed most of these topics through the course of the book, but some may be new to you, especially if you have not deployed MySQL in large numbers—either with replication or a similar configuration.

The following sections elaborate on these areas by providing advice (and in some cases, examples) to follow so that you can evaluate whether to incorporate them into your plans for your InnoDB Cluster. Do not think of these as mandatory so much as highly recommended.

User Account

The preceding chapter covered securing InnoDB Cluster with SSL and a whitelist of servers. What wasn't discussed is the user account you use to administer InnoDB Cluster. Thus far, the user account we've used is the root account. Although you can continue to use that account effectively, a more secure option would be to dedicate a specific user account to that task. Some may be hesitant to do this, because that requires remembering yet another user account and password, but it is considered more secure than using the root account because the root account is often used by more than one person for all manner of MySQL-related actions. Using a separate account for InnoDB Cluster means potentially fewer people will use it to do other things.

The user account used to administer must be assigned full read and write privileges on the InnoDB Cluster metadata database tables in addition to full MySQL administrator privileges (same as root: SUPER, GRANT OPTION, CREATE, DROP, and so forth.). You can create the user manually with the CREATE USER and GRANT SQL commands as follows:

```
CREATE USER idc_admin@'%' IDENTIFIED BY 'secret';
GRANT ALL ON mysql_innodb_cluster_metadata.* TO idc_admin@'%' WITH GRANT
OPTION;
```

However, the preferred method is to use the clusterAdmin and clusterAdminPassword options with the dba.configure_instance(), dba.configure_local_instance(), and cluster.add_instance() methods:

```
dba.configure_instance('root@localhost:3306', {'clusterAdmin': "idc_
admin@'%'", 'clusterAdminPassword': 'secret'})
```

If you need to monitor your cluster performance and metadata, you can create a read-only account using a more restricted privileges. The following example creates the user and grants read-only privileges:

```
CREATE USER idc_mon@'%' IDENTIFIED BY 'secret';
GRANT SELECT ON mysql_innodb_cluster_metadata.* TO idc_mon@'%';
GRANT SELECT ON performance_schema.global_status TO idc_mon@'%';
GRANT SELECT ON performance_schema.replication_applier_configuration TO
idc_mon@'%';
GRANT SELECT ON performance_schema.replication_applier_status TO idc_mon@'%';
GRANT SELECT ON performance_schema.replication_applier_status_by_
coordinator TO idc_mon@'%';
GRANT SELECT ON performance_schema.replication_applier_status_by_worker TO
idc_mon@'%';
GRANT SELECT ON performance_schema.replication_connection_configuration TO
idc_mon@'%';
GRANT SELECT ON performance_schema.replication_connection_status TO
idc_mon@'%';
GRANT SELECT ON performance_schema.replication_group_member_stats TO
idc_mon@'%';
GRANT SELECT ON performance_schema.replication_group_members TO idc_mon@'%';
GRANT SELECT ON performance_schema.threads TO idc_mon@'%' WITH GRANT OPTION;
```

Hostname

Although choosing a hostname may not seem like something you want to plan for, consider the example deployment from Chapter 7 that used hostnames such as `cluster-rpi1` and `cluster-rpi2`. These hostnames were chosen to help identify the server used in the cluster. In this case, the hostnames were chosen as a mimic of the name of the cluster. However, you could use the name of the cluster with a prefix or postfix to help further identify the server. The bottom line is, it is recommended to choose a hostname that helps you manage your servers. Other than that, the hostname is merely a string, and you can use whatever you want within the limits of defining the hostname on your system or network.

We already know that each machine in the cluster must have its own hostname. We have also seen one technique for assigning hostnames and using the `/etc/hosts` file to manage access without a domain name system (DNS). More specifically, each machine must be able to resolve the hostname for the other servers in the cluster. However, if you have a DNS on your network, you can assign the hostnames and map them accordingly by using that service.

Also, remember to configure the `report_host` server option for each server in the cluster. This will be used by InnoDB Cluster to report the hostname to the cluster and stored in the metadata (and configuration files). This value should match the hostname of the machine. You also saw how to do this in the demonstrations from previous chapters.

Metadata

You discovered how to change the metadata in Chapter 9. We can set certain options when we create the cluster in the form of a JSON set of key/value pairs. The following is a list of the options available in the `dba.create_cluster()` method. Recall, we also provide the name of the cluster as a separate parameter for this method. Be sure to choose a name for the cluster that is both descriptive and unique among your infrastructure.

- `multiMaster`: If `True`, define an InnoDB cluster with multiple writable instances.

- `force`: If `True`, confirms that the `multiMaster` option must be applied.

- adoptFromGR: If True, create the InnoDB cluster based on existing replication group.

- memberSslMode: SSL mode used to configure the members of the cluster.

- ipWhitelist: The list of hosts allowed to connect to the instance for Group Replication.

- clearReadOnly: If True, confirm that super_read_only must be disabled.

- groupName: The Group Replication group name UUID to be used instead of the automatically generated one.

- localAddress: The Group Replication local address to be used instead of the automatically generated one.

- groupSeeds: A comma-separated list of the Group Replication peer addresses to be used instead of the automatically generated one.

When planning your cluster, you should review this list to see if you need to set any of these options. You have already seen how to use the options to set the SSL mode and establish a whitelist. If you are migrating from a Group Replication deployment, you may want to consider some of those options. We will talk about migrating from Group Replication in a later section. We also discuss the multiple master option in the next section.

Logging

If you have done any form of administration of systems or diagnosis of problems including debugging code, you are familiar with logs and logging. MySQL Shell provides a robust debug-level logging feature that can help you manage your clusters. This is especially helpful when working with server instances. To turn on logging in MySQL Shell, use the -log-level option as follows:

```
$ mysqlsh root@cluster-rpi1:3306 --log-level=DEBUG3
```

The DEBUG3 value is the most verbose option and recommended for diagnosis. You can always restart the shell if you want to default to no additional logging or use a different level. See the MySQL Shell online reference for more details about logging.

You can also increase the verbosity (logging) from the AdminAPI by setting the dba.verbose member variable to one of the following values:

- 0 or OFF: (Default) provides minimal output and is the recommended level

- 1 or ON: Adds verbose output from each call to the AdminAPI

- 2: Shows additional debug output along with the verbose output (developer-level)

Listing 10-1 shows an example of using the shell with logging and the verbosity member variable, and the output you can expect to see. In this case, we use level 2, which is the most verbose option. The example shows we need to re-add an instance to the cluster: one machine had an issue and had to be repaired, including reinstalling MySQL. The listing is rather long because we have turned on maximum verbosity, but it gives great insight into the many things that happen behind the scenes in the shell and AdminAPI. Some of the more mundane sections have been excluded for brevity. Take some time to dig through this listing. It reveals a lot about the way the add_instance() method works.

Listing 10-1. Using the Verbosity Setting in MySQL Shell

```
MySQL  cluster-rpi1:3306 ssl  Py > dba.verbose=2
MySQL  cluster-rpi1:3306 ssl  Py > cluster = dba.get_cluster()
MySQL  cluster-rpi1:3306 ssl  Py > cluster.add_instance('root@cluster-
rpi2:3306')
A new instance will be added to the InnoDB cluster. Depending on the amount of
data on the cluster this might take from a few seconds to several hours.

Please provide the password for 'root@cluster-rpi2:3306': ****
Adding instance to the cluster ...

Validating instance at cluster-rpi2:3306...

This instance reports its own address as cluster-rpi2
DBA: mysqlprovision: Executing printf '[{"server":{"host":"cluster-
rpi2","passwd":"****","password":"****","port":3306,"scheme":"mysql","user
":"root"},"verbose":2}]\n.\n' | /usr/local/mysql/bin/mysqlsh --log-level=8
--py -f /usr/local/mysql/share/mysqlsh/mysqlprovision.zip check
=========================== MySQL Provision Output ===========================
```

DEBUG: MySQL query: SHOW VARIABLES LIKE 'READ_ONLY'
Running check command.
DEBUG: MySQL query: SELECT GROUP_NAME FROM performance_schema.replication_
connection_status where CHANNEL_NAME = 'group_replication_applier'
Checking Group Replication prerequisites.
DEBUG: The server: 'cluster-rpi2:3306' has been set to check
DEBUG: Option checking started: {'log_slave_updates': {'ONE OF': ('ON',
'1')}, 'binlog_format': {'ONE OF': ('ROW',)}, 'relay_log_info_repository':
{'ONE OF': ('TABLE',)}, 'binlog_checksum': {'ONE OF': ('NONE',)}, 'report_
port': {'ONE OF': ('3306',)}, 'enforce_gtid_consistency': {'ONE OF': ('ON',
'1')}, 'master_info_repository': {'ONE OF': ('TABLE',)}, 'log_bin': {'ONE
OF': ('1', 'ON')}, 'gtid_mode': {'ONE OF': ('ON',)}, 'transaction_write_
set_extraction': {'ONE OF': ('XXHASH64', '2', 'MURMUR32', '1')}}
DEBUG: Checking option: 'log_slave_updates'
DEBUG: MySQL query: SELECT @@log_slave_updates
DEBUG: Option current value: '1'
DEBUG: OK: value 1 is one of ('ON', '1')
DEBUG: Checking option: 'binlog_format'
DEBUG: MySQL query: SELECT @@binlog_format
DEBUG: Option current value: 'ROW'
DEBUG: OK: value ROW is one of ('ROW',)
...
DEBUG: MySQL query: SHOW VARIABLES LIKE 'VERSION'
DEBUG: Server version: [8, 0, 11]
DEBUG: Server version check result: True
* Checking server version... PASS
Server is 8.0.11
...
DEBUG: MySQL query: show plugins
* Verifying Group Replication plugin for server 'cluster-rpi2:3306' ...
DEBUG: MySQL query: show plugins
WARNING: The group_replication plugin has not been installed/loaded in
'cluster-rpi2:3306'
Group Replication plugin: Not loaded
DEBUG: MySQL query: SELECT PLUGIN_NAME, PLUGIN_STATUS FROM INFORMATION_
SCHEMA.PLUGINS WHERE PLUGIN_NAME LIKE 'group_replication%'

```
DEBUG: Plugin group_replication is not installed
================================================================================

Instance configuration is suitable.
DBA: mysqlprovision: Executing printf '[{"group_seeds":"cluster-
rpi3:33061,cluster-rpi4:33061,cluster-rpi1:33061","rep_user_
passwd":"****","replication_user":"mysql_innodb_cluster_r0000124900","ssl_
mode":"REQUIRED","verbose":2},{"host":"cluster-rpi2","passwd":"****","pas
sword":"****","port":3306,"user":"root"},{"host":"cluster-rpi1","passwd"-
:"****","port":3306,"user":"root"}]\n.\n' | /usr/local/mysql/bin/mysqlsh
--log-level=8 --py -f /usr/local/mysql/share/mysqlsh/mysqlprovision.zip
join-replicaset
=========================== MySQL Provision Output ===========================
DEBUG: MySQL query: SHOW VARIABLES LIKE 'READ_ONLY'

Running join command on 'cluster-rpi2:3306'.
Checking Group Replication prerequisites.
DEBUG: MySQL query: SHOW VARIABLES LIKE 'READ_ONLY'
DEBUG: MySQL query: SELECT GROUP_NAME FROM performance_schema.replication_
connection_status where CHANNEL_NAME = 'group_replication_applier'
DEBUG: MySQL query: SELECT MEMBER_STATE FROM performance_schema.replication_
group_members as m JOIN performance_schema.replication_group_member_stats as
s on m.MEMBER_ID = s.MEMBER_ID AND m.MEMBER_ID = @@server_uuid
DEBUG: MySQL query: SELECT @@have_ssl
DEBUG: MySQL query: SELECT @@group_replication_recovery_use_ssl
DEBUG: MySQL query: SELECT @@group_replication_ssl_mode
DEBUG: ->parse_server_address
  host: %
  address_type: host like
DEBUG: Using replication_user: mysql_innodb_cluster_r0000124900@'%'
DEBUG: ->rpl_user_dict {'replication_user': "mysql_innodb_cluster_
r0000124900@'%'", 'rep_user_passwd': '******', 'host': '%', 'recovery_
user': 'mysql_innodb_cluster_r0000124900', 'ssl_mode': u'REQUIRED'}
DEBUG: MySQL query: select MEMBER_HOST, MEMBER_PORT from performance_
schema.replication_group_members
```

DEBUG: MySQL query: SHOW VARIABLES LIKE 'READ_ONLY'
DEBUG: MySQL query: SHOW VARIABLES LIKE 'READ_ONLY'
DEBUG: MySQL query: SHOW VARIABLES LIKE 'READ_ONLY'
DEBUG: The server: 'cluster-rpi2:3306' has been set to check
DEBUG: Option checking started: {'log_slave_updates': {'ONE OF': ('ON',
'1')}, 'binlog_format': {'ONE OF': ('ROW',)}, 'relay_log_info_repository':
{'ONE OF': ('TABLE',)}, 'binlog_checksum': {'ONE OF': ('NONE',)}, 'report_
port': {'ONE OF': ('3306',)}, 'enforce_gtid_consistency': {'ONE OF': ('ON',
'1')}, 'master_info_repository': {'ONE OF': ('TABLE',)}, 'log_bin': {'ONE
OF': ('1', 'ON')}, 'gtid_mode': {'ONE OF': ('ON',)}, 'transaction_write_
set_extraction': {'ONE OF': ('XXHASH64', '2', 'MURMUR32', '1')}}
DEBUG: Checking option: 'log_slave_updates'
DEBUG: MySQL query: SELECT @@log_slave_updates
DEBUG: Option current value: '1'
DEBUG: OK: value 1 is one of ('ON', '1')
DEBUG: Checking option: 'binlog_format'
DEBUG: MySQL query: SELECT @@binlog_format
DEBUG: Option current value: 'ROW'
DEBUG: OK: value ROW is one of ('ROW',)
DEBUG: Checking option: 'relay_log_info_repository'
DEBUG: MySQL query: SELECT @@relay_log_info_repository
DEBUG: Option current value: 'TABLE'
DEBUG: OK: value TABLE is one of ('TABLE',)
DEBUG: Checking option: 'binlog_checksum'
DEBUG: MySQL query: SELECT @@binlog_checksum
DEBUG: Option current value: 'NONE'
DEBUG: OK: value NONE is one of ('NONE',)
DEBUG: Checking option: 'report_port'
DEBUG: MySQL query: SELECT @@report_port
DEBUG: Option current value: '3306'
DEBUG: OK: value 3306 is one of ('3306',)
DEBUG: Checking option: 'enforce_gtid_consistency'
DEBUG: MySQL query: SELECT @@enforce_gtid_consistency
DEBUG: Option current value: 'ON'
DEBUG: OK: value ON is one of ('ON', '1')
DEBUG: Checking option: 'master_info_repository'

DEBUG: MySQL query: SELECT @@master_info_repository
DEBUG: Option current value: 'TABLE'
DEBUG: OK: value TABLE is one of ('TABLE',)
DEBUG: Checking option: 'log_bin'
DEBUG: MySQL query: SELECT @@log_bin
DEBUG: Option current value: '1'
DEBUG: OK: value 1 is one of ('1', 'ON')
DEBUG: Checking option: 'gtid_mode'
DEBUG: MySQL query: SELECT @@gtid_mode
DEBUG: Option current value: 'ON'
DEBUG: OK: value ON is one of ('ON',)
DEBUG: Checking option: 'transaction_write_set_extraction'
DEBUG: MySQL query: SELECT @@transaction_write_set_extraction
DEBUG: Option current value: 'XXHASH64'
DEBUG: OK: value XXHASH64 is one of ('XXHASH64', '2', 'MURMUR32', '1')
DEBUG: Options check result: True
* Comparing options compatibility with Group Replication... PASS
Server configuration is compliant with the requirements.
DEBUG: Checking option: 'transaction_write_set_extraction'
DEBUG: MySQL query: SELECT @@global.transaction_write_set_extraction
DEBUG: MySQL query: SELECT @@global.transaction_write_set_extraction
DEBUG: expected value: XXHASH64 found
* Comparing options compatibility with the group of the given peer-
instance... PASS
Server configuration is compliant with current group configuration.

Option name	Required Value	Current Value	Result
transaction_write_set_extraction	XXHASH64	XXHASH64	PASS

DEBUG: Server version checking: 5.7.17
DEBUG: MySQL query: SHOW VARIABLES LIKE 'VERSION'
DEBUG: Server version: [8, 0, 11]
DEBUG: Server version check result: True
* Checking server version... PASS
Server is 8.0.11

DEBUG: checking server id uniqueness
DEBUG: MySQL query: SELECT @@server_id
DEBUG: server id = 102
DEBUG: MySQL query: SELECT variable_source FROM performance_schema.
variables_info WHERE variable_name='server_id'
DEBUG: MySQL query: SELECT @@server_id
DEBUG: Verifying the peer 'cluster-rpi3:3306' ...
DEBUG: The peer 'cluster-rpi3:3306' have a different server_id 103
DEBUG: MySQL query: SELECT @@server_id
DEBUG: Verifying the peer 'cluster-rpi4:3306' ...
DEBUG: The peer 'cluster-rpi4:3306' have a different server_id 104
DEBUG: MySQL query: SELECT @@server_id
DEBUG: Verifying the peer 'cluster-rpi1:3306' ...
DEBUG: The peer 'cluster-rpi1:3306' have a different server_id 101
* Checking that server_id is unique... PASS
The server_id is valid.

DEBUG: MySQL query: SELECT @@slave_parallel_workers
* Checking compatibility of Multi-Threaded Slave settings... PASS
Multi-Threaded Slave settings are compatible with Group Replication.

DEBUG: MySQL query: show plugins
* Verifying Group Replication plugin for server 'cluster-rpi2:3306' ...
DEBUG: MySQL query: SELECT @@global.super_read_only
Initializing group_replication plugin on 'cluster-rpi2:3306'
DEBUG: MySQL query: show plugins
DEBUG: MySQL query: SELECT @@version_compile_os
DEBUG: MySQL query: INSTALL PLUGIN group_replication SONAME 'group_
replication.so'
DEBUG: The group_replication plugin has been successfully install in
server: 'cluster-rpi2:3306'
DEBUG: MySQL query: SELECT PLUGIN_NAME, PLUGIN_STATUS FROM INFORMATION_
SCHEMA.PLUGINS WHERE PLUGIN_NAME LIKE 'group_replication%'
DEBUG: Plugin group_replication has state: ACTIVE and not the expected: DISABLED
WARNING: Not running locally on the server and can not access its error log.
DEBUG: MySQL query: SELECT MEMBER_STATE FROM performance_schema.
replication_group_members as m JOIN performance_schema.replication_group_

member_stats as s on m.MEMBER_ID = s.MEMBER_ID AND m.MEMBER_ID = @@server_uuid
DEBUG: local_address to use: cluster-rpi2:33061
DEBUG: MySQL query: show plugins
DEBUG: MySQL query: SELECT @@global.group_replication_local_address
DEBUG: MySQL query: SELECT @@group_replication_single_primary_mode
DEBUG: MySQL query: SELECT @@server_id
DEBUG: Trying to retrieve group replication name from peer server.
DEBUG: MySQL query: show plugins
DEBUG: MySQL query: SELECT GROUP_NAME FROM performance_schema.replication_
connection_status WHERE CHANNEL_NAME='group_replication_applier'
DEBUG: Retrieved group replication name from peer server: dc7cb30b-701a-
11e8-bc94-b827eb2bc4f3.
Joining Group Replication group: dc7cb30b-701a-11e8-bc94-b827eb2bc4f3
DEBUG: Setting Group Replication variables
DEBUG: group_replication_group_seeds = cluster-rpi3:33061,cluster-
rpi4:33061,cluster-rpi1:33061
DEBUG: MySQL query: SET SQL_LOG_BIN=0
DEBUG: MySQL query: SET PERSIST group_replication_group_seeds = ?, params
(u'cluster-rpi3:33061,cluster-rpi4:33061,cluster-rpi1:33061',)
DEBUG: MySQL query: SET SQL_LOG_BIN=1
DEBUG: group_replication_single_primary_mode = 'ON'
DEBUG: MySQL query: SET SQL_LOG_BIN=0
DEBUG: MySQL query: SET PERSIST group_replication_single_primary_mode = 'ON'
DEBUG: MySQL query: SET SQL_LOG_BIN=1
DEBUG: group_replication_group_name = dc7cb30b-701a-11e8-bc94-b827eb2bc4f3
DEBUG: MySQL query: SET SQL_LOG_BIN=0
DEBUG: MySQL query: SET PERSIST group_replication_group_name = ?, params
('dc7cb30b-701a-11e8-bc94-b827eb2bc4f3',)
DEBUG: MySQL query: SET SQL_LOG_BIN=1
DEBUG: group_replication_recovery_use_ssl = 'ON'
DEBUG: MySQL query: SET SQL_LOG_BIN=0
DEBUG: MySQL query: SET PERSIST group_replication_recovery_use_ssl = 'ON'
DEBUG: MySQL query: SET SQL_LOG_BIN=1
DEBUG: auto_increment_offset = 2

```
DEBUG: MySQL query: SET SQL_LOG_BIN=0
DEBUG: MySQL query: SET PERSIST auto_increment_offset = ?, params (2,)
DEBUG: MySQL query: SET SQL_LOG_BIN=1
DEBUG:   group_replication_ssl_mode = 'REQUIRED'
DEBUG: MySQL query: SET SQL_LOG_BIN=0
DEBUG: MySQL query: SET PERSIST group_replication_ssl_mode = 'REQUIRED'
DEBUG: MySQL query: SET SQL_LOG_BIN=1
DEBUG:   group_replication_start_on_boot = ON
DEBUG: MySQL query: SET SQL_LOG_BIN=0
DEBUG: MySQL query: SET PERSIST group_replication_start_on_boot = ?,
params ('ON',)
DEBUG: MySQL query: SET SQL_LOG_BIN=1
DEBUG:   group_replication_local_address = 'cluster-rpi2:33061'
DEBUG: MySQL query: SET SQL_LOG_BIN=0
DEBUG: MySQL query: SET PERSIST group_replication_local_address = 'cluster-
rpi2:33061'
DEBUG: MySQL query: SET SQL_LOG_BIN=1
DEBUG:   auto_increment_increment = 1
DEBUG: MySQL query: SET SQL_LOG_BIN=0
DEBUG: MySQL query: SET PERSIST auto_increment_increment = ?, params (1,)
DEBUG: MySQL query: SET SQL_LOG_BIN=1
* Running change master command
DEBUG: MySQL query: SET SQL_LOG_BIN=0
DEBUG: MySQL query: CHANGE MASTER TO MASTER_USER = /*(*/ 'mysql_innodb_
cluster_r0000124900' /*)*/, MASTER_PASSWORD = /*(*/ '******' /*)*/ FOR
CHANNEL 'group_replication_recovery';
DEBUG: MySQL query: SET SQL_LOG_BIN=1
Attempting to join to Group Replication group...
DEBUG:
DEBUG: * Starting Group Replication plugin...
DEBUG: MySQL query: START group_replication
Server 'cluster-rpi2:3306' joined Group Replication group dc7cb30b-701a-
11e8-bc94-b827eb2bc4f3.
================================================================================
The instance 'root@cluster-rpi2:3306' was successfully added to the cluster.
```

Notice the many statements that come from the MySQL Provision script. This is a special script hidden in the shell and used to interact with the servers for you. As you can see, a lot of things need to be done. If you look deeper into the listing, you will also see statements about configuring Group Replication. Now, if that doesn't convince you that InnoDB Cluster is easier, nothing will!

Server Deployment

One area that we haven't talked a lot about is choosing how many servers should be in the cluster and how should they be deployed in your infrastructure. This section presents considerations for determining the number of primary (read/write) and secondary (read-only) servers you should start with, along with considerations for physical and networking choices.

Primary Servers

Most deployments of InnoDB Cluster are based on the default single-primary mode that has one primary (read/write) server in the cluster at any given time. However, another mode, called *multi-primary*, provides for more than one read/write server in the group. We use multi-primary mode for write scaling—dividing up the writes to two or more primaries to improve write performance.

Setting up multi-primary in InnoDB Cluster is not documented well but is supported. Most of the documentation for multi-primary is included in the "Group Replication" chapter of the online reference manual. However, the documentation for InnoDB Cluster regarding multi-primary states that the cluster will be created with all servers participating as read/write servers, which may not be what you want.

If you want to have a subset of the server participating as read/write servers, you should consider setting up Group Replication first with that configuration and then adopt the configuration into the new cluster. See the following section on how to adopt a "Upgrading from Group Replication" to InnoDB Cluster.

To enable multi-primary mode in InnoDB Cluster, we must do it when we create the cluster by using the `multiMaster` and `force` options, as shown next. Once again, this will enable all servers to participate as read/write servers.

```
dba.create_cluster('RPI_Cluster_MP', {'multiMaster':True, 'force': True})
```

Let's see this in action. Listing 10-2 shows an excerpt of creating an InnoDB Cluster in multi-primary mode. Notice that all the servers are listed as read/write servers.

Listing 10-2. Creating a Multi-Primary Mode Cluster

```
MySQL  cluster-rpi1:3306 ssl  Py > cluster = dba.create_cluster
('RPI_Cluster_MP', {'multiMaster':True, 'force': True})
...
MySQL  cluster-rpi1:3306 ssl  Py > cluster.add_instance('root@cluster-
rpi4:3306')
...
MySQL  cluster-rpi1:3306 ssl  Py > cluster.add_instance('root@cluster-
rpi3:3306')
...
MySQL  cluster-rpi1:3306 ssl  Py > cluster.add_instance('root@cluster-
rpi2:3306')
...
MySQL  cluster-rpi1:3306 ssl  Py > cluster.status()
{
    "clusterName": "RPI_Cluster_MP",
    "defaultReplicaSet": {
        "name": "default",
        "ssl": "REQUIRED",
        "status": "OK",
        "statusText": "Cluster is ONLINE and can tolerate up to ONE
        failure.",
        "topology": {
            "cluster-rpi1:3306": {
                "address": "cluster-rpi1:3306",
                "mode": "R/W",
                "readReplicas": {},
                "role": "HA",
                "status": "ONLINE"
            },
            "cluster-rpi2:3306": {
                "address": "cluster-rpi2:3306",
                "mode": "R/W",
```

```json
                    "readReplicas": {},
                    "role": "HA",
                    "status": "ONLINE"
                },
                "cluster-rpi3:3306": {
                    "address": "cluster-rpi3:3306",
                    "mode": "R/W",
                    "readReplicas": {},
                    "role": "HA",
                    "status": "ONLINE"
                },
                "cluster-rpi4:3306": {
                    "address": "cluster-rpi4:3306",
                    "mode": "R/W",
                    "readReplicas": {},
                    "role": "HA",
                    "status": "ONLINE"
                }
            }
        },
        "groupInformationSourceMember": "mysql://root@cluster-rpi1:3306"
}
```

When you bootstrap the router for a multi-primary mode cluster, you get some
interesting results. The following example bootstraps the router with the multi-primary
mode cluster:

```
$ sudo /usr/local/mysql/bin/mysqlrouter --bootstrap root:root@cluster-
rpi4:3306 --user=pi --directory=/usr/local/mysql/lib/test_mp --name=test_mp

Bootstrapping MySQL Router instance at '/usr/local/mysql/lib/test_mp'...
Module " not registered with logger - logging the following message as
'main' instead
MySQL Router 'test_mp' has now been configured for the InnoDB cluster 'RPI_
Cluster_MP' (multi-master).
The following connection information can be used to connect to the cluster.
Classic MySQL protocol connections to cluster 'RPI_Cluster_MP':
```

- Read/Write Connections: localhost:6446

X protocol connections to cluster 'RPI_Cluster_MP':

- Read/Write Connections: localhost:64460

Unlike single-primary mode, we have only one port for read/write connections and no ports for read connections. Once again, using multi-primary is a special use case. The default and recommended mode for InnoDB Cluster deployment is single-primary mode.

Tip   For more information about using the multi-primary mode with InnoDB Cluster, see the "Multi-Primary Mode" section of the online reference manual, which describes how it works from a Group Replication perspective.

Secondary Servers

The initial number of secondary (read-only) servers needed in a cluster was defined as a function of the number of unrecoverable faults you want your cluster to tolerate. The number of servers (S) is equal to 2 times the number of faults (f) you want to tolerate, plus 1:

$S = 2f + 1$ So, if we want our cluster to tolerate up to three faults, we should have at least seven servers in the cluster.

Tip   See the "How Do I Calculate the Number of Faults a Group Can Handle?" sidebar in Chapter 3 for more explanation of this formula.

For read scale-out, the function is a good start, but you may need to add more read-only servers to keep up with demands. How many are needed will depend on a variety of factors, which can be summarized using the following simplified formula:[1]

$$AverageLoad = (\sum ReadLoad + \sum WriteLoad) / \sum Capacity$$

The average load on a server is the sum of the read load plus the write load divided by the maximum capacity. This is because each read-only server must satisfy not only the read requests, but also all the write requests from the read/write (primary) server while performing the read requests.

---

[1]This formula is simplified in the case that it is a tool of approximation rather than specification. Use it accordingly.

Let's consider an example. Suppose you have a secondary that, through experimentation or recommendation (target goal), can process 20,000 transactions per second without noticeable performance loss. Suppose also there is a stable average write load of 5,000 transactions per second to the cluster and an average read load of 10,000 reads per second (2:1 ratio of reads to writes) to one of the read-only servers. Using the preceding formula, we find that the server is at only 75% of capacity, which is a safe margin for operating for most applications:

```
(10,000 + 5,000) / 20,000 = 0.75 = 75%
```

However, consider that the average load can have peak times when there are more read or write, or both, requests. When this happens, capacity could be reached, and you could experience lag among the servers. To guard against that, you should plan the number of read-only servers so that the load remains between about 50–75%. You can adjust that threshold depending on how often (or if) your applications experience periods of peak demand.

So, how does this help us for InnoDB Cluster? Recall, the router, by default, cycles through the read-only servers, dividing the read requests among them. If we factor in the round-robin algorithm for distributing reads, we can modify the formula as follows:

$$AverageLoad = ((\sum ReadLoad/NumSecondaries) + \sum WriteLoad) / \sum Capacity$$

Here, we can divide the read load across the set of secondaries, making a more accurate approximation of the read capacity of the cluster. Going back to our example, if we have four secondaries, the average load for a read-only server is considerably less:

```
((10,000 / 4) + 5,000) / 20,000 = 0.375 = 37.5%
```

Thus, the cluster can safely handle an average of 10,000 reads across the read-only servers. If you monitor the number of read requests made on average to the cluster, you can use the formula to determine when average load is greater than the threshold you've chosen—and when that occurs, you should add more read-only servers.

Tip   For an excellent explanation of planning for read scale-out, see "MySQL Replication Scale-Out" in *MySQL High Availability* Second Edition by Charles Bell et al. (O'Reilly, 2014).

Physical Deployment

The physical location of the server computers that participate in InnoDB Cluster is seldom considered. Most simply place the servers in their designated climate-controlled laboratories and let the attendants who manage those laboratories decide and manage. Although that is all well and good for most, you may want to consider certain aspects.

First, we should consider the hardware configuration. A best practice for any form of high-availability system is choosing like hardware for all the servers participating. Although it is true that a single read/write (primary) instance may require more memory and could benefit from a faster processor, that adage is not adequate for InnoDB Cluster because the cluster can decide to elect a new primary at any time. You should plan to make all your servers in the cluster the same hardware configuration.

In addition, placing the machines near each other—either in the same rack, as part of the same blade server array, or on the same shelf—can help make hardware repairs of the machines easier. If one machine goes down, you can repair it from spares on hand purchased for the group; you would require having only one set of spares. Furthermore, if you adopt the practice of having standby machines (machines not powered on but ready to swap), you can do this without having to lug hardware around in the laboratory.

Network Considerations

Another area for consideration in the laboratory is the networking configuration for the servers in the cluster. It is recommended that the servers be on their own subnet and switch to limit traffic to the cluster. The routers that talk to the cluster should have access to that subnet through a high-speed connection (or they too can be on the subnet). If this is an option you want to explore, consult network expertise to ensure that you either have the equipment you need, or you acquire the correct equipment to make this work correctly.

On the other hand, if the networking in your laboratory is sufficiently fast and free from network lag, you may want to consider waiting to implement this later. Still, planning for a subnet first may help avoid downtime needed to retrofit it into your cluster deployment.

Upgrading from Group Replication

The last area that may require deliberate planning is deploying InnoDB Cluster by using an existing Group Replication deployment. Because InnoDB Cluster uses Group Replication, this should be an easy thing to do, yes? The answer is it is easy, but only if you create your cluster with a special option named adoptFromGR set to True and specified with the dba.create_cluster() method. However, you should understand three considerations.

First, if your Group Replication topology includes MyISAM (or other storage engine) tables, you must convert them to InnoDB. This can be accomplished via the ALTER TABLE SQL command.

Second, the new InnoDB Cluster will be configured using the mode of Group Replication. If Group Replication is in single-primary, so too shall InnoDB Cluster. The only issue may be if you want to change the mode. In that case, it is not possible to specify the multiMaster option when creating the cluster from an existing Group Replication topology.

Third, if any instance has super_read_only set to ON, the AdminAPI will set it to OFF when the instances are added to the cluster.

Let's look at a Group Replication topology running as separate instances on a single machine (not in a sandbox). Listing 10-3 shows an example of an existing Group Replication topology using two queries on the performance schema database. The first selects the group members, and the second identifies the primary in the group.

Listing 10-3. Existing Group Replication Topology

```
> SELECT * FROM performance_schema.replication_group_members \G
*************************** 1. row ***************************
   CHANNEL_NAME: group_replication_applier
      MEMBER_ID: ab44d8c1-70c0-11e8-9776-d4258b76e981
    MEMBER_HOST: oracle-pc
    MEMBER_PORT: 24801
   MEMBER_STATE: ONLINE
    MEMBER_ROLE: PRIMARY
 MEMBER_VERSION: 8.0.13
```

```
*************************** 2. row ***************************
  CHANNEL_NAME: group_replication_applier
     MEMBER_ID: b1bf7839-70c0-11e8-b7ee-d4258b76e981
   MEMBER_HOST: oracle-pc
   MEMBER_PORT: 24802
  MEMBER_STATE: ONLINE
   MEMBER_ROLE: SECONDARY
MEMBER_VERSION: 8.0.13
*************************** 3. row ***************************
  CHANNEL_NAME: group_replication_applier
     MEMBER_ID: b83fcc48-70c0-11e8-9d84-d4258b76e981
   MEMBER_HOST: oracle-pc
   MEMBER_PORT: 24803
  MEMBER_STATE: ONLINE
   MEMBER_ROLE: SECONDARY
MEMBER_VERSION: 8.0.13
*************************** 4. row ***************************
  CHANNEL_NAME: group_replication_applier
     MEMBER_ID: be81348f-70c0-11e8-8ce4-d4258b76e981
   MEMBER_HOST: oracle-pc
   MEMBER_PORT: 24804
  MEMBER_STATE: ONLINE
   MEMBER_ROLE: SECONDARY
MEMBER_VERSION: 8.0.13

> SELECT member_id, member_host, member_port FROM performance_schema.
global_status JOIN performance_schema.replication_group_members ON
VARIABLE_VALUE=member_id WHERE VARIABLE_NAME='group_replication_primary_
member';
+--------------------------------------+-------------+-------------+
| member_id                            | member_host | member_port |
+--------------------------------------+-------------+-------------+
| ab44d8c1-70c0-11e8-9776-d4258b76e981 | oracle-pc   |       24801 |
+--------------------------------------+-------------+-------------+
```

441

Here the primary is currently the server running on port 28401. Now, let's see how we can convert this Group Replication topology to InnoDB Cluster. Because Group Replication is already set up, we just need to create the cluster. Listing 10-4 shows the transcript for converting the Group Replication to InnoDB Cluster for a cluster named GR_Cluster.

Listing 10-4. Converting an Exiting Group Replication Topology to InnoDB Cluster

```
MySQL  192.168.1.80:24801 ssl  Py > cluster = dba.create_cluster('GR_
Cluster', {'adoptFromGR':True})
A new InnoDB cluster will be created based on the existing replication
group on instance 'root@192.168.1.80:24801'.

Creating InnoDB cluster 'GR_Cluster' on 'root@192.168.1.80:24801'...
Adding Seed Instance...
Adding Instance 'oracle-pc:24802'...
Adding Instance 'oracle-pc:24803'...
Adding Instance 'oracle-pc:24804'...

Cluster successfully created based on existing replication group.

 MySQL  192.168.1.80:24801 ssl  Py > cluster.status()
{
    "clusterName": "GR_Cluster",
    "defaultReplicaSet": {
        "name": "default",
        "primary": "oracle-pc:24801",
        "ssl": "DISABLED",
        "status": "OK",
        "statusText": "Cluster is ONLINE and can tolerate up to ONE
        failure.",
        "topology": {
            "oracle-pc:24801": {
                "address": "oracle-pc:24801",
                "mode": "R/W",
                "readReplicas": {},
                "role": "HA",
```

```
                "status": "ONLINE"
            },
            "oracle-pc:24802": {
                "address": "oracle-pc:24802",
                "mode": "R/O",
                "readReplicas": {},
                "role": "HA",
                "status": "ONLINE"
            },
            "oracle-pc:24803": {
                "address": "oracle-pc:24803",
                "mode": "R/O",
                "readReplicas": {},
                "role": "HA",
                "status": "ONLINE"
            },
            "oracle-pc:24804": {
                "address": "oracle-pc:24804",
                "mode": "R/O",
                "readReplicas": {},
                "role": "HA",
                "status": "ONLINE"
            }
        }
    },
    "groupInformationSourceMember": "mysql://root@192.168.1.80:24801"
}
```

The create_cluster() method automatically finds the instances and configures them for the cluster. The primary is still the server running on port 24801. There is one other thing to note: the state of the SSL option. It is currently disabled. This is expected because the servers in the group are running without SSL. Thus, this example also demonstrates that you do not need to convert your servers to use SSL in order to use them in InnoDB Cluster (but it is recommended for better security).

We also see in the status output that we do indeed have a working cluster. Cool! So, you do not need to drop your current Group Replication topologies to adopt InnoDB Cluster. In fact, it's easier to migrate to InnoDB Cluster.

Tip   For more information about working with Group Replication, see the "Group Replication" chapter in the online reference manual (`https://dev.mysql.com/doc/refman/8.0/en/group-replication.html`).

Limitations

Fortunately, using InnoDB Cluster has only a few limitations. The limitations that may be significant for planning your InnoDB Cluster deployment include the following. Notice the list is short and applies to noncritical areas:

- Results that contain multibyte characters sometimes may not align to columnar output.

- Nonstandard character sets may not display correctly in results.

- The AdminAPI does not support UNIX socket connections.

- Adding non-sandbox server instances to a cluster in the sandbox may prevent MySQL Shell from persisting configuration changes in the instance's configuration file.

- Using the `--defaults-extra-file` option to specify an option file is not supported by InnoDB cluster server instances.

Tip   See `https://dev.mysql.com/doc/refman/8.0/en/mysql-innodb-cluster-limitations.html` for the latest list of limitations and possible workarounds. You should also see the "Group Replication Limitations" section for limitations that may affect InnoDB Cluster.

Planning for MySQL 8

Although this book is not a tutorial on upgrading to MySQL 8, you should consider some things before adopting MySQL InnoDB Cluster, which will likely result in upgrading your existing MySQL servers.

There are several ways you can go about learning how to do an upgrade. The most obvious and recommended route is to read the online reference manual, which contains a section on upgrading MySQL (providing critical information you must know). However, some higher-level or general practices apply to any form of upgrade or migration. This section presents upgrade practices that will help you avoid some of the trouble with upgrading a major system like MySQL.

This section covers the types of upgrades you will encounter with MySQL as well as general practices for planning and executing the upgrade. We conclude the section with a brief discussion about reasons for performing the upgrade. We discuss the reasons for doing an upgrade last so that you will have a better understanding of what is involved, including implied risks.

Let's begin by looking at the types of upgrades you are likely to encounter.

Types of Upgrades

The online reference manual and similar publications describe two basic upgrade methods, which are strategies and procedures for how to do the upgrade. The following is a summary of the methods:

- *In-place*: MySQL Server instances are upgraded with binaries by using the existing data dictionary. This method employs various utilities and tools to ensure a smooth transition to the new version.

- *Logical*: The data is backed up before installing the new version over the old installation, and data is restored after the upgrade.

These two general strategies for upgrading MySQL don't cover all possible options. In fact, you will see another method in a later section. After all, your installation is likely to be slightly different—especially if you've been using MySQL for a long time or have a lot of MySQL servers configured for high availability or are using third-party applications and components with your own applications. These factors can make following a given, generic procedure problematic.

Rather than try to expand on the upgrade methods, let's look at it from the point of view of a system administrator. Specifically, what do we do if we have version x.y.z and want to upgrade to a.b.c? The following sections describe upgrades based on versions.

Caution   Oracle recommends upgrades of only GA versions. Upgrading other releases is not recommended and may require accepting additional time to migrate and accepting potential incompatibilities. Upgrade non-GA releases at your own risk.

MYSQL VERSION NUMBER TERMINOLOGY

MySQL uses a three-digit version number in the form of major, minor, and revision (oddly, it is also called the *version* in the documentation). This is often expressed with dot notation. For example, version 5.7.20 defines the major version as 5, the minor version as 7, and the revision as 20. Often, the version number is followed by text (called the *suffix* in the documentation) indicating additional version history, stability, or alignment—such as general availability (GA), release candidate (RC), and so forth. For a complete explanation of the version number in MySQL, see `https://dev.mysql.com/doc/refman/8.0/en/which-version.html`.

Revision Upgrade

In the simplest form of upgrade, only the revision number is changed. This is commonly referred to as the z in the x.y.z version number, or simply *the version of the major.minor release*. For example, version 5.7.20 is revision 20, or version 20 of 5.7.

Upgrading at this version level is generally safe and, although not guaranteed to work flawlessly, is low risk. However, you still should take the precaution of reading the release notes before executing the upgrade. This is especially true if you are working with non-general-availability (GA) releases. If the release is not a GA release, you must pay attention to the release notes and upgrade section in the reference manual. Although they are rare, sometimes special considerations exist that you must plan for and overcome to achieve the upgrade. Fortunately, Oracle does an excellent job of communicating any necessary steps and procedures; you just need to read the documentation! For example, see the release notes at `https://dev.mysql.com/doc/relnotes/mysql/8.0/en/` to learn more about changes from one version to another.

Minor Upgrade

In the next form of upgrade, the minor number is changed. This is commonly referred to as the y in the x.y.z version number. For example, you might upgrade from 5.6 to 5.7.

Upgrades are generally acceptable and documented for single-digit increments of the minor version. For example, the upgrade from 5.6 to 5.7 is supported, but an upgrade from 5.0 to 5.7 is not directly supported. This is because too many differences exist between the versions to make an upgrade viable (but not impossible).

Nevertheless, you can upgrade minor version changes with manageable risk if you plan accordingly. You'll see more about managing the risk in later sections.

Major Upgrade

In the next form of upgrade, the major number is changed. This category—aside from the incompatible versions—is the one with the most risk and potentially the most likely to require more work.

Upgrades of versions at the major version are rare and occur only when Oracle has released a new, major set of changes (hence the name) to the server. MySQL Server version 8 contains many improvements over MySQL 5. Most have brought tremendous increases in performance, advanced features, and stability. However, a few changes have rendered some features in older versions incompatible.

For example, after MySQL 8.0 is released as GA, upgrading from MySQL 5.7 to MySQL 8.0 is supported, but you may have to migrate certain features to complete the upgrade.

Fortunately, Oracle has documented all the problem areas in detail, providing suggestions for migrating to the new features.

Incompatible Upgrades

As you may have surmised, some upgrades are not recommended either because of a lack of features to support the upgrade or major incompatibilities. For example, you should not consider upgrading from MySQL 5.0 to MySQL 8.0. This is simply because there is no support for some of the older 5.0 features in 8.0. These types of upgrades are not common, so we summarize some of the incompatible upgrades in the following list. The subject of the incompatibility isn't the new version to which you want to upgrade; it is the old version that you want to upgrade.

- *Skipping major versions*: Upgrading major versions may introduce incompatible changes.

- *Skipping minor versions*: Some upgrades of minor versions may introduce incompatible changes.

- *Upgrading incompatible hardware*: Upgrading hardware of one endianness may not be compatible with another. For example, big-endian to little-endian may not be compatible.

- *Versions that change the InnoDB format*: Some upgrades result in changes to the InnoDB storage engine internals. Most have been planned for compatible minor.revision upgrades (for example, 5.7.3 to 5.7.12), but some have required a few extra steps to prepare the data.

- *New features*: Less often, new features are introduced that may result in incompatibilities. For example, the data dictionary was added, rendering the .frm metadata obsolete.

- *Platform changes*: Some upgrades that include changing platforms may require additional work or introduce potential incompatibilities. An example is moving from a platform without case sensitivity support in the file system to one that does support case sensitivity.

- *Upgrading non-GA releases*: Upgrades from a non-GA to a GA, GA to non-GA, and among non-GA releases is not recommended.

Clearly, the incompatibilities are dependent on certain features, hardware, or internal storage mechanisms. In most cases, the online documentation outlines what you can do to ensure success. Sometimes this requires following a specific upgrade path, such as first upgrading to one version before upgrading to your target version.

WHAT IF I MUST UPGRADE AN INCOMPATIBLE VERSION?

If your upgrade strategy falls into one of these categories of incompatible upgrades, do not despair. You may still be able to perform the upgrade, but it may be costlier and require more work. For example, you could perform a logical upgrade by backing up your data using SQL statements with mysqldump or mysqlpump, installing the new version, and then working with the SQL files to adjust them to remove any incompatibilities. Although this does introduce considerable risk that you can still import all your data cleanly, it is still possible. If you find yourself in this situation, be sure to spend more time on addressing risks using such strategies as parallel installation and extended periods of testing.

Now that you have a good idea about the types of upgrades that are possible, let's look at some best practices for performing the upgrade.

Upgrade Practices

When upgrading any system, we should adhere to general practices or at least use them as a guide. This section describes some fundamental practices you should consider when upgrading your MySQL servers. Although some of these may be familiar, others may not be ones you would consider when upgrading MySQL. Further, some of these are not outlined in the online reference manual.

As you will see, these practices are not necessarily sequential or even prerequisites of the next. For example, planning should also include time for testing. The practices discussed here are in a general order of importance but should not be considered or implemented in this order.

Check Prerequisites

The first thing you should do when upgrading MySQL is to check the documentation for any prerequisites. Sometimes the prerequisite is only to safely back up your data, but can also include factors such as the utilities and tools you need to use to migrate certain features (or data). Be sure you have all the prerequisites met before you begin the upgrade.

The upgrade documentation will also include incompatibility issues. Most often, this occurs when upgrading major versions, but sometimes incompatibilities can happen for minor versions. Fortunately, these are outlined in the online reference manual. Checking the prerequisites can also help you by providing details you can use to plan the upgrade.

Caution   The online reference manual section on upgrading should be your first stop, not your last, when things go wrong. Reading the upgrade section and release notes may help you avoid unnecessary rework and problems during the upgrade.

Once you've read through the documentation, one of the things you will want to do as a prerequisite is to use the mysqlcheck utility to check your MySQL installation for compatibilities. For example, one of the prerequisites for upgrading to MySQL 8 is that, per the online reference manual, "there must be no tables that use obsolete data types, obsolete functions, orphan .frm files, InnoDB tables that use nonnative partitioning, or triggers that have a missing or empty definer or an invalid creation context." We can use the mysqlcheck utility to identify any of these conditions, as shown in Listing 10-5.

Listing 10-5. Using mysqlcheck to Identify Upgrade Issues

```
$ mysqlcheck -u root -p --all-databases --check-upgrade
Enter password:
library_v1.authors                            OK
library_v1.books                              OK
library_v1.books_authors                      OK
library_v1.notes                              OK
library_v1.publishers                         OK
library_v2.books                              OK
library_v2.notes                              OK
library_v2.publishers                         OK
library_v3.books                              OK
...
mysql.user                                    OK
sys.sys_config                                OK
```

For best results, you should use the mysqlcheck utility from the version to which you want to upgrade. This will ensure that the utility is the most up-to-date and should identify more upgrade issues.

Plan the Upgrade

When you have all the prerequisites mapped out and have identified any features that require special handling to solve incompatibilities, it is time to plan for upgrading your server. This may be an obvious thing to do if you have thousands of servers, but less obvious to those with only a few (or even one) server to upgrade.

You should resist the temptation to simply run the upgrade without planning what you are going to do. We want to ensure that the upgrade goes smoothly by reducing (or eliminating) risk. This is much more critical for production environments, but any potential loss of availability, performance, or data can result in loss of productivity.

You can get most of what you need to plan from the documentation, but the documentation won't be specific to your installation, servers, platform, and so forth. You must fill in those blanks and adapt the procedures suggested in the documentation to your own installation. You can learn quite a lot by reading the section, "What's New in MySQL 8.0" (https://dev.mysql.com/doc/refman/8.0/en/mysql-nutshell.html) and paying attention to any subsections labeled "Ramifications for Upgrades" in the server online reference manual. There, you will find tips that may help you avoid complicated decisions or, better, avoid complex repairs.

This step also includes making sure you have the right personnel on hand to do the upgrade or to be ready to engage in case something goes wrong.[2] For example, don't forget your developers, web administrators, and other critical roles.

The form of the plan is up to you; however, it is suggested that you put down in writing what you plan to do and share it with others. This way, everyone in the chain of ownership of the upgrade will know what is to be done. You will be surprised how much a little communication can do to reduce the risk of things going wrong.

Caution   If you are using or plan to use a platform that supports automatic updates, and those facilities include repositories that monitor MySQL, you may want to consider excluding MySQL from automatic updates. This is especially true for production environments. You should never automatically update MySQL in a production environment for any mission-critical data.

Document Your Results

One of the qualities that some of the best administrators, architects, and planners have is they write everything down. They keep notes on what they've tried and the results. This includes both things that go right and things that go wrong. You should always consider keeping an engineer's notebook for all your projects.

---

[2]It is always shocking for a database or web administrator to get a call (often in the middle of the night) to fix something gone wrong in an upgrade—especially when they have no knowledge that such an upgrade was planned! Yes, it does happen, far too often.

Some keep a single notebook with their notes logged chronologically. Others may keep several notebooks, each devoted to a specific project or experiment. The notebook need not be a deluxe, leather-wrapped tome with triple locks for security, but it should be a typical notebook in the sense that the pages are not removable and it is small enough to be placed alongside your workstation.

It is strongly recommended that you use ink to record your thoughts, experiments, setup, configuration, and observations so that you are not tempted to erase them. If you make drawings, you should consider using pencil because drawings often change or may need to be modified for accuracy. You should mark all your entries with the date and optionally the time.

Also, be sure to keep your notebook nearby so that you are not tempted to "write it down later." Sometimes the heat of the moment of diagnosis or experimentation takes precedence. Only routine and habit will ensure that you keep your notes complete.

Finally, be mindful of the security aspects of the information in your notebook. For example, if you are working on projects that contain company private or other information that should not be seen by others, you should store the notebook in a place designated by company policy for such information. If you cannot do this or do not have such a mechanism in your company policy, you should avoid writing down any such information. Although that may make the notes less than complete, it is far better than accidentally sharing the information if someone happens upon your notebook without access to such data.[3]

Consider Parallel Deployment

One practice that can help the most when upgrading systems that require more than a trivial amount of work is installing the new version in parallel to the existing version. This is a practice known to software engineering and is designed to ensure that the existing data and applications remain unchanged while the new system is being installed and configured. The new version (installation) would be considered a development platform and is often made a production deployment after sufficient testing of the migration is complete.

---

[3]The most common response I've seen to why engineers don't use notebooks is they don't want to risk exposing the data. But once again, taking care and establishing or following policies on data protection can help overcome such fears.

Although this isn't an upgrade per se (it's a new installation), having a new version of MySQL running in parallel gives considerable freedom in how to attack the migration of your existing data and applications. After all, if something goes wrong, your data is still operational on the old system.

This practice also provides another benefit: you can change platforms or other major hardware without having to risk your existing data. If your existing servers have hardware that is to be updated at the same time, you can use a parallel installation to install MySQL on the new hardware, thus isolating the risks with the new hardware.

Finally, employing a parallel installation may help you with scheduling and planning your migration by ensuring that the existing systems are fully capable. And, better, you can always go back to the old system if something goes wrong during the migration.

Parallel deployment often includes keeping both systems running for a certain period. The length of time may depend on the amount of risk you're willing to take or on the amount of time it takes to fully switch over all your applications.

Unfortunately, some may not have the resources available to consider parallel deployments. Consider that having two installations of MySQL running at the same time may place a greater burden on developers, administrators, and support personnel. Given the benefits of parallel development, it may be worth adding extra resources or accepting less productivity of some personnel for a short period.

However, even this safety net is tenuous if you don't perform enough testing.

Test, Test, Test!

Testing, along with planning, is often overlooked or given far less importance than it should have. Sometimes this is due to external forces such as not having the right personnel available or failures in planning resulting in no time for extensive testing. Regardless of the excuse, failing to adequately test your upgrade increases risk beyond what most would be willing to endure.

Testing should include ensuring that all the data has been migrated, all applications work fully, and all access (user accounts, permissions, etc.) is functional. However, don't stop there. You should also ensure that all your operational practices have been modified for the new version. More specifically, your maintenance scripts, procedures, and tools all work correctly with the new version.

Furthermore, your testing should result in a go/no-go decision for accepting the upgrade. If things are not working or there are too many issues, you may need to decide to keep or reject the upgrade. The parallel installation practice can help in this manner because you don't destroy the existing data or installation until you are certain everything is working. Writing those criteria into your plan will ensure success.

Tip   Be sure to test all existing operational procedures as part of your acceptance criteria.

Production Deployment Strategies

If you have a production and development (or test) environment, you should also consider how to move the development or test deployments to production. If you are using parallel installations, you might switch application routers and similar appliances and applications. If you are using in-place installations, the process may be more involved. For example, you may need to plan for a period of downtime to complete the migration.

For parallel installations, planning downtime may be more precise and involve a shorter period because you have more time to test things. However, for in-place upgrades, you may need to set aside a period to complete the migration. Naturally, you will want to minimize downtime by doing as much of the migration as you can. But in the base of MySQL, this may be nothing more than forming a plan and gathering resources. The bottom line is, don't forsake including production deployment in your plan.

Now that we've discussed upgrade practices, let's take a moment to discuss reasons for performing an upgrade, which clearly can be an involved process with a certain amount of risk.

Reasons for Upgrading

If you're like most avid users of platforms or systems, you will want to upgrade to the latest and greatest versions whenever a new one is released. Savvy administrators and planners know there is little room in a production database environment for such behavior. Reasons for upgrading will require some genuine bang for the buck. The upgrade must be worth your while. The main driving reasons for upgrading MySQL include the following:

- *Features*: A new feature is released that can improve your applications or data. Examples include the Document Store, Group Replication, and InnoDB Cluster.

- *Performance*: The newer version improves performance, making your applications better. For example, the latest 5.7 release is many times faster than previous versions, and MySQL 8 is promising to improve upon that.

- *Maintenance*: New features can help you maintain the system better. Examples include the new data dictionary, Group Replication, and ancillary tools such as MySQL Enterprise Backup.

- *Bug fixes*: Defects in older versions may require workarounds or limitations. Newer versions may contain fixes for critical bugs, so you can remove the workarounds and limitations caused by the defect.

- *Compliance*: Your platform, standard operating procedures, or external entities require the upgrade for compliance. For example, you may be required to run a specific version of MySQL for contractual agreements.

The bottom line is you must answer the question, "Why should I upgrade?" and that answer must result in a benefit for you, your data, clients, workforce, and the company's future. It makes little sense to spend resources on an upgrade that has little or no benefit, which is another reason companies often skip version upgrades. Alas, skipping too many upgrades can make later upgrades more problematic. However, given all the improvements in MySQL 8.0 as compared to MySQL 5.7 and earlier, many will want to upgrade to MySQL 8.

Tip   For more details about migrating to MySQL 8, including platform-specific steps, see `http://dev.mysql.com/doc/refman/8.0/en/upgrading-from-previous-series.html`.

SO, SHOULD I UPGRADE TO MYSQL 8 OR NOT?

The discussion in this section may be casting some doubt on whether you should upgrade to MySQL 8. That is not my intent. This book should convince you to upgrade to MySQL 8 as soon as you can do so in a safe, risk-free manner. This section suggests that you need to plan your upgrade and execute it carefully in order to ensure success. If you start migrating to MySQL 8 now, by the time MySQL 8 has had a revision or minor upgrade released as GA, you will be ready to upgrade.

Considerations for Upgrading to MySQL 8

Several compatibility issues are identified in the online reference manual for MySQL 8.0. The following are a few that you should be aware of when planning your MySQL 8.0 upgrade:

- *Data dictionary*: The new metadata, transactional storage mechanism is a major change in the architecture. If you have DevOps that work with .frm files and other metadata, you may need to make changes to migrate to using the data dictionary.

- *Authentication plugin*: The default authentication plugin has changed. This may result in connection issues for those who use older authentication mechanisms.

- *Error Codes*: Some error codes have changed. If you have applications that use error codes, explore these changes to avoid application errors after upgrading.

- *Partitioning*: The default partitioning storage engine support has been removed. If you are using a custom storage engine (or an old one), ensure that an upgraded version exists for use with MySQL 8.

- *INFORMATION_SCHEMA*: Minor changes have been made to the views. If your applications or DevOps teams use these views, be sure to check whether any of the views you are using have been removed or changed.

- *SQL commands*: This version has some new and obsolete SQL commands. Be sure to check your SQL statements to see if you are using some of the older, removed commands.

- *Default charset*: The default character set has been changed to utf8mb4. If you have character set support in your applications, you may need to test with the new default to ensure compatibility.

Once again, be sure to read the online reference manual section "Verifying Upgrade Prerequisites for Your MySQL 5.7 Installation" as well as the section "Changes Affecting Upgrades to MySQL 8.0" for the most up-to-date information about these and other prerequisites and migration tasks needed to upgrade to MySQL 8.0.

Other excellent resources are the engineering blogs at `https://mysqlserverteam.com/`. These blogs often discuss new features before they are released as GA and are a fountain of knowledge about how those features work as well as any upgrade issues that the engineering team has identified or is working to overcome. Watching the blogs will give an excellent early warning of changes.

Summary

The task of planning an InnoDB Cluster installation is not overly complex but does require some forethought and a deliberate plan. As with any technology, we should start small with a simple experimental installation for testing as many aspects of the technology as possible. This includes not only the mechanics of setting up the cluster, but also the specifics of configuring the router and your application for use with the cluster. More important, we must document all our results—including the mistakes and things that do not work—so we can avoid them when we deploy InnoDB Cluster for production.

In this chapter, you learned some important considerations for planning an InnoDB Cluster, including planning adoption of MySQL 8. This completes your introduction to InnoDB Cluster. With this newfound knowledge of the way InnoDB Cluster works, you are fully prepared to adopt MySQL InnoDB Cluster in your own environment.

This is an exciting time for MySQL users. Oracle continues to keep its promise not only to continue developing MySQL, but also to pour resources into improving and expanding the feature set. Keep a close watch on more excellent features and further refinement and updates. MySQL 8 is here, and now is the time to jump on board. Look for more titles from Apress on MySQL 8!

Index

A

Admin application programming interface (AdminAPI), 65

Administration

backup and restore, 397–401

general

checking, cluster status, 377

describing cluster, 377–378

getting cluster, 377

instances

cluster.add_instance() method, 381

cluster.rejoin_instance() method, 381–382

cluster.remove_instance() method, 382

cluster status, 379–381

customization, cluster metadata, 382

dba.check_instance_state() method, 379

group name, 383

group seeds, 383

local address, 383

methods, 379

whitelist, 382

MySQL Shell, 375–376

no shutdown and restart, 397

security

data breaches, 403

Internet, 403

MySQL, authentication plugin, 404

passwords, 403

router, 415, 417–418

server whitelist, 406

SSL connections (*see* Secure Sockets Layer (SSL) connections)

think group, not independent servers, 402

troubleshooting (*see* Troubleshooting)

Application (500) errors, 329

Application server, 228

ARM64, 231

Atomicity, consistency, isolation, and durability (ACID), 48

B

Binary log, 11, 57

C

Clustered index, 49

Comma-separated values (CSV) files, 47

Cross-site request forgery (CSRF) protection, 308, 312–313

D

Default section, router, 218

logger section, 219

metadata, 219

routing section, 220–221

Printed in the United States
By Bookmasters